THE DO-IT-YOURSELF GUIDE TO
HOME EMERGENCIES

THE DO-IT-YOURSELF GUIDE TO

HOME EMERGENCIES

From Breakdowns and Leaks to Cracks and Critters

Step-by-Step Solutions to the Toughest Problems a Homeowner Will Ever Face

Don Best

Rodale Press, Inc.
Emmaus, Pennsylvania

OUR MISSION

We publish books that empower people's lives.

RODALE BOOKS

Printed in the United States of America on acid-free ∞, recycled ♻ paper

Library of Congress Cataloging-in-Publication Data

Best, Don, date
    The do-it-yourself guide to home emergencies : from breakdowns and leaks to cracks and critters : step-by-step solutions to the toughest problems a homeowner will ever face / Don Best.
        p.   cm.
    Includes index.
    ISBN 0-87596-713-2 (paperback : alk. paper)
    1. Dwellings—Maintenance and repair—Amateurs' manuals.
I. Title.
TH4817.3.B473   1996
643'.7—dc20   96-10201

Distributed in the book trade by St. Martin's Press

2 4 6 8 10 9 7 5 3 1 paperback

THE DO-IT-YOURSELF GUIDE TO HOME EMERGENCIES EDITORIAL AND DESIGN STAFF
Editors: **Kenneth S. Burton, Jr.**
        Robert A. Yoder
Coordinating Designer: **Marta Mitchell Strait**
Interior Book Designer: **Robert E. Ayers,**
    AYERS/JOHANEK PUBLICATION DESIGN, INC.
Interior Illustrator: **John Gist**
Interior Book Layout: **Susan Smerker, AYERS/JOHANEK
    PUBLICATION DESIGN, INC.**
Interior Photographer: **Kurt Wilson**
Interior Photo Stylist: **Troy Schnyder**
Cover Designer: **Robert E. Ayers**
Front Cover Photographer: **Mitch Mandel**
Front Cover Photo Stylist: **Dale Mack**
Back Cover Illustrator: **John Gist**
Back Cover Photographers: **Kurt Wilson (top) and
    Betty Kussmaul (bottom)**
Copy Editor: **Nancy N. Bailey**
Manufacturing Coordinator: **Patrick T. Smith**
Indexer: **Christine J. Smith**
Editorial Assistance: **Nancy Kutches and
    Stephanie Wenner**

RODALE HOME AND GARDEN BOOKS
Vice President and Editorial Director: **Margaret Lydic
    Balitas**
Managing Editor: **Kevin Ireland**
Art Director: **Michael Mandarano**
Associate Art Director: **Mary Ellen Fanelli**
Studio Manager: **Leslie Keefe**
Copy Director: **Dolores Plikaitis**
Manufacturing Manager: **Helen Clogston**
Office Manager: **Karen Earl-Braymer**

If you have any questions or comments concerning the editorial content of this book, please write to:
    Rodale Press, Inc.
    Book Readers' Service
    33 East Minor Street
    Emmaus, PA 18098

To Frank and Jeanette,
whose Faith and Love equipped me
for life's emergencies

Contents

1 HOPE FOR THE BEST...

2 WATER & SEWAGE EMERGENCIES

3 ELECTRICAL EMERGENCIES

4 HEATING & COOLING EMERGENCIES

5 STRUCTURAL EMERGENCIES

6 NATURAL EMERGENCIES

7 SELF-INFLICTED EMERGENCIES

A WORD OF THANKS

The author gratefully acknowledges the generous help of many individuals, companies, and institutions. Prominent among these are the following:

Abatron, Inc.; American Academy of Allergy, Asthma, and Immunology; American Gas Association; American Lung Association; Bat Conservation International; Jack Bevington, F. E. Myers Co.; Jeff Bishop; Brick Institute of America; Steven Bukosky; Carpet and Rug Institute; Cedar Shake Bureau; Harold Chapdelaine; Kevin Clark, Critter Control, Inc.; Consumer Product Safety Commission; Roger Corn, Enviro-Chem, Inc.; George Craft, American Water Works Association; Dale Crowley, Crowley Lightning Protection, Inc.; Raymond Desjardins, EnergyNorth; Bob DiCello, EverDry Waterproofing, Inc.; Terry Eck, E-Poxy Industries; Bill Eich, Bill Eich Construction; Electric Power Research Institute; Genova Products; Georgia Poison Control Center; Dr. Thad Godish, Ball State University; David Grimsrud, Minnesota Building Research Center; Ken Hall, Edison Electric Institute; Tom Hasbrouck, Hasbrouck Associates; Lloyd Hitchins, Hitchins Construction; Dan Holohan; Joe Iorio, Atlantic Heating and Air Conditioning; *Journal of Light Construction;* Elizabeth Kussmaul; Terry Lasky; Peter W. Lewis, Intermatic, Inc.; Amanda Lollar; Joe MacAniff; Ward Malisch, Portland Cement Association; Bill Marquard, Oatley Co.; Lee Martin; Fred Mellini, Goulds Pumps, Inc.; Frank Mueller, Reynolds Metals Company; National Association of the Remodeling Industry; National Association of Waterproofing Contractors; National Center for Health Statistics; National Concrete Masonry Association; National Fire Protection Association; National Institutes of Health; National Pest Control Association; National Safety Council; New Hampshire Department of Health and Human Services; Marty Obando; Ohio Sealants, Inc.; Mike Phelps; Dave Poindexter, Roofing Industry Education Institute; Don Provencher; John Quaregna; Ken Roberts, Wespac Enterprises; Chuck Romick, Roto-Rooter Corp.; Larry Sanford, Macklanburg-Duncan, Inc.; Dave Shanohan, Keller Ladders, Inc.; Parker Silva, New England Lightning Protection, Inc.; Dr. Dennis Slate, U.S. Department of Agriculture; Tom Smith, National Roofing Contractors Association; Dr. Stephen Smulski, Wood Science Specialists, Inc.; Tony Sobaski; Roseanne Soloway, American Association of Poison Control Centers; Joe Stiburek, Building Science Corp.; Steve Thomas; Underwriters Laboratories, Inc.; Bob VanLaningham; Water Quality Association; Larry Weingarten, Elemental Enterprises; Wood Shingle and Shake Association; Pat Zumbush, Geomet, Inc.

Hope for the Best...

Prepare for the Worst

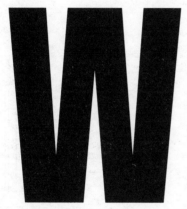

While it is my earnest hope that no emergency will ever afflict your home, I urge you—with equal fervor—to do everything you can to be prepared for one.

With that in mind, I encourage you to read through this book before any emergencies arise. That way you'll be forearmed with information and have a feel for how the book is organized.

You'll find that each chapter begins with "Quick Response" and "Hazards" sections to help you safely stabilize an emergency situation. This is followed with in-depth information on how to repair the damage and—perhaps most important of all—how to avert such an emergency in the future.

This introductory chapter is the key to using the rest of the book. It teaches you not only how to deal with an emergency but also how to prevent one from interrupting your busy life in the first place. It's divided into three sections—"Understanding How Your House Works," "Preparing for an Emergency," and "Performing Good Maintenance"—plus it has sources for further reading on the subject. (See "For More Information" on page 16.)

Understanding How Your House Works

Understanding how the plumbing, electrical, gas, and heating and cooling systems in your house work is essential to dealing with an emergency. Take the time to familiarize yourself with the various parts of each operating system and to understand—if not in practice, at least in theory—how they work. *Above all else, learn how to shut down these systems in a hurry.*

NOTE: While the illustrations presented here are necessarily generic, they depict the key elements found in most houses.

UNDERSTANDING YOUR PLUMBING SYSTEM

Every homeowner should know at least how to shut off the water in the event of an emergency. Otherwise, a relatively small problem can end up causing thousands of dollars in needless water damage. So, do some detective work and locate the important parts of your plumbing system. You should become familiar with how each operates before an emergency sneaks up on you.

Main shutoff valve. Start by locating the point where your main water line enters the house, as shown in *Your Plumbing System* on this page.

On municipal water systems, this is usually a 1-inch-diameter pipe that comes through the foundation wall on the street side of your house. You'll find the water meter and the main shutoff valve near the point where the pipe penetrates the wall.

In cold climates, the shutoff valve is usually located indoors, in a basement or utility room, close by the wall where the pipe enters. In climates where there's no danger of freezing, the shutoff valve is sometimes located outdoors.

On private well water systems, the main water line, which might be metal or plastic, usually comes in through the wall from the direction of the well. The shutoff valve is found on the supply line coming out of the storage tank.

In the event of a leak or other plumbing emergency, simply close the main valve to prevent water damage. If the valve fails to close, call your city water authority immediately and have them turn the water off at the main.

If the main valve fails to close on a pumped well system, shut off the electricity to the pump and call a plumber or well water technician for help.

Your plumbing system not only supplies water— hot and cold—to your sinks, dishwasher, lavatories, and toilets, but it must also drain it away efficiently.

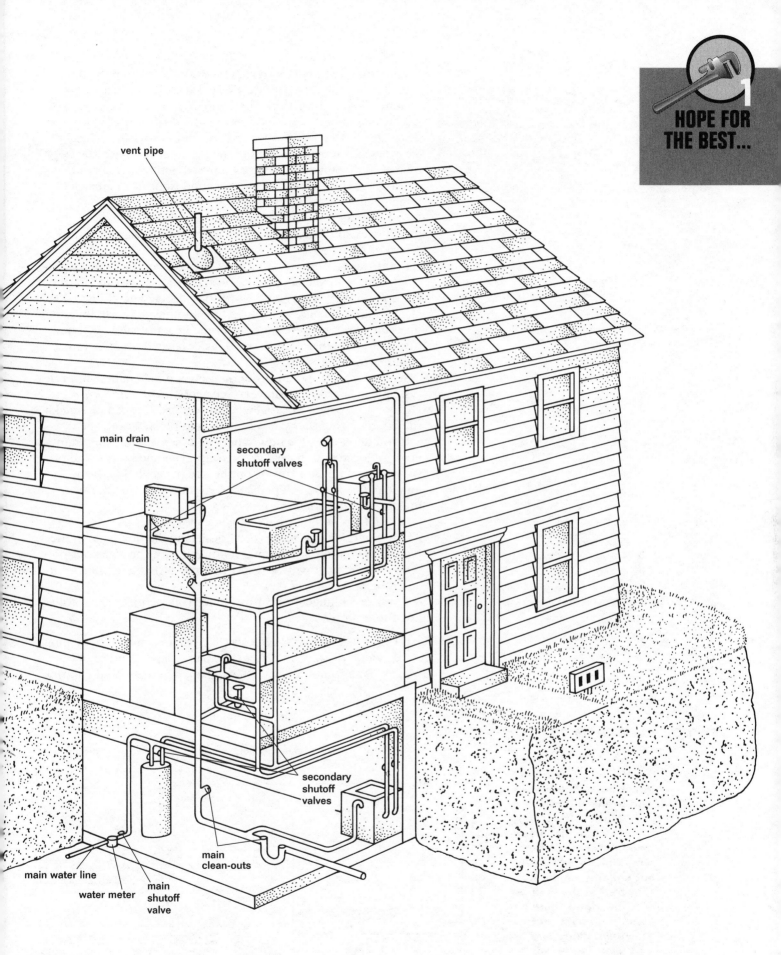

vent pipe

main drain

secondary shutoff valves

secondary shutoff valves

main clean-outs

main water line

water meter

main shutoff valve

Secondary shutoff valves. Once you know how to shut off the main supply valve, locate all the secondary valves in the system. As shown in *Your Plumbing System* on page 2, a typical, well-plumbed house will have individual shutoff valves for the water heater, each toilet and sink, and the dishwasher. Showers and washing machines may or may not have their own shutoff. Some houses are plumbed with zone valves that control the flow of water to the second floor or to a particular wing of the house.

By knowing the location of these valves, you can isolate single fixtures, appliances, or zones without depriving the entire house of water.

Clean-outs. Modern plumbing codes require that houses provide main drain and secondary clean-outs for access to clogged drainpipes. (See "Clogged Fixture" on page 42 and "Clogged Main Drain" on page 51.) Take a few minutes to locate these so that you'll know where they are in the event of an emergency. If you discover that your house doesn't have clean-outs, hire a plumber to install them.

Septic system. When properly used and maintained, a septic system can last almost forever. (See *Septic Tank and Drain Field* on this page.) But if neglected or abused, it can be quickly ruined, requiring thousands of dollars to repair or replace.

If you don't already know where your septic tank and drain field are located, find out. Their location should be detailed on your original house plans or on the site plans filed with the municipality. If no such plans exist, ask the prior owner or builder to show you where they are.

Failing that, you may have to get a shovel, find the point where the drainpipe leaves the house, and dig down along the pipe until you locate the tank. If you're lucky, the clean-out port on top of the tank will be near the surface. If you're unlucky, it could be buried 4 feet down.

To ensure a long and healthy life for your septic system, follow these simple rules:

● Don't flush harsh chemicals (like paint thinner) or anything that won't dissolve in water (like baby diapers and sanitary napkins) into the septic system. Soap, detergent, and chlorine

SEPTIC TANK AND DRAIN FIELD

Bacteria living inside the tank can digest most household waste and break it down into nitrate-rich water, which is dispersed through the drain field. The indigestible waste that collects on the bottom of the tank as sludge should be pumped out by a professional every two or three years.

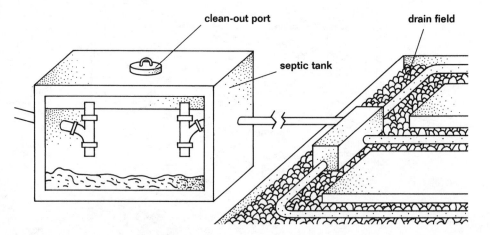

clean-out port

drain field

septic tank

bleach—used in *moderation*—generally won't harm the waste-digesting bacteria that live inside the tank.

● Don't use disinfectants, enzymes, or other additives that claim to "improve" septic system performance. Most such products provide no benefit and some may actually do harm.

● Have your tank pumped out every two or three years to remove sludge. The two-year cycle is recommended for families of four or more and for families that use garbage disposals. Failure to have the tank pumped will eventually cause scum and sludge to flow into the drain field and ruin it. Such neglect can also cause sewage to back up into your house.

● Don't direct the runoff from rain gutters or foundation drains into the septic tank.

● Keep the ground above the tank and drain field free of trees and large plants. Their roots can play havoc with the underground tank and pipes.

● Don't let heavy equipment run over the drainpipe, tank, or drain field.

● Don't burn brush fires over the drain field. It might generate enough heat to melt the underlying pipe if it's plastic.

DRAINING THE PLUMBING SYSTEM

If you're going to close up your house for a season, be sure to shut off the main water valve and drain all the pipes and fixtures. The main drain valve should be located at the lowest point in the system.

All faucets and supply valves should be left open as you drain the system to ensure that no water is trapped under a vacuum. Double-check the clothes washer and dishwasher—including their drain lines—to make sure there's no trapped water. Don't

Smells like Trouble

If you smell sewage around the septic tank or over the drain field, it's a sure sign of trouble. So is the presence of black or gray water oozing up from the drain field. It may contain bacteria or viruses harmful to people and pets. Lose no time in calling a firm that specializes in septic systems. ●

Provide Tank Access

If the septic tank's clean-out port is buried deeply, line the hole you dig with a steel barrel and top plate so that you don't have to redig the hole every time you have the tank pumped out. I used a steel 55-gallon oil drum, as shown here. Since I don't own a welding machine or cutting torch, I had it fabricated at a local metal working shop for about $20. ●

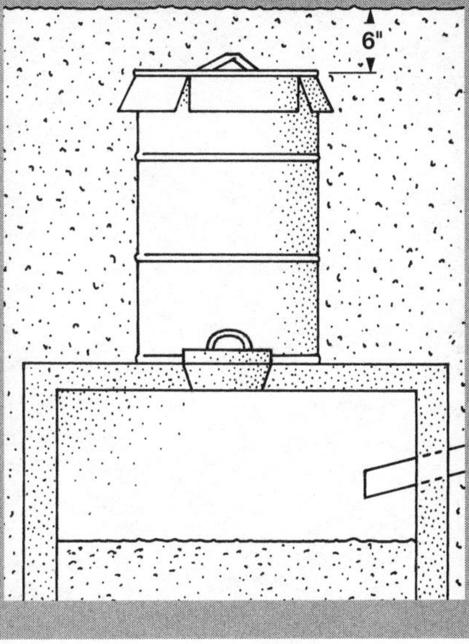

The barrel's top and bottom were cut off, and the top plate was saved to act as the lid.

> **Learn from a Pro**
> If you're insecure about draining your plumbing system yourself, hire a plumber to do it for you the first time. Watch and take notes, so the next time you can do it yourself. ●

forget to open and drain all outdoor faucets, the sump pump's discharge line, and, if you have a well system, the pressurized holding tank.

CAUTION: Make absolutely sure that the power supply to the water heater is turned *off* before you drain it. (See "Leaky Water Heater" on page 84.)

After the plumbing is drained, pour about a pint of antifreeze into each toilet and a cup of antifreeze into each sink trap to ensure that they don't freeze.

UNDERSTANDING YOUR ELECTRICAL SYSTEM

As shown in *Your Electrical System* on the opposite page, the utility service line typically ties into a service entrance head that's secured to the gable end of the house. Electricity then flows through a metal- or plastic-covered conduit to the meter and into the back of your main service panel.

To protect your health and property during an emergency, it's vitally important that you know how to turn off the electricity. In modern construction, this is usually done by switching off the main double-pole breaker at the top of the service box.

Other configurations are possible. Sometimes the main breaker has its own smaller service box located indoors (near the service panel) or outdoors (near the meter).

Older houses may have one or more pull-out fuse blocks that disconnect the electricity when they're removed. Still other designs, with exposed cartridge fuses in the main panel, will have an *ON/OFF* lever to one side. Always switch the lever into the *OFF* position before you open the main panel.

In addition to knowing how to cut off electricity to the whole house, it's prudent to clearly mark all the circuit breakers (or fuses) inside the main service panel so that you can selectively cut power to an individual circuit. (See "Adding Up the Amps" on page 104.) Be sure to store a good flashlight inside the service panel and, if needed, an assortment of replacement fuses.

Before you attempt to service the panel in any way, carefully read the section "Electrical Emergencies," which begins on page 99, and especially the box, "Electrical Safety Tips," on page 102.

As shown in the table "Four Seasons Maintenance" on page 18, I recommend that all circuit breakers and ground fault circuit interrupters be tested once a year. (Also, see "GFCI Spells Electrical Safety" on page 265.)

YOUR ELECTRICAL SYSTEM

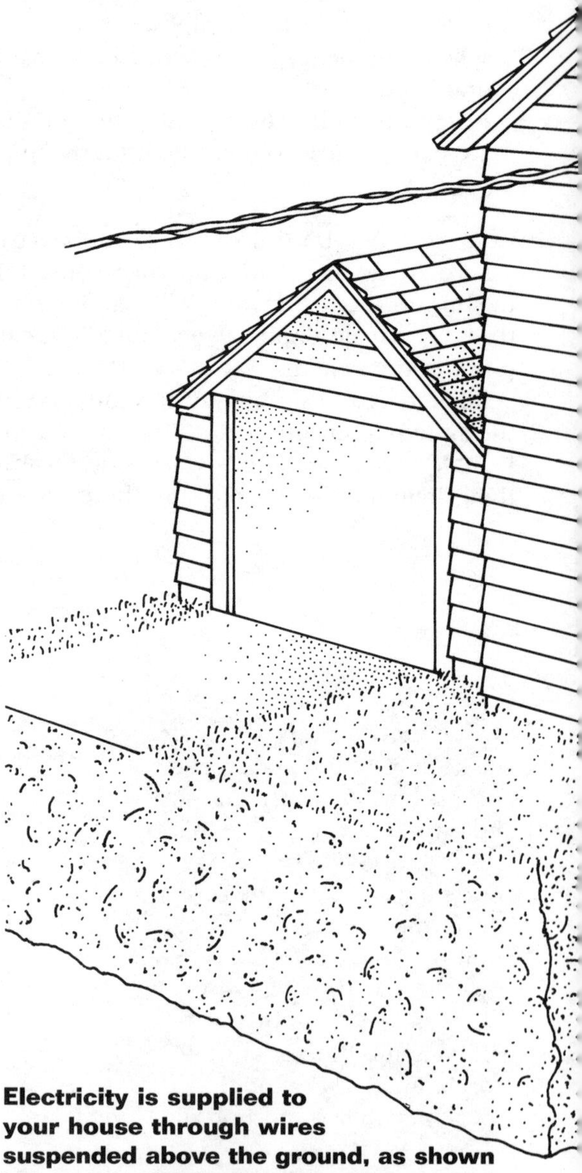

Electricity is supplied to your house through wires suspended above the ground, as shown here, or through wires encased in a conduit that runs underneath the ground. Once the electricity reaches your house, it is divided up at the main service panel and fed to different parts of your home.

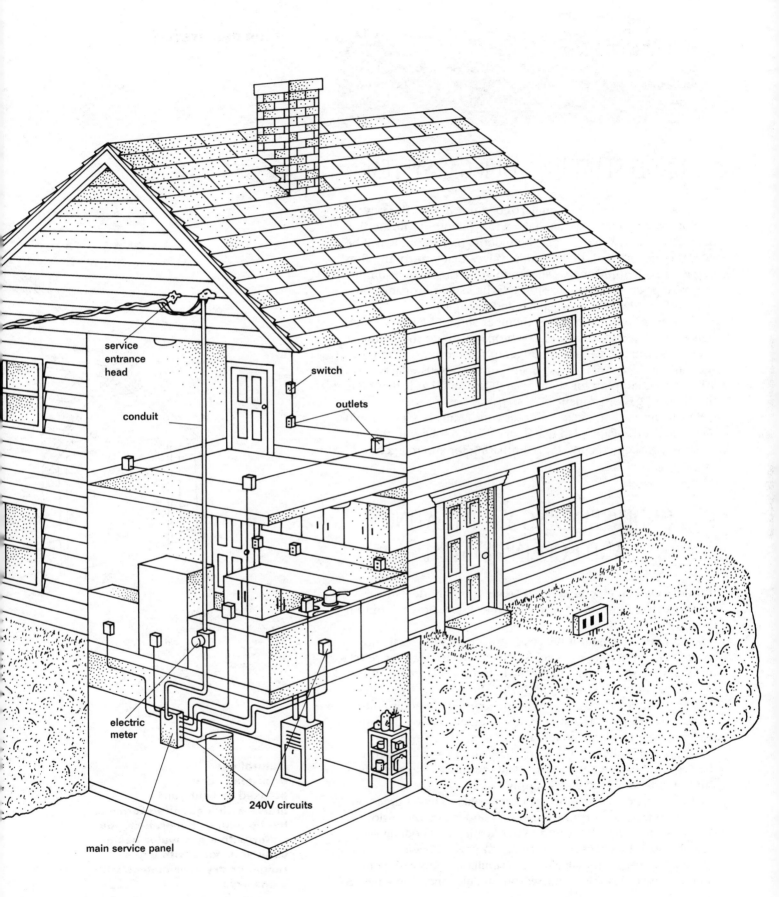

service
entrance
head

switch

conduit

outlets

electric
meter

240V circuits

main service panel

It's Alarming

If anyone in your family has an impaired sense of smell, consider installing an electronic gas alarm. (See "Gas Leak" on page 118.) ●

UNDERSTANDING YOUR GAS SYSTEM

In the same way that you familiarized yourself with the valves on your water supply system, take a few minutes to locate the main gas shutoff valve—it may be indoors or out, but it will be near the meter—and the individual valves that control the flow of gas to each appliance, as shown in *Your Gas System* on the opposite page. See "How to Shut Off the Gas or Propane" on page 119 for detailed instructions and drawings.

To protect your family, every member should be able to recognize the smell of leaking gas or propane. To do this, gather everyone around the kitchen range, turn a burner on for a few seconds, and let everyone get a sniff of uncombusted gas. Or ask your gas supplier for some scratch-and-sniff cards that emit the smell of gas or propane.

Equally important, make sure that your family has a clear and well-practiced escape plan that everyone can follow in the event of a gas emergency. (See "Preparing for an Emergency" on page 10.)

UNDERSTANDING YOUR HEATING AND COOLING SYSTEM

If there's ever an emergency that stems from or affects your heating or cooling system, you'll need to know how to shut off the system quickly and safely.

Since most heat pumps, electric furnaces, and central and room air conditioners run exclusively on electricity, they're relatively easy to shut down. Simply switch the system control to *OFF* or cut power to the circuit inside the main service panel.

Gas and oil furnaces are a bit more complex. In addition to cutting electricity to the system, it's prudent to close the valve that feeds gas or oil to the furnace.

Gas and oil boilers may require three steps to safely secure the system during an emergency: Cut the power, close the fuel valve, and turn off the water supply valve.

Of course, no two systems are exactly alike. Thus, I urge you to *read* your owner's manuals carefully and locate the various switches and valves that control your heating and cooling system. Reading the chapters "No Heat" on page 126 and "No Cooling" on page 141 will also help familiarize you with your system as will the table "Four Seasons Maintenance" on page 18.

Natural gas or propane can be used to heat your house with a gas-fired furnace, heat pump, or boiler, heat your water with a gas water heater, cook your food with a gas range, or dry your clothes with a gas dryer.

gas meter

main shutoff valve

secondary
shutoff valves

Preparing for an Emergency

While it may sound strange to "plan" for an emergency, that's precisely what you need to do to protect your family and property from harm.

The plan outlined here constitutes one of the best insurance policies you can get. Not only will it reduce the odds of an emergency ever occurring, but it will also lessen the likelihood of serious injuries and material damage if one ever does.

So don't procrastinate! Draw up your plan and lay in the proper safety equipment and supplies.

Eliminate fire hazards. Using *Fire Hazards in Your Home* on the opposite page as your guide, take a thorough inventory of your house and eliminate any existing fire hazards.

Install smoke detectors. The National Fire Protection Association (NFPA) estimates that installing smoke detectors in your home will cut your risk of dying in a fire by half.

With that in mind, make sure you have a working smoke detector on each floor—preferably one outside each bedroom—and that the batteries are fresh. (Maintenance routines are detailed in the table on page 18.) If you have plug-in type detectors, be sure that they're clamped fast into their receptacles.

The *best* installation option of all is to have smoke detectors hard-wired into a permanent electric circuit.

Equip your home with fire extinguishers. Place a fully charged fire extinguisher in your kitchen, basement, and garage. Rooms that have fireplaces or woodstoves are also prime candidates for fire extinguishers.

Fire extinguishers are rated Class A, B, or C—or combinations thereof—according to what type(s) of fire they are designed to put out. Class A fires involve wood, paper, household rubbish, and other ordinary combustibles. Class B fires involve oil, grease, paint, or other flammable liquids. Class C refers to electrical fires.

If you're buying a new fire extinguisher, opt for a multipurpose type that's rated ABC—that means it's safe to use on all common household fires.

Never store gasoline inside the house.

Keep garage free of clutter.

Fire Alarm Box

If there's a fire alarm box in your neighborhood, everyone should know where it is and how to use it. ●

If you are aware of fire hazards in your home, you can eliminate them and keep your family safe. Check out these areas for potential dangers.

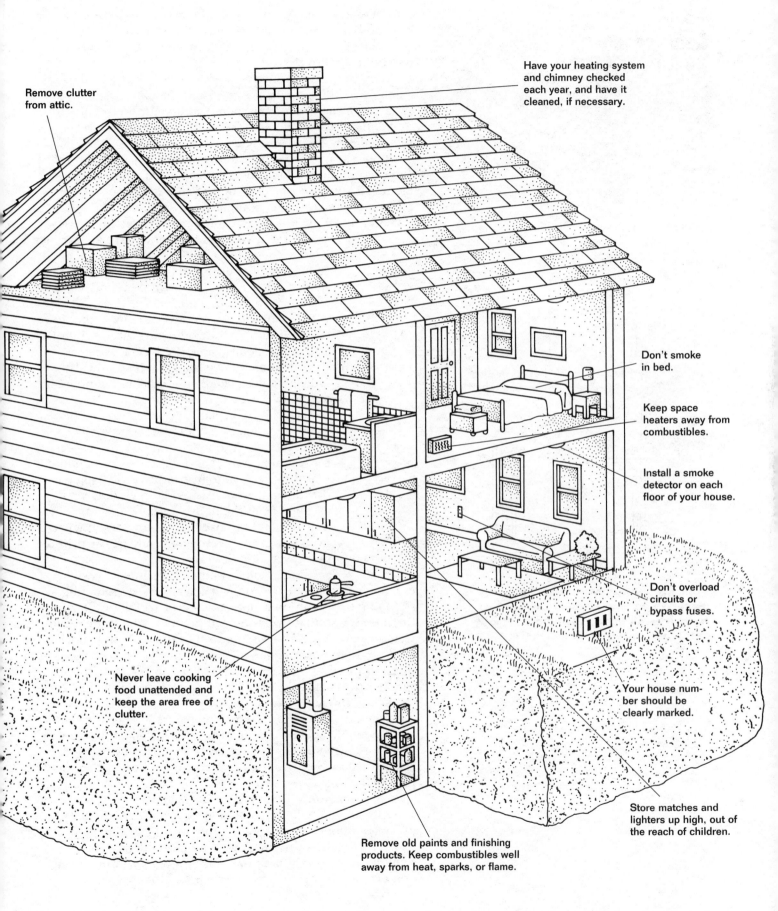

Remove clutter from attic.

Have your heating system and chimney checked each year, and have it cleaned, if necessary.

Don't smoke in bed.

Keep space heaters away from combustibles.

Install a smoke detector on each floor of your house.

Don't overload circuits or bypass fuses.

Your house number should be clearly marked.

Never leave cooking food unattended and keep the area free of clutter.

Remove old paints and finishing products. Keep combustibles well away from heat, sparks, or flame.

Store matches and lighters up high, out of the reach of children.

ESCAPE PLAN

FIRE ESCAPE PLAN

meet under old oak

collapsible ladder

garage roof

fire extinguisher

bedroom

bedroom

porch roof

telephone

smoke detector

first aid kit

porch roof

bathroom

bedroom

Your fire escape plan should show at least two escape routes from each room as well as the location of smoke detectors and fire extinguishers.

Generally speaking, the bigger the fire extinguisher you buy the better, as long as you don't buy one that's too heavy or unwieldy for the smallest adult member of your household to handle effectively.

Mount the extinguisher on a wall in plain sight, within easy reach of an adult. Learn how to work the extinguisher, then teach all of the other adult members of your household, too. *Remember, there'll be no time to read the instructions during an emergency.* (See "Fire!" on page 244.)

All fire extinguishers have a test button or gauge that tells you the pressure, which should be checked about once a month. If you discover that the pressure has dropped, replace or recharge the extinguisher.

Develop an escape plan. In the midst of an emergency, everyone in your family should have a clear idea of how to get out fast. Start by drawing a good floor plan of your house that shows the location of every room, door, window, and stairway, as shown in *Escape Plan* on this page.

The plan should also mark the location of fire extinguishers, smoke detectors, utility shutoffs, telephones, collapsible fire ladders, first-aid kits, and emergency supplies. It should also indicate a designated spot outside the house where everyone agrees to meet.

Make the floor plan large and clear, so that even the youngest children in your family can understand it. And make several extra copies for teaching purposes. Explain to your children that they can't hide from a fire or leaking gas; they must get out. Also, that once they've escaped from the house during an emergency, they're not to go back in for any reason whatsoever, not even to rescue a family pet or prized possession.

Using a colored pen, chart at least two escape routes from each room. Then stage periodic drills—sounding the alarm on a smoke detector will get everyone in the mood!—so that everyone can practice what they're supposed to do. Stage at least one drill in the dark and another at ant time to teach family members how to crawl out of the house if there's heavy smoke. (During the early stages of a smoky fire, a safety zone of breathable air will remain 12 to 24 inches above the floor.)

If you have elderly or disabled members in your household who require a special escape plan, ask your local fire department for advice on how to set it up. The fire department can also provide window decals to mark any rooms that are occupied by infants.

Post emergency phone numbers. Make a clear and complete list of emergency phone numbers and post them by every telephone. Or photocopy the form *Emergency Phone Numbers* on the opposite page, fill in the information required, and hang it next to your phone. *Print* the information clearly for the young readers in your home. Also put a

Emergency Phone Numbers

My Family Name: _____

My Phone Number: _____

My Address: _____

My Town: _____

My County: _____

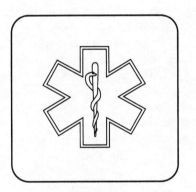      

Ambulance   Fire   Police/Sheriff

Mother   Father   Other

Source: The Federal Emergency Management Agency

If a room lacks two escape routes, store a collapsible ladder near the window and drill the occupant on how to use it. ●

list in your survival pantry. (See **Build a survival pantry** below.) The telephone list should include the following numbers:

- Police
- Fire department
- Ambulance
- Poison control center
- Hospital
- Family physician
- Electric, gas, and water utilities

Even very young children can be taught to call for help during an emergency, especially since 911 service is so widely available. If your child can't read, use a picture chart like the one on page 13.

Get first-aid training. See to it that at least one family member—and preferably more—is trained in cardiopulmonary resuscitation (CPR) and other first-aid techniques.

Build a survival pantry. Most parts of the United States are subject to natural disasters that can isolate a neighborhood or community from vital services for days at a time. While hurricanes and earthquakes tend to grab the biggest headlines, other natural threats, including tornadoes, floods, blizzards, and wildfires, can be equally devastating.

No matter where you live, it makes sense to keep a cache of emergency supplies on hand, as shown in *Emergency Supplies* on this page, and to check its contents periodically.

EMERGENCY SUPPLIES

In a real emergency, a well-stocked cache of emergency supplies can save you or your family.

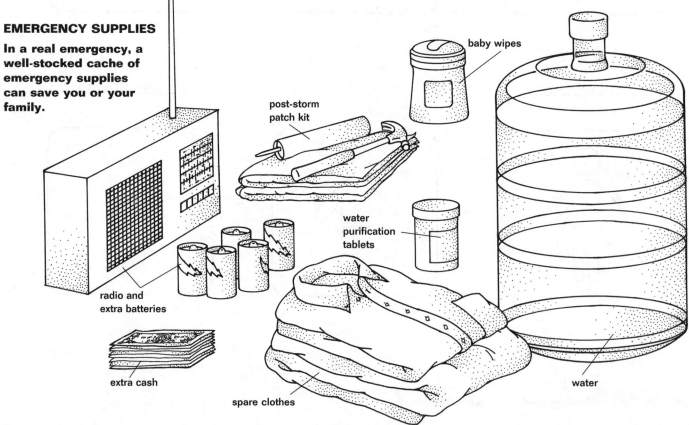

baby wipes

post-storm patch kit

water purification tablets

radio and extra batteries

extra cash

spare clothes

water

Should a natural disaster strike, disrupting food and water supplies and severing transportation and communications links, a survival pantry can mean the difference between life and death. Even if the situation isn't life-threatening, a stash of emergency supplies can make a bad situation a lot more bearable.

Whatever the emergency, here's the Golden Rule: *Neither your house nor your car nor your boat nor anything else you own is as important as your life.* When an evacuation order comes, grab your important papers and your wedding pictures and get out.

If you live in one of the 18 coastal states that are vulnerable to Atlantic hurricanes, know your evacuation routes ahead of time. If tornadoes are a frequent menace in your area, give some forethought to where you would take your family for shelter should a twister threaten your neighborhood.

Here's a checklist of items that can help protect your family and home when nature runs wild. Make it a point to check your supplies from time to time to make sure everything is fresh and usable.

● *Water:* Water is your family's most basic necessity. Keep several large containers on hand that can be quickly filled if

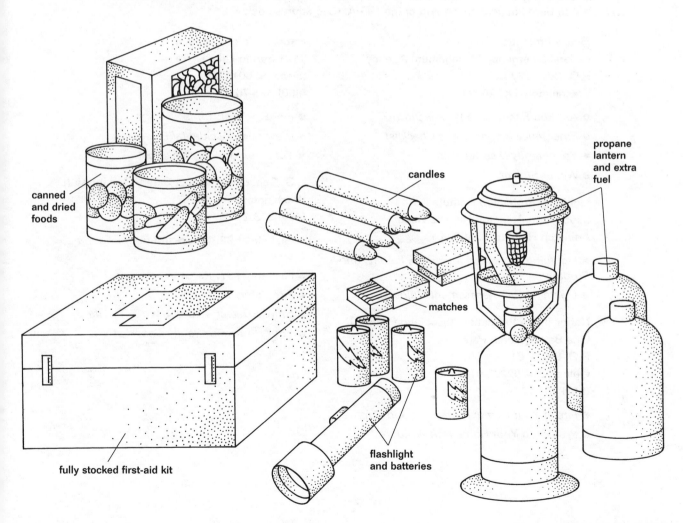

canned and dried foods

candles

propane lantern and extra fuel

matches

fully stocked first-aid kit

flashlight and batteries

a storm, flood, or other event threatens to disrupt your water supply. Also fill your sinks and bathtubs. Once that's done, shut off the main shutoff valve to the house to protect the water that's already in the system. In an emergency, you can get 30 to 60 gallons of safe water by draining your pipes and water heater. (Be sure to turn off the water heater first. Leaving the power on could cause an explosion or burn out the heating element.) The pressurized tank on well systems can also provide a reservoir of emergency water. If you have trouble draining water out of the system, open a faucet at the highest point in your house to break the vacuum.

● *Water purification tablets*: If you have to use water of questionable quality, treat it with purification tablets first. These are sold at most drug stores. Another alternative, provided you have a heating source, is to boil the water for ten minutes to kill any disease-causing bacteria.

For More Information

These booklets and brochures are available (generally free for single copies) by sending a self-addressed stamped envelope to the appropriate organization. For information on fire safety for people with disabilities and other high-risk groups, contact the Learn Not to Burn Foundation, an arm of the NFPA. (See address below.)

Family Protection Program
Federal Emergency Management Agency
P.O. Box 70274
Washington, DC 20024

● *Are You Ready for a Winter Storm?*
● *Emergency Preparedness Checklist*
● *Your Family Disaster Plan*
● *Winter Storms*

Lightning Protection Institute
3365 North Arlington Heights Road
Arlington Heights, IL 60004

● *Lightning Protection for Home, Family, and Property*
● *Lightning Risk Assessment Guide*

National Fire Protection Association (NFPA)
One Batterymarch Park
P.O. Box 9101
Quincy, MA 02269-9101
(617) 984-7274

● *Fire in Your Home: Prevention and Survival*
● *Protecting Your Home from Wildfire*

National Safety Council
1121 Spring Lake Drive
Itasca, IL 60143
(800) 621-7615

● *Fire Safety at Home*
● *Preventing Accidental Poisoning*
● *Your Home Safety Checklist*

U.S. Consumer Product Safety Commission
Washington, DC 20207
(800) 638-2772

● **Fact sheet 92:** *Wood and Coal Burning Stoves*
● **Fact sheet 97:** *Kerosene Heaters*
● *Fire Safety at Home*
● *Smoke Detectors Can Save Your Life*
● *Your Home Fire Safety Checklist*

● *Food:* Stock a generous supply of canned goods and other nonperishable foods. If your electricity goes off, leave the freezer door closed as long as possible. As meats and other foods begin to thaw, cook them before they spoil. A fireplace, woodstove, or even a fondue pot can be used for emergency indoor cooking; a camp stove, gas grill, or charcoal cooker can be used outdoors.

● *First-aid kit:* Be sure to include an extra supply of any special medications the family needs.

● *Flashlight:* Include an extra set of fresh batteries. Kerosene lamps are generally discouraged because of the fire hazard.

● *Propane lantern:* Keep a few extra propane cannisters on hand for refueling. Use candles only as a last resort.

● *Portable radio:* Stock an extra set of batteries.

● *Cash:* Keep some emergency cash on hand. In a crisis, you may not be able to find an open bank or an automated teller machine that works.

● *Baby wipes:* Even if you haven't got a baby, these disposable wipes are great for hand showers. (If you *do* have a baby, stock some extra disposable diapers, too.)

● *Change of clothes*

● *Emergency phone numbers:* See page 13.

● *Post-storm patch kit:* If possible, keep a roll of thick plastic sheeting and a tub of roofing cement or adhesive caulk on hand. Homeowners who are able to make temporary roof and window repairs following a storm may prevent thousands of dollars in additional damage to the home's interior in the days that follow.

For more information on dealing with sudden emergencies, be sure to read "No Electric Power" on page 109 and "Thunderstorm Safety Tips" on page 184.

Happy New Year

Make it a habit to check emergency supplies at a memorable time of year like New Year's Day or your birthday. Special days serve as effective reminders. ●

Performing Good Maintenance

It's a fact! A home that's well maintained is *much* less likely to experience emergencies than one that's cluttered and rundown. As your home ages, it needs your constant tender loving care to stay in top shape. With attentive care, emergencies will be less likely to sneak up on you and catch you off guard. The table "Four Seasons Maintenance" starting on page 18 details the key maintenance routines that will help you avert big trouble later on.

FOUR SEASONS MAINTENANCE

Good maintenance is the best way to prevent home emergencies. Follow the schedule below and keep your home safe and healthy.

THE PLUMBING SYSTEM

Task	Season	Comments
CLEAN SHOWERHEADS, AERATORS, AND DRAIN STRAINERS.	As needed	Soak in hot vinegar. Use pin to clean clogged openings.
TREAT SLOW DRAINS.	As needed	See "Do Drain Cleaners Really Work?" on page 46.
TEST SUMP PUMP.	Spring	Pour water into sump pit to make sure float and switch respond.
PROTECT OUTDOOR FAUCETS FROM FREEZING.	Fall	Unless faucet is freeze-proof type, it must be drained or isolated.
ADJUST WATER HEATER BURNER AND PILOT.	Summer	Best left to pro; schedule when furnace or boiler is to be serviced.
CHECK PIPES, VALVES, AND FIXTURES FOR LEAKS.	Any season, once a year	Look for corrosion, vibration, slow leaks, or failed valves.
OPEN AND CLOSE MAIN AND SECONDARY WATER VALVES.	Any season, once a year	Close and open each valve to ensure that each is in working order.
TEST WATER HEATER RELIEF VALVE.	Any season, once a year	Lift handle on valve. If water comes out, valve is in good working order. If no water is discharged, replace valve immediately. (See "Replacing a Water Heater Relief Valve" on page 94.)
DRAIN SLUDGE OUT OF WATER HEATER.	Any season, once a year	Mineral sludge can build up in bottom of water heater and reduce efficiency. (See "Leaky Water Heater" on page 84.)
HAVE SEPTIC TANK PUMPED.	Every 2–3 years	Solids that build up in septic tank can eventually block tank outlets. Call pro to pump out your tank. (See **Septic system** on page 4.)

THE ELECTRICAL SYSTEM

Task	Season	Comments
INSPECT RECEPTACLES AND CORDS FOR WEAR.	Any season, once a year	As electrical cords age, they can become brittle and crack, exposing you and your family to risk of shock and fire.
SWITCH MAIN AND SECONDARY CIRCUIT BREAKERS ON AND OFF.	Any season, once a year	Toggling switches will help prevent corrosion and sticking.

THE ELECTRICAL SYSTEM—CONTINUED

TASK	SEASON	COMMENTS
TEST GROUND FAULT CIRCUIT INTERRUPTERS (GFCIs).	Any season, once a year	GFCIs generally have test button that, when pushed, trips built-in circuit interrupter. Pressing reset button should return circuit to normal. If GFCI doesn't operate properly, replace it. (See "GFCI Spells Electrical Safety" on page 265.)

THE HEATING AND AIR CONDITIONING SYSTEM

TASK	SEASON	COMMENTS
HAVE SYSTEM PROFESSIONALLY CLEANED AND TUNED.	Oil-fired heating systems and heat pumps—annually; gas heating systems and central and room air conditioners—every 2 years.	It is difficult to get fast, reliable heating or cooling service by dialing number in Yellow Pages. Some heating and cooling companies offer reasonably priced maintenance contracts for their customers. Try to line one up before you need service.
HAVE DUCTWORK PROFESSIONALLY CLEANED.	Every 2–5 years as needed	Contact National Air Duct Cleaners Association, 1518 K Street NW, Suite 503, Washington, DC 20005, for list of members in your area.
CLEAN OR REPLACE AIR FILTERS.	As needed	Clogged furnace or air conditioning filter will reduce system's efficiency and degrade indoor air quality.
CLEAN FAN(S).	Summer	Scrape blades clean with screwdriver or putty knife.
CHECK FAN BELTS FOR SNUGNESS, ALIGNMENT, AND WEAR.	Summer	Loose belt can reduce fan speed, squeak, and wear more quickly than one that is properly adjusted. (See "No Heat" on page 126.)
LUBRICATE FANS, PUMPS, AND MOTORS.	Summer	Use oil sparingly, as prescribed in owner's manual. Some newer fans, pumps, and motors with sealed bearings don't require oil.
MAKE SURE REGISTERS ARE PROPERLY ORIENTED AND FREE OF OBSTRUCTIONS.	Summer	Rugs, furniture, and other obstructions can block flow of heated or cooled air.
CHECK, REPAIR, OR UPGRADE DUCT OR PIPE INSULATION.	Summer	You can patch failed duct with tape, but it takes pro with right equipment to test and seal system properly. Hot water and steam system pipes should be fitted with compressed fiberglass insulation only.
CLEAN HUMIDIFIER.	Summer	Follow manufacturer's instructions.
CLEAN RADIATORS AND CLEAR AWAY OBSTRUCTIONS.	Summer	Hot water and steam heating systems only

(continued)

THE HEATING AND AIR CONDITIONING SYSTEM—CONTINUED

TASK	SEASON	COMMENTS
BLEED AIR OUT OF SYSTEM.	Once or twice each heating season	Hot water and steam heating systems only
DRAIN EXPANSION TANK.	Summer	Hot water and steam heating systems only (not required on modern diaphragm-style expansion tanks)
MAKE SURE SYSTEM HAS PROPER AMOUNT OF WATER.	Summer; also check during heating season.	Hot water and steam heating systems only
ADD CORROSION INHIBITOR AND ANTIFREEZE.	Summer	Hot water and steam heating systems only
CLEAN INDOOR COIL WITH VACUUM OR BRUSH.	Summer	Heat pump and central air conditioning systems only; use vacuum cleaner with brush attachment to remove dust and old toothbrush and mild detergent to remove grime.
CUT GRASS AND OTHER FOLIAGE AWAY FROM OUTDOOR UNIT.	As needed	Heat pump and central air conditioning systems only
COVER OR REMOVE UNIT FOR WINTER.	Fall	Room air conditioners only
SEAL GAPS BETWEEN UNIT AND ADJOINING WALL OR WINDOW.	Spring	Room air conditioners only
CLEAN CATALYTIC CONVERTER.	Summer	Woodstoves only; follow manufacturer's instructions.
SWEEP CHIMNEY.	Summer	Woodstoves only

GENERAL MAINTENANCE

TASK	SEASON	COMMENTS
INSPECT FOR TERMITES.	As needed	See "Termites, Beetles, and Carpenter Ants" on page 231.
INSPECT FOR WOOD ROT.	Summer	See "Rotting Wood" on page 168.
WASH AND REPAIR VINYL, ALUMINUM, OR CLAPBOARD SIDING.	Spring	See "Damaged Siding" on page 150.
CHECK ROOF FOR DAMAGED SHINGLES.	Spring	Repair damaged shingles immediately before leaks develop. (See "Leaky Roof" on page 24.)

GENERAL MAINTENANCE—CONTINUED

TASK	SEASON	COMMENTS
CHECK UNDERSIDE OF ROOF (IN ATTIC) FOR WATER STAINS.	Spring	Water stains indicate leak that can lead to wood rot. (See "Leaky Roof" on page 24.)
CLEAN VEGETATION OFF ROOF.	Fall	Cut away vines and branches. Sweep off pine needles with broom. Use power sprayer to remove moss, lichen, or fungus from wooden shingles (not asphalt shingles).
REPAINT OR RESTAIN WEATHERED SIDING OR TRIM.	Summer	Wind and weather can strip wood of finish and leave it open to rot. Refinish wood before it is damaged.
COAT WOOD DECKS WITH WATER REPELLENT.	Spring	See "Hot Spots for Rot" on page 170.
CLEAN AND REPAIR RAIN GUTTERS AND DOWNSPOUTS.	Spring and fall	See "Clogged Rain Gutter" on page 33 and "Damaged Rain Gutter" on page 37.
PAINT GALVANIZED STEEL GUTTERS AND FLASHING.	As needed	Try Rustoleum flat brown oil paint primer 7769.
CLEAN OUT WINDOW WELLS AND CELLARWAYS.	Fall	Leaves, grass clippings, and fallen sticks in window wells and cellarways will clog drains and attract vermin.
REPLACE WORN WEATHER-STRIPPING.	Fall	Worn weatherstripping will let warm air out and cold air into house.
RECAULK WINDOWS, DOORS, AND SIDING.	Fall	Splits and gaps in old caulking let water and cold air into house.
TRIM BACK OVERGROWN TREES AND SHRUBS THAT ABUT HOUSE.	Summer	Tree limbs, ivy, and dense vegetation can damage roofing and siding and give pests access to house. (See "Critter-Proofing Your Home" on page 223.)

SAFETY EQUIPMENT

TASK	SEASON	COMMENTS
CHECK FIRE EXTINGUISHERS.	Once a month	Make sure pressure is at proper levels.
TEST SMOKE DETECTORS.	Once a month	Press test button and listen for alarm.
PRACTICE FIRE DRILL.	Every six months	Involve children in mapping escape routes.
REPLENISH SURVIVAL PANTRY.	Every six months	See *Emergency Supplies* on page 14.
REPLACE SMOKE DETECTOR BATTERIES.	Once a year	Plan to change batteries every New Year's Day.

Water & Sewage Emergencies

Leaky Roof

DIVERTING THE LEAK

Quick Response

1. Position buckets or plastic sheet in attic to catch leaking water.

2. Inspect underside of roof to pinpoint leak.

rafter or truss

tack

rag

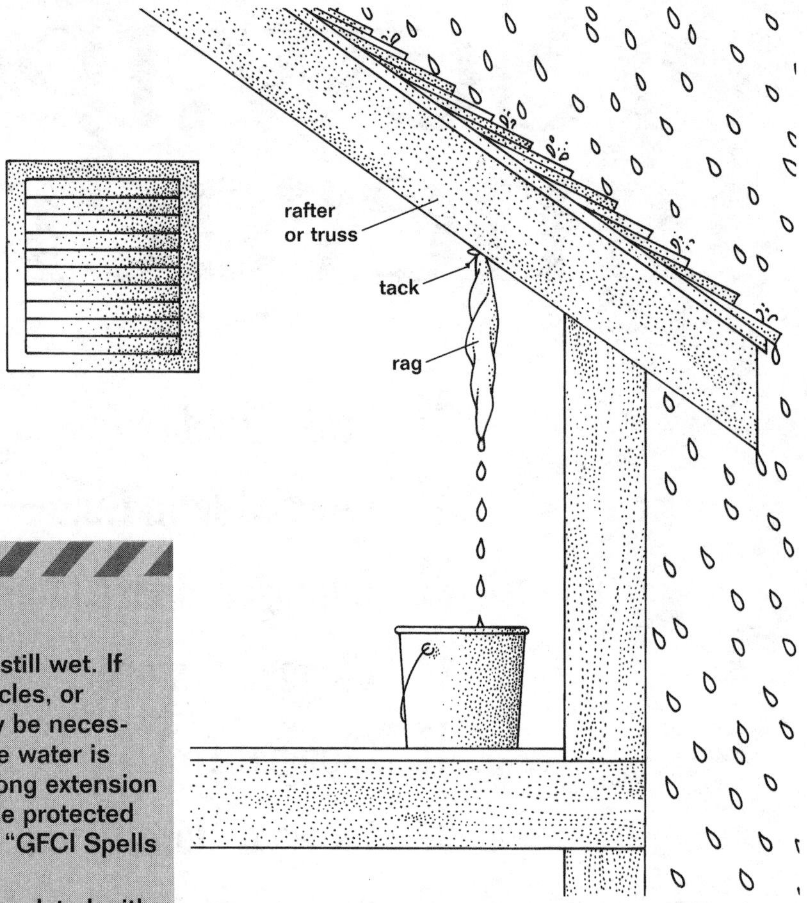

Using a tack and rag, it's sometimes possible to divert the leak into the bucket.

Hazards

● Do not attempt to get up on the roof while it's still wet. If water has leaked near electric switches, receptacles, or cords, beware of shock. For safety's sake, it may be necessary to turn off the electricity to the area until the water is cleaned up. If electric tools are required, use a long extension cord (to another circuit) plugged into a receptacle protected by a ground fault circuit interrupter (GFCI). (See "GFCI Spells Electrical Safety" on page 265.)

● If you're working in an unfinished attic that's insulated with loose or unfaced fiberglass, wear protective clothing, gloves, goggles, and a dust mask.

● If your roof is pitched more than 4 in 12 (that is, it rises more than 4 feet for every 12 horizontal feet), let a professional roofing contractor do the work.

● When working up on the roof, observe the safety precautions spelled out in "12 Steps to Ladder Safety" on page 35. Wear soft, rubber-soled shoes that provide a good grip and won't scuff the protective mineral surface on asphalt shingles. Avoid walking on ridge, hip, or valley areas, on loose or damaged shingles, or across portions of the roof that may be structurally unsound.

● If your roof has asbestos-cement shingles, call in a pro. Apart from the potential health hazards, asbestos-cement shingles are brittle and difficult to repair. (Replacement shingles have to be crafted out of substitute materials.) Asbestos-cement shingles are usually gray in color and have a thick, hard appearance. Some are hexagonal.

● Always wear gloves when working with metal flashing.

ATTACKING THE LEAK

Professional roofers claim that leaks *always* appear directly above an expensive computer system or over a grand piano—usually when the owner isn't home.

All jokes aside, water leaking through the roof can end up almost anywhere, even in the basement of a three-story house. Sometimes the leak is so subtle that it's easily overlooked, appearing as a damp or dark spot on the ceiling or under a strip of wallpaper that's peeled loose. Other times, when water comes streaming down the face of the chimney or splatters noisily on the dining room table, there's no subtlety at all.

Whatever the case, your first priority is to pinpoint the source of the leak. Plumbing leaks, attic condensation, or leaks coming through a wall can sometimes masquerade as a leaky roof. (See "Tracking Hidden Leaks" on page 57.)

If the roof really is to blame, move quickly to intercept the leak before it can cause any further damage.

CONTROLLING THE LEAK

Armed with a good flashlight, climb up in the attic and try to find the spot where the roof is leaking. It may not be directly above the place where the leak appeared in the lower part of the house, since water often takes a roundabout course.

If you find wet insulation underneath the leak, pull it out and stuff it in a plastic bag for disposal. (However, fiberglass insulation can sometimes be dried out and reused.) Lay boards across the joists to create a steady platform, then position a bucket or pan to catch the leak. Check the bucket frequently to make sure that it's not overflowing or that the leak hasn't moved.

Another tactic, if buckets and pans aren't practical, is to spread plastic sheets over the joists, overlapping and taping the seams. The sheets need to be turned up and taped around the edges to create a catch basin for the water. They must be sponged or mopped off frequently to keep too much water from pooling.

Water leaking down the face of a chimney or plumbing vent pipe is devilishly hard to control. Using duct tape or a thin bead of adhesive caulk, try attaching a sheet of plastic to the chimney or pipe so that the plastic intercepts the water and diverts it into a shallow pan or onto another plastic sheet, as described above. The seam must be flat and tight to keep water from winding under or around it.

Water trickling along the bottom edge of a rafter can sometimes be diverted into a bucket by hanging a rag from the rafter, as shown in *Diverting the Leak* on the opposite page. Just tack the rag into place so that it intercepts the water, which will wick down through the rag and drip into the bucket.

No Visible Damage?

Even if the leak isn't causing any damage in the lower part of the house, it's imperative to fix it quickly. Once moisture gets under the sheathing and into the rafters, rot will quickly follow. (See "Rotting Wood" on page 168.) ●

Once the water is controlled, take the time to mark the underside of the roof with a crayon or other waterproof marker so that you can remember the exact position of the leak. When things dry out and you're ready to do repairs, drive a nail up through the spot so it's easy to find when you get up on the roof.

SLEUTHING FOR THE LEAK

If you weren't able to catch the leak in the act, you'll have to do some patient detective work.

Check the insulation for clues—leaking water will often leave a funnel-shaped indentation in insulation, almost as if someone poked a finger into it.

Also look for residual water marks on the underside of the roof sheathing along the rafters, on the attic floor, or on the framing lumber around the chimney, vent pipe, or skylight. Since water usually travels downhill (see the exception cited below), track the water marks up to their highest point and mark the spot with a waterproof marker.

In older roofs, which may have leaked and been repaired before, water marks don't necessarily indicate an active leak. The only way to know for sure is to mark the spot and return to the attic when it's raining. Or you can string a garden hose up on the roof and drench the suspected area from the outside. Start just below the leak point and work your way up *slowly*.

As you proceed in your sleuthing, bear in mind that most roof leaks occur where the plane of the roof is penetrated by a chimney, vent pipe, skylight, or exhaust fan terminal or where a first-story roof intersects a wall on a two-story house, as shown in *Common Areas of Leaks* on page 26. Such leaks occur when water finds its way down through the protective flashing that is supposed to waterproof the seam between the two surfaces.

COMMON AREAS OF LEAKS

Leaks are tricky to track, but there are a few potential trouble spots you can target first. Check out these areas on your roof for damage that could lead to leaks.

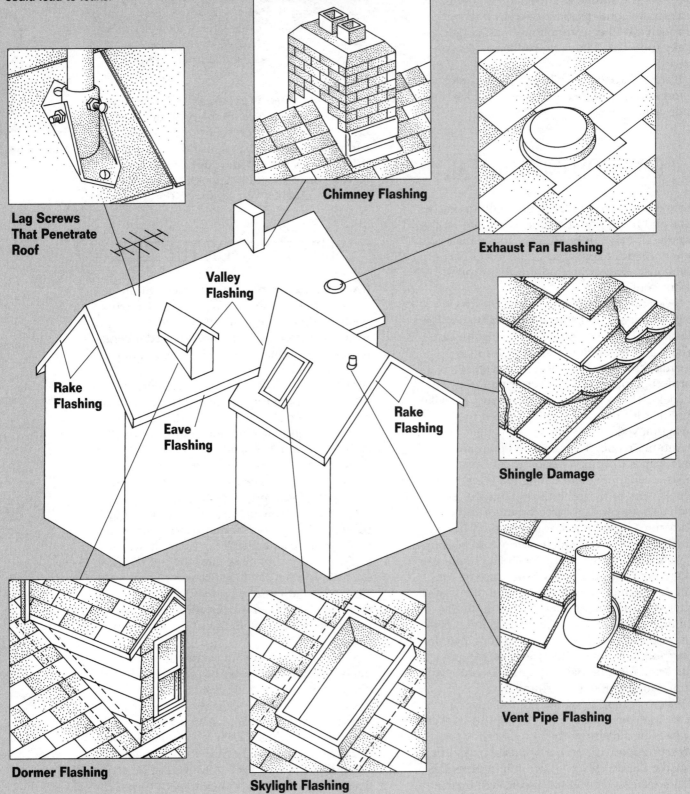

Lag Screws That Penetrate Roof

Chimney Flashing

Exhaust Fan Flashing

Valley Flashing

Rake Flashing

Eave Flashing

Rake Flashing

Shingle Damage

Dormer Flashing

Skylight Flashing

Vent Pipe Flashing

The lack of proper drip-edge flashing along the roof's eaves and rakes can also cause leaks, especially when the rain gutters aren't working properly and/or when ice dams are a problem. (See "Clogged Rain Gutter" on page 33, "Damaged Rain Gutter" on page 37, and "Avoiding Ice Dams" on page 41.)

When drip-edge flashing is absent or in poor repair, water can actually defy gravity, wicking its way up into the wood sheathing by capillary action. If the problem is not addressed, this type of leak will rot the sheathing along the lower part of the roof.

Cracked, loose, or missing shingles are the second leading cause of roof leaks. Such damage can occur suddenly, as when fallen tree limbs or storm winds rake the roof, or can occur as the inevitable result of weathering.

Once you've inspected the underside of the roof, go topside and look for additional clues. Wherever there are protrusions, valleys, or intersecting walls—as detailed in *Common Areas of Leaks* on the opposite page—check to see if the flashing or the cement holding the flashing is missing, cracked, or punctured. Also survey the plane of the roof, looking for damaged or missing shingles. The odds are good that the external damage is close to where the water appeared inside the attic.

If careful sleuthing doesn't reveal an obvious point of failure, call in a pro. Some leaks, such as those that occur underneath interwoven valleys and those that occur only when there's wind-driven rain, seem to defy detection.

STOPPING THE LEAK

The simple flashing and shingle repairs shown in the illustrations on this page and on pages 28 to 32 will stop most leaks. But even high-quality asphalt roofing cement, which is recommended for such repairs, will fail after a few years under the sun; thus, the leak will reappear and the patch will have to be made again. Likewise, a weatherworn roof that has suffered one shingle failure is bound to suffer more. Thus, there comes a point when patchwork simply isn't cost effective anymore. (See "Too Far Gone to Patch?" on page 30 and "How to Shop for a New Roof" on page 31.)

Buy a can or tube of good-quality asphalt roofing cement and a roll of fiberglass tape or asphalt-saturated cotton, available at most hardware stores and lumberyards. Canned cement

is generally less expensive than a tube but must be applied with a putty knife or trowel.

Of course, even good-quality roofing cement will wear out after a few years, requiring more maintenance. If the flashing or roofing is badly deteriorated, you are probably better off hiring a professional roofer to replace it.

REPAIRING FLASHING

To patch a flashing joint: Though fresh roofing cement can be applied over old, it's better to clean the joint first, using a stiff wire brush or a cold chisel and hammer to chip off the old cement. Using a caulk gun, reseal the joint with a generous, overlapping bead of roofing cement, as shown in *Patching a Flashing Joint* on this page. If the leak is in the cap flashing on a chimney and the flashing is loose, wedge a small piece of sheet metal into the mortar joint to secure the flashing before you reseal the joint, as shown in *Securing Chimney Flashing* on this page.

PATCHING A FLASHING JOINT

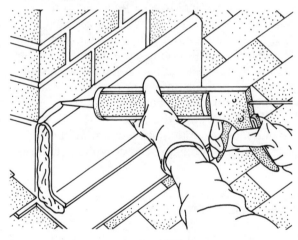

Chip away the old roofing cement before applying new cement. Apply it around the edges of leaking flashing.

SECURING CHIMNEY FLASHING

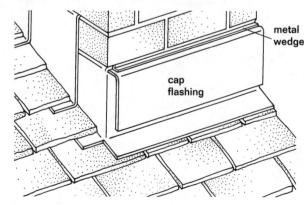

metal wedge

cap flashing

Wedge a V of sheet metal into the joint, if necessary, to secure the flashing.

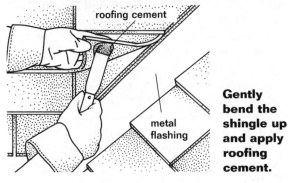

Sunny and Mild

Try to schedule repairs for a warm day, when asphalt shingles are pliable and easy to work with. In cold weather, asphalt shingles are brittle and easily broken. In hot weather, they're tacky and easily scuffed (and *you* get heat exhaustion). ●

To patch a small hole: Brush the rust off the metal flashing with a wire brush or sandpaper, and wipe the surface clean. Fill the hole with roofing cement, overlapping the edges by 1/2 inch. Polyurethane sealant is another good choice for patching small holes and narrow splits that are less than 1/8 inch wide.

To patch a large hole or split: Brush the rust off the metal flashing, and wipe it clean. Fill the hole with a thick, even bed of roofing cement, overlapping the edges by 2 inches or more. Cut a piece of fiberglass cloth large enough to lap the hole by 1 inch or more on every side. Embed the cloth evenly in the cement and cover it with another layer of cement, as shown in *Patching a Hole or Split* on this page.

To repair a leaking valley: An open valley, which is usually flashed with sheet metal or rolled roofing felt (and not with shingles), can be patched with roofing cement and fiberglass cloth, as described above. A patch can also be cut out of a similar metal or roofing felt and applied with roofing cement.

If a shingle along the edge of the valley has come loose or curled up, pack roofing cement under it and gently press it down on the flash-

ing, as shown in *Repairing an Open Valley* on this page. (No nails, please!) If the slope of the roof permits, you can set a brick or other weight on top of the shingle to hold it down while the cement sets. Otherwise, hold the shingle in place for a few minutes until the cement has a chance to grab.

REPAIRING AN OPEN VALLEY

roofing cement

metal flashing

Gently bend the shingle up and apply roofing cement.

A closed valley, which is covered with interwoven shingles, is more difficult to repair because the leak is usually hidden under the shingles. One repair method, which avoids tearing off the shingles, is to slip a piece of metal flashing up under each course of shingles, as shown in *Patching a Closed Valley* on the opposite page. Cut the patches out of a sheet of 0.024-inch-thick aluminum. Make them 7 inches square, bending them across opposite corners to match the angle of the valley.

Start with the bottom course of shingles, where the valley meets the eave. Apply roofing cement to the entire underside of the metal patch and to the top half of the top side. Slip the patch up under the shingle and press or

PATCHING A HOLE OR SPLIT

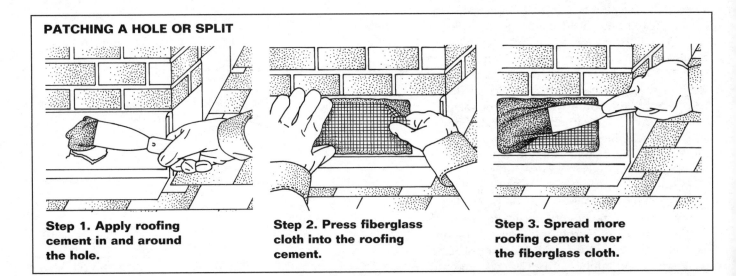

Step 1. Apply roofing cement in and around the hole.

Step 2. Press fiberglass cloth into the roofing cement.

Step 3. Spread more roofing cement over the fiberglass cloth.

PATCHING A CLOSED VALLEY

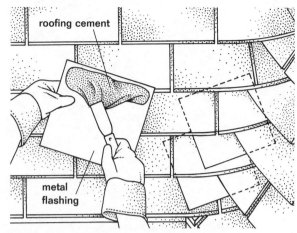

roofing cement

metal flashing

Slide a 7" square of flashing up under each course of the interwoven shingles.

weight the shingle until the cement holds. Proceed on up the valley until each course is done. While this type of repair isn't always successful, it's well worth a try. If it fails to stop the leak, hire a professional to remove the shingles and reflash the entire valley with painted aluminum, copper, or stainless steel.

FIXING
AN ASPHALT SHINGLE

If the edge of the shingle is curling up: Apply a quarter-size dab of roofing cement to the edge, as shown in *Repairing a Curled Edge* on this page, and gently press the shingle down. If the slope permits, weight the shingle down with a brick until the cement sets.

If the shingle is cupped or bulging: Check under the shingle to see if a roofing nail is backing out of the sheathing. If so, remove it with a slotted pry bar and drive in a new nail to one side. Don't try to bend the overlapping shingles back to hammer the nail directly—they're liable to break. Instead, set the end of your pry bar on the nail head and drive it indirectly by hammering on the pry bar, as shown in *Hammering a Popped Shingle Nail* on this page. Cap the old hole and the new nail with dabs of roofing cement.

If the shingle has torn loose from its nails: Using a slotted pry bar, remove the old nails and fill the holes with roofing cement. Reposition the shingle and drive new nails

Add Some Texture

To make asphalt shingle repairs more durable and attractive, mix ceramic granules in with the asphalt cement before you start, or press them into the patch once you're finished. The granules are available from roofing supply outlets. Or you may be able to scavenge a handful of old granules from the rain gutter, where they've washed down off the roof. ●

alongside the old holes. (To keep from damaging the overlapping shingles, use the hammering technique described above and shown in *Hammering a Popped Shingle Nail* on this page.) Cover the new nail heads with roofing cement.

If the shingle is split or cracked: Spread a layer of roofing cement under the tear and reposition the torn parts. Gently press or weight the shingle with a brick until the cement holds. Spread more cement along the top of the crack, overlapping the edges. Cut a strip of fiberglass cloth, press it evenly into the

REPAIRING A CURLED EDGE

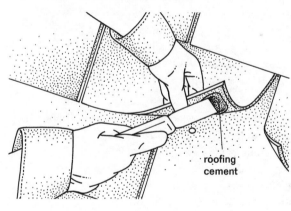

roofing cement

Dab a spot of roofing cement under the corner of the curled shingle, then press the shingle down.

HAMMERING A POPPED SHINGLE NAIL

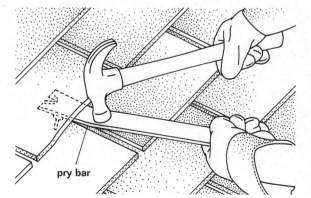

pry bar

Insert a slotted pry bar on top of the popped nail, then drive the nail by striking the pry bar with a hammer.

REPAIRING AN ASPHALT SHINGLE

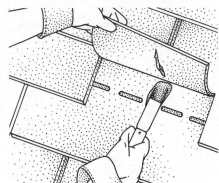

Step 1. Gently lift the shingle and spread roofing cement under the split.

Step 2. Press the shingle down and spread a thin coat of cement over the split.

fiberglass cloth

Step 3. Press fiberglass cloth into the cement and cover it with more cement.

Too Far Gone to Patch?

Deciding whether to repair or replace a leaky roof is a tough choice. Here are a few tips to help you decide.

● Asphalt shingles can last anywhere from 10 to 40 years, depending on their original quality and how much heat and ultraviolet light they're subjected to. At some point, they lose most of their protective coating of ceramic granules and then begin to shrink and curl. If you can easily break off a piece of shingle and crumble it between your fingers or if you find widespread curling, cracking, or splitting, the roof is ready to be reshingled.

● Wood shingle roofs can last decades if they have a chance to dry out between rains. If not, moss and rot become a problem and the roof may fail in as little as ten years. When there's no moisture problem, wood shingles eventually dry out, warp, and split. If you're losing pieces or whole shingles off the roof with annoying frequency, it's probably time to reroof.

● Tile and slate roofs are generally long-lived, though individual tiles or pieces may have to be replaced. The felt underlayment will probably crumble and fail first. In that case, the tile or slate is removed, new underlayment and flashing is installed, and then the tile or slate is remounted. This job is best left to a professional experienced with these roofs.

● If kept properly painted, galvanized steel roofs will last for decades. Unpainted, they quickly develop pinholes, which rust into larger holes. A steel roof will eventually become so riddled with holes that it can't be patched.

● Hire a qualified home inspector to give you an expert, *independent* assessment. (See "Hiring a Pest Control Professional" on page 238.)

cement so that it bridges the crack, and cover with more cement, as shown in *Repairing an Asphalt Shingle* on this page.

If a shingle is damaged beyond repair (or is missing): Try to find a replacement shingle stashed away in your garage, attic, or basement. (Roofers often leave a few shingles behind for just such needs.) If you can't find any originals, buy some new shingles, matching the color as closely as you can. (Remember that light-colored shingles will darken over time and dark-colored shingles will lighten.)

Using a slotted pry bar, remove the two rows of nails that hold the damaged shingle in place. Start by lifting the shingle that's two courses *above* the one you want to remove. Slip the pry bar in and remove the nails (usually four). Now lift the shingle that's directly above the damaged shingle and remove that row of nails as well, as shown in Step 1 of *Replacing an Asphalt Shingle* on the opposite page. This should free the damaged shingle so you can easily remove it.

Once you've removed the damaged shingle, use roofing cement to patch any holes in the roofing felt or surrounding shingles. Then slide the new shingle into place, aligning the bottom, as shown in Step 2 of *Replacing an Asphalt Shingle*. If you have a hard time sliding the new shingle into place, clip off the corners a little and try again.

Once the new shingle is in place, set the top row of nails first (but *not* in the old holes), nailing from one side to the other to avoid a

Let the Sun Shine In

Contrary to what scam artists might tell you, light showing through the underside of your roof doesn't necessarily mean it needs to be replaced. It's natural for light to shine in along the eaves, where soffit vents admit light, and around certain types of chimney flashing. Likewise, a wooden shingle or slate roof that admits light into the attic may be perfectly sound. ●

REPLACING AN ASPHALT SHINGLE

Step 1. Remove the nails that fasten the old shingle with a pry bar.

Step 2. Slip the new shingle in place and fasten it with roofing nails.

---

buckle in the middle. Use the indirect hammering technique described above and shown in *Hammering a Popped Shingle Nail* on page 29. Drive the bottom row of nails in the same manner. Cap each nail head with a dab of roofing cement.

How to Shop for a New Roof

● Hire an honest, experienced roofer who has an established business and a great reputation.

● It's usually best to replace *all* of the flashing when the roofing is replaced. However, copper or stainless steel flashing that's in good shape can be kept. So can the metal cap flashing around the chimney, provided it's in good condition and tuck-pointed into the mortar as it should be. *NOTE*: Unless it's spelled out in the contract, the roofer isn't obliged to replace the flashing.

● Though codes generally permit roofers to lay new asphalt shingles on top of old ones, thereby saving the homeowner money, the practice makes it impossible to inspect the condition of the sheathing or lath underneath or to replace worn flashing. Installing wooden shingles over existing roofing is especially discouraged since it's almost impossible to get an even, aesthetically pleasing installation that way.

● Specify No. 30 felt underlayment. Though some roofers use a lighter felt (No. 15) or no felt at all, the better-quality felt provides better protection against leaks.

● Ask for metal valleys made out of painted aluminum (0.024 inch thick or better), copper (16 ounces per square foot or more), or stainless steel (26 or 28 gauge). Closed valleys, interwoven out of shingles, are born to leak.

● Make sure the eaves and rakes are equipped with a proper drip edge. If ice dams are a problem, the eaves can be protected with a broad ice shield. (See "Avoiding Ice Dams" on page 41.)

● Unless the chimney straddles the ridge, it should have a small A-framed rise—called a "cricket"—installed on the up-roof side to keep water and debris from lodging in the crack.

● If there's rot in the fascia board, sheathing, or rafters, this is the ideal time to deal with it. It's also a good time to have rain gutters repaired or installed.

● The weight, asphalt content, color, and warranty of asphalt shingles are important considerations. Generally speaking, organic-reinforced asphalt shingles have more asphalt and a longer life than fiberglass-reinforced asphalt shingles. Discuss these points with the honest, experienced roofer you've hired.

● If you live in a hot climate, consider buying light-colored shingles. They'll help keep the roof temperature down, prolonging the life of the shingles. Providing plenty of ventilation in the attic also helps to lower roof temperatures and extend shingle life.

● Ask your roofer to leave behind a bundle of replacement shingles for that faraway day when you need to patch the roof.

● If you're going to reroof with cedar shakes, consider buying ones treated with fire-retarding and/or rot-preventing chemicals.

● Ask your local building inspector to look in on the job while the work is in progress and again when it's finished. Quality roofers won't mind this at all.

REPAIRING
A WOODEN SHINGLE

If the shingle is split (with both pieces still in place): Cut a metal patch out of a sheet of 0.024-inch-thick dark-painted aluminum. Make the patch 2 to 4 inches wide and long enough to extend 1 inch up under the overhanging shingle. To keep the patch from slipping out of place, bend the bottom corners down at a 45-degree angle so they'll wedge into the shingle below, as shown in *Patching a Wooden Shingle* on this page. Using a block of wood and hammer, tap the patch into place, until it's flush with its neighbors.

If the shingle is damaged beyond repair (or missing): Split the damaged shingle with a wood chisel and remove it piece by piece, as shown in Step 1 of *Replacing a Wooden Shingle* on this page. Cut the nails off with a hacksaw blade, as shown in Step 2 of *Replacing a Wooden Shingle*. (Wrap the blade with masking tape on one end to form a makeshift handle.) Trim the new shingle to fit (leaving a ¼-inch gap on either side) and tap it gently into place (but not quite flush with the shingles on either side). Drill pilot holes through the new shingle at a 45-degree angle,

up under the butt of the overhanging shingle. Using a hammer and nail set, drive the new nails in at a 45-degree angle, as shown in Step 3 of *Replacing a Wooden Shingle*. As you do, the shingle should pull up flush with its neighbors as the nail heads disappear up under the butt of the overhanging shingle. Cover the nail heads with roofing cement.

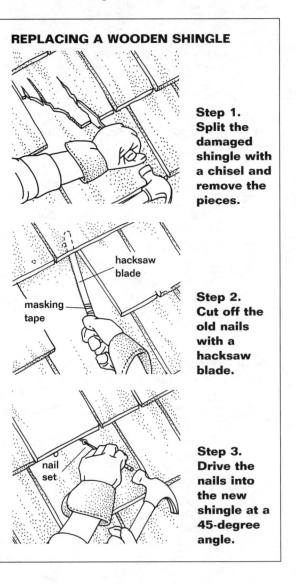

REPLACING A WOODEN SHINGLE

Step 1. Split the damaged shingle with a chisel and remove the pieces.

hacksaw blade

masking tape

Step 2. Cut off the old nails with a hacksaw blade.

nail set

Step 3. Drive the nails into the new shingle at a 45-degree angle.

PATCHING A WOODEN SHINGLE

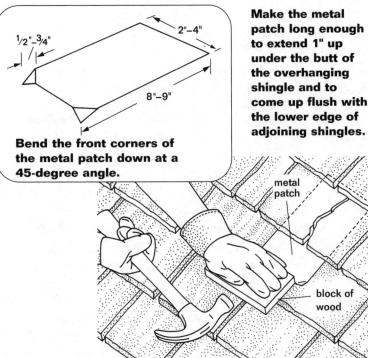

½"–¾"

2"–4"

8"–9"

Bend the front corners of the metal patch down at a 45-degree angle.

Make the metal patch long enough to extend 1" up under the butt of the overhanging shingle and to come up flush with the lower edge of adjoining shingles.

metal patch

block of wood

REPAIRING OTHER
TYPES OF ROOFING

While asphalt and wooden shingles account for more than 80 percent of all residential roofing, many other kinds of materials are used, including slate, tile, metal, and synthetics. Repairing leaks in these types of roofs is best left to a professional who specializes in their repair.

Clogged Rain Gutter

CLEANING THE GUTTERS

garden trowel

Cleaning gutters isn't so bad if you have the proper tools, including a sturdy ladder.

Quick Response

1. While it's raining, survey gutters and downspouts to see exactly where they are clogged and overflowing.

2. Check drop outlet on each downspout. Often leaves and other debris will gather there and back whole system up.

3. Clean out blockage as soon as possible.

DEALING WITH CLOGGED GUTTERS

Though a clogged rain gutter or downspout may not *seem* like much of an emergency, it needs to be treated like one. If you delay in fixing it, the weight of backed-up water and debris can cause the gutters to sag and leak. If the water should freeze, it can destroy the watertight seals that join gutter sections together or split the walls of the downspout.

Procrastination invites other problems as well. When the gutters are clogged, thousands of gallons of rainwater and snow melt that would ordinarily be diverted away from your

Hazards

● When you're working on your gutters, there is always the danger of falling—a danger not to be taken lightly.

● If you plan to work from the roof, wait for a dry day and wear shoes with nonskid soles. If your roof rises more than 4 feet for every 12 horizontal feet, work from a ladder.

● If you're going to work from the ground, use a sturdy ladder that's safely positioned and have a helper on hand to make the job safer and easier. (See "12 Steps to Ladder Safety" on page 35.)

● Wear work gloves. Gutters, especially metal types, have sharp, sometimes rusty, edges.

Bucket Elevator

To make cleaning gutters safer and easier, use a bucket to collect the refuse. Tie a stout line to the bucket's handle so that you can easily lower the bucket to the ground. You can use the bucket to raise and lower tools as well. ●

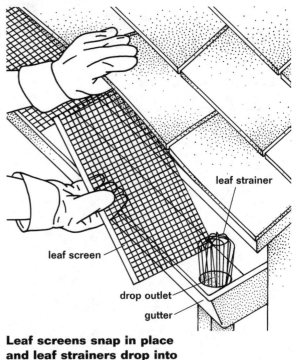

leaf strainer

leaf screen

drop outlet

gutter

Leaf screens snap in place and leaf strainers drop into the downspout.

house suddenly have no place to go. The water backs up into the fascia and soffit boards, promoting rot. It also bleeds down the side of your house, degrading the paint, and pools around the foundation, setting the stage for a wet basement. (See "Leaky Basement" on page 61.)

Start at the downspout or at the low end of the gutter, and work toward the high end. Use a garden trowel to scoop out leaves and twigs, and dump them into a bucket, as shown in *Cleaning the Gutters* on page 33.

As you clean the gutter, keep a roll of duct tape in your pocket so that you can tag any holes, scratches, low spots, or damaged seams you find. Stick the tape markers on the outer face of the gutter where they can be easily seen from the ground. This will speed things along when it comes time to make repairs. (See "Damaged Rain Gutter" on page 37.)

Once the entire length of gutter is cleaned, use a garden hose or bucket of water to flush it out. Watch the water as it flows from the high end to the low end and note any places where the gutter has sagged, allowing water to pool. Tighten or reposition the gutter's support brackets to bring the low spots back into proper alignment. (See "Leveling a Sagging Gutter" on page 38.)

To help keep the gutter from clogging again, install leaf screens across the top, as shown in *Installing Leaf Screens and Strainers* on this page. These lightweight metal or plastic screens, available at hardware stores and home centers, are designed to fit various gutter configurations.

CLEANING OUT
THE DOWNSPOUT

Using a garden hose with an adjustable nozzle, direct a high-pressure stream of water up into the downspout. Work the nozzle up the spout until it hits the clog at close range, as shown in

Cleaning the Downspout on this page. If that doesn't succeed in breaking the clog loose, try working from above, pushing the nozzle down into the drop outlet.

CLEANING THE DOWNSPOUT

Work a garden hose with a nozzle up into the downspout and turn on the water. The forceful stream should loosen the clog.

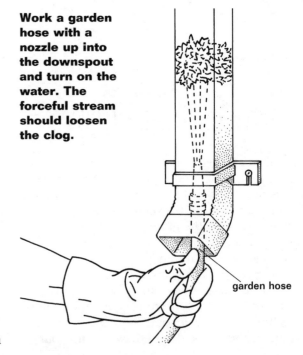

garden hose

12 Steps to Ladder Safety

Using a ladder is so fundamental to many repairs that many homeowners don't give a second thought to jumping on one. But a ladder can be as dangerous as a power saw, and who would use one of *those* without taking a few precautions? Here, then, is a list of guidelines for safe ladder use.

1. The ladder should be in good physical shape and of adequate strength and length for the job. Check the rating label on the ladder before you use it. Its weight capacity (counting you and your equipment) will range from 200 pounds (light duty—Type III) to 300 pounds (extra heavy duty—Type IA). The ladder should be long enough so that you don't have to work off the topmost rungs or stretch beyond a safe distance. A ladder equipped with non-skid, vinyl "shoes" is less likely to slip on smooth surfaces, such as concrete, for example, and won't mar flooring.

2. Wear shoes with nonskid soles when you're on a ladder, and never work on a ladder when it's raining, icy, or windy.

3. Check to see what's overhead before you move the ladder. Be extremely cautious around utility lines and tree branches. Use a fiber-glass or wooden ladder if there's any chance of the ladder coming in contact with an overhead power line.

4. Enlist a helper to help you move and steady the ladder and to assist you with your tools.

5. Position the ladder so that it sits firmly on the ground. If the ground is uneven or soft, use broad, stiff boards to create a steady platform. If necessary, cleat the ladder (or the boards) to keep it from slipping.

6. Tilt the ladder at about a 75-degree angle to the building. (The distance from the foot of the ladder to the building will be about one-fourth the length of the ladder.)

7. If you're using the ladder to climb up on the roof, adjust the ladder so that it extends at least 2 feet above the eave. If you have to lean the ladder up against a rain gutter, choose a spot where it will rest against a gutter support bracket. Take two short 2 × 4s and a towel up the ladder with you the first time you go. Set the 2 × 4s into the gutter to provide additional bracing. If you want to protect the gutter's finish, drape the towel between the gutter and the ladder.

8. Use a side- or rear-hanging tool belt to avoid snagging the rungs with your tools. Or raise and lower your tools in a bucket.

9. Keep yourself centered between the two rails of the ladder as you work. Don't lean out to extend your reach—get down and move the ladder to a better position.

10. Never stand on the top rungs of the ladder. Keep your waist below the level of the top rung.

11. Never permit more than one person on the ladder at a time.

12. If you're going to lean the ladder against the side of the house, equip the rails with rubber bumpers or rollers so that they don't scar the siding.

cleat

If water pressure fails to clear the downspout, use a drain auger. The tools and techniques are exactly the same as those used in cleaning out clogged house drains. (See "Using a Drain Auger" on page 53.)

To keep the downspout from clogging up again, install a metal or plastic strainer—sometimes called a "spider"—over each drop outlet, as shown in *Installing Leaf Screens and Strainers* on page 34.

CLEANING OUT THE DRAINPIPE AND DRY WELL

In some homes, downspouts flow directly into an underground drainpipe that carries rainwater to a storm sewer or dry well.

If the drainpipe is clogged, disconnect the downspout from it and use a drain auger to clean out the line. The technique for using an auger is explained in detail in "Clogged Main Drain" on page 51.

The auger won't work, of course, if the drainpipe has collapsed, rusted out, or become choked with tree roots. In that case, the pipe needs to be excavated and replaced or augered out by a professional.

Another possible problem, if your system empties into a dry well, is that the dry well has become so clogged with leaves, twigs, silt, and other debris that it can't perform its job—namely, to hold large amounts of incoming rainwater until it can be absorbed into the surrounding soil. If that is the case, the only remedy is to dig up the dry well and recondition it. Be advised, however, that even a new dry well, fully functioning, can overfill and back up in a heavy, prolonged rain. (See "Troubleshooting Guide to Wet Basements" on page 66.)

MAINTAINING GUTTERS

To keep your rain gutters and downspouts trouble-free, inspect them in late fall when the last leaves are down and again in the spring to check for ice damage. Clean off the leaf

Cleaning Out the Gutter

Though a tennis ball or the occasional deceased squirrel may clog a rain gutter, fallen leaves and twigs are the more typical culprits. These are most easily removed right after a rainstorm, when they're still wet and pliable.●

screens and strainer caps, and remove any debris that's filtered down into the gutter. Make sure that the downspout extension, splash block, or other accessory used to direct water away from the foundation is working properly. (See *Your Home's Primary Lines of Defense* on page 64.)

Carefully prune back any tree limbs that extend out over the roof or gutters. Not only will this reduce the amount of leaves and twigs you have to remove each season, it will also reduce the chance that a fallen limb will damage the roof or gutter system.

Since neither plastic nor aluminum gutters rust, they require little surface maintenance. But galvanized steel gutters *are* susceptible to rust, especially when the coating gets scratched. If you find a deep scratch, clean off any rust, and cover the spot with a thin layer of roofing cement. Be sure to feather the cement out so that it doesn't leave a lump or ridge to impede the flow of water. Steel can also be painted, provided you clean the surface with a 50–50 solution of vinegar and water and apply a rust-resistant primer coat first.

Wooden gutters, which are prone to split and rot, typically need to be painted every two or three years. If the inside of the gutter is split and worn beyond the help of paint, you can extend the wood's life by lining it with fiberglass. This is done by embedding fiberglass cloth in a thin, smooth bed of resin. Two more coats of resin on top of the cloth are usually recommended with ample drying time allowed for each. Follow the instructions on the kit.

If the wood is in really poor condition, the cost and effort involved in maintaining it may not be justified. Replacing it with a low-maintenance plastic or aluminum gutter system might be more cost-effective.

Damaged Rain Gutter

Gutters and downspouts come in several different shapes and sizes. Materials include aluminum, vinyl, and steel.

Quick Response

1. Use duct tape as temporary patch for leaky gutter.

2. If gutter is dangling from eaves, go ahead and pull it down.

3. Plan to make repairs as soon as possible to avoid increased repair costs and more damage.

TAKING NATURE'S ABUSE

Because rain gutters and downspouts are on the front line in protecting your house from water, they take a lot of abuse from the elements. While high winds or falling branches can inflict quick and dramatic damage, it's the slower, more mundane forces of nature that usually cause the problems. These include the relentless expansion and contraction of gutter sections, rust, rot, and the sheer weight of ice, snow, and rainwater. (See "Avoiding Ice Dams" on page 41.) Even fallen leaves must be perceived as enemies, since their weight puts additional stress on the support brackets, and the tannic acid produced as they decay promotes corrosion.

Hazards

● Always read the safety precautions when working with sealants and caulks. Some are hazardous to touch or inhale; others are highly flammable.

● See "Hazards" on page 33 and "12 Steps to Ladder Safety" on page 35.

REPAIRING A LEAKING GUTTER JOINT

As outdoor temperature changes, the joints in the gutters and downspouts expand and contract, which can cause them to leak.

If you have vinyl gutters that snap together (no adhesives), remove the slip-joint connector that's leaking and replace the rubber seals. Replacement seals should be available from the dealer or manufacturer at little or no cost.

If you have vinyl gutters that are glued together (or if you can't find replacement seals for a snap-together system), you can fix a leaking joint, as shown in *Sealing a Gutter Joint* on this page.

The type of "Band-Aid" joint shown in *Sealing a Gutter Joint* is also recommended to stop leaking joints in aluminum or galvanized steel gutters. If you prefer, you can use neutral-cure silicone instead of Kraton rubber sealant on metal gutters, but silicone must be thinned at the edges so that it doesn't leave a pronounced ridge. (Kraton, being less viscous than silicone, will flatten across the patch without tooling.)

On a metal gutter system, you may discover that one or more of the seams is lapped backwards, allowing water to run into the seam. If this is the case, take the sections apart and reassemble them before you seal the joints. Sections of gutter or downspout should overlap on the downhill side, like shingles on a roof. After the gutters and downspouts are properly lapped, seal the joints with Kraton rubber sealant or neutral-cure silicone (for metal only) so that water can't back into them.

LEVELING A SAGGING GUTTER

A rain gutter should be pitched so that water flows gradually and uniformly down to the drop outlet. A 1-inch drop for every 16 feet of run is a good rule of thumb, though it need not be precise. If there's a sag anywhere along the gutter, it will collect standing water, debris, and ice, putting additional weight on the sag.

It's easy to spot a low point: Simply pour a bucket of water into the high end of the gutter and watch it flow to the downspout. Water will pool in the valley.

Your first step in leveling the gutter should be to inspect the fascia board or rafter ends for rot, especially where the gutter's support

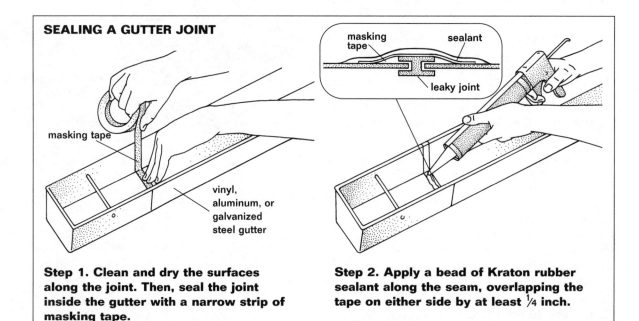

SEALING A GUTTER JOINT

masking tape

sealant

leaky joint

masking tape

vinyl, aluminum, or galvanized steel gutter

Step 1. Clean and dry the surfaces along the joint. Then, seal the joint inside the gutter with a narrow strip of masking tape.

Step 2. Apply a bead of Kraton rubber sealant along the seam, overlapping the tape on either side by at least ¼ inch.

brackets are attached. If you can push a screwdriver into the wood with little or no resistance, the board is probably rotten to the point that it can't support the brackets, causing them to sag. If this is the case, take the gutter down, brackets and all, and replace the rotten fascia board. You'll then have a good solid surface on which to mount the gutters.

If you discover rot on the end of a rafter or other structural parts, it needs to be treated—and perhaps braced—before you can continue. (See "Rotting Wood" on page 168.)

If the wood is solid, you may be able to adjust a sagging gutter simply by tightening one or more support brackets, which are secured to the fascia board or rafter ends with spikes, screws, or nails, as shown in *Typical Gutter Support Systems* on this page. Another tactic—for metal gutter systems—is to gently bend the support brackets up with a pair of pliers, as shown in *Adjusting a Gutter Bracket* on this page.

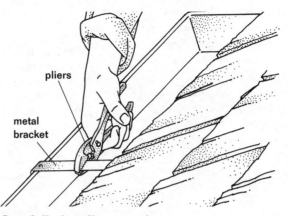

Carefully bending metal brackets up can adjust the gutter height.

ADDING A GUTTER BRACKET

If the original gutter installation wasn't properly braced, it may be necessary to add new support brackets, as shown in *Adding Brackets* on this page. A well-braced system should have support brackets every 24 inches on center in climates that have lots of snow and ice. Check with a local gutter installer to see what spacing is common in your area.

If you do add new brackets, try to sink the screws, nails, or spikes through the fascia into a rafter end, as shown in *Adding Brackets*. The rafters provide much better support than the fascia board alone. (Rafters or trusses are usually spaced across the roof at either 16 or 24 inches on center.)

As a last resort, you may have to remove one or more of the support brackets and move it

TYPICAL GUTTER SUPPORT SYSTEMS

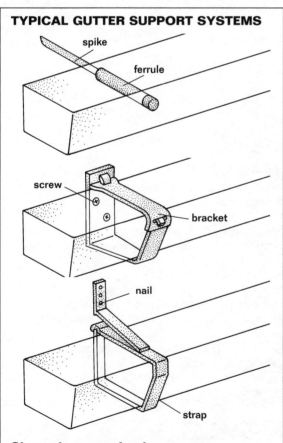

Shown here are the three most common systems for hanging gutters: spike and ferrule (*top*), bracket (*center*), and strap (*bottom*).

ADDING BRACKETS

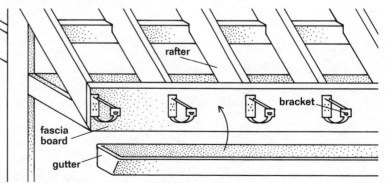

Try to attach brackets to rafter ends, if possible.

higher, filling the old holes in the fascia board or rafter end with wood putty.

If the support brackets are attached to the roof up underneath the shingles, be careful not to break the shingles as you lift them. It's easier if you wait for a warm day when the shingles become pliant. Wooden shingles, tiles, and slate have to be removed to access this type of gutter bracket.

PATCHING HOLES

Of the three primary gutter materials in use—vinyl, aluminum, and galvanized steel—only steel, which is vulnerable to rust, is likely to develop holes.

If the entire gutter is rusted and developing holes, it is probably wiser to replace it than to keep sinking time and money into repairs. Check out the table "Buying New Gutters" on this page for an overview of the various gutter systems available.

To patch large holes, refer to *Patching a Hole* on this page. This type of patch works

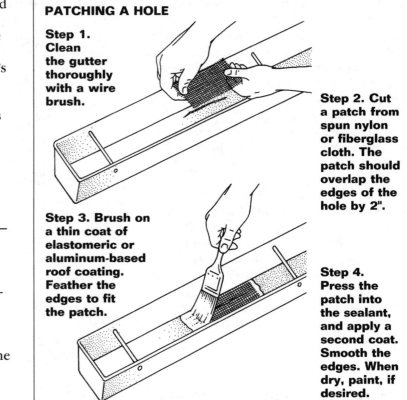

PATCHING A HOLE

Step 1. Clean the gutter thoroughly with a wire brush.

Step 2. Cut a patch from spun nylon or fiberglass cloth. The patch should overlap the edges of the hole by 2".

Step 3. Brush on a thin coat of elastomeric or aluminum-based roof coating. Feather the edges to fit the patch.

Step 4. Press the patch into the sealant, and apply a second coat. Smooth the edges. When dry, paint, if desired.

BUYING NEW GUTTERS

MATERIAL	COST *	INSTALLATION *	MAINTENANCE	COMMENTS
GALVANIZED STEEL	Least expensive	Challenging	Moderate	Subject to rust; available with baked-on enamels in various colors
VINYL	Moderately expensive	Easy	Low	Won't rust; limited color selection; may discolor over time; not easily painted
ALUMINUM	Moderately expensive	Challenging	Low	Won't rust; available with baked-on enamels in various colors; thin-gauge aluminum gutters (0.032 inch) dent easily, so heavier gauge (0.070 inch) is recommended
WOOD	Most expensive	Challenging	Heavy	Won't rust; preserves the original beauty of older, classic homes; can provide a special architectural touch to new homes; subject to rot
COPPER	Most expensive	Professional installation recommended	Low	Won't rust; preserves the original beauty of older, classic homes; can provide a special architectural touch to new homes

* If you're getting cost estimates for a professional installation, make sure they include an evaluation of the fascia board or rafter ends.

well with aluminum, copper, and wooden gutters, too. And it can be painted to match the rest of the gutter.

To patch a very small hole, knock the rust off the spot with a wire brush, clean the surface with paint thinner, let it dry, and seal the hole with a dab of neutral-cure silicone caulk. (*NOTE:* For galvanized steel gutters that are less than six months old, the surface should be treated with a 50/50 solution of vinegar and water to clean and etch the surface so that the sealant will stick.)

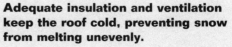
Patching a downspout is much more difficult—especially if the rust hole is large—because the patch has to go on the outside where it's subjected to constant water pressure. It's easier just to replace the damaged section.

Avoiding Ice Dams

One of the most common causes of roof and gutter damage is ice buildup along the eaves. These so-called ice dams are formed when snow melts off the upper portion of the roof and then refreezes further down, forming a ridge of ice.

HOW ICE DAMS FORM

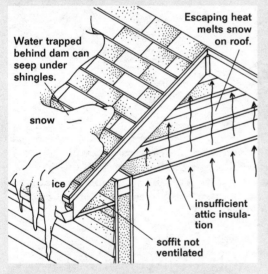

Water trapped behind dam can seep under shingles.

Escaping heat melts snow on roof.

snow

ice

insufficient attic insulation

soffit not ventilated

Water refreezes at the eave, forming an ice dam. The sheer weight of the ice dam can damage gutters.

If you have chronic problems with ice dams, as shown in *How Ice Dams Form*, it's a good bet that your attic isn't sufficiently insulated and/or ventilated. Thus, heat escaping up into the attic warms the underside of the roof, causing the snow above to melt. When the snow melt trickles down to the eaves, where the roof is colder, it refreezes.

The first step in preventing ice dams, as shown in *Preventing Ice Dams*, is to make sure that your attic insulation meets or exceeds the energy code requirements for your region. The standards range from R-19 (6 inches of fiberglass batt or equivalent) in the Deep South to R-49 (15 inches) in the far North. If you're unsure how much insulation you need, check with your local utility or code officials, or contact the Energy Efficiency and Renewable Energy Clearinghouse, P.O. Box 3048, Merrifield, VA 22116; (800) 523-2929.

A properly ventilated attic should have 1 to 3 square feet of unimpeded vent area (ridge, soffit, gable, or other) for every 300 square feet of attic. The low end of the range is adequate if the vents are covered with large-mesh screen wire (1/4 inch) only. More total vent area is required if the vents are covered with smaller mesh screen wire (1/8 or 1/16 inch) and/or louvers, since they impede the flow of air.

If natural temperature swings still cause ice dams—even though your attic is properly insulated and ventilated—you can install a protective aluminum or copper shield—sometimes called an "ice belt"—along the eaves. The shield is available through lumberyards and roofing supply outlets.

PREVENTING ICE DAMS

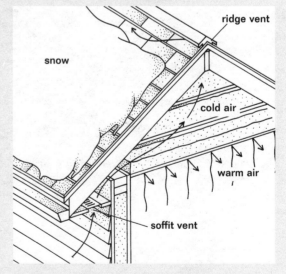

ridge vent

snow

cold air

warm air

soffit vent

Adequate insulation and ventilation keep the roof cold, preventing snow from melting unevenly.

Clogged Fixture

Quick Response

1. Clean drain stopper.

2. Use plunger.

3. Open and clean trap.

4. Use drain auger or hydraulic nozzle to clear clog.

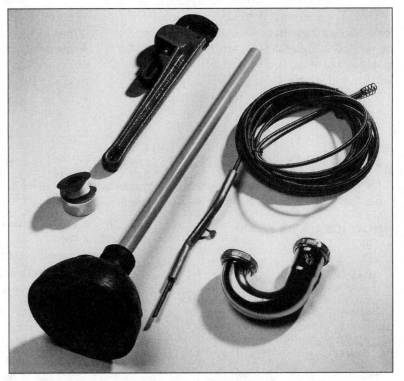

Here are a few of the common characters you will become acquainted with when dealing with plumbing problems (*clockwise from left*): Teflon tape, pipe wrench, simple drain auger or "snake," sink trap, and funnel cup plunger (funnel cup retracted).

Hazards

- Do *not* use chemical or biological drain cleaners if the drain is *completely* stopped up. Chemical drain cleaners can release noxious fumes and burn unprotected skin. When they fail to do the job, you're left with a sink or tub full of dangerous chemicals. (See "Do Drain Cleaners Really Work?" on page 46.)
- Wear rubber gloves to protect your hands.

UNCLOGGING A SINK DRAIN

If the sink is the *only* fixture in the bathroom that's backing up, it's a good bet that the clog is right there in the pop-up stopper or in the trap underneath. If other bathroom fixtures are also clogged, the stoppage may be further along, possibly in the branch drain (see below) or in the main house drain. (See "Clogged Main Drain" on page 51.)

To unclog a sink, start by removing the pop-up stopper, as shown in the first part of *Removing the Stopper* on the opposite page. In some models, this can be done simply by turning the stopper a quarter turn and pulling it out. In others, you have to get underneath the basin with a monkey wrench, and disconnect the lift lever and nut that hold the stopper in place, as

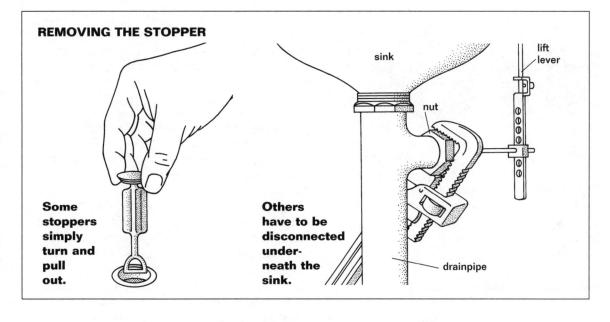

REMOVING THE STOPPER

sink

lift lever

nut

Some stoppers simply turn and pull out.

Others have to be disconnected underneath the sink.

drainpipe

shown in the second part of *Removing the Stopper.* Position a bucket or pan underneath to catch any spilling wastewater.

Once the stopper is out, remove any soap, hair, or debris that's stuck to it. If that doesn't unclog the sink drain, reach for your plunger.

USING A PLUNGER

For unclogging sinks and tubs, you'll need a plunger with a flat-faced profile or a conical-shaped plunger with the bulb retracted.

But before you get started, make sure the plunger will work on your sink. Sometimes the size or shape of the basin makes it impossible to fit a plunger in snug against the drain for effective use. Or perhaps you have a wall-hung sink that isn't braced well enough to support the forceful pushing action that a plunger requires. In either case, forget the plunger and disassemble the trap, as described below.

If a plunger *can* be used, first plug the overflow hole with a wet rag so that the pumping action won't be dissipated. If the fixture has a double basin (as is common with kitchen sinks), plug all drains but the one you're working on.

Start with a few inches of water in the basin. Allow the cup to fill with water, then press the plunger firmly down over the drain and pump it vigorously up and down for about 1 minute.

If the water level drops, *congratulations!* You've succeeded in moving the clog. Keep plunging until the drain is completely cleared, and then flush the line with 3 or 4 gallons of boiling water, which will help dissolve any remaining soap or grease that are in the line.

(Be careful not to burn yourself!) If the plunger doesn't do the trick, try cleaning out the trap.

CLEANING THE TRAP

Some sinks, especially those with older copper plumbing, have a clean-out plug built into the bottom of the trap. With a bucket or bowl under the trap to catch the water, remove the plug and let it drain, as shown in *Cleaning a Trap with a Clean-Out Plug* on this page. Insert a coat hanger or other stiff wire up into the trap and see if you can find and dislodge the clog.

If fishing a wire up through the clean-out plug doesn't help (or if you didn't have a

CLEANING A TRAP WITH A CLEAN-OUT PLUG

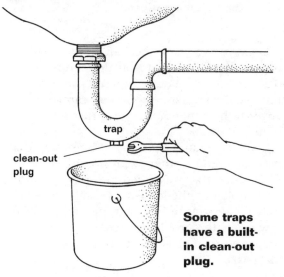

trap

clean-out plug

Some traps have a built-in clean-out plug.

clean-out plug to start with), go ahead and take the trap apart, as shown in *Removing a Trap* on this page. This is an easy task if the trap has coupling nuts or slip joints to unscrew—and fortunately, that's how most chrome and plastic traps are plumbed.

REMOVING A TRAP

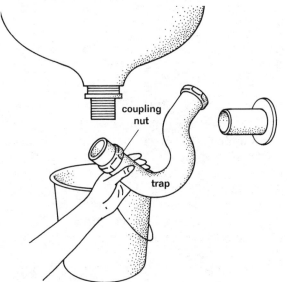

Most modern sink traps are easy to disassemble. Simply loosen the coupling nuts, and slide the trap off at the adjoining pipes.

Once you've taken the trap apart, clean it thoroughly. If the clog isn't there, don't despair—the next step requires you to remove the trap anyway so you can get an auger or hydraulic nozzle into the line behind the sink.

If you have an old-fashioned brass trap that was soldered together (with no union) or a plastic trap that was glued into place without any slip joints, the job isn't so simple. Your only recourse is to cut the pipe with a hacksaw. Once the problem is resolved, you'll then have to replace the trap with new materials.

If this is your fate, be sure to cut the pipe squarely, leaving a 2- or 3-inch stub protruding from the wall or floor to accommodate a rubber or plastic coupling for the new trap.

USING A DRAIN AUGER

A drain auger or plumber's "snake," as it's sometimes called, is essentially a long, stiff cable with a hook or spring on the end that's pushed down into the drain line to bore through or snag debris.

To use an auger, start by releasing the setscrew on the handle and push as much of the cable down into the open drain as you can, as shown in *Operating a Drain Auger* on this page. When you feel the tip hit the clog, set the screw and push on the cable as you crank it clockwise. As the clog begins to break up and move on down the drain line, extend the cable and keep pushing and cranking until the clog is pushed out of the branch drain into the main drain (the large vertical drain of the system) beyond. At that point, you'll feel the resistance on the cable go slack and perhaps hear the tip of the auger flopping around inside the drainpipe.

If the clog can't be pushed, perhaps you can snag it on the cable tip and pull it out. If you do snag part or all of the clog, continue turning the coil spring clockwise as you retrieve it. You may have to go in and out

OPERATING A DRAIN AUGER

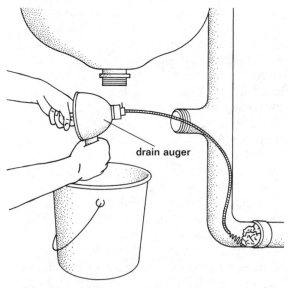

Feed the auger in until it reaches the blockage, then turn the crank clockwise to break up the clog.

several times before you actually snag and remove the entire clog. Keep some rags handy to wipe the cable clean as you pull it back out of the drain.

After the clog is removed, reassemble the trap and flush the drain with 3 or 4 gallons of boiling water. (Again, be careful not to scald yourself.) For additional information about buying and using an auger, see "Using a Drain Auger" on page 53.

USING A HYDRAULIC NOZZLE

Another effective way to clean out the branch drain behind your sink is to use a hydraulic nozzle, or "flush bag," as it's called in the trade. This simple device consists of an expandable rubber bladder and a nozzle that screws onto the end of an ordinary garden hose. With the water supply to the hose turned off, the hydraulic nozzle is inserted into the open drain as far as possible, ideally right to the point of the clog. When the water is turned on, the nozzle's built-in bladder expands to form a watertight collar against the walls of the drain line while the nozzle releases a powerful jet of water against the clog. When you turn the water off, the bladder automatically deflates itself. For more details, see "Using a Hydraulic Nozzle" on page 54.

UNCLOGGING A TUB DRAIN

If your tub has a pop-up stopper in the drain hole, as shown in *Pulling the Stopper Out of a Tub* on this page, start by pulling it out and cleaning off the hair and soap scum. Also disassemble the drain assembly that runs through the overflow drain and clean it. If there's no pop-up stopper—that is, only a strainer plate—remove the strainer and fish a wire down into the drain hole to see if you can snag and pull out the clog.

If that fails, try a plunger. But first unscrew the overflow plate, pull the drain assembly out, and stuff the hole with a wet rag. Otherwise, a lot of the force you exert on the plunger will be lost up through the overflow hole.

Once the rag is in place, fill the tub with a few inches of water and follow the steps in "Using a Plunger" on page 43. If vigorous plunging doesn't unclog the line, try a drain auger. (See "Using a Drain Auger" on the opposite page.)

Check the Nozzle Size

Hydraulic nozzles come in several sizes to fit different-size drainpipes. When you buy one, make sure that it's suitable for residential-size drains, which are typically 2 to 4 inches in diameter. ●

It's much easier to unplug a tub if you don't have to run the auger through the trap. Some older houses are plumbed so that you can access the tub's trap through a removable floor plate. Others have an access panel in the wall behind the tub. If you have neither, it may be possible to get to the trap from the basement or floor below. In any case, removing the trap is the best way to gain access for your auger.

If you can't get into the trap, the best alternative is to work the auger cable down

PULLING THE STOPPER OUT OF A TUB

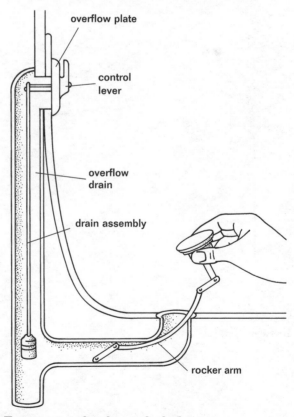

To get at a clog in a tub drain, you will have to pull the stopper out, and clear away any debris. For tough clogs, you may also need to remove the overflow plate and the drain assembly.

through the overflow drain on the tub, as shown in *Clearing a Tub Drain with an Auger* on this page. (*Don't* try going through the drain hole.)

Using the techniques described in "Using a Drain Auger" on page 44, work the cable down the drainpipe until it reaches the main drain. Once the drain is cleared, put the pieces back together and flush the pipe with boiling water. (Take care not to burn yourself!) Finally, clean off the drain assembly and screw it back into place.

NOTE: Using a hydraulic nozzle to clear a backed-up tub isn't recommended. These devices have a nasty habit of becoming stuck in tub drain lines.

CLEARING A TUB DRAIN WITH AN AUGER

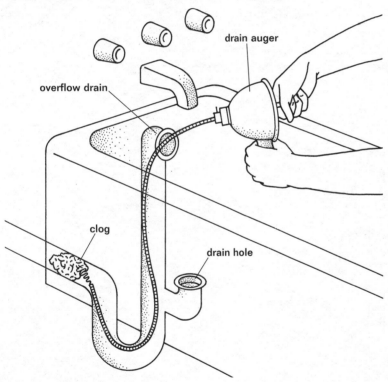

drain auger

overflow drain

clog

drain hole

If you can't access the trap, feed the auger through the overflow drain.

Do Drain Cleaners Really Work?

While chemical drain cleaners can sometimes help open a drain that's *partially* clogged, professional plumbers generally discourage their use (despite what TV commercials might lead you to believe).

For one thing, these products contain powerful acids or alkalis that can burn your skin. They can be hard on your plumbing, too. What's more, if a chemical drain cleaner doesn't solve the problem and it becomes necessary to take the trap apart or remove clean-out plugs in the system, the now-toxic slush inside your pipes makes the job a lot more *interesting*. (If you end up calling a plumber after trying a chemical drain cleaner, warn him before he goes to work or he might be burned by the drain cleaner residue.)

The so-called "biological" drain cleaners are much safer and usually more effective for opening a slow drain. These products work by introducing helpful strains of bacteria into the clogged drain, where they feast on the organic matter that's choking the pipe. In just a few days, these hard-working bacteria can actually double the flow rate of a slow drain and will diligently continue working to keep it open.

If you opt for a biological treatment, be sure to read and follow the instructions carefully. Some products require that you discontinue using the drain for a specified time so that the bacteria can establish themselves. Others call for repeated applications to be effective. Still others are harmful if they're swallowed or come in contact with your skin.

Two biological drain cleaners with proven track records are Plumb Clean, an inexpensive powder made by Kinzie and Payne Biochemical in St. Louis, and Roto-Rooter Concentrated Drain Cleaner, which won high praise from *Consumer Reports* magazine.

Clogged Toilet

USING A PLUNGER

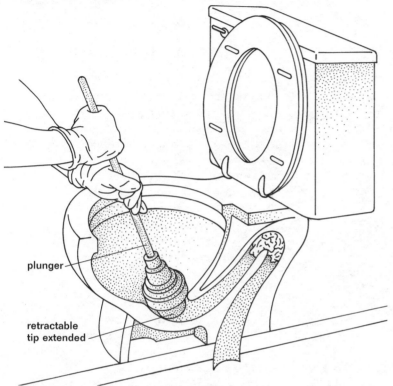

plunger

retractable
tip extended

Plunging should remove most toilet clogs. Be sure to use a plunger with a retractable tip. Extend the tip and try to create a seal around the outlet as you plunge.

Quick Response

1. Stop using toilet.

2. Clean up any overflow. (See "Spills" on page 247.)

3. Use rubber plunger to clean out trap.

4. If plunger fails to unclog toilet, try closet auger.

5. If necessary, remove toilet to clean out trap or drain.

USING YOUR HEAD

When someone reports a stopped-up toilet, your first instinct is to test-flush it to see for yourself. *Don't!* You're liable to end up with a bathroom full of muck.

Instead, calmly take the lid off the toilet tank and operate the stopper valve by hand, letting a little water flow into the bowl. If the toilet is indeed plugged, you'll see the water rise in the toilet bowl and you'll be able to stop the water before it overflows the rim.

Hazards

● Do *not* use chemical or biological drain cleaners. These are unlikely to work on a toilet that is completely stopped up, especially if the clog is located below the trap. What's more, chemical drain cleaners can release noxious fumes and burn unprotected skin. When they fail to do the job, you're left with a toilet full of dangerous chemicals.

● If sewage-laden water has backed up onto the floor, wear rubber gloves and boots while you clean it up. Afterward, thoroughly clean and disinfect the area, your tools, and—most importantly—*yourself*. (See "Spills" on page 247.)

LOCATING THE CLOG

By checking to see if other plumbing fixtures are stopped up, you can usually guess where the clog is located. If only the one toilet is affected, it's a good bet that the clog is right there in the toilet's internal trap.

If the tub and sink in the same bathroom are also plugged, the clog has to be somewhere below the toilet trap, perhaps in the horizontal drain line that's immediately behind the toilet or somewhere in the main drain. (See *Your Plumbing System* on page 2.) If *all* of your household drains are stopped up, see "Clogged Main Drain" on page 51.

If the clog appears to be in the toilet trap or the drain pipe immediately behind the toilet, read on to see how to get things flowing again.

PLUNGING THE TOILET

All toilets, regardless of their design, have a built-in trap that prevents sewer gas from backing up into the house. When too much paper gets caught in the trap or foreign objects are accidentally flushed and wedged inside it, the trap has to be cleared.

Since cleaning out a stopped toilet can be pretty grubby work, dress in old work clothes, rubber boots, and long rubber gloves. Protect the bathroom floor around the toilet with a thick mat of newspapers or a plastic sheet.

With rubber gloves on and a bucket standing by, remove any visible debris in the bowl. Once that's done, reach down into the trap and see if you can feel the clog. There's a chance—albeit slim—that you can remove the stoppage by hand.

If that doesn't work, try using a rubber plunger. The most effective type of plunger for working on a toilet has a conical bulb on the tip that fits right down into the narrow part of the bowl, as shown in *Using a Plunger* on page 47. Since the bulb is retractable, this type of plunger can also be used on other household drains.

To plunge the toilet, fill the bowl about three-quarters full with clean water. With the bulb extended, insert the plunger into the toilet and let it fill with water. Then insert the bulb firmly into the bowl and pump it vigorously for about one minute (or until you hyperventilate). It's important that the toilet bowl and the plunger cup be full of water to exert maximum pressure on the clog.

If the water level falls, you've succeeded in dislodging the clog. Keep plunging until the drain line is completely cleared and the toilet flushes normally. If plunging doesn't work, catch your breath, then borrow, rent, or buy a closet auger.

USING A CLOSET AUGER

A closet auger is a specialty tool with just one purpose in life: cleaning out clogged toilet traps. As shown in *Operating a Closet Auger* on this page, the plastic or rubber tip of the auger is shaped to slip up into a toilet's trap without chipping or scratching the porcelain.

Don't use an ordinary drain auger for this job; it's more difficult to work with and quite likely will damage your toilet.

To use a closet auger, start with the toilet three-quarters full of water so that the clog remains under pressure. With the auger's coil spring pulled all the way back into the sleeve, slip the tip of the auger down into the bowl and around the bend. Turning the auger handle *clockwise*, work the coil spring through the twists and turns of the toilet's trap until you feel it run into the clog.

It takes strength and coordination—plus a sensitive touch—to effectively work the auger.

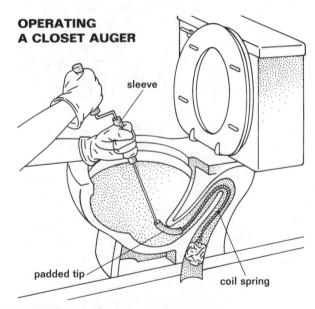

OPERATING A CLOSET AUGER

sleeve

padded tip

coil spring

Turn the auger handle clockwise into the toilet's trap until you feel the resistance of the clog.

Since the coil spring must be turned while it's pushed forward, the job is a lot easier with two people. Be sure to keep the tip of the auger tight against the top of the lip at the beginning of the trap; otherwise, the coil spring will begin to twist and knot up on you.

If you snag part or all of the clog, continue turning the coil spring clockwise as you gently pull it back out of the toilet. You may have to go in and out several times before you snag and remove the entire clog. If you can't snag the clog and pull it out, it may be possible to push it on down the line to the sewer.

If neither of these tactics work—as is sometimes the case when a toy or toothbrush is wedged tightly inside the trap—you'll have to remove the toilet to clean things out. It's also possible that the clog is beyond the short reach of the closet auger, which would also necessitate a "toiletectomy."

REMOVING THE TOILET

Before you start the job, buy a new wax ring or neoprene gasket to replace the old wax ring, which will self-destruct when you pull the toilet up. Also buy a new set of brass closet bolts to replace the old ones.

If you can, draft someone to help you with the job, especially when it comes time to lift the toilet up off the floor. It's especially important to have a helper if you're removing a heavier, two-piece toilet. It may prove easier to remove the tank from the bowl instead of muscling out both pieces together. If you do separate the two pieces, you'll probably also have to replace the rubber gasket that joins the tank and bowl when you reassemble them.

Start by removing the tank lid and placing it in a safe spot—it's easy to break and hard to replace. Next, turn off the small valve under the tank that controls the water supply to the toilet.

Once the water is off, flush the toilet and use a cup to bail the water out of the bowl. Better yet, use a shop vac, which can pull additional water up out of the trap. That way you'll have less to spill when you lift the toilet off the floor.

Use pliers or a small crescent wrench to loosen both compression nuts on the water supply line. Remove the line and set it aside so that it won't be damaged as you maneuver the toilet off the closet flange.

Now loosen the old closet bolts that hold the toilet to the floor. If the nuts are stuck,

Neoprene instead of Wax

When you reinstall the toilet, consider replacing the old wax ring with a neoprene gasket. Neoprene provides a crackproof seal that won't self-destruct if you have to remove the toilet again. ●

give them a shot of WD-40 penetrating oil and try again. If they still won't budge, cut them off with a hacksaw or a reciprocating saw equipped with a thin blade.

You're ready now to remove the toilet, as shown in *Disassembling a Toilet* on page 50. But first, decide exactly what you're going to do with the thing. If you plan to move it into the garage, workshop, or out in the yard to work on it, be sure to line your path through the house with newspapers or plastic sheets to catch any spills. And have a large flat pan ready in the bathroom so that you can empty out the trap before you move the toilet.

With your helper there to assist you, tip the toilet forward and lift it off the floor. You may get a little resistance and noise as the old wax ring breaks apart. Slide the drip pan into place and turn the toilet sideways so that the water

Time for a New John?

If you have to remove your old toilet to clean out the trap or get into the branch drain behind it, give some serious thought to replacing it.

The new gravity and pressurized tank toilets that are on the market today are dynamos of efficiency, using only 1.6 gallons per flush compared to the 3.5, 5, or even 7 gallons per flush used in older models.

While the new toilet will cost you between $100 and $600 (depending on how fancy you want to get), the investment could save you $20 to $70 a year in water and sewage fees. The payback will vary depending on how much you pay for water and sewage services and how often the toilet is flushed.

If you do decide to go shopping for a new toilet, check to see if your state or municipality offers a cash incentive or rebate. In an effort to conserve water and reduce sewage, many cities—including New York, Los Angeles, Denver, and Tampa—give homeowners generous rebates for installing a new toilet.

If you're on a private well and septic system, a new water-saving toilet can significantly reduce the demand on your well and cut the load on your septic system.

DISASSEMBLING A TOILET

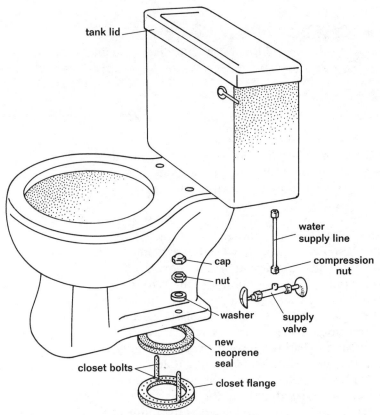

tank lid

water supply line

cap

compression nut

nut

washer

supply valve

new neoprene seal

closet bolts

closet flange

Disconnect a toilet in this order: Remove the tank lid, turn off the supply valve, flush the tank, bail the water from the bowl, disconnect the water supply line, loosen the closet bolts, and finally, lift the toilet off its wax seal.

can drain out of the trap safely into the pan.

Be sure to cover the open drain line with a heavy cover that will keep tools, toys, and little feet from going down the hole.

If you have a toilet with a wall-mounted tank, think about replacing it while you have the chance. The time and frustration involved in putting it back together isn't worthwhile, and it's probably a water guzzler to boot. (See "Time for a New John?" on page 49.)

Once the toilet is out in the garage or yard, you can sometimes reach up into the trap from underneath and remove the obstruction. Another tactic is to thread a line through the trap with a rag attached to one end so that you can really swab the passage out.

If you discover that there's no obstruction in the trap, set the toilet aside and redirect your efforts to the open branch drain in the bathroom. The best way to attack a clog in the

Protect the Porcelain

If you have to cut your toilet free from its mounting bolts, cover the porcelain with duct tape to prevent it from being scarred by the saw blade. ●

branch drain is with a drain auger or hydraulic nozzle. (See "Using a Drain Auger" on page 44 and "Using a Hydraulic Nozzle" on page 45.)

Before you reset the toilet, use a putty knife to scrape the wax off the toilet base and closet flange so that there's a good clean seat for the new wax ring or neoprene gasket. Put the ring or gasket in place. Stand the new closet bolts in their proper position, using a little dab of putty to keep them from moving while you lower the toilet into place. Your helper can help by aligning the toilet on the bolts.

Once the toilet is seated, snug the nuts into place (not *too* tight, or you'll break the porcelain). If the bolts are too long to fit a cosmetic cap over them, cut their tips off with a hacksaw.

Finally, reconnect the water line, taking care not to bend it or overtighten the nuts, and reopen the water supply valve.

The Ring's the Thing

Should a wedding ring or other valuable take a dive into the toilet, there's a fair chance of recovering it before it disappears forever into the sewer.

Act quickly to make sure that the toilet isn't flushed. Turn off the water or disconnect the handle, if necessary.

Wearing long rubber gloves to protect yourself, remove any visible debris from the toilet and bail out all the water you can. Use a shop vac to suck the remaining water out of the toilet and trap. If you're lucky, the lost valuable will come up with the water and can be recovered out of the shop vac.

If that doesn't work and you suspect your treasure is still there, remove the toilet. (See "Removing the Toilet" on page 49.)

Clogged Main Drain

OPENING THE CLEAN-OUT PLUG

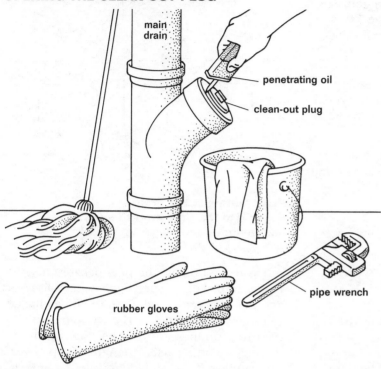

- main drain
- penetrating oil
- clean-out plug
- pipe wrench
- rubber gloves

Apply penetrating oil to the plug threads to facilitate removing it.

Quick Response

1. Stop using toilets, tubs, washers, and other fixtures that feed into main drain.

2. Locate clog.

3. Use drain auger or hydraulic nozzle to clean out drain.

LOCATING THE CLOG

By checking to see if the drains on various plumbing fixtures around the house work, you should be able to determine the approximate location of the clog. If the drainage problem is limited to a single fixture or to just one bathroom, refer to "Clogged Fixture" on page 42 or "Clogged Toilet" on page 47.

If the drains on *all* of your plumbing fixtures are backed up, you are left with the following possibilities:

- **The municipal sewer line is blocked.** Call your neighbors on both sides to see if their houses are affected, too. Or call the municipal department that oversees the sewer system.

Hazards

- Do *not* use chemical or biological drain cleaners. These are unlikely to work on a drain that's completely clogged. Moreover, chemical drain cleaners can release noxious fumes and burn unprotected skin. When they fail to do the job, you (or your plumber) have the added worry of working on a drain that's filled with hazardous chemicals.
- When working with sewage-laden water, wear rubber gloves and boots. Once the work is completed, thoroughly clean and disinfect the work area, your tools, and, last but not least, yourself. (See "Spills" on page 247.)

- **Your septic tank is full.** Locate the tank, open the access port, and take a peek. If the tank is full, arrange to have it pumped out immediately. (If the soil above the leach field is soggy and smells like sewage, more serious problems are indicated. Consult a septic professional as soon as possible.)
- **The main house drain is clogged.** See "When to Call a Plumber" on page 54.
- **The main house drain is broken.** See "When to Call a Plumber."
- **The main house drain to the municipal sewer or septic tank is clogged.** Open the main clean-out plug, as described below, and use a drain auger or hydraulic nozzle to clean the drain.

Once you've determined that the main house drain is clogged, you can open its clean-out plug and attack the problem.

OPENING THE CLEAN-OUT PLUG

At the base of the main house drain (the main vertical drainpipe in your house) is a Y- or T-shaped fitting called the *clean-out plug,* as shown in *Opening the Clean-Out Plug* on page 51. Its express purpose is to provide access to the main house drain if the drain becomes clogged. Depending on the layout of your house and plumbing system, the clean-out plug could be located on the first floor or in the basement or crawl space. (In an older house, there may not be a clean-out, as such. However, you may be able to access the drain through a U-shaped fixture called the *house trap,* which is shown in *Cleaning a Floor Trap* on this page.)

Before you attempt to open the clean-out (or house trap), position a large bucket or pan to catch the wastewater that's backed up in the pipes, as shown in *Opening the Clean-Out Plug.* Also, have some extra containers standing by as well as a mop and some dry rags.

Using a large monkey wrench or crescent wrench, loosen the clean-out plug enough to let a stream of water drain out. Tighten the plug while you change buckets, if necessary, and then loosen the plug again. When all of the wastewater has drained out, go ahead and remove the plug.

CLEANING A FLOOR TRAP

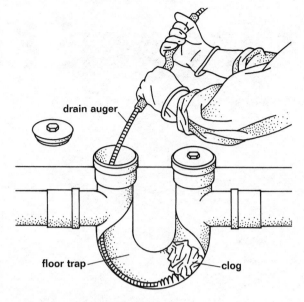

Push and twist the drain auger into the floor trap to snag and dislodge the clog.

If you can't budge the plug because it's rusted in place, try spraying it with WD-40 or another penetrating oil. Give the oil a chance to go to work, then give the wrench another try. (You can increase your leverage on the wrench by fitting a short length of pipe over the handle.) If the plug doesn't let go, give it another squirt of oil and allow a little more time for things to loosen up. If the plug still won't budge, you will have to drill it out.

Before you start drilling, buy a replacement plug made of plastic or expandable rubber; these won't corrode and stick like brass or iron plugs do. Also prepare yourself for what could be a high-velocity spurt of wastewater when the drill first breaks through the plug.

To drill out the old plug, use a power drill fitted with a 3/8-inch bit. Drill a circle of holes toward the outside of the plug, as shown in *Removing an Uncooperative Plug* on the opposite page. Then break the plug up with a hammer and cold chisel. Take care not to let the broken chunks fall into the drain line, or retrieve them if they do.

Once you've got the clean-out open, you're ready to use a drain auger or hydraulic nozzle, as described below.

NOTE: If no wastewater comes out of the clean-out when you open it, the clog has to be located somewhere higher in the line. After cleaning and wrapping the plug's threads with Teflon tape, screw it back into

REMOVING
AN UNCOOPERATIVE PLUG

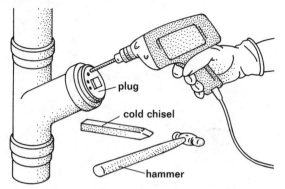

plug

cold chisel

hammer

**Drill through the plug and
then break it out with a hammer and cold chisel.**

place. Now look for another clean-out, somewhere higher in the system. Modern plumbing codes require numerous clean-outs in residential plumbing systems, but older houses
or plumbing systems not built to code may
not have them. In such cases, the only access
may be through the roof vent. (See "When to
Call a Plumber" on page 54.)

USING A DRAIN AUGER

A drain auger, or plumber's "snake," is a
long coil-spring cable with a hook on the
end that's pushed into the drain line to
remove a clog.

   After all of the wastewater has drained from
above the clean-out, release the setscrew on
your auger and push as much of the cable
down into the drain as possible, toward the
municipal sewer line or septic tank, as shown
in *Operating a Drain Auger* on this page.

   When you feel the tip of the auger hit the
clog, set the screw and push on the cable as
you crank it clockwise. If you can snag part
or all of the clog, continue turning the cable
clockwise as you retrieve it. You may have
to work the cable in and out of the drain
several times before you snag and remove
the entire clog. Wipe the cable clean with
a rag each time you pull it out.

   If you can't snag the clog and pull it out,
try pushing on it. You may be able to break
the clog up into small pieces that can be
flushed away. Once the obstruction is
cleared, flush the drain with clean water to
clear away any remaining debris.

Reel It In

If you decide to buy a drain auger, get one
of the new canister types that have an easy-
to-use reeling mechanism. Unlike the old-
style augers, which let the unused portion
of the cable thrash around on the floor, the
new canister types enable you to play out
or take in the cable with a simple
turn of the crank. ●

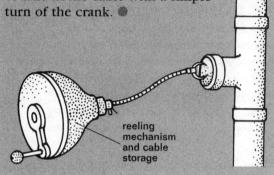

reeling
mechanism
and cable
storage

OPERATING A DRAIN AUGER

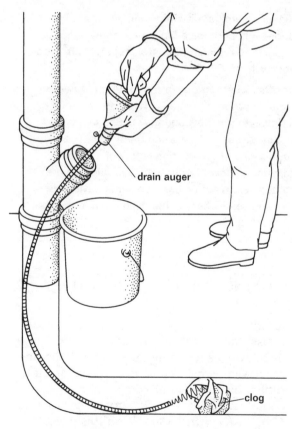

drain auger

clog

**Turn the crank to feed the
auger into the drain.**

When to Call a Plumber

Sometimes, as Shakespeare put it, discretion is the better part of valor. In the realm of clogged drains, that means being smart enough—when the situation warrants—to call a plumber rather than to try to do it yourself.

Here are some situations where it's probably more cost- and time-effective (not to mention *safer*) to call in a professional.

● *No clean-out:* If you find that your house has no clean-out at the base of the main house drain, have a plumber install one.

● *Roots in the main house drain:* Tree roots, especially willows, elms, and poplars, love the warm water and nutrients that come surging through the drain. Roots get a start by penetrating a tiny crack or joint in the pipe. Once inside, they can quickly expand, clogging the whole works. Clearing these out is a good job for Roto-Rooter or another professional who's trained to use a power auger equipped with a special root-cutting blade.

● *Broken sewer pipe:* The 3- or 4-inch-diameter drainpipe that runs between your house and the municipal sewer (or to your septic tank) can break for a number of different reasons, including old age (corrosion), root pressure, a shift in the water table, an earthquake, or by being crushed under the weight of heavy equipment.

Whatever the reason, a broken drainpipe will usually cause a soggy, smelly spot—and perhaps a sinkhole—somewhere in the yard. Digging up and replacing the broken pipe isn't a job for most do-it-yourselfers.

● *Leaves, ice, or other obstructions in the main drain vent:* (See *Your Plumbing System* on page 2.) This can cause all of your household drains to run slow and may cause toilets and other fixtures to burp sewer gas back into the house. The only way to clean out this kind of obstruction is to work a drain auger or hydraulic nozzle down through the vent pipe on the roof, another job best left to a plumber. The same advice holds true if you have a clog somewhere in the main drain, above the clean-out.

USING A HYDRAULIC NOZZLE

Another effective way to unclog your main house drain is to use a hydraulic nozzle, or *flush bag*, as it's sometimes called. This simple device, which consists of an expandable rubber bladder and nozzle, screws onto the end of an ordinary garden hose, as shown in *Using a Hydraulic Nozzle* on this page.

With the hose turned off, insert the hydraulic nozzle into the open drain as far as it will go—ideally, right to the point of the

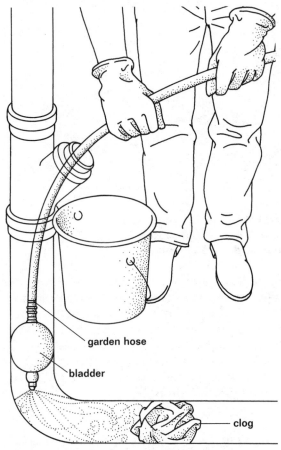

garden hose

bladder

clog

Insert the hydraulic nozzle into the drain as far as possible and turn on the water.

clog. When the water is turned on, the nozzle's built-in bladder expands to form a water-tight collar against the walls of the drain while the nozzle directs a powerful jet of water against the clog. When you turn the water off, the bladder will automatically deflate itself.

After you've finished using the nozzle, be sure to clean it thoroughly. Also clean the outside of the hose and let water run through it to flush out any debris that's gotten inside.

While it may seem inconvenient to run a garden hose into your basement or under your crawl space, hydraulic nozzles are effective in unclogging drains. They're sold under various trade names (for example, Oatey Clog Buster and Dr. Fixit Drain Flusher) for less than $20.

If the hydraulic nozzle doesn't work on the clog—or if the drain is cleared momentarily only to clog up again—you probably have tree roots growing into the drain. (See "When to Call a Plumber" on this page and "Getting to the Root of the Matter" on the opposite page.)

REPLACING THE CLEAN-OUT PLUG

When you've finished working on the drain, put a plug back into the clean-out. If you removed a brass or iron plug that's still in usable condition, clean the threads and wrap them with Teflon tape (five or six turns) before you screw the plug back in, as shown in *Wrapping the Plug* on this page. If you find the original plug rusted or showing wear on the threads, replace it with a plastic or expandable rubber plug, which won't corrode.

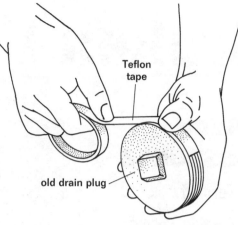

WRAPPING THE PLUG

Teflon tape

old drain plug

Wrap the old plug thread with Teflon tape before replacing it in the drain.

Getting to the Root of the Matter

Chuck Romick, a long-time resident of Los Angeles, has a passion for getting to the root of the matter. In fact, for more than 20 years now he's been pulling tree roots—and just about everything else you can imagine—out of people's clogged-up drains.

Testifying to Chuck's prowess as a root killer are the three first-place trophies that he's won in Roto-Rooter's "Monster Root Contest," a national competition involving more than 200 franchises. (Chuck is president of the Los Angeles franchise.) One of his most impressive "kills," which won him the 1990 prize, was a 46-foot tree root that he pulled out of a drain in—where else?—Hollywood.

Of course, tree roots aren't the only culprits when it comes to clogged-up drains. "You'd be surprised at the things that come out of people's drains," he says. "Dentures. Diapers. Dolls. I've seen it all."

But the strangest clog of all, he says, was of the *living* variety. "We arrived at the man's house thinking it was just another stopped-up toilet," says Chuck. "Then he mentioned to us that his 14-foot boa constrictor was *missing*.

"Well, sure enough, when we removed the toilet, the tip of that little fellow's tail was sticking up through the flange hole. We grabbed

hold of it—as best we could—and tried to pull him out. But I'm here to tell you that 14 feet of snake can put up quite a little tussle."

While Chuck's epic struggle with the boa constrictor makes a great tale (tail?), it's not by any means unique. Starting in 1990, Roto-Rooter Corporation began to poll its service technicians around the United States and document some of the weird things they pull out of people's drains. Among the hundreds of items documented, here are just a few.

- Alarm clock
- Baby pigs
- Diamond engagement ring (worth $4,000)
- Eight ball
- 14 pairs of men's XL briefs
- Glass eye
- Hockey stick
- Hummingbird feeder
- Live groundhog
- Marijuana and pipe in plastic bag
- Meat loaf
- Tear-gas canister
- Teenage Mutant Ninja Turtle
- Toupee

Broken Pipes

Quick Response

1. Turn off water.

2. Position a pan or pail to catch leak.

3. Limit water damage by moving furniture, rugs, and other valuables out of harm's way.

4. Clean up spill. (See "Spills" on page 247.)

5. If pipe has frozen, thaw it out quickly before further damage occurs.

Pipe leaks demand quick action because they can cause extensive damage to your home.

Hazards

● If leaking water has come in contact with appliances, electrical lines, or extension cords, wear rubber-soled shoes and rubber gloves to avoid shock. If necessary, turn off electricity to the area until the water is cleaned up.

● Any electrical tools or appliances used in cleanup or repair should be plugged into a receptacle protected by a ground fault circuit interrupter (GFCI). (See "GFCI Spells Electrical Safety" on page 265.)

● If the break is in a sewage pipe and sewage or gray water is leaking out, don't use toilets, bathtubs, sinks, or appliances that drain into that line. Take special care to avoid contact with spilled sewage. Wear rubber-soled boots and rubber gloves. Afterward, thoroughly clean and disinfect the area as well as your tools. (See "Spills" on page 247.)

● Do **NOT** use a propane torch, candles, or other open-flame devices to thaw frozen pipes.

TURNING OFF THE WATER

Don't procrastinate fixing a small water leak. It will only get worse over time. Your water supply pipes are charged with 30 to 80 pounds of pressure per square inch—should that small leak you've been ignoring suddenly get ambitious, the damage can be impressive. Begin the repair by shutting off the water supply.

Locate and close the valve on the water supply line that feeds the leak. If the point of the leak is hidden, there's no valve in the branch line, or the branch valve won't close properly, you'll have to close the main water shutoff valve to the entire house. (See "Understanding Your Plumbing System" on page 2.)

After you've closed the supply line or the main shutoff valve, water will continue to leak from the broken pipe until there's no pressure left in the line.

LOCATING THE LEAK

Sometimes the biggest challenge in fixing a leak is finding the point where the pipe is broken. Leaking water often follows a long and winding road before it finally is apparent. If you have a hidden leak, read "Tracking Hidden Leaks" on this page for some helpful tips.

Once you've found your leak, *Three Patching Options* on this page, *Repairing Copper Pipe*, *Repairing Plastic Pipe*, and *Repairing Cast-Iron Pipe* on page 58, and *Repairing Steel Pipe without Cutting New Threads* on page 60 show some tried and trusted methods—both

temporary and permanent—for making repairs. Generally speaking, leaks in copper and plastic pipes and fittings are relatively easy to fix, while repairing leaks in galvanized steel and cast-iron pipes is more challenging. For major repairs, you're better off calling a pro.

THREE PATCHING OPTIONS

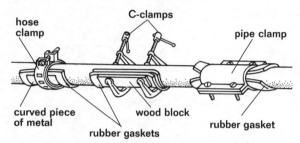

The clamping methods shown here combined with gaskets cut from an old inner tube make good, temporary patches.

Tracking Hidden Leaks

Because leaking water can travel a long way before it shows itself, pinpointing its source can be a real challenge. Here are some questions to help you with your detective work.

● *Is the leak steady or intermittent?* A steady leak suggests a break in a supply line, such as to a sink, toilet, or water heater. Intermittent leaks, on the other hand, point to a broken drain line. (To track the leak, you'll probably have to turn the water back on so that the leak can show itself.)

● *Is the leak directly below or adjacent to water pipes, fixtures, or appliances?* Proximity is usually a good clue. For example, if you have a steady leak showing underneath a bathroom, it's a good bet that a supply pipe or gasket in the toilet, sink, or tub has failed. If the leak is *intermittent*—occurring, for example, only when someone showers—then the water is more likely coming through a crack in or around the tub or shower seal or drain or perhaps leaking through the floor tiles.

● *Can you associate the leak with a certain household activity?* For example, if the leak appears only when the dishwasher is running or a certain toilet is flushed, you've got strong evidence that either the appliance or fixture or the drain line below it is leaking.

● *Is the leaking water gray or have a bad odor?* These are telltale signs that the leak is in a drain line. Supply pipes should have fresh, clean water in them.

● *Does the leak occur only during and immediately after a rainstorm?* Water that's coming through a leaky roof can sometimes travel a long way—even down to the basement—masquerading as a plumbing problem.

● *Does the "leak" coincide with hot, muggy weather?* When conditions are just right, water can condense on pipes, water heaters, toilets, and other fixtures. Sometimes it can run and pool, imitating a plumbing leak.

● *Is water visible under appliances or fixtures?* Check the pipes and fittings on the water heater, clothes washer, dishwasher, shower, tub, sinks, and toilets. If there's a plumbing access panel next to the tub or shower, remove it and look inside.

Cutting into a Wall or Ceiling

Sometimes, when a leaky pipe is hidden inside a wall or ceiling, the only option is to get out a utility knife or keyhole saw and perform a little exploratory surgery. But be sure that you've eliminated *all* of the other possibilities before you start cutting.

If you do have to cut into a wall or ceiling, use the location of visible plumbing fixtures and a tape measure to find the position of the hidden pipe. Locate surrounding studs or joists by tapping on the drywall or using an electronic stud finder. Make a small and shallow cut so that your blade doesn't snag a pipe or electric cable inside the wall. (See "What's Inside That Wall?" on page 267.)

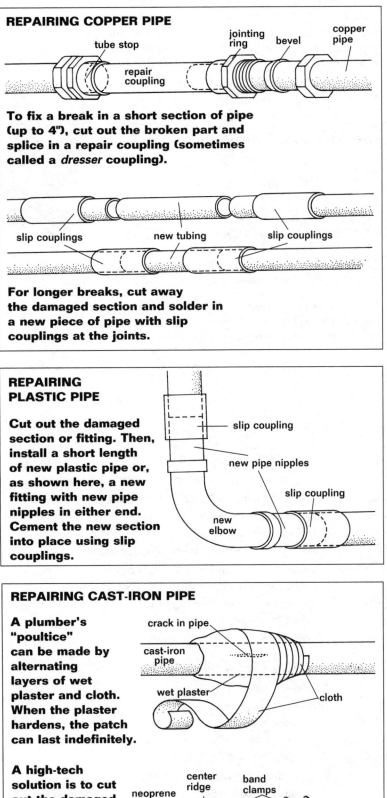

REPAIRING COPPER PIPE

tube stop · jointing ring · bevel · copper pipe · repair coupling

To fix a break in a short section of pipe (up to 4"), cut out the broken part and splice in a repair coupling (sometimes called a *dresser* coupling).

slip couplings · new tubing · slip couplings

For longer breaks, cut away the damaged section and solder in a new piece of pipe with slip couplings at the joints.

REPAIRING PLASTIC PIPE

Cut out the damaged section or fitting. Then, install a short length of new plastic pipe or, as shown here, a new fitting with new pipe nipples in either end. Cement the new section into place using slip couplings.

slip coupling · new pipe nipples · slip coupling · new elbow

REPAIRING CAST-IRON PIPE

A plumber's "poultice" can be made by alternating layers of wet plaster and cloth. When the plaster hardens, the patch can last indefinitely.

crack in pipe · cast-iron pipe · wet plaster · cloth

A high-tech solution is to cut out the damaged section of pipe and then splice in a new section of pipe using neoprene hubless pipe connectors.

center ridge · band clamps · neoprene sleeve · hubless iron pipe · new section of hubless iron pipe · stainless steel sleeve

ADDRESSING THE CAUSE

While freezing is the most common source of damaged pipes, leaks can also be caused by corrosion, vibration, and impact.

Thawing Frozen Pipes

When ice forms inside a pipe, it cuts off the flow of water to whatever fixtures the pipe serves. By taking *fast* action, you may be able to keep the pipe from bursting or at least prevent the ice from spreading down the pipe and causing more damage. Here are the proper steps to follow.

1. Open all faucets and valves in the frozen line. This gives the ice (and water melting off the ice) room to expand, alleviating pressure on the wall of the pipe, joints, and/or valve components.

If the pipe has already burst and is leaking damaging amounts of water, close the main water shutoff valve. (See *Your Plumbing System* on page 2.)

2. If your home's primary heating system is turned off, get it started. Use supplementary heat, such as a woodstove, fireplace, or electric space heater, to provide added heat to the effected area.

3. Locate the point of the freeze as precisely as possible. This is easy if the pipe is already bulging or leaking water. If there are no visible clues, run a damp rag or sponge along the pipe—the frozen area will frost over. Or move your hand along the pipe, feeling for the coldest spot. Generally, pipes will freeze in proximity to exterior walls, unheated basements, attics, and crawl spaces. On a vertical pipe run, the frozen spot will generally be lower in the pipe than higher because cold air settles.

4. Heat the pipe. Use a hair dryer or heat gun (on *LOW*) to apply heat, as shown in *Heating the Pipe*. Start applying heat at the nearest open valve or faucet that's level with or below the frozen spot in the pipe. This guarantees that water melting out of the ice plug has a clear path to drain away. Work the hair dryer or heat gun gradually toward the frozen spot.

If you don't have a hair dryer or heat gun, you can dip rags or towels in hot water and wrap the pipe. Wet the fabric with more hot water as necessary. Wrapping a frozen pipe with electric

All types of metal pipes are vulnerable to corrosion over time, particularly if the water is extremely acid or alkaline. Even good-quality copper pipe can corrode to the point that it's walls can be crushed with a firm squeeze of the hand.

Vibration can also take its toll on household plumbing and eventually cause leaks, especially at the joints. One common source of vibration—known as *water hammer*—can be both annoying and damaging. It occurs when you suddenly turn off a faucet and the surging

heating cables, hot pads, or even hot water bottles will also do the job, though not as quickly.

CAUTION: If you use electric heating cables, be sure to follow the manufacturer's instructions. Older-style cables may create a fire hazard when wrapped incorrectly. ***Never use a propane torch, Bunsen burner, candles, lit paper, or other sources of open flame to thaw frozen pipes.*** These can produce a dangerous steam pocket inside the pipe and present the risk of igniting wood and other flammable materials nearby. Plastic pipe will actually melt and release toxic fumes when exposed to direct flames.

Getting to Hidden Pipes

If the frozen pipe is enclosed inside a ceiling or wall, applying direct heat to it becomes much more difficult. On some ceilings, it's possible to remove individual tiles or dropped panels to gain access to the plumbing above. Or you may be able to gain access through the attic.

Thawing frozen pipes that are buried inside walls can be especially troublesome. A tactic that sometimes works with *metal* pipes is to heat the pipe where it emerges from the wall (or ceiling) cavity. Hopefully, the pipe will conduct enough heat back to the point of the freeze to thaw the blockage. If there is a gap between the emerging pipe and the surrounding drywall, aim your hair dryer through the gap and pump some warm air down the pipe and into the cavity. If there's no gap, use a utility knife or keyhole saw to cut one. You can patch the hole later, *after* you've rescued your frozen pipes.

Unfortunately, if the ice plug is more than 1 or 2 feet away, it's unlikely that enough heat will spread back along the pipe to melt it. And of course, the method won't work at all with plastic pipe because plastic is such a poor heat conducter.

In such cases, it may be necessary to cut a hole through the drywall to get in close to the frozen section of pipe. The best way to do this is to locate the studs on either side of the suspect pipe and cut a hole between them just above the baseboard. (If you

HEATING THE PIPE

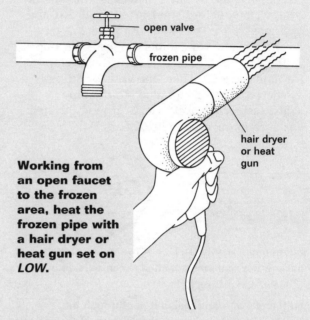

open valve

frozen pipe

hair dryer or heat gun

Working from an open faucet to the frozen area, heat the frozen pipe with a hair dryer or heat gun set on *LOW*.

don't have an electronic stud finder, tap your knuckles across the face of the drywall. The studs are typically spaced 16 inches on center and give off a solid "thud" compared to the hollow sound of the cavity.) Make the hole 3 or 4 inches square—large enough to admit the tip of a hair dryer or heat gun. *CAUTION:* Take care that your saw blade doesn't damage the pipe or electric cables inside the wall. (See "What's Inside That Wall?" on page 267.)

Once the hole is cut, use your hair dryer or heat gun to pump hot air into the wall cavity. While this tactic may seem extreme, the cosmetic damage to the drywall is relatively easy and inexpensive to repair compared to what might happen if the pipe would burst inside the wall.

Of course, leaving a hole in the wall is *not* a viable way to protect your pipes over the long term. For one thing, the hole lets warm, moist air into a cold wall cavity, which invites condensation and rot. The wiser course is to make permanent changes to your plumbing and house that will prevent pipes from freezing again.

water inside the pipe comes to an abrupt stop. The shock vibrates back through the plumbing, producing a loud hammering noise. The damage that results can be especially quick and severe if pipes aren't properly supported, as the vibration will bend and twist them at the joints.

A third cause of leaks is impact, which may occur when a pipe, joint, or fixture is accidentally punctured by a nail, shovel, pick, saw blade, drill bit, or other man-made implement. (See "Think Before You Dig" on page 261 and "What's Inside That Wall?" on page 267.)

Finally, valves and joints can just wear out enough to leak. Such leaks usually develop around the joint where the valve or fitting is soldered, threaded, or glued to the pipe. Valves can also develop leaks around the stem or even in the casting itself.

The Little Thing Overlooked

It was a mild, late-summer day when Don Provencher moved the telephone service box that was attached to the outside of his Chesterfield, New Hampshire, home.

"When I snipped the old wire and pulled it out through the wall, I noticed that it left a tiny hole—maybe ¼ inch—through the sill plate," he says. "Well, I thought to myself at the time, 'I ought to caulk that.' But *you* know how it is. It's one of those little things that you never quite get around to."

A few months later, on a cold December morning, Don woke up to find that he didn't have any water.

"I checked the pump first," he says. "When that didn't show any problem, I began to check the pipes. Sure enough, I found a place where the copper supply line had frozen."

Don used a hair dryer to thaw out the frozen pipe, which luckily hadn't ruptured. He thought it strange that after so many years of living in the house without any problems, he would suddenly be confronted with a frozen pipe.

"I was *really* puzzled when I woke up the next morning and it'd happened again!" he relates. "Same pipe. Frozen in the same place. Then I noticed a tiny spot of light showing through the wall. It was that little hole from the telephone wire that I'd never caulked, about 3 inches away from the pipe."

Don got his caulking gun out and solved the problem faster than you can say "protect your pipes from cold winter drafts." He counts himself lucky that the pipe survived the experience without bursting, which could have made the lesson a lot more costly.

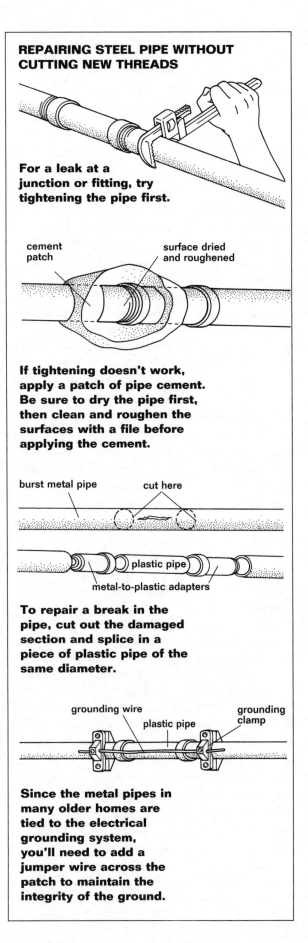

REPAIRING STEEL PIPE WITHOUT CUTTING NEW THREADS

For a leak at a junction or fitting, try tightening the pipe first.

cement patch

surface dried and roughened

If tightening doesn't work, apply a patch of pipe cement. Be sure to dry the pipe first, then clean and roughen the surfaces with a file before applying the cement.

burst metal pipe

cut here

plastic pipe

metal-to-plastic adapters

To repair a break in the pipe, cut out the damaged section and splice in a piece of plastic pipe of the same diameter.

grounding wire

plastic pipe

grounding clamp

Since the metal pipes in many older homes are tied to the electrical grounding system, you'll need to add a jumper wire across the patch to maintain the integrity of the ground.

Leaky Basement

A WELL-CONSTRUCTED FOUNDATION DRAIN

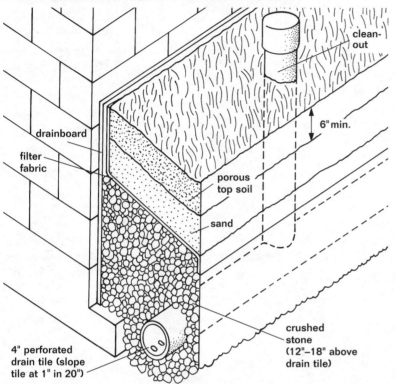

- clean-out
- drainboard
- filter fabric
- porous top soil
- sand
- 6" min.
- crushed stone (12"–18" above drain tile)
- 4" perforated drain tile (slope tile at 1" in 20")

Quick Response

1. Clear away rugs, furniture, and other items.

2. Patch leaking cracks or holes.

3. If water is more than 1 inch deep, rent a pump. (See "Spills" on page 247.)

Ideally, a foundation drain should be installed when the foundation is laid. As a retrofit, it is an effective, although labor-intensive, solution to a leaky basement.

PUTTING THE LEAK IN PERSPECTIVE

Leaky basements are more common and produce more anxiety than just about any other home repair problem known to man.

But don't panic. Having a damp wall or a crack oozing water doesn't mean your basement wall is going to collapse. Don't be stampeded into buying an expensive waterproofing job before you have a good diagnosis of the problem.

Also, resist rushing out and buying an interior brush-on product. The odds are good that it *won't* solve your problem. (See "Solutions in a Can? Let the Buyer Beware!" on page 62.)

Hazards

● Do not enter the basement if standing water may have become "energized" through contact with live electric cords, switches, or receptacles. If necessary, turn off electricity to the area until the water is cleaned up.

● Wear rubber-soled boots and rubber gloves as an added safeguard against shock.

● Any electrical tools or appliances used in cleanup or repair work should be plugged into a receptacle protected by a ground fault circuit interrupter (GFCI). (See "GFCI Spells Electrical Safety" on page 265.)

● When applying epoxy, caulk, or other materials, wear rubber gloves and goggles. Carefully read the product's safety instructions, especially regarding the need for ventilation.

PATCHING OBVIOUS LEAKS

If you have a leak that needs immediate attention—that is, a crack or hole in the basement wall that's oozing water—patch it with fast-setting hydraulic cement, as shown in *Patching Cracks and Holes* on this page. For a stronger, more durable patch, use epoxy, as discussed in "Cracks in Concrete, Masonry, and Stucco" on page 157.

If you're lucky, an indoor patch may solve your problem permanently—provided there's not much water pressure on the outside of the basement wall. Such pressure can vary a lot from season to season with the occurrence of

Solutions in a Can? Let the Buyer Beware!

Hardware stores and home centers are brimming with ready-mix products—available in cans, buckets, and bags—that purportedly cure leaky basements with a single coat or two. But nine times out of ten—unless the seepage is extremely mild—these brush-on coatings only mask the problem and may, in fact, cause damage to the wall.

It isn't necessarily water pressure that causes these coatings to fail, but rather the buildup of waterborne salts—called *subflorescence*—that crystallize behind the coating and deep inside the wall. In time, these salt deposits will pop the coating off, usually taking some of the concrete wall or masonry with it. (When this powdery white deposit is visible on the surface of the wall, it's called *efflorescence*. To clean the wall, see "Removing Efflorescence" on page 67.)

An additional hazard, especially in the spring and fall, is that water trapped inside the wall will undergo freeze-thaw cycles that can further damage the wall. If the interior coating is truly impermeable, leaving the water no place to evaporate, the water may wick its way up into the sill plate and produce rot.

The wisest course—if you can't address the root cause of the problem—is to let the basement go ahead and leak. An ordinary latex paint can be used as a cosmetic or sacrificial coat until the real source of the problem can be diagnosed and corrected.

Only for *very* mild instances of seepage, where the wall is merely damp, are waterproofing paints advisable.

Independent tests conducted at the *Consumer Reports* laboratories ranked epoxy-based paints such as Atlas Epoxybond Waterproof Sealant and the Barrier System Epoxy Paint highest in water resistance. But be advised that epoxy systems are *a lot* more expensive than regular paint, trickier to mix, and more difficult to apply.

Also scoring well in the tests and less expensive than the epoxies were Glidden Spred Waterproof Basement Paint, a ready-to-use oil-based paint, and Bondex Waterproof Cement Paint. Both of these products required two coats to effect a good seal.

All of the aforementioned coatings require that the surface be carefully cleaned and prepped beforehand. Be sure to follow the manufacturer's instructions carefully, especially regarding safety precautions.

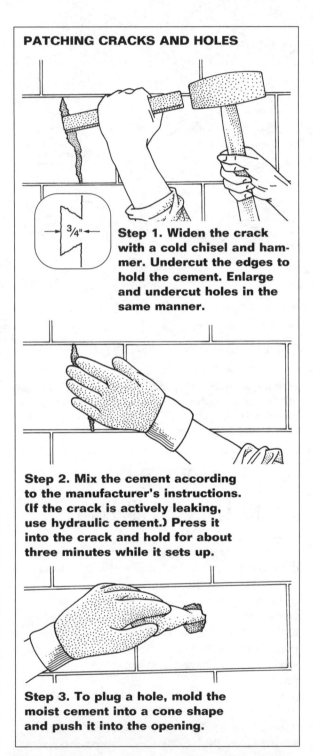

PATCHING CRACKS AND HOLES

3/4"

Step 1. Widen the crack with a cold chisel and hammer. Undercut the edges to hold the cement. Enlarge and undercut holes in the same manner.

Step 2. Mix the cement according to the manufacturer's instructions. (If the crack is actively leaking, use hydraulic cement.) Press it into the crack and hold for about three minutes while it sets up.

Step 3. To plug a hole, mold the moist cement into a cone shape and push it into the opening.

rainwater, snow melt, and/or ground-water. As the soil around the foundation approaches the saturation point, the pressure against the wall increases.

If there *is* substantial water pressure, interior patchwork is doomed. Over time, the water will either push the patch off or stealthily find its way through other cracks and holes.

NOTE: In all but the mildest cases, the key to repairing a wet basement is to relieve the water pressure against the outside wall and/or from under the floor.

TROUBLESHOOTING A WET BASEMENT

If you have damp walls and/or floors in your basement and the source of the moisture is not apparent, you may have a condensation problem due to excessive indoor humidity rather than a leak.

To find out, dry 1 square foot of wall or floor area with a hair dryer or heat gun. Fasten a piece of aluminum foil over the dry area, with the edges tightly sealed with duct tape, and leave it for a couple of days. If there's moisture under the foil when you remove it, it proves there's water coming in from outside. If the foil is dry underneath, but moisture has formed on the face of it, high indoor humidity is the villian. See "Controlling Indoor Humidity" on page 217.

Water trickling down from a broken pipe or plumbing fixture—even from a leaky roof—can also masquerade as a leaky basement. So can water that's backed up through a floor drain after a particularly heavy rain. Patient exploration—perhaps with some expert help—is the only way to ferret out the source of the water. For some tips on figuring out where the water is coming from, see "Leaky Roof" on page 24 and "Tracking Hidden Leaks" on page 57.

If water *is* leaking into the basement from outside, there's a good chance that you can diagnose and correct the problem yourself. The vast majority of leaks—say 95 percent—occur because water control systems on the *outside* of the house haven't been properly maintained or were never installed in the first place. (See *Your Home's Primary Lines of Defense* on page 64.)

Broken rain gutters and downspouts, surface drainage problems, poorly sealed construction

Keep It Dry

Move quickly to solve basement water problems. Water that infiltrates cracks, holes, mortar joints, and the voids in concrete blocks can freeze, causing serious structural damage. Moisture from the basement will invariably find its way into other parts of the house, warping wood floors and causing premature paint failure. A wet basement also attracts insects and other vermin and sets the stage for mildew and rot. The spores produced from mildew will quickly migrate from the basement into the upper portions of your house, causing allergic reactions and other health problems. (See "Mold and Mildew" on page 213.) ●

joints, and leaky window wells are among the prime suspects. When one or more of these faults exist, water can build up around the basement wall, where it seeps in through cracks or wicks its way through the wall via capillary action.

Such failures can often be diagnosed simply by putting on your raincoat and inspecting the outside of your home during a rainstorm. (See "Troubleshooting Guide to Wet Basements" on page 66.)

FACING MORE CHALLENGING REPAIRS

Hopefully, your wet basement problem can be solved by some of the simple and inexpensive measures suggested in "Troubleshooting Guide to Wet Basements" on page 66, such as repairing rain gutters, correcting the grade, or recaulking basement windows and doors.

If not, you'll be faced with more difficult and expensive choices, as follows:

Install a coving system. This system makes no attempt to keep water from coming through the basement wall. Instead, it effectively collects the leaking water in a watertight plastic channel that's glued into place around the perimeter of the basement floor. Water that is tapped from the bottom course of concrete block or that is flowing down the poured concrete wall enters the back side of the plastic channel and flows by gravity to a floor drain or sump pit. (See *A Typical Coving System* on page 65.)

YOUR HOME'S PRIMARY LINES OF DEFENSE

The best way to deal with water in your basement is to prevent it from getting there in the first place. So, set up strong lines of defense around your home to block nature's onslaught.

If you live at the base of a hill, dig a swale to divert water around your house. The swale should be 2' to 3' wide and 6" deep.

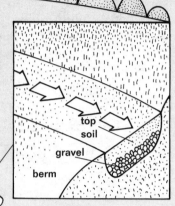

Make sure gutters and downspouts are clean and sloped properly. Use splash blocks to divert water away from the house.

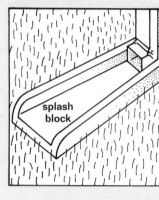

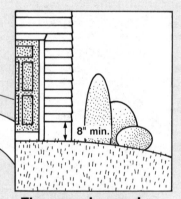

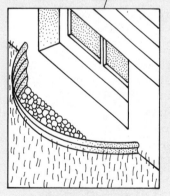

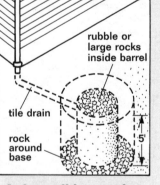

Basement window wells should be well drained with a layer of gravel at the bottom. Side walls should extend 1" to 2" above grade. Add a plastic bubble cover, if necessary, to keep wells from filling with snow and water.

A dry well is even better than a splash block. Bury the drain tile leading away from house at a pitch of about 1/4" to 1/2" per foot. The top of the barrel should be 18" to 24" below the soil surface. Puncture the barrel with small holes to let water out.

The ground around your house should slope away from your foundation, dropping about 6" over a distance of 10'. Keep shrubs well trimmed so the sun can dry out the soil next to the house. Your house's foundation should extend about 8" above grade before the siding begins.

A TYPICAL COVING SYSTEM

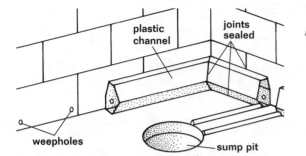

A coving system is like a hollow baseboard installed around the basement's perimeter. Water enters the coving through weepholes drilled at intervals along the wall and is diverted to a sump pit where it can be pumped away.

One concern with coving systems is that they do nothing to protect the structural integrity of the foundation wall. Water steadily seeping through cracks or mortar joints will eventually weaken the wall, especially if it is subject to freeze-thaw cycles.

Since coving systems are designed to control water—not to keep it out—installing one obviously won't give you a bone-dry basement. But if you're looking for a relatively low-cost fix (compared to the options that follow) and are willing to live with some dampness, a coving system may be your ticket. Some manufacturers, such as Beaver Water Control Corporation and Channel Drain, have designed their systems for do-it-yourself installation.

Excavate and repair the foundation wall and footing drain. While this strategy is much more expensive than a coving system, it's likely to provide better long-term results. *NOTE:* I recommend that you use an experienced waterproofing contractor to do this kind of work.

Since the work requires excavating a deep trench around the outside of your house (down to the foot of the foundation), any trees, shrubs, and flowers abutting the house

Install a Clean-Out

Ask your contractor to install a vertical clean-out riser on the new foundation drain. For very little additional cost, the riser provides an easy way to access and flush the drain. ●

Insulate and Save

While you have the basement wall exposed, consider adding a band of rigid foam insulation. (Some types of drainboard that incorporate insulation can do double duty.) Adding exterior insulation is a wise move for two reasons. First, it will cut your annual heating and cooling costs. Second, it will raise the temperature of the basement wall, thereby reducing or eliminating condensation inside. ●

will probably perish in the process. (Not a bad idea anyway, since they're probably part of the problem. See the table on page 66.) Patios, walks, and driveways abutting the foundation may also have to be torn up and later repaired, which contributes significantly to the overall cost of the project.

The repair crew, working down in the trench, will first clean and repair the exposed foundation wall. Cracks, depending on their type and size, will be filled with cement or epoxy. If it's a block wall, a fresh coat of cement, called a *parging* coat, may be added.

Once the wall is restored, a waterproof membrane will be applied. Some contractors apply a layer of polymer-modified asphalt overlaid with a thick sheet of polyethylene that's carefully lapped and taped along the seams. Other contractors prefer to use plastic or fiberglass drainboard, which is mounted flush to the basement wall. Whether the drainboard is configured with dimples, is in a mesh, or is a solid mat, it can provide an excellent drainage channel to the foundation drain below.

If there is no exterior drainpipe along the footing, your contractor will probably recommend one. (See *A Well-Constructed Foundation Drain* on page 61.) The pipe, often made of corrugated plastic and perforated to admit water, is laid in a bed of washed gravel at the bottom of the footing. The pipe is protected from silt by a wrap of man-made filter cloth and a thick layer of washed riverbed gravel.

The pipe collects water percolating down from the surface and discharges it. If you're lucky, your house is on a rise and has natural drainage downhill. If there's no suitable discharge point on your property, the drainpipe will have to be connected to a municipal storm drain (code permitting), dry well, or an interior sump pit.

TROUBLESHOOTING GUIDE TO WET BASEMENTS

COMMON CAUSE	WHAT TO LOOK FOR
BROKEN WATER OR SEWER PIPE	Ground dampness or puddling may occur even in dry weather. Leak may show up indoors where pipe penetrates wall. Turn off water at street, or pump, then monitor results. Sewage leaks stink.
LOCALIZED LEAK THROUGH CRACK OR WHERE UTILITY PIPE OR VENT PENETRATES BASEMENT WALL	Assuming wall is exposed, this type of leak will be evident during rainstorm or spring melt.
HOUSE LACKS RAIN GUTTERS, OR CLOGGED OR LEAKING GUTTERS FAIL TO DIVERT WATER AWAY FROM FOUNDATION.	Go outside in rainstorm and see if gutters or downspouts are overflowing or leaking. Water pooling along foundation is telltale sign.
CLOGGED OR BROKEN STORM DRAIN OR DRY WELL CAUSES RAINWATER TO BACK UP AGAINST FOUNDATION.	Disconnect downspout at ground level. Using flexible or rigid extension pipe, temporarily divert runoff away from foundation. If the leak stops, you've found culprit.
IMPROPER GRADING OR SETTLING CAUSES SURFACE WATER TO POOL NEAR FOUNDATION. PLANTS WITH ROOTS TOO CLOSE TO FOUNDATION WALL AGGRAVATE PROBLEM.	Tape plastic sheet along bottom of siding and drape it out away from house so that it sheds water away from foundation. If the leak disappears, it points to surface drainage problem. You may be able to spot this problem simply by walking around house in rainstorm. Is shallow moat of water forming along foundation?
BASEMENT WINDOW WELLS OR BULKHEAD DOORS ARE POORLY FLASHED AND CAULKED. DRAIN IS CLOGGED.	Leak will be localized around or below basement window or door frame. If drain is clogged, well will fill with rainwater during storm.
THE JOINT BETWEEN DRIVEWAY, PATIO, PORCH, OR WALK AND ABUTTING FOUNDATION ISN'T PROPERLY SEALED. PROBLEM WORSE IF SURFACE SLOPES TOWARD HOUSE.	Check pitch with level. It should slope away from foundation at ¼" per foot (minimum). Check condition of joint.
FOUNDATION DRAIN IS CLOGGED OR BROKEN, FAILING TO DRAIN SUBSURFACE WATER AWAY FROM FOUNDATION.	If mouth of outlet pipe is visible, check its discharge after a good rain. If it's dry or barely flowing, clogged foundation drain may be at fault. (*NOTE:* Many houses, especially older ones, don't have foundation drains. Consult construction blueprints or building department records.)
WATER TABLE RISES TO POINT WHERE IT FORCES WATER UP THROUGH CRACKS IN SLAB OR THROUGH JOINT BETWEEN SLAB AND WALL.	May cause constant or seasonal leaks. Wetness usually appears on lower wall or at joint between wall and slab. A clear leak in middle of floor is an even stronger indicator. In some cases, water pressure beneath the slab can buckle floor.

WHAT YOU CAN DO

Call plumber and city water or sewage authority. Together, determine location of leak and, therefore, who has responsibility to make repair.

Find crack on wall, excavating if necessary. Patch with hydraulic cement, butyl rubber caulk, or epoxy. (See "Cracks in Concrete, Masonry, and Stucco" on page 157.)

Install or repair gutters. (See "Clogged Rain Gutter" on page 33 and "Damaged Rain Gutter" on page 37.)

Have professional drain cleaning service clean out tree roots and silt. Or excavate and repair damaged drain or dry well. Or abandon drain, diverting runoff instead into a swale (a shallow drainage ditch). (See *A Well-Constructed Foundation Drain* on page 61.)

Remove flower beds and shrubs planted within 3' of foundation. To correct grade, remove 4"–6" of dirt 3' adjacent to foundation; backfill with clay soil sloped away from house at 2" per foot. Continue the slope out for another 3' at 1" per foot.

Clean out clogged drains and make sure they drain away from house. Raise window-well walls a few inches above grade to prevent flooding. Repair faulty window and door frames and flashing. Recaulk joints. Install plastic window-well covers and/or new bulkhead doors.

For temporary abatement, clean joint and caulk it with Dymeric or other swimming pool caulk. Or fill crack to ½" below surface with foam backer rod and pour in liquid asphalt crack filler. For lasting relief, correct pitch problem.

Flush drain with hose and pressure nozzle via vertical clean-out riser. Or contract with reputable drain-cleaning service that has high-pressure water jet equipment. As last resort, have pro excavate around foundation and repair drain.

Hire experienced contractor to install interior drain and sump pump. (See *Use pumps to address a chronically high water table* on page 68.)

Double-Duty Drains

With forethought, interior and exterior footing drains can sometimes do double duty as part of a radon-control system. Be sure to test your home for radon before your basement plans are formalized and, if radon mitigation is needed, ask your contractor about designing a dual-purpose system. (See "Radon" on page 205.)

Finally, with delicate care, the contractor will backfill the trench so that the foundation wall, drainpipe, and waterproofing material aren't damaged. The surface is regraded so that it falls away from the foundation at least ½ inch per foot and is planted with grass.

For houses that sit at the foot of a slope, it may also be necessary to excavate a shallow drainage ditch, called a *swale,* to divert surface water away from the house. Swales are positioned at least 10 feet from the foundation—and often much further—providing a first line of defense against incoming water.

This type of exterior repair work will usually come with the contractor's guarantee that there won't be any further leaks through the basement wall, but subsequent leaks up through the floor of the basement or through the cove joint between the floor and the wall typically aren't covered.

Install a French drain under the basement floor. Some contractors prefer to install

Removing Efflorescence

Efflorescence is the salty deposit that's left on the surface of concrete and masonry walls by moving water.

If you can't remove the white powder by simply dry- or wet-brushing the wall, use a 10-percent solution of muriatic acid (1 ounce of crystals to 10 ounces of water).

Dampen the wall with clean water before you start. Apply the acid to a small area (less than 4 square feet) and let it sit for five minutes. Then scour the salt off with a stiff brush and flush the wall with clean water.

CAUTION: Muriatic acid can affect your skin and eyes and your breathing. Be sure to wear rubber gloves, goggles, and protective clothing. Make sure the area is well ventilated and that you observe the safety precautions on the label.

a foundation drain on the *inside* of the basement wall rather than outside, particularly when the leak is coming up through the basement floor or through the cove joint.

Using a pneumatic or electric hammer to break through the floor, the contractor will excavate a trench around the perimeter of the basement wall. Gravel and a perforated drainpipe are laid in the trench, pitched so that water will drain to a sump pit, as shown in *A French Drain* on this page. Weepholes are drilled through the basement wall, just above the footing, so that water collecting outside can flow through the wall into the drainpipe channel. Fresh concrete is then poured to seal the open trench.

Some French drain systems also employ a coving mechanism—typically sheets of rigid plastic paneling affixed to the wall—to channel water down into the subfloor drain.

Installing a French drain creates a mess in the basement and requires the installation of a sump pit and pump, with the energy and maintenance costs that accompany them.

A FRENCH DRAIN

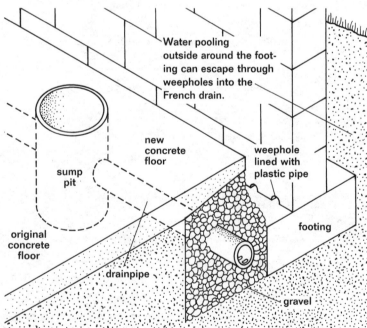

Water pooling outside around the footing can escape through weepholes into the French drain.

sump pit

new concrete floor

original concrete floor

drainpipe

weephole lined with plastic pipe

footing

gravel

A French drain laid inside the footing is another heavy-duty solution to water problems. Retrofitting one is a messy job and often requires installing a sump pump.

Contractors who install interior drain systems typically guarantee that there won't be any further leaks up through the floor. But the guarantee usually doesn't cover any subsequent leaks through the wall.

Install a system that employs both exterior and interior drains, combining the two previous options. This is an expensive but effective approach for serious water problems. The work should prevent any further leakage through the basement floor, cove joint, or walls and be guaranteed to that effect.

Use pumps to address a chronically high water table. When clear water rises through cracks in the basement slab or through the joint between the floor and the wall, it's strong evidence that you have a high-water-table problem. The flow will typically wax and wane with seasonal variations in rainfall—rising, for example, several days after a heavy rain. Sometimes the uplifting pressure of the water is enough to buckle or heave the slab.

Unfortunately, the only solution to a chronically high water table is to pump the water out faster than it can come in—a complicated and expensive proposition. (Fortunately, only about 5 percent of all basement leaks are caused by water-table problems!)

Using collection pits and pumps, the strategy is to lower the water table under or around the house by creating a "zone of influence." Most contractors prefer to install the pits and pumps inside the basement because it's simpler and less expensive than placing them outdoors.

Broken Sump Pump

You have two choices when buying a sump pump. You can choose the newer submersible type (*above left*) or the older pedestal type (*above right*).

Quick Response

1. Stop incoming water.

2. Attempt emergency repairs on pump.

3. Rent or buy replacement pump.

4. Clean up. (See "Spills" on page 247.)

Hazards

● To avoid shock, shut off electricity to the sump pump while you inspect the pump and diagnose the problem. Wear rubber-soled shoes and rubber gloves as an added precaution against shock.

● If sewage has spilled into the sump pit or onto the surrounding floor from a backed-up or broken drain, take special care to avoid infection. Wear rubber gloves and boots. Thoroughly clean and disinfect the area, your tools, and yourself. (See "Spills" on page 247.)

DOWN IN THE SUMPS

Sump pumps are designed to protect your home from water damage, even when you're away. They are typically installed in a pit, or sump, in the lowest part of the house, where leaking water collects first. When water rises around the base of the pump, it activates a built-in switch that automatically turns the electric motor on. The pump then draws water out of the sump and discharges it to a proper drain.

STOPPING INCOMING WATER

If the sump pump fails to come on, your first priority should be to stop the incoming water, if possible. Here are some pointers.

● If water is coming from a break in a supply pipe or ruptured water heater, close the nearest branch valve or main water shutoff valve. (See *Your Plumbing System* on page 2.)
● If the water is coming from a broken drain line, quit using the toilets, showers, sinks, or appliances that feed into the broken drain. (See "Broken Pipes" on page 56.)
● If the source of the water is a temporary or seasonal leak through a cement wall or up through the slab, turn your attention to making emergency repairs on the sump pump until you can get to the root of the problem later. (See "Leaky Basement" on page 61 for remedies for those leaks.)

MAKING EMERGENCY REPAIRS

If the motor is running but the pump isn't moving water, proceed with repair options 1, 2, and 3 below until you have diagnosed the problem.

If the motor isn't running, jump ahead to repair options 4, 5, and 6. In either case, refer to *Anatomy of a Pedestal-Type Sump Pump* and *Anatomy of a Submersible Sump Pump* on this page to get your bearings.

1. If the motor and pump are working but the drain line has broken, allowing water to spill back down in the pit, shut the pump off and repair the drain line. Various temporary and permanent repairs for metal and plastic pipe are discussed in "Broken Pipes" beginning on page 56.
2. If the motor is running, but water isn't draining from the sump pit, the pump may be clogged with silt or debris.

To clean it, first unplug the pump and pull it out of the pit. If the discharge line is made of metal or rigid plastic pipe, you'll have to disconnect the pipe before you can remove the pump.

Once the pump is out, unscrew the intake screen and clean it thoroughly, as shown in *Cleaning Your Sump Pump* on the opposite page. Use an old toothbrush and rinse with clean water. If your pump is the type that

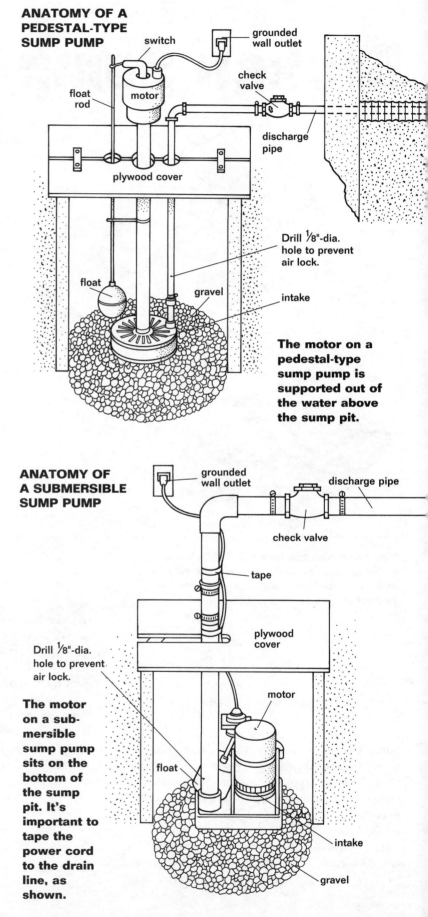

ANATOMY OF A PEDESTAL-TYPE SUMP PUMP

switch
grounded wall outlet
float rod
motor
check valve
discharge pipe
plywood cover
Drill ⅛"-dia. hole to prevent air lock.
float
gravel
intake

The motor on a pedestal-type sump pump is supported out of the water above the sump pit.

ANATOMY OF A SUBMERSIBLE SUMP PUMP

grounded wall outlet
discharge pipe
check valve
tape
Drill ⅛"-dia. hole to prevent air lock.
plywood cover
motor
The motor on a submersible sump pump sits on the bottom of the sump pit. It's important to tape the power cord to the drain line, as shown.
float
intake
gravel

A Pedestal-Type Sump Pump

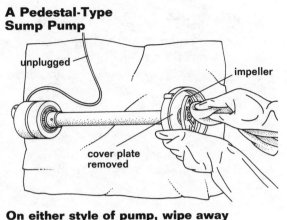

unplugged

impeller

cover plate removed

A Submersible Sump Pump

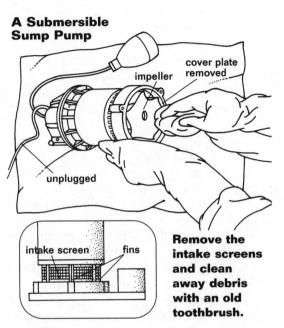

cover plate removed

impeller

unplugged

intake screen   fins

On either style of pump, wipe away dirt and debris that has accumulated. Then remove the cover plate, and clean the inside of the pump with a rag. Make sure the impeller spins freely. If it is too tight or too loose, it needs professional service.

Remove the intake screens and clean away debris with an old toothbrush.

has louvers (finlike partitions) behind the intake screen, wipe them clean with a cloth or paper towel.

Finally, unscrew the pump cover plate and clean off the impeller that's housed inside. Remove any sand or other gunk that may have accumulated in the chamber. The impeller should turn freely on the shaft and without much wobble. If it's locked in place or excessively wobbly, take the pump in for service or replacement.

If the impeller looks and feels sound, put the pieces back together and set the pump back down in the pit for a test run.

3. If the motor is running, but water isn't draining from the pit (and you've already cleaned the pump, as suggested in repair option 2), you probably have a clogged drain line or defective check valve (a valve in the line that prevents water from siphoning back through the line after the pump shuts off).

If you suspect the drain line or check valve is frozen and plugged with ice, use a hair dryer or heat gun on *LOW* to thaw the line or valve. Don't use a propane torch or other open flame device to thaw it. (See "Thawing Frozen Pipes" on page 58.)

If freezing isn't the problem, the check valve may be jammed with debris or corroded to the point where it's stuck closed. (The check valve can also fail in an open

position, which lets water pumped out of the discharge pipe drain back into the pit when the pump cuts off.)

To test the valve, you'll need to disconnect the drain line from the pump. If the line is made of rigid plastic or metal pipe, you'll have to open a slip joint, pipe clamps, or a union in the line to remove the valve.

Using a garden hose, direct a stream of water through either end of the check valve to see how well it performs. Water should flow easily through the valve in line with the arrow marked on the outside—but *not* in the opposite direction.

If the check valve isn't badly corroded, it may be possible to clean the gunk out of it and put it back into service. If that doesn't work, replace it with a new one.

4. If the motor is not working, use a test lamp or volt-ohm meter to make sure there's power to the outlet or subpanel that runs the

Pump Up the Heat

One way to thaw out a frozen sump drain line (if the flooding isn't too severe) is to bail out the sump pit with a bucket and refill it with hot water. Pumping hot water into the frozen line should unplug it in fairly short order. ●

pump. If there is, move on to option 5.

If the test lamp or meter indicates a dead circuit, it's a good bet that a short circuit or overload has occurred. Thus the circuit breaker (or fuse) that protects that circuit will have shut down the power.

Do not reset the circuit breaker or replace the fuse until you have been able to diagnose and correct the problem.

The motor itself may be the problem, either because it has seized up, such as when the bearings fail, or because it has an internal short circuit. Either way, you're probably better off buying a new sump pump than dickering over repairs.

A second possibility is that the circuit serving the pump is overloaded, that is, drawing more than its rated amperage. To calculate the load, see "Adding Up the Amps" on page 104.

Finally, it's possible that the circuit breaker has failed or that there's been a short circuit in the house wiring. (See "Circuit Breaker Trips or Fuse Blows" on page 100.)

5. If your sump pump has a float-activated switch, make sure the float can move freely up and down. (You may have to

Maintaining Your Sump Pump

At least once a year—and perhaps as many as four times a year—it's wise to test your sump pump so that it won't fail you in an emergency.

Start by cleaning out any debris that may have fallen into the sump pit and make sure that the pump is firmly seated on its base. Then use buckets of water or a garden hose to fill the pit with water and observe the action as the water rises.

While some pumps come equipped with a manual *ON* button, *don't* rely on it to test your pump. Filling the pit with water is the *only* way to test the pump's automatic function, which is critical in protecting your home while you're away.

Here are three additional tips to help increase the reliability and extend the life of your pump.

● Do not sweep or dump refuse or waste-laden water of any kind into the sump pit.

● Keep 1 inch or so of clean water in the pit year-round.

● While the bearings on most sump pumps are permanently sealed and lubricated, some older-type pedestal models may require oiling. If yours has an oil port on it, service it with a couple drops of lightweight oil once a year or as prescribed in your owner's manual.

Pump Start

Your sump pump should switch on automatically when a few inches of water (less than 10, typically) accumulate around the base. If the pump is slow in coming on, adjust the float stops (on pedestal-type pumps) or shorten the tether (on submersible types that have a tethered float switch). Sump pumps with pressure-activated diaphragm switches are preset at the factory and can't be adjusted. ●

bail some water out of the sump pit to get a good look at it.) If the float is stuck on the float rod or jammed against the side of the pit, free it so that it can move. If the float had been punctured and become waterlogged, replace it with an *exact* duplicate. As a short-term measure, you can "trick" the pump into working by holding the switch lever up (on pedestal-type pumps) or by unplugging the motor from the switch (on submersible models with tethered switches) so that the motor can be plugged directly into the outlet.

6. If none of the above measures has solved the problem, you're left with the prospect of a failed switch or motor. Rent a sump pump to handle the emergency while you replace the switch to determine if that is where the problem lies. (See "Replacing the Switch" on this page.) If the old switch is faulty, you're all set. If not, the motor must be bad. Since a motor isn't cost-effective to replace, it's time for a new sump pump.

REPLACING THE SWITCH

If the sump pump is heavily corroded and showing other signs of age, it's probably wise to be done with it and buy a new one. But if the sump pump is still in good shape, it may be worth your while to replace the switch. (It isn't cost-effective to hire an electrician or plumber to do this for you because the price of their labor would quickly exceed the cost of buying a new sump pump.) But make sure you're comfortable with the procedure before attempting this or any other electrical repair.

Since switch designs can vary a lot from one sump pump model to the next, be sure that the new switch you buy is an exact replacement for the old one. When you remove the old switch, work with the owner's manual close at hand. Take careful notes and use taped-on labels so that screws, clamps, float stops, and electrical leads can be reassembled in their proper positions. And be sure to save all of the parts, packaging, and receipt that come with the new switch so that it can be returned for credit if for some reason it doesn't work.

If you have a submersible sump pump with a separate, tethered switch (either a float or diaphragm type), you'll find that the motor plug and switch plug are joined in piggyback fashion at the electrical outlet. This is known as a *series plug*. To test it, remove the switch plug so that you can plug the motor directly into the outlet. If the motor *doesn't* work, there's no use replacing the switch; go buy yourself a new sump pump.

If the motor *does* run, you can happily conclude that the problem is in the switch, which is literally a snap to replace.

To replace a tethered float switch, simply loosen the clip or clamp that holds the tether to the motor housing and put the new switch—a $20 to $30 item—in place. Make sure that the new tether is adjusted to the same length as the old one.

Diaphragm-type switches—sometimes called *pressure-activated* switches—are replaced by removing a single bolt or fastener that secures the switch to the pump housing. No adjustment is necessary. Some older-style diaphragm switches are sealed in the pump housing, making them difficult to service or replace. Ask your dealer or manufacturer about the cost-effectiveness of replacing one versus buying a new pump.

Replacing a faulty switch on a pedestal-type sump pump is an easy job. The new switch, which costs $10 to $25, mounts directly on top of the motor. The problem is, unless you tested the old switch with a volt-ohm meter beforehand, you have no way of knowing for sure that it's faulty until the new switch is mounted in place. If the pump still doesn't work once the new switch is in place, you've discovered the hard way that the motor was the culprit all along. That's why it's always smart to save your packaging and receipt.

REPLACING YOUR PUMP

Since a new sump pump costs under $200—with some as low as $75—it doesn't make much sense to invest a lot of time and money in repairing an old one. If you think you can pull off a quick and cost-effective repair—such as the switch repairs described above—it might make sense to rent a sump pump for a day or two to get you through the crisis. *NOTE:* Watch your costs. The price of renting a sump pump for a few days will probably buy you a new one.

If you do go shopping for a new sump pump, you'll find both pedestal types and submersible models for sale. While there's no marked difference in the way they perform, pedestal types may have a slight edge in reliability while submersible models tend to run quieter.

Try to get some expert help in sizing the new pump to meet your needs. Depending on how much horsepower they have, sump pumps can handle from 700 to 3,000 gallons per hour. Whatever the type and capacity rating, choose a pump that's made out of stainless steel, plastic, or a combination of the two, so the pump won't corrode.

Finally, if leaking water is a serious, recurring problem, consider some of the permanent water control strategies outlined in "Leaky Basement" on page 61.

No Water

Quick Response

1. Check for frozen pipes. (See "Broken Pipes" on page 56.)

2. If you use municipal water, call city to see if supply has been disrupted at main.

3. If you have private well, check your pump and circuit box.

When you go for a nice cool glass of nature's best and your faucet just sputters and coughs a drop or two, it's time for some quick action.

Hazard

Once you've diagnosed and fixed the problem, make sure that the water is safe to drink. A broken pipe, for example, may have left contaminated water in the pipes or well. As a first precaution, flush out affected pipes and fixtures by running fresh water through them for five minutes. If you still suspect there's contamination in the system, have the water professionally tested. (See "Contaminated Drinking Water" on page 185.)

SITTING HIGH AND DRY

When you turn on the faucet for a nice cool drink of water and nothing happens, it's no joke. Not only do we depend on a reliable supply of water for drinking and cooking, but we also need it for washing ourselves and flushing the toilets. You should always keep a supply of water on hand, as described in "Preparing for an Emergency" on page 10. In the following text, you'll find several possible causes for your water shortage (depending on whether you get your water from a well or from a municipal system) and some steps you can take to correct them.

DEALING WITH CITY WATER

If you're on a municipal water system, there are three reasons why the water pressure might fail.

You have frozen pipes. See "Thawing Frozen Pipes" on page 58.

The municipal supply is disrupted. Call your neighbors to see if they're experiencing problems, too. If so, call the city water authority to notify them of the problem and to determine how long the water will be off.

The supply line between the main and your house is broken. This usually leaves a soggy patch—and perhaps a sinkhole—on your lawn or close to the foundation wall where the water line enters your house. Have the city water authority turn off your water at the main and call a plumber to repair the line.

DEALING WITH PRIVATE WELL WATER

If you draw water from your own well, there are seven possible reasons why you've lost water pressure.

You have frozen pipes. See "Thawing Frozen Pipes" on page 58.

The circuit breaker (or fuse) serving the pump has tripped (or blown). Before you reset the breaker or replace the fuse, check the condition of the motor. If the housing is unusually warm—after a long period of running—let it cool down before you restore power to the circuit. If the motor made unusual noises just before the outage—a sign that the bearings may have failed—have it repaired or replaced before you reset the breaker or replace the fuse. (See **The motor has failed** on page 78.)

If the motor seems sound, the problem may have been an overloaded circuit. This can occur only if there are other appliances or lights on the same circuit with the water pump and their combined load temporarily exceeded the circuit's capacity. The problem is easily solved by reducing the demand on the circuit before you reset the breaker or replace the fuse. (See "Adding Up the Amps" on page 104.)

Finally, it's possible that the circuit breaker that protects the pump circuit has failed or that there's been a short circuit in the house wiring. (See "Circuit Breaker Trips or Fuse Blows" on page 100.)

The water level in the well is low. Some pumps have a low-water cutout switch that protects the pump by shutting it off if the water level in the well falls too low. A low-water condition may be a seasonal occurrence, such as in dry conditions, or can result from increased demand on the water table, such as when new wells are drilled nearby. Once the well has recharged itself, the cutout switch must be manually reset. (Consult your owner's manual.)

The water supply line between the well head and the storage tank is broken. This causes the pump motor to run continually without building pressure in the storage tank.

The problem is easily diagnosed on an indoor jet-pump system, as shown in *A Typical Well with a Jet-Siphon Pump* on page 76, because you can hear the pump running. If the jet pump is located in an underground pit, you'll have to remove the lid and listen to tell if the pump is cycling off when it should.

On a submersible pump system, as shown in *A Typical Well with a Submersible Pump* on page 76, in which the motor and pump are located down inside the well, there's no telltale sound to alert you. In some cases—if the break in the pipe is between the well head and the house, for example—you'll find a soggy patch of ground to help you identify the problem. But if the pipe is broken down inside the well, you'll have no clues to guide you, except for the lack of pressure in the tank.

If you suspect there's a broken pipe, move quickly to cut off the power. The motor can overheat and burn itself up if left to run, and the seals inside the pump aren't designed to run dry.

If the point of the break is obvious, it's fairly simple to dig up the pipe and repair it. (See "Broken Pipes" on page 56.) But if the break is down inside the well, call a plumber.

NOTE: A stuck check valve, which normally prevents water from flowing backward in the line, can produce similar symptoms. If the check valve is accessible, you can clean or replace it yourself. If it's at the bottom of the well, call a pro.

The pressure tank has sprung a leak. This is usually an easy failure to spot, since leaking water will pool around the base of the tank. A tank that has corroded to the point that it's leaking is generally not worth repairing.

The pressure switch is faulty. The pressure switch is the device that turns the pump motor on when the water supply in the pres-

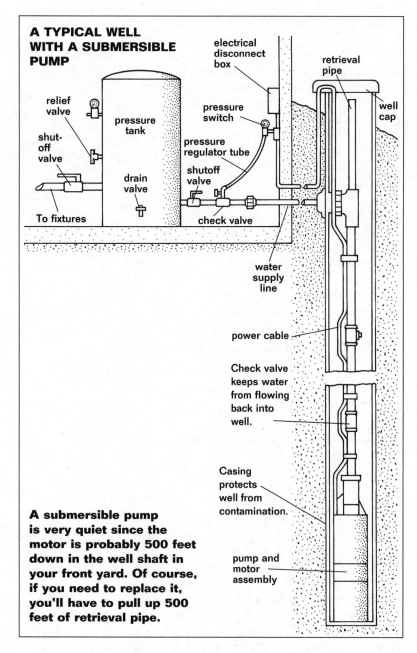

A TYPICAL WELL WITH A SUBMERSIBLE PUMP

relief valve

shut-off valve

pressure tank

drain valve

To fixtures

electrical disconnect box

pressure switch

pressure regulator tube

shutoff valve

check valve

retrieval pipe

well cap

water supply line

power cable

Check valve keeps water from flowing back into well.

Casing protects well from contamination.

pump and motor assembly

A submersible pump is very quiet since the motor is probably 500 feet down in the well shaft in your front yard. Of course, if you need to replace it, you'll have to pull up 500 feet of retrieval pipe.

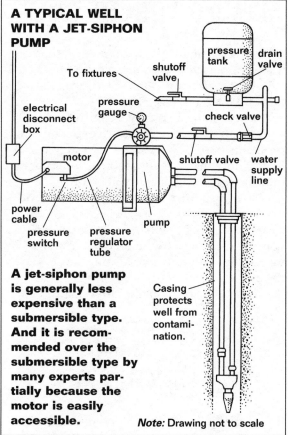

A TYPICAL WELL WITH A JET-SIPHON PUMP

To fixtures

shutoff valve

pressure tank

drain valve

check valve

electrical disconnect box

pressure gauge

motor

power cable

pressure switch

pressure regulator tube

pump

shutoff valve

water supply line

Casing protects well from contamination.

A jet-siphon pump is generally less expensive than a submersible type. And it is recommended over the submersible type by many experts partially because the motor is easily accessible.

Note: Drawing not to scale

sure tank is depleted below a set point. If the motor isn't coming on, there may be a problem with this switch.

Start by turning the power off at the pump's subpanel or at the main service panel and releasing any remaining water pressure from the tank—simply open a faucet until all water flow ceases.

Now remove the small metal or plastic pressure regulator tube that connects the pressure switch to the pump or tank. If the tube is clogged, it will prevent the switch from sensing the pressure drop in the tank and turning the pump on. You can clean the tube by snaking a thin wire through it, or you can

get a replacement for about 50 cents.

If the tube is clear, the pressure switch itself may have failed. If you feel confident working around electricity and know how to use a volt-ohm meter, you can test the switch yourself. If not, don't hesitate to call an electrician.

To test the switch, use the volt-ohm meter to check the line voltage running to it to make sure there's adequate power. Set the volt-ohm meter on the 250-volt AC scale. With the electricity to the pump turned back on, remove the cover of the switch and carefully touch the meter's probes to the line-in terminals (those coming from the service panel), as shown in *Testing Voltage to the Motor* on page 78.

CAUTION: When using a volt-ohm meter on live wires and equipment, be very careful not to touch the test leads together or to any ground (like a metal switch box). Touching the leads or grounding them can create a short circuit that can ruin your equipment and/or give you a nasty shock.

If the pump motor is wired at 115 volts, the meter should read *at least* 104 volts (allowing for a 10 percent fluctuation in the motor's operating voltage). A motor wired at 230 volts should test at least 207 volts. If the

Low Pressure Blues

Lack of water pressure, whether throughout your whole house or in just a single fixture, is a nettlesome problem that often has a cure. Here are some of the most common causes and solutions.

ALL HOUSEHOLD FIXTURES RUN SLOW

Possible Cause	Solution
City water pressure low	Work with city authority to solve problem. As last resort, install pump and pressurized holding tank.
Supply valve partly closed	Make sure all supply valves are fully open.
Supply pipe too small to meet increased demand (e.g., new bathroom)	Water pressure may be increased by replacing globe valves with gate valves (see your plumbing supplier), installing a new water meter, and straightening pipe runs.
Supply pipes clogged with sediment	Hire plumber or other professional to flush out pipes.
Supply pipes clogged with mineral deposits	Replace pipes. Installing water softener will help prevent further buildup of minerals in pipes but won't address existing flow problems.
Water purification system or water softener clogged	Change filter(s) and provide other necessary maintenance service.
Pressure regulator set too low *	Adjust pressure regulator.
Too much or too little air pressure in storage tank*	Have tank properly charged.
Pump impeller clogged or worn *	Clean or replace impeller.
Pump orifice clogged*	Clean out orifice.
Strainer and/or check valve at foot of well clogged*	Have strainer or valve professionally cleaned. Installing in-line filter will help keep silt out of pump.
Storage tank leaking*	Replace.

SINGLE FIXTURE RUNS SLOW

Possible Cause	Solution
Supply valve partly closed	Make sure all supply valves are fully open.
Faucet aerator clogged	Remove and clean aerator with pin or old toothbrush.
Showerhead clogged	Remove and clean showerhead.
Dirty strainer (on dishwashers, clothes washers, and some valves)	Remove dirty or calcified strainer and clean it with warm vinegar, then soapy water. Or replace strainer.
Worn or corroded washer or valve seat	Repair affected faucet or valve.
Water purification unit clogged	Change filter(s) and provide other necessary maintenance service.

*Problem occurs on well water systems only.

TESTING VOLTAGE TO THE MOTOR (WITH POWER ON)

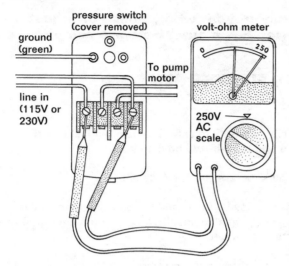

For motors wired at 115V, the meter should register at least 104V to be within 10 percent of required voltage. For motors wired at 230V, the minimum is 207V.

meter reads below those levels, you have a low-voltage problem; call an electrician.

If the voltage is okay, turn the power off again at the subpanel or main service panel so that you can check the switch for continuity. Start by disconnecting the line-in lead wires from their switch terminals, as shown in *Testing the Pressure Switch* on this page. Now set your volt-ohm meter on the RX-1 scale and touch the probes to the line-in terminals. The meter should read less than 9 ohms, indicating there is no resistance in the switch. (The motor accounts for 7 to 8 ohms of resistance.)

If the reading is 9 ohms or more, try cleaning the screw terminals on the switch with a piece of fine sandpaper. If that doesn't bring the reading below 9 ohms, replace the switch.

As you remove the old switch, be sure to tag the leads with tape so you can wire the new switch properly. If possible, buy the replacement switch from the same manufacturer who supplied the original, so you can get an exact replacement.

The motor has failed. If none of the above-mentioned possibilities is the culprit, the motor itself has probably failed. Repairing or replacing it is a job for a licensed electrician.

TESTING THE PRESSURE SWITCH (WITH POWER OFF)

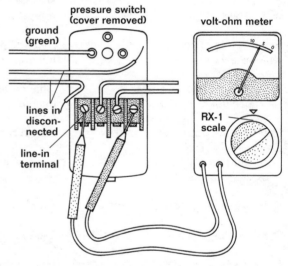

If the switch is okay, the meter should read less than 9 ohms.

No Hot Water

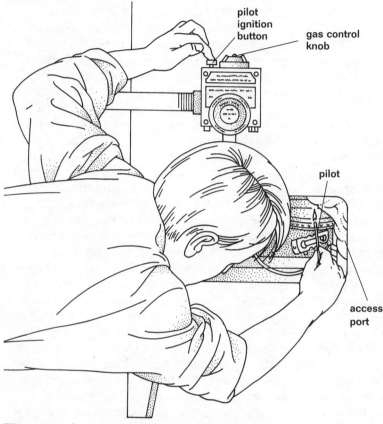

pilot ignition button

gas control knob

pilot

access port

The controls on gas water heaters are similar, and you should be able to relight yours easily by following the directions on page 80.

2

WATER & SEWAGE EMERGENCIES

Quick Response

1. If you have gas water heater, check to make sure it's getting fuel and that pilot is on.

2. If you have electric water heater, check circuit breaker or fuses that serve it.

FACING A COLD SHOWER

Losing your hot water is inconvenient, but a cold shower never killed anyone—at least I don't *think* it has. So don't do anything rash. Before you run out and buy a new water heater or hire an expensive repairman, check out the troubleshooting sections that follow for gas or electric water heaters. If you are out of hot water for a couple of days but save a couple hundred bucks by fixing the problem yourself, the brief inconvenience is probably worth it.

Hazards

● Even simple water heater repairs must be approached with caution. Carelessness can result in an explosion, fire, asphyxiation (from gas), shock, or scalding. If you're not sure what you're doing, don't be afraid to call in a pro.

● If you smell gas (except for a whiff while lighting the pilot), call your gas or propane company at once. (See "Gas Leak" on page 118.)

TROUBLESHOOTING A GAS WATER HEATER

If your gas water heater is working but doesn't supply enough hot water, consult the table "Not Enough Hot Water?" on page 82. If you have no hot water at all, consider the following possibilities:

The fuel supply is off. Double-check to make sure that all gas valves are open and the control setting on the tank itself is on. If other gas appliances in your house aren't getting fuel, call the gas or propane company to see why the supply has been interrupted. *NOTE:* Some older-style propane tanks have a pressure gauge or pop-up flag that signals when the tank is empty.

The power vent has stopped working. Some gas and propane water heaters are vented directly through the wall and rely on a small electric blower to properly exhaust the unit. If the fan stops for whatever reason, one or more safety switches automatically shut the water heater down so that exhaust fumes can't backdraft into the house. If you own a power-vented water heater, check your owner's manual for detailed information on how to diagnose and fix it. The problem may call for a professional.

The pilot light has gone out. To relight the pilot, first remove the access panel on the bottom of the water heater. Look for the manufacturer's instruction plate or tag that provides specific instructions on how to relight the pilot. (The procedure varies a little from one model to the next.) Your owner's manual will also help.

If there is no plate, tag, or manual to assist you, follow the steps outlined here and as shown in *Relighting the Pilot* on page 79.

1. Open windows and doors in the room to provide ventilation.
2. Remove the access panel at the bottom of the water heater. (Some models may have an additional panel that covers the pilot assembly. Remove this cover, too.)
3. Turn the gas control knob to *PILOT.*
4. Press the pilot ignition button (what is known as the reset button) for a few seconds, and then hold a lighted match or twist of paper near the tip of the pilot. (If there's no button, try pressing the gas control knob, which serves a dual purpose on some mod-

els.) After the pilot flame has established itself (it may take a few matches to get it going), keep the button (or knob) pressed in for about a minute, then slowly release it. Make sure the pilot stays lit.
5. Turn the control knob to *ON.* This should ignite the main burner.

If the pilot light keeps going out, turn the gas off and stick a needle into the orifice to clean out any debris that may be blocking the flow of gas, as shown in *Cleaning the Pilot Orifice* on this page. (You may have to take the pilot assembly apart to do this.) Also check to see if there are strong drafts through the area that may be extinguishing the pilot, and, if so, eliminate them.

If neither of these measures helps and the pilot won't stay lit, the thermocouple is apt to be the problem. (See "Replacing the Thermocouple" on the opposite page.)

The electronic ignition has failed. Some gas water heaters use an electric spark or hot-surface ignition (rather than a conventional pilot light) to light the main burner. A spark-type ignition makes a distinctive snap sound as it lights the burner. If you hear the ignition snapping, responding to the need for hot water, you can conclude that it's working properly but that there's no gas to ignite in the main burner. (See **The fuel supply is off** on this page and **The thermostat or main gas valve has failed** on the opposite page.)

If the ignition isn't snapping, make sure that there's electric power to the circuit that runs

CLEANING THE PILOT ORIFICE

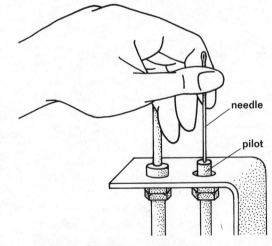

If the pilot orifice is clogged, work a fine needle in and out of the orifice to clean it.

Carry a Big Stick

Long-sticked fireplace matches (those with 9 to 10-inch sticks) are handy for relighting pilot lights. ●

the ignition. Consult your owner's manual and, if necessary, the manufacturer for more specific troubleshooting information.

The thermostat or main gas valve has failed. If all of the above possibilities have been eliminated, then either the thermostat or the gas valve has failed. Call a plumber to make the repairs. If the water heater is badly

corroded, see "Buying a New Water Heater" on page 90 for some advice on replacing it.

TROUBLESHOOTING AN ELECTRIC WATER HEATER

If your electric water heater is working but doesn't supply enough hot water, consult the table "Not Enough Hot Water?" on page 82. If you have no hot water at all, consider the following possibilities:

The circuit breaker has tripped (or the fuse has blown). Reset the circuit breaker or

Replacing the Thermocouple

The thermocouple is a low-voltage electrical circuit that holds a water heater's gas valve open as long as the pilot light is burning. If the pilot light goes out, the thermocouple quickly shuts off the flow of gas so there's no chance of a fire, explosion, or asphyxiation. Follow these steps.

1. To replace a faulty thermocouple, first shut off the main gas valve to the water heater. (In its *OFF* position, the valve handle should be perpendicular to the gas line, as shown.) Also turn the control knob on the water heater to *OFF*.

2. Open the access panel on the bottom of the water heater and locate the thermocouple. Of the three lines coming out of the bottom of the control unit, it's the line with the smallest diameter, as shown in *Replacing the Thermocouple.* Use an adjustable wrench to loosen the nut that fastens the thermocouple to the control and then gently pull it out.

The other end of the thermocouple, located in the same bracket that holds the pilot, is typically fastened by a second nut or bushing. Unscrew it and pull the tip of the thermocouple out of the bracket. (On some models, it may be necessary to remove the pilot—perhaps even the main burner—to free the thermocouple.)

3. Take the old thermocouple with you to the plumbing supply outlet or hardware store. If you can't get an exact replacement, it's okay to buy a thermocouple that's a little longer than the original, but *not* shorter, since it can't be stretched to fit.

4. Install the new thermocouple, reversing the steps outlined above. Be careful not to overtighten the nuts or bushings or you may strip the threads.

Once the water heater is back in service, with the pilot light burning, take a few minutes to carefully check all of the gas lines and fittings for leaks—especially any that you took apart and reassembled. Using a small brush, coat the pipes and fittings with a 50–50 solution of liquid soap and water. If there's a gas leak, it will show itself by bubbling up underneath the solution.

REPLACING THE THERMOCOUPLE

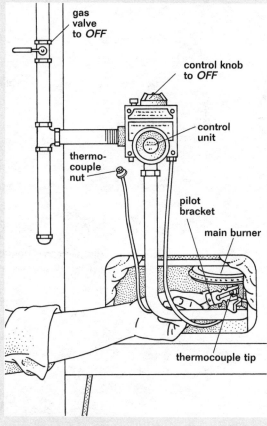

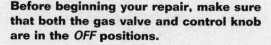

Before beginning your repair, make sure that both the gas valve and control knob are in the *OFF* positions.

Not Enough Hot Water?

If your water heater is working but falls short of meeting your water needs, here are some possible reasons and the corresponding steps to take.

Possible Cause	Solution
Thermostat set too low	Turn up thermostat. A setting between 115–120°F is recommended.
Hot water being wasted	Reduce hot water use. Install water-saving showerheads and faucet aerators, use cold water for family wash and other cleaning chores, and run dishwasher only when it's fully loaded.
Tank filled with sediment	Flush out tank. (See "Maintaining Your Water Heater" on page 89.)
Damaged dip tube	Replace dip tube. (See "Maintaining Your Water Heater" on page 89.)
Heat dissipates in long plumbing runs	Insulate pipes.
Tempering valve stuck (common with solar water heating systems)	Have valve repaired or replaced.
Water heater too small for (growing) family	Install larger-capacity water heater.
Dirty gas valve or other problem with main burner*	Have valve and burner professionally serviced.
Low gas pressure (small flame)*	Have gas company check line pressure or refill propane tank.
Low voltage**	Replace substandard wiring. Or check for low voltage from utility. (See "Spikes, Brownouts, and Blips" on page 111.)
Heating elements are scaled up**	Clean or replace elements.
Burned out lower element or thermostat**	Replace defective part.

*Gas and propane water heaters only
**Electric water heaters only

Save During Vacation

A great way to save money is to turn your water heater off while you're away on vacation. But if you do this, remember to turn it back on when you return. ●

replace the fuse. (See "Circuit Breaker Trips or Fuse Blows" on page 100.) If the problem repeats itself, it's a good bet that one of the heating elements has shorted out or the controls have malfunctioned, causing an overload. If the water heater is newly installed, another possibility is that it was wired incorrectly to begin with. Call a professional plumber to diagnose the problem and fix it.

The high-limit switch has tripped. If the water temperature inside the water tank exceeds the high-limit setting, a built-in safety switch will automatically shut the water heater off.

RESETTING THE HIGH-LIMIT SWITCH

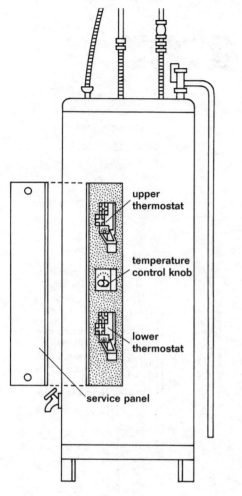

upper thermostat

temperature control knob

lower thermostat

service panel

To reset the switch, open the upper panel on the water heater, and push the red button, as shown in *Resetting the High-Limit Switch* on this page.

If the high-limit switch continues to cut out, it's possible that the switch itself is faulty or that either the upper or lower thermostat is malfunctioning. Have a licensed plumber test the circuits and make repairs or, if the water heater is on its last leg, replace the unit. (See "Buying a New Water Heater" on page 90.)

The upper or lower thermostat is malfunctioning. Since testing the voltage and various circuits is a complex and potentially dangerous job, it's best left to an experienced plumber.

The upper or lower heating element has failed. Have a plumber test the elements and replace them, if necessary.

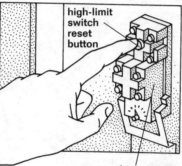

high-limit switch reset button

upper thermostat

To reset the high-limit switch, open the service panel on your electric water heater and press the red high-limit switch reset button.

Leaky Water Heater

Quick Response

1. Turn off power to water heater.

2. Turn off water to water heater.

3. Clean up. (See "Spills" on page 247.)

ANATOMY OF A WATER HEATER

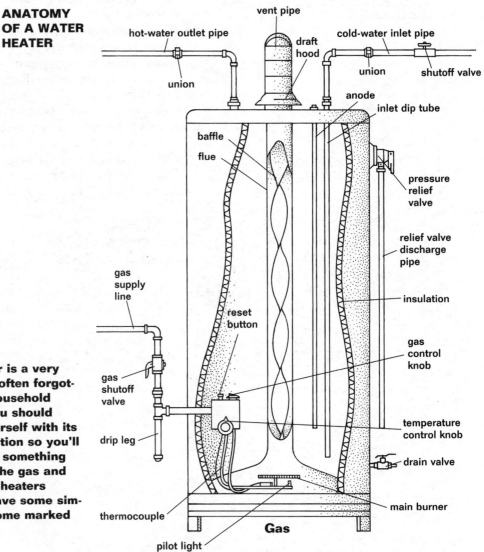

A water heater is a very important but often forgotten piece of household equipment. You should familiarize yourself with its parts and function so you'll be prepared if something goes wrong. The gas and electric water heaters shown here have some similarities and some marked differences.

Hazards

● If leaking water has come in contact with appliances, electrical lines, or extension cords, wear rubber-soled shoes and rubber gloves to avoid shock. If necessary, turn off electricity to the area until the water is cleaned up.

● Any electrical tools or appliances used in clean up or repair should be plugged into a receptacle protected by a ground fault circuit interrupter (GFCI). (See "GFCI Spells Electrical Safety" on page 265.)

TAKING CARE

With good care and maintenance, a hot-water heater can last 20 years or more. But all too often, this appliance slowly disintegrates while it faithfully pumps out gallon after gallon of hot water. This neglect can cause your water heater to fail. Should you find yourself with a leaky or nonfunctioning water heater, start by shutting off the gas and/or electric and water to the heater before assessing the problem.

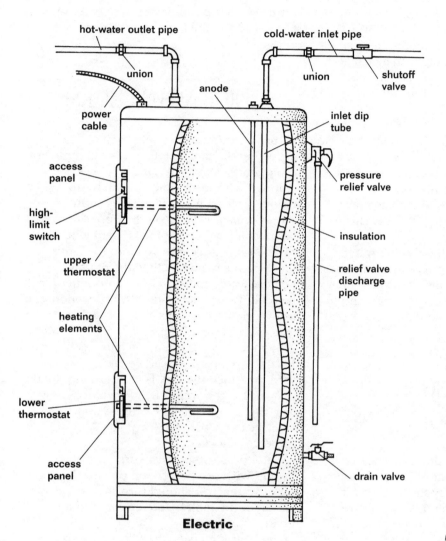

hot-water outlet pipe

union

power cable

access panel

high-limit switch

upper thermostat

heating elements

lower thermostat

access panel

cold-water inlet pipe

union

shutoff valve

anode

inlet dip tube

pressure relief valve

insulation

relief valve discharge pipe

drain valve

Electric

TURNING OFF THE ENERGY SOURCE

On a gas water heater, turn the gas control knob (usually a red or black knob located on the thermostat) to *OFF* and close the gas shut-off valve in the gas line. If your water heater has an electronic ignition, unplug the transformer or turn off the switch. If the ignition is hardwired into the wall, turn it off at the circuit breaker panel.

If you have an electric water heater, go to the circuit box and switch off the circuit breaker that serves it. It's typically a 30-amp, double-pole breaker. In some electrical layouts, the breaker for the water heater may be in a smaller, separate box close to the main box or on the wall near the water heater.

Homes that are equipped to use off-peak electricity for water heating will have *two* circuit breakers for the water heater, one for on-peak electricity, the other for off peak. Be sure to switch off both breakers.

If none of the circuit breakers is clearly marked *WATER HEATER*, the safest course is to switch off *all* of the breakers that are 20 amps or more.

If you have an oil-fired water heater, turn off the toggle switch that's located on the side of the tank or nearby. Also, close the valve in the fuel line.

TURNING OFF THE WATER

When the energy source has been turned off, the water supply to the heater should be shut off to take pressure away from the leak. Most water heaters have a gate or ball shutoff valve located in the cold-water inlet pipe that runs into the tank, as shown in *Anatomy of a Water Heater* on the opposite page and this page. Locate the valve and shut it off.

If there's no valve on the water heater's cold-water inlet pipe or if the valve fails to close properly, you'll have to shut off water to the whole house. (See "Understanding Your Plumbing System" on page 2.)

ASSESSING THE PROBLEM

Just because you've found water around the base of the water heater doesn't *necessarily* mean that it's leaking. When the relative humidity is high and the tank is being repeatedly filled with cold water during periods of heavy use, enough condensation can form on the pipes and tank to collect on the floor and give the appearance of a leak. With a change in the humidity and/or less demand for hot water, the tank will quit sweating and the "leak" will disappear.

Standing water can also come from a relief valve that isn't connnected to a proper drain. The relief valve is designed to release excess heat and pressure from the tank to prevent an explosion. It can discharge hot water for a number of different reasons, including failure of the valve itself. (See "Leaky Water Heater Relief Valve" on page 93.)

Finally, it's possible that the leaking water originates from other appliances or water lines nearby or from water seeping in through the wall or up through the floor. (See "Broken Pipes" on page 56 and "Leaky Basement" on page 61.)

FINDING SHORT-TERM SOLUTIONS

If the leak *is* coming from the water heater, it's important to remember that not all leaks are fatal. You may be able to repair the leak without replacing the entire water heater. And even if the water heater does need to be replaced, you still have time to make smart choices. In other words, don't panic yourself into making bad decisions. (See "Buying a New Water Heater" on page 90.)

If the leak is only a trickle (most are), you can probably keep using the water heater for a few days while you select your best course of action. A drip pan and/or an occasional mopping up is all that's needed to buy that extra time.

Another option is to turn the power and water back on when you need to bathe or wash clothes, then turn them off again.

Obviously, a "let-it-leak" approach won't work if the leaking water is threatening an expensive carpet or oak floor, or if the water heater is located in the attic. In such cases, it's best just to leave the power and water off until you can diagnose the problem.

Water heaters that experience a "catastrophic" tank failure that sends water streaming or gushing onto the floor are ready for the junkyard. If you have that kind of failure—not to be confused with a broken pipe or fitting—leave the power and water off, and skip ahead to "Buying a New Water Heater" on page 90.

PROBING FOR LEAKS

By turning the water supply back on and inspecting the tank carefully, it's often possible to pinpoint a slow leak. (If the tank is wrapped with insulation, you'll have to remove it to get a good look.) As shown in *Checkpoints for Leaks* on the opposite page, the most likely points of failure are where valves or pipes are screwed into the tank. These points would include the drain valve, the cold-water inlet and hot-water outlet pipes, the relief valve, the anode rod connection, the heating element gaskets (on electric water heaters), and the thermostat.

If you have good plumbing and mechanical skills, the repair work can be fairly straightforward, provided the leak is in or around the fittings, not in the welds. Be forewarned, however, that an unskilled or careless approach to water heater repair can leave you seriously burned or shocked.

While pros sometimes work on water heaters with the power still on and the tank full of water, *you* should turn the power off and drain the tank before attempting any repairs.

On electric models, the first step is to open the access panel on the upper heating element and locate the points where the exposed wires are connected to the uppermost terminals. This is just above the red high-limit switch. Using a volt-ohm meter, check each of these terminals, grounding one of the volt-ohm meter probes to the tank to make doubly sure that the electricity is off, as shown in *Power Off?* on the opposite page. *CAUTION: Electric water heaters are typically wired with 240 volts at 30 amps. This is not kids' stuff!*

On gas models, double-check to make sure that the gas valve on the thermostat is in the *OFF* position and the gas shutoff valve in the gas line is closed.

CHECKPOINTS FOR LEAKS

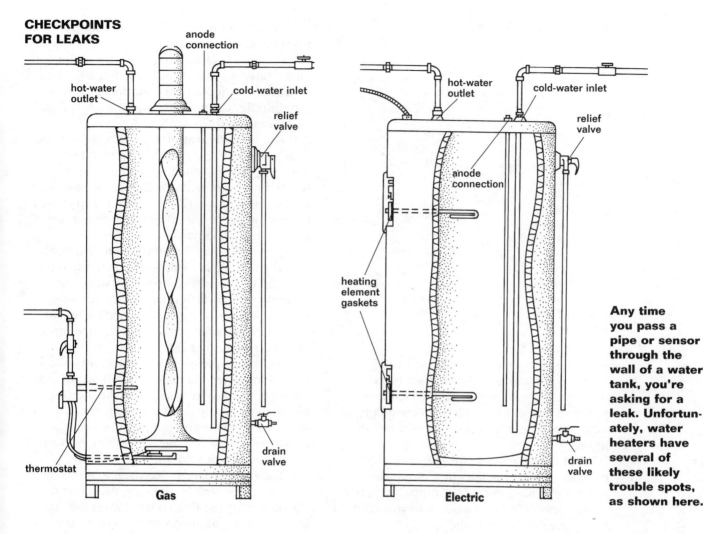

anode connection

hot-water outlet

cold-water inlet

relief valve

hot-water outlet

cold-water inlet

relief valve

anode connection

heating element gaskets

drain valve

thermostat

Gas

drain valve

Electric

Any time you pass a pipe or sensor through the wall of a water tank, you're asking for a leak. Unfortunately, water heaters have several of these likely trouble spots, as shown here.

POWER OFF?

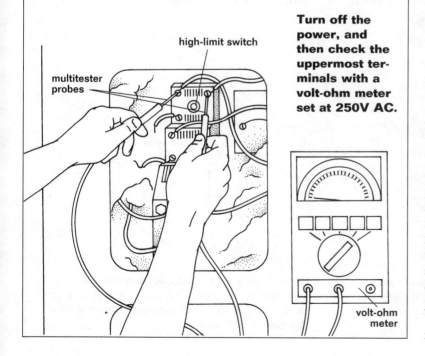

high-limit switch

multitester probes

Turn off the power, and then check the uppermost terminals with a volt-ohm meter set at 250V AC.

volt-ohm meter

Once you're sure the power and water are shut off, drain the tank completely, as shown in *Draining the Tank* on page 88. Attach a hose to the drain valve and run it to a proper indoor or outdoor drain, or position a bucket under the valve. You'll need to open a hot-water faucet somewhere in the house to break the vacuum, then open the drain valve and let the tank drain. Keep in mind that if the tank hasn't had time to cool, the water may be scalding hot.

Most fittings on a water heater are ¾ inch in diameter and can be removed with an ordinary pipe wrench. The two exceptions are the anode rod nut, which generally takes a 1 1/16-inch socket and the screw-in–type elements found on some electric water heaters, which take a 1½-inch socket. Inexpensive 1½-inch sockets, made expressly for removing this type element, are available at hardware stores and plumbing supply outlets.

If the drain valve is leaking: If the valve is made out of cheap plastic (most are), remove

DRAINING THE TANK

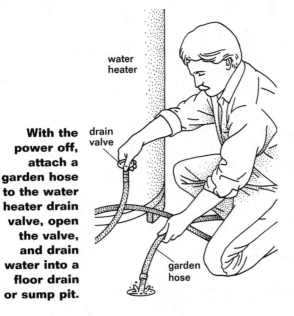

water heater

drain valve

With the power off, attach a garden hose to the water heater drain valve, open the valve, and drain water into a floor drain or sump pit.

garden hose

it and install a new ¾-inch brass ball valve, as shown in *Installing a Brass Ball Valve* on this page. A brass ball valve is much less prone to leak than the plastic variety and makes draining the tank a cinch rather than a hassle.

You'll need to insert a plastic-lined steel pipe nipple into the tank first. Wrap the threads on either end of the nipple with five or six turns of Teflon tape before you screw it into place. Then screw the new ball valve onto the nipple. Finally, screw a male adapter into the ball valve that will fit the female adapter on your garden hose. This makes it

easy to attach the hose the next time you want to drain the tank.

If the tank is already equipped with a good metal valve and the leak is confined to the threaded connection, try putting in a new pipe nipple, carefully wrapped with Teflon, and reseating the valve.

If the inlet or outlet pipe nipple is leaking: To remove the nipple, you must first open the union in the line with a pipe wrench or disconnect the flex connector with a crescent wrench. (If there's no union or flex connector in the line, you'll have to cut the pipe with a hacksaw.)

Once you've removed the nipple, examine it. If the threads are still good, clean them off with a pipe die, a wire brush, or steel wool, wrap them with Teflon tape, and then snug the nipple back into place. If the threads on the nipple are shot, replace it with one made of plastic-lined steel.

Once the nipple is back in place, reconnect the union or flex connector. If you had to cut the pipe, the easiest way to remake the connection is by using a flex connector with a suitable compression fitting on one end. (See *Installation Tips* on page 91.) This avoids any pipe threading or soldering.

If the relief valve is leaking: Remove the valve from the tank by opening the union or disconnecting the flex connector on the drain line. (If there's no union *or* flex connector, you may have to cut the pipe with a hacksaw, as described above, and later reconnect the pipes using a flex connector.)

INSTALLING A BRASS BALL VALVE

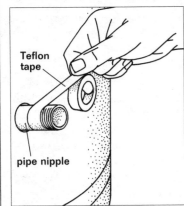

Teflon tape

pipe nipple

Step 1. Wrap the Teflon tape around the pipe nipple threads five or six times.

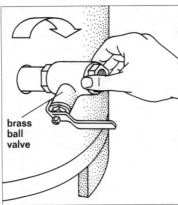

brass ball valve

Step 2. Turn the new brass ball valve onto the pipe nipple and snug with a wrench.

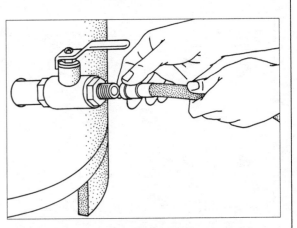

Step 3. Buy a pipe nipple with one end adapted to fit a garden hose, wrap Teflon tape around the threads, and insert it into the brass ball valve.

wrench (for screw-type elements) or an adjustable wrench (for bolted flange types). Throw away the old gasket, clean the gasket's seating area, and then reinstall the element with a new gasket. If you're working with a screw-type element, be sure to clean and wrap the threads with Teflon tape before you screw the element back in so that it can be easily removed in the future.

Sometimes the element itself is the culprit, leaking at the terminals, the flange, or through ruined threads. If so, replace both the element (a heavy-duty incoloy element is recommended) and the gasket. Make sure that the replacement element is the same wattage as the old one. A lower-wattage element will reduce the tank's heating capacity while a higher-wattage element could overload the circuit and create a fire hazard.

If the thermostat is leaking: On gas water heaters, gently disconnect the three tubes (thermocouple, pilot, and main burner) that are connected to the thermostat. Using a pair of large groove joint pliers or an adjustable wrench, unscrew the thermostat from the tank. If the threads look good, clean them, wrap them with Teflon tape, and reseat the thermostat.

NOTE: Modern electric water heaters don't experience leaks around the thermostat because the thermostat doesn't penetrate the wall of the tank.

If none of the above-mentioned fittings is leaking, you can conclude that the tank itself has failed and the water heater will have to be replaced.

MAINTAINING
YOUR WATER HEATER

Before you put the water heater back in service, pull the anode rod out of the top of the tank and check it for deterioration, as shown in *Checking the Anode* on page 92. (The hex-head nut takes a 1 1/16-inch socket.) The anode's role is to "sacrifice" itself to corrosion so that the tank won't rust. (*NOTE:* Plastic-lined water heaters don't require an anode because the lining makes them impervious to corrosion.)

If the anode is corroded to the point that 6 inches of its core wire are showing, replace it with a new one, wrapping the threads

(*continued on page 92*)

If the leak is in the threaded stem of the relief valve and the threads look good, try cleaning them with a wire brush or steel wool, wrapping them with Teflon tape, and snugging the valve back into place. If the threads are shot or the valve itself is leaking, replace it. (See "Leaky Water Heater Relief Valve" on page 93.)

If the anode is leaking: Remove the anode rod by loosening the nut with a socket wrench. Try cleaning the threads, wrapping them in Teflon, and reinserting the anode. If the rod is badly corroded, replace it. (See "Maintaining Your Water Heater" on this page.)

If the electric elements or gaskets are leaking: Remove the element with a socket

Buying a New Water Heater

If your old water heater can't be repaired, don't *panic!* Your family can survive a day or two without hot water while you take the time to make a smart decision.

Selecting a New Heater

Here are some key points to consider in selecting a new water heater.

● Gas water heaters come in a variety of tank sizes ranging from 20 to 75 gallons; electric models range in size from 30 to 80 gallons. To choose the proper size, first estimate how many gallons of hot water your family uses during an hour of *peak* usage. Your plumber or appliance dealer can help you make the estimate, based on the size of your family, peak hour activities, and the type of hot-water appliances you use. The estimate of peak hour usage is then matched to the water heater's "first hour rating."

NOTE: If you expect the number of people living in your home to grow or shrink in the years ahead, consider installing a larger or smaller tank to accommodate your changing needs.

Also, ask your local electric utility about "off-peak" water heating, a money-saving option that may require a larger tank.

● Water heaters that come equipped with twin anodes and carry an eight- or ten-year warranty are usually worth the extra money. Or you can get the same results for less money by adding a second anode to a less expensive tank. (In this case, the second anode and hot-water outlet pipe are combined in one fixture.) Best of all, but very expensive, are the new plastic-lined tanks offered by State Industries and Rheem Manufacturing that come with a lifetime warranty. (See "Suppliers" on page 89.)

● The water heater is one of the home's biggest energy users. It's smart to pay a little extra for a high-efficiency model, which can save you hundreds of dollars in fuel costs over its life. Use the water heater's Energy Factor rating (listed on the side of the tank) to compare its efficiency with other models using the same fuel (but do not, for example, compare a gas model to an electric one).

● If electricity is expensive in your area, consider switching from an electric water heater to a gas or propane model, which can reduce fuel costs by as much as two-thirds. Some state-of-the-art gas-fired models can be vented directly through the wall without any need to build an expensive chimney or run a flue pipe up through the roof.

● If you're going to install a gas or propane water heater, consider a "sealed combustion" model, which draws its combustion air from *outside* the house. With sealed combustion, you get high efficiency and eliminate the risk of backdrafts.

● No matter what model you choose, make sure that the anode rod is easily accessible at the top of the tank (except for plastic-lined models, which don't need an anode) and that the water heater has an insulation rating of at least R-16.

● Buy from a reputable firm. There are a lot of shysters out there who love to do quick-and-dirty installations at twice the going rate.

Installation Considerations

Don't try to install your own water heater unless you are confident that you can safely carry out the manufacturer's instructions. This requires basic plumbing skills, using flexible connectors and/or unions to hook the new unit up. (See *Installation Tips* on the opposite page.)

On electric models, you'll have to connect the wires in the unit's junction box—two hot lines and a ground—to your house wiring. Following the manufacturer's instructions, make sure that you use the proper wire (typically 10-gauge copper) and that the water heater is properly grounded and fused.

Gas water heaters must be safely connected to the gas line and equipped with a safe exhaust vent to the outside. They also require plenty of ventilation for combustion air (except closed combustion models) and minimum clearance to combustible surfaces, as the code prescribes.

Since water heaters weigh 100 pounds or more, you'll probably need a friend to help you muscle the tank into position.

The alternative to doing the installation yourself is to pay a plumber $25 to $75 an hour for the work (typically two to four hours). Thus your savings on labor would range from about $50 to $300.

Regardless of who does the work, use dielectric unions and plastic-lined steel nipples so that copper and brass fittings don't come in direct contact with the steel tank. This is to avoid the electrolytic corrosion that occurs when two dissimilar metals come in contact.

Also, equip your new water heater with heat traps (to keep hot and cold water from rising and falling in the pipes), a curved dip tube (to help clean sediment out the tank), earthquake strapping, and a brass ball valve (replacing the plastic drain valve that comes standard on most models). It's also a smart idea to position a drain pan underneath the new water heater and fit it with a 1-inch drain line into an appropriate drain.

If you install the water heater yourself, be sure to have the work checked by a local building inspector or someone from the fire department. Installations that don't meet code can put you and your family at risk and could void your homeowner's insurance if there's an accident.

INSTALLATION TIPS

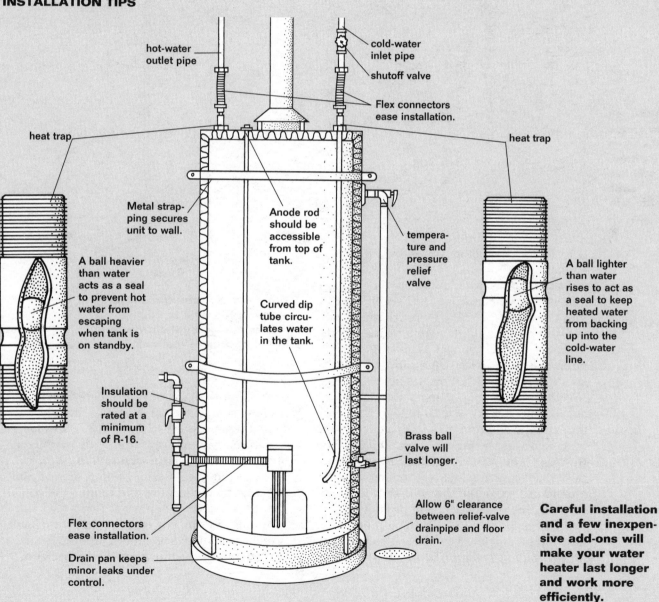

hot-water outlet pipe

cold-water inlet pipe

shutoff valve

Flex connectors ease installation.

heat trap

heat trap

Metal strapping secures unit to wall.

Anode rod should be accessible from top of tank.

temperature and pressure relief valve

A ball heavier than water acts as a seal to prevent hot water from escaping when tank is on standby.

Curved dip tube circulates water in the tank.

A ball lighter than water rises to act as a seal to keep heated water from backing up into the cold-water line.

Insulation should be rated at a minimum of R-16.

Brass ball valve will last longer.

Flex connectors ease installation.

Drain pan keeps minor leaks under control.

Allow 6" clearance between relief-valve drainpipe and floor drain.

Careful installation and a few inexpensive add-ons will make your water heater last longer and work more efficiently.

CHECKING THE ANODE

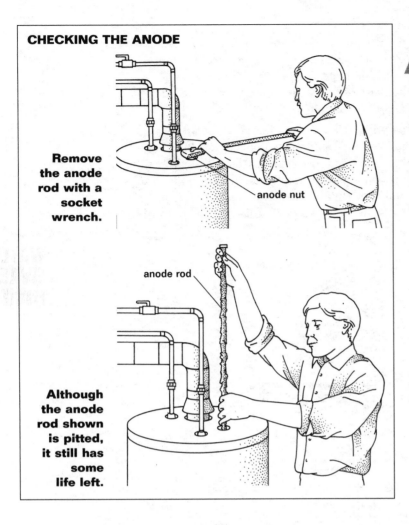

Remove the anode rod with a socket wrench.

anode nut

anode rod

Although the anode rod shown is pitted, it still has some life left.

CURVED DIP TUBE

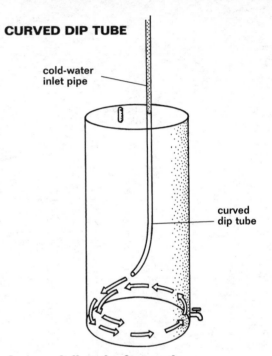

cold-water inlet pipe

curved dip tube

A curved dip tube forces the water in the tank to circulate as shown by the arrows in the bottom of the tank.

with Teflon tape before you screw the new one into place.

If the anode is inaccessible or you can't get it loose from the tank, put in a second one. This can be simply done by purchasing a new hot-water–outlet nipple with a built-in anode. If headroom over the tank is limited to the point that you can't install a conventional anode, buy one with short, flexible links.

With the tank drained and your tool box already out, this is the ideal time to remove the dip tube and replace it with a curved one (a $5 item), as shown in *Curved Dip Tube* on this page. The new curved tube needs to be positioned so that it swirls incoming water around the bottom of the tank, thus keeping the tank free of sediment and promoting a good flush. Be sure to mark the top of the new dip tube before you insert it so that you'll know which way the tip is oriented as you

tighten it into place. For the most efficient flushing action, the curved tip of the tube should point inward so that incoming water will travel the long way around the perimeter of the tank to reach the drain valve.

To put the water heater back in service, simply close the drain valve and reopen the cold-water inlet valve. When water flows back out of an opened sink faucet, you'll know the tank is full. Close the faucet, check all fittings for watertightness, and turn the power back on.

Leaky Water Heater Relief Valve

Quick Response

1. If necessary, position bucket to catch overflow.

2. Carefully open hot-water faucet to check for superheated water or steam.

3. Shut off power to water heater. (See "Turning Off the Energy Source" on page 85.)

You'll find your water heater's relief valve on top of the tank (*as shown above*) or on the side of the tank. If it is spitting hot water or steam, take fast action to shut the heater down.

LETTING OFF SOME STEAM

The water heater relief valve is a safety device that responds to two interrelated problems: excessive temperature and/or pressure inside the tank. Should the water temperature near the top of the tank hit 210°F or the internal pressure reach 150 pounds per square inch (typical threshold settings), the relief valve is designed to pop open, releasing hot water from the tank before there's any chance of a rupture or explosion.

Hazards

● Under some circumstances, a malfunctioning water heater can explode.

● If your water heater is overheating, turn it off, then warn family members not to use any hot water—for fear of scalding—until the heater is repaired or replaced. Also beware of burning yourself on hot water escaping from the relief valve itself.

When the valve discharges hot water, it can indicate either a major malfunction or a minor problem. But until you know otherwise, treat the situation seriously because the potential is there for a real nightmare. As described in "The Night of the Shooting Water Heater" on page 97, a failed relief valve can sometimes have disastrous consequences.

But even when there's no chance of explosion, high-temperature or high-pressure conditions need to be addressed since they will shorten the life of the water heater and can damage other plumbing fittings and fixtures as well. High water temperature also can scald people, especially children and the elderly, who may not be able to react quickly.

TROUBLESHOOTING A RELIEF VALVE

There are several reasons why a relief valve will suddenly start to drip or discharge water. The most dangerous of these is a faulty control that permits the water temperature inside the tank to exceed the desired setting. Super-heated water or steam coming out of fixtures is a sure sign that the controls have failed. If this should occur, quickly shut off power to the water heater, then see **Faulty controls can fail to shut the burner or electric elements off** on page 96. If the water temperature seems normal, consider some other potential causes on page 96.

Install a Regulator

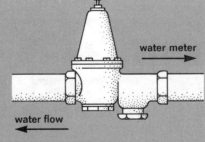

water meter

water flow

If high water pressure (above 80 pounds per square inch) is a constant or recurring problem in your house, install a water pressure regulator at the water meter, as shown here. You can determine the water pressure with help from the municipal water authority or by checking it yourself with a pressure gauge. (A water pressure gauge is a $15 hardware store item that screws onto any faucet. Once the faucet is opened, the analog dial on the gauge reads the water pressure, from 0 to 200 pounds per square inch.) ●

Replacing a Water Heater Relief Valve

If you have any doubts about your ability to properly install a new relief valve, let a professional plumber do it. Remember, the valve is your last line of defense against a ruptured tank, water damage, scalding, or even an explosion—should other controls fail. If you're confident in your plumbing skills, however, this is not a difficult job.

1. Start by turning the thermostat on the water heater to *OFF*, then shut off the electricity, gas, or oil supply to the heater.

2. Next, close the cold water inlet valve. (See "Turning Off the Energy Source" and "Turning Off the Water" on page 85.)

For safety's sake, it's best to let the tank cool down a few hours—even overnight—before you work on it. (If you can't afford to wait, be extra careful not to scald yourself.)

3. Once the water inside the tank has had time to cool, open the drain valve and draw off some water. If the relief valve is located on top of the tank, about a gallon should suffice. If the valve is on the side of the tank, drain 4 or 5 gallons.

4. As shown in *Installing a New Relief Valve*, remove the discharge pipe from the relief valve, using a pipe wrench to disassemble the union or—if necessary—a hacksaw to cut the pipe.

5. Once the discharge pipe is removed, unscrew the old relief valve. If the valve won't budge, you may need a helper to steady the tank while you apply some real muscle to the wrench. As you remove the old valve, note how far the temperature-sensing element extends into the tank. To be effective, the tip of the rod should reach at least 6 inches into the tank. If it doesn't, you should buy a valve with a longer probe (up to 8 inches).

6. Once the valve is removed, locate the identification plate on the water heater and write down the model number and its BTU input rating. (BTU, short for British thermal unit, represents the heat required to raise 1 pound of water 1°F. For practical purposes, 1 BTU equals the amount of energy released by a kitchen match.) A typical rating for a residential water heater is 35,000 BTUs.

INSTALLING A NEW RELIEF VALVE

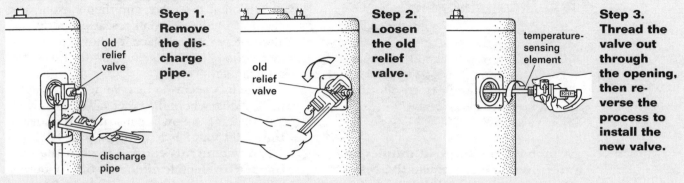

Step 1. Remove the discharge pipe.

old relief valve

discharge pipe

Step 2. Loosen the old relief valve.

old relief valve

Step 3. Thread the valve out through the opening, then reverse the process to install the new valve.

temperature-sensing element

Take the old valve and the model number and BTU rating you recorded from the heater to your local plumbing supply. A standard-size relief valve (rated at 100,000 BTUs and 150 pounds per square inch of pressure) costs about $10 and will work with most residential water heaters. Nevertheless, it's prudent to double-check, making sure that the new valve's American Gas Association (AGA) BTU rating is higher than the BTU input rating you copied off your water heater's identification plate.

The temperature and pressure settings on the new valve are preset at the factory at 210°F and 150 pounds per square inch, respectively, and are not adjustable.

7. Before you screw the new relief valve into place, wrap the threads with five or six turns of Teflon tape.

8. Reassemble the discharge pipe using a union or flex connector so that the pipe can be easily removed in the future. If you're using threaded pipe, wrap the threads with Teflon tape before screwing the pipe into place.

The discharge pipe, whether metal or plastic, should be the same diameter as the valve outlet (usually ¾ inch) with no valves, reductions, or obstructions along it. It should run downhill as directly as possible, with no dips or bends. Leave at least a 6-inch gap between the end of the pipe and the floor drain or ground below it, as shown in *Positioning the Discharge Pipe,* to eliminate any chance of polluted water back-flowing into the pipe. An outdoor discharge pipe isn't recommended for cold climates, where snow and ice can clog the end.

9. Once you've plumbed the discharge line, open the water supply valve, turn the power back on, and put the water heater into service.

10. When it's resumed normal operating temperature, test the relief valve to make sure it's working properly. To do this, simply lift the test lever on the valve, as shown in *Testing the Relief Valve.* If it's working properly, water should flow out the end of the discharge pipe. When you push the lever down, the discharge should stop completely. Repeat this test once or twice a year as a safety precaution.

POSITIONING THE DISCHARGE PIPE

discharge pipe

6" minimum

The discharge pipe can open over a floor drain, as shown, or run through an exterior wall to discharge outside.

TESTING THE RELIEF VALVE

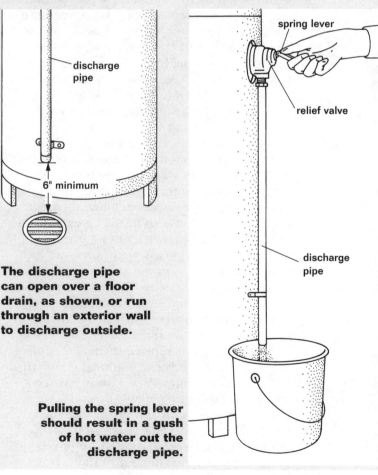

spring lever

relief valve

discharge pipe

Pulling the spring lever should result in a gush of hot water out the discharge pipe.

Test the Relief Valve

Because corrosion can build up inside your water heater's relief valve and cause it to stick—a dangerous situation—make it a point to test the valve at least once a year. See "Replacing a Water Heater Relief Valve" on page 94 for details.

A momentary surge in municipal water pressure can cause the relief valve to drip or possibly release a large volume of water. Opening a faucet will temporarily relieve the pressure. However, if the valve doesn't stop leaking once the water pressure has dropped back to normal, open the spring lever on the valve, let some water flush through it, and then close the lever again. If the valve continues to leak after a few tries, it may be faulty, as explained below.

In some cases, water pressure can build up inside your pipes even though the municipal water pressure is quite normal. This can occur when there's a backflow preventor and/or pressure regulator in the supply line leading to the water heater. (A backflow preventor is a type of check valve that keeps water from flowing back through the line toward the main.) As water is heated inside the water heater, it has nowhere to expand—the backflow preventor or pressure regulator won't let it. So the excess pressure bleeds out through the relief valve. This problem is often misdiagnosed as a failed relief valve, which is mistakenly replaced—sometimes two or three times—before the real problem becomes apparent.

The real solution is to install an expansion tank above the water heater or a diversion valve that shunts excess water pressure into a toilet tank.

On well water systems, high water pressure can result from a malfunctioning pump control, which overpressurizes the system to the point where the relief valve leaks. It's important to fix or replace the faulty control quickly, because it puts additional stress on the motor and pump. (See **The pressure switch is faulty** on page 75.)

A relief valve can fail from old age, generally because the valve seat or threads have been damaged by corrosion. If water is leaking out of the valve

itself—that is, out the end of the discharge pipe—open the spring lever, let some water run through the valve, and then close it again. If the valve won't reseat properly after a few tries, replace it following the instructions in "Replacing a Water Heater" on page 94.

If the leak seems to be coming from around the threads, where the relief valve is screwed into the tank, follow the instructions under **If the relief valve is leaking** on page 88.

Faulty controls can fail to shut the burner or electric elements off. Modern water heaters are equipped with a safety device called an *energy cutoff* or *high-limit switch* that automatically cuts power or fuel to the water heater when the water temperature exceeds the high-limit setting, typically 160°F. If the cutoff circuit fails, the water temperature inside the tank can keep right on climbing until it hits 210°F, which will open the relief valve. If the relief valve doesn't open, the stage is set for disaster.

Overheating can also occur if the gas valves on a gas water heater get dirty or corroded, preventing them from closing properly in response to the thermostat. The gas line into the heater should always be equipped with a sediment trap to help keep debris out of the valves. The sediment trap—also called a *drip leg*—is a short length of capped pipe that's plumbed into the bottom of the gas line. Any debris coming through the line falls into the sediment trap before it can lodge in the valves. (See *Anatomy of a Water Heater* on page 84.)

If you have a control failure that produces excessively hot water or steam, shut off the fuel source or power to the water heater immediately. Leave the heater off until you can have a licensed plumber check and repair the controls.

Check for Tampering

In some cases, serious—even fatal—accidents have occurred because someone tampered with the high-limit switch in a misguided effort to get more hot water. Before you move into a new house or apartment, have this control checked as part of a complete home inspection.

The Night of the Shooting Water Heater

It was 6:23 in the morning when a rocket exploded up through Tony Sobaski's bedroom floor—missing his bed by 2½ feet and blasting a 5-foot hole in the ceiling. "As rude awakenings go, it was about as extreme as you can get," says Tony, of South St. Paul, Minnesota. "As I dashed out the front door, furniture was still flying."

It wasn't until days later that Tony, assisted by a platoon of investigators, understood exactly what had happened.

In the basement of Tony's house—directly under his bedroom—was a 66-gallon electric water heater. Sometime during the night, after he'd taken a shower, the thermostat on the heater stuck. Instead of shutting off the electric elements, as it should have, the tank kept right on heating. The relief valve, unfortunately, had been installed too far away from the water heater to accurately sense the extreme temperature and pressure that were building up inside the tank.

Finally, something had to give—the bottom of the tank ruptured. As the superheated water hit air, it flashed into steam, blasting the water heater up through the house. After exploding through Tony's bedroom, the tank rocketed on through the attic and punched through the roof, finally landing 150 feet downrange in a neighbor's yard.

The force of the explosion lifted the house off the foundation and left it a complete wreck. "We were fortunate that my daughter wasn't in the house at the time," says Tony. "I believe she would have been killed."

Other people, in fact, have been killed by exploding water heaters. In Spencer, Oklahoma, a teacher and six children died in 1982 when a gas water heater exploded at the Star Elementary School, demolishing the school cafeteria.

In August 1993, just a month after Tony Sobaski's water heater went ballistic, a man in El Torito, California, was killed in a water heater explosion.

Is there a moral to the story?

"You bet there is!" exclaims Tony. "Be sure that your water heater has a relief valve that's properly installed and operating. And make it a habit—every few months—to pull that test lever on the valve to make sure it's working."

Electrical Emergencies

3
ELECTRICAL EMERGENCIES

Circuit Breaker Trips or Fuse Blows

Quick Response

Do not reset circuit breaker or replace fuse until you've diagnosed problem.

TYPICAL ELECTRICAL SERVICE EQUIPMENT

Service Panel with Circuit Breakers

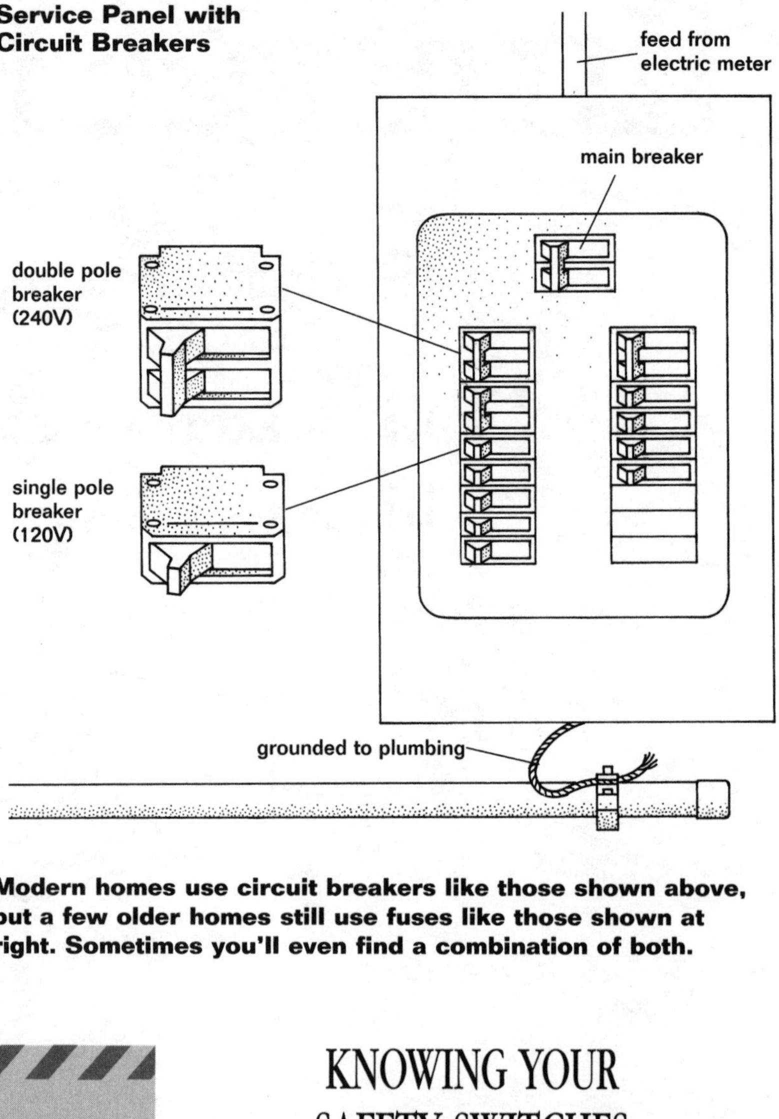

feed from electric meter

main breaker

double pole breaker (240V)

single pole breaker (120V)

grounded to plumbing

Modern homes use circuit breakers like those shown above, but a few older homes still use fuses like those shown at right. Sometimes you'll even find a combination of both.

Hazard

Working with electric circuits and appliances requires an extra measure of caution. Please read and observe the tips in "Electrical Safety Tips" on page 102.

KNOWING YOUR SAFETY SWITCHES

Circuit breakers and fuses are electro-mechanical safety switches that protect the electric circuits and appliances in your home from damage. (See *Typical Electrical Service Equipment* on this page.) They are built into the main electric service panel, where electric-

**Service Panel
with Fuses**

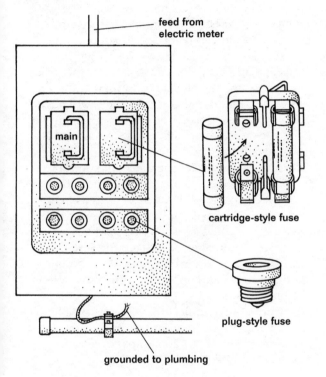

feed from
electric meter

main

cartridge-style fuse

plug-style fuse

grounded to plumbing

Breaker Calisthenics
As part of your annual maintenance routine, switch each circuit breaker off and on three or four times to keep its mechanical parts from sticking. ●

amps or more (protecting the whole electrical system). If a short circuit or overload occurs, the breaker "trips" to its center position, or the fuse blows, cutting off the flow of current to the entire circuit.

TROUBLESHOOTING CIRCUIT BREAKERS AND FUSES

There is more than one way to trip a breaker or blow a fuse, so you need to play detective and eliminate the possibilities until you find the true cause.

OVERLOADED CIRCUIT

Problems can often be diagnosed simply by reviewing the situation in your house just before the breaker tripped or the fuse blew. For example, if a large number of electrical devices were running simultaneously, you may have overloaded a circuit. Unplug or turn off some of the devices that were in use, especially those that have electric heating elements, such as toasters, skillets, space heaters, and hair dryers.

A good diagram or key explaining the layout of your electric circuits should be affixed to the door of the main service panel—in fact, it's required by the National Electric Code. Unfortunately, electricians often neglect to leave a diagram or key behind, which leaves the homeowner—if not literally, at least figuratively—in the dark. Other times, the diagram or key is illegible, outdated, or so poorly done that it's next to worthless. Fortunately, it's a relatively simple task to create a circuit map

ity from the utility—after passing through the meter—enters your house.

Inside the service panel, electricity is divided into various branch circuits, each protected by a breaker or fuse. Some houses have circuit breakers only, others use fuses only, and still others have a combination of the two.

Circuit breakers and fuses are rated by how much current—or amperage—they are designed to handle, ranging from 15 amps (protecting a light-duty branch circuit) to 200

Electrical Safety Tips

● If an appliance, tool, plug, or cord sparks, smokes, or shocks, do not touch it again until you're sure the power to the circuit is off.

● Do not work on the service panel if it's wet inside or has been damaged by lightning or fire.

● Wear thick rubber gloves when working inside the electric service panel and use one hand only.

● Stand slightly to one side as you work at the service panel. In the unlikely event that a breaker or fuse should explode, this is the safer position.

● Keep a nonmetallic flashlight in or near the service panel. If the panel has exposed cartridge fuses, keep an insulated fuse puller on hand as well. (See "Breakers and Fuses" on page 106.)

● A blown fuse *must* be replaced by a fuse of *exactly* the same amperage. Keep a proper assortment of replacement fuses handy.

● Be careful not to overload extension cords. Check the cord's amperage rating (10 amps is typical for household extension cords) and make sure that any appliance or tool plugged into it does not exceed that amperage limit.

● Do not cut the grounding prong off a three-pronged plug or otherwise try to fit a three-pronged plug into a two-slot receptacle.

● To prevent serious shocks, have ground fault circuit interrupters (GFCIs) installed in receptacles that are close to water (for example, bathrooms, kitchen, laundry, and outdoors). (See "GFCI Spells Electrical Safety" on page 265.)

● In case of emergency, everyone in your home—even older children—should know where the main electric service panel is located and how to turn off the power. (See "Understanding Your Electrical System" on page 6.)

● In case of electrical fire, keep at least one ABC-type extinguisher on hand. *CAUTION:* Do not use water on an electrical fire! (See "Fire!" on page 244.)

● Make sure that everyone in the family knows what to do in case of fire. Learn your escape routes. Stage drills. Post a list of emergency numbers by each phone and on the service panel door.

● *CAUTION:* Do *not* touch a person who is being shocked—the current could flow into you. Instead, unplug the appliance that's causing the shock or turn the electricity off at the main service panel. If that's not possible, use a wooden broom handle or other nonmetallic stick to separate the victim from the power source.

Once the victim is free, check to see if he or she is breathing—if not, start CPR immediately. Call 911 for emergency help.

Key to Success

Nothing makes diagnosing electrical problems easier than a proper circuit diagram or key. If your service panel lacks one, or if the one it has is outdated, take the time to make up a new one. Or, if your house is new or you've had electrical work done recently, call the electrician back to do it. (See "Adding Up the Amps" on page 104.) ●

for your home. For advice on how to go about it, see "Adding Up the Amps" on page 104.

Once you've "shed" some of the load from the circuit, you can reset the affected circuit breaker or replace the blown fuse. (See "Breakers and Fuses" on page 106.) If the problem recurs, look for a way to permanently shift some lights or appliances from the overloaded circuit to a lesser used one. With a good circuit map, it's easy to determine how much load is on a particular circuit.

If there is heavy electrical use on several branch circuits, exceeding your home's total amperage capacity, the main breaker will trip or the main fuse will blow, shutting everything down. Again, the key is to shed load *before* you reset the breaker or replace the fuse and to learn through the experience what combination of lights and appliances push the system past its capacity.

If overloaded circuits are a chronic problem, consider updating your service panel (for example, from 100 to 200 amps) or adding new branch circuits.

SHORT CIRCUIT

A short circuit occurs when two wires carrying electricity come in contact with each other or when a single wire carrying electricity comes in contact with a ground, such as a water pipe or the metal housing of a tool or appliance.

Often, you can diagnose the problem by reviewing what happened just before the breaker tripped or the fuse blew. Was someone plugging in or starting an electrical device? Perhaps there was a visible spark or sound when the short circuit occurred. If so, you have only to unplug the faulty device before you reset the breaker or replace the fuse and see to it that the device is repaired before anyone tries to use it again.

If you can't locate the short circuit, unplug or turn off *everything* that's on the affected circuit. Again, an accurate circuit diagram or key is indispensable. (See "Adding Up the Amps" on page 104.) After everything is unplugged or switched off, reset the breaker or replace the fuse. (See "Breakers and Fuses" on page 106.) If the circuit shorts out again, the problem has to be somewhere in the house's permanent wiring. Leave the circuit dead and call an electrician.

If the breaker or fuse holds, systematically test each light and appliance that's on the circuit—one at a time—until the faulty device reveals itself by tripping the breaker or blowing the fuse again. *CAUTION: For safety's sake, wear thick rubber gloves and rubber-soled shoes as you run the tests.*

Once you've isolated the faulty device, repair it, replace it, or throw it away.

FAILED MOTOR

The electric motors on large appliances, such as well pumps, clothes washers, and clothes dryers, are designed to shut themselves off if there's a problem, without tripping a circuit breaker or blowing a fuse. Usually, the motor housing remains cool to the touch, though the cord or cable may signal a problem by getting warm.

However, if the motor seizes—that is, abruptly jams, as a vacuum cleaner might if it gobbles up something it shouldn't—it may trip the breaker or blow the fuse.

By code, most large appliances should be on a dedicated 20- or 30-amp circuit by themselves, with their own breaker or fuse. Circuits that serve large, motorized appliances are sometimes equipped with a special time-delay fuse or breaker that provides the motor its necessary start-up voltage without blowing the fuse or tripping the breaker. Smaller motorized appliances, such as a kitchen blender, usually share a 15- or 20-amp circuit with other small appliances, receptacles, or lights and don't require a special fuse or breaker.

LOW VOLTAGE

Though household appliances are designed to run at either 120 or 240 volts, the actual voltage delivered by your utility may fluctuate. If the voltage is low, it can cause a breaker to trip or a fuse to blow, especially if the low voltage coincides with the start-up of a motorized

appliance. For information on how to diagnose, measure, and correct low-voltage problems, see "Spikes, Brownouts, and Blips" on page 111.

LIGHTNING

The effect of lightning on residential electrical systems is not easily predicted. A near hit might, under the right circumstances, trip one or more breakers or blow one or more fuses without causing any permanent damage. A direct hit can produce dramatic, even explosive damage to unprotected breakers and fuses, start an electrical fire, and compromise branch circuits and receptacles. Since damaged circuits may still be live, such situations can be extremely dangerous and even more so if there is storm-related water in the service panel or on the floor. *Leave such repairs to a utility emergency team or qualified electrician.* (See "Lightning Strikes!" on page 180.)

FAULTY CIRCUIT BREAKER

Like any mechanical device, a circuit breaker can fail, which causes it to shut down the circuit periodically when in fact there's no overload, short circuit, or other problem. If, by process of elimination, you conclude that the breaker is faulty, here's how to replace it. (See *Inside a Service Panel* on page 108.)

1. Buy a replacement breaker that's the same amperage as the old one, preferably made by the same manufacturer. (Different makes are not always interchangeable.)
2. Turn the main power off by throwing the main house breaker or by removing the main fuse. (See "Understanding Your Electrical System" on page 6.)
3. Loosen the screws that hold the service panel's cover plate in place, and remove the plate.
4. Once the breakers are exposed, test the affected circuit with a volt-ohm meter to

(continued on page 108)

Adding Up the Amps

Before you can calculate how much load is on a given circuit, you have to know where the circuit runs and what's on it. Check the inside of your service panel to see if a good electrical diagram or key has already been done, as shown in *A Well-Mapped Service Panel*. If so, jump ahead to "Simple Math" on the opposite page. If not, here's how to map the circuits.

Start by tagging each breaker or fuse inside the service panel with a small adhesive label, numbering them sequentially 1, 2, 3, and so on. The tags should be mounted alongside the corresponding breakers and fuses, where

they won't interfere. Tape a large piece of lined paper or white cardboard to the inside of the service panel door so that you can neatly list the outlets, switches, and appliances that correspond to the numbered breakers or fuses.

One at a time, turn each circuit off by switching the breaker to its *OFF* position or unscrewing the fuse. (See "Breakers and Fuses" on page 106.) As each circuit is turned off, patrol the house and make a list of what *isn't* working. Use a test light to check receptacles, as shown in *Using a Test Light*.

A WELL-MAPPED SERVICE PANEL

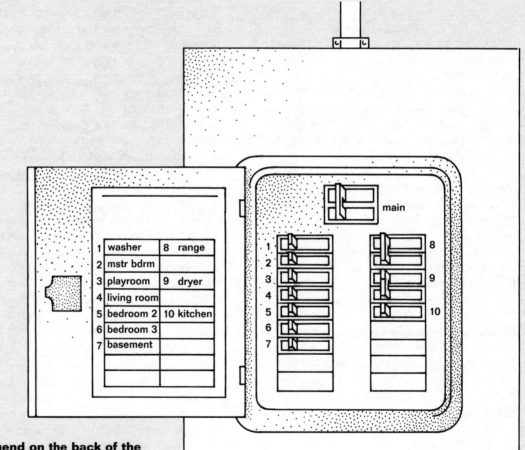

1	washer	8	range
2	mstr bdrm		
3	playroom	9	dryer
4	living room		
5	bedroom 2	10	kitchen
6	bedroom 3		
7	basement		

The legend on the back of the service panel door is keyed to the circuit breakers inside. Each breaker should be clearly identified by the portion of the house it controls.

USING A TEST LIGHT

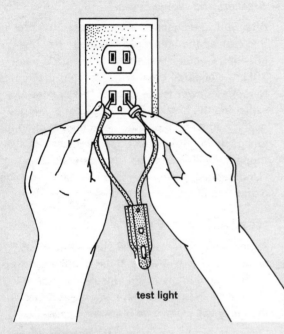

test light

When mapping your household circuits, use a test light to see which outlets are dead.

Generally, 15- and 20-amp breakers and fuses protect circuits that power lights and receptacles. Large appliances (drawing 1000 watts or more) will each have their own circuit (usually 30 amps or more) with a dedicated breaker or fuse. Such appliances would include the water heater, electric range, clothes dryer, well pump and, possibly, heating and air conditioning systems.

The best way to identify the electric water heater circuit is by process of elimination, since it would take hours for the water inside the tank to cool down enough to reveal that it's off. Electric water heaters are typically protected by a 30-amp breaker or fuse, which may be located apart from the other breakers or fuses or situated in a small service box of its own.

Once you know how the electric circuits run through your home and what's on them, it's a simple matter to calculate how close

they are to full capacity. That knowledge, in turn, may help you shift lights or small appliances from overloaded to underutilized circuits or perhaps spur you to update your electric service.

Simple Math

To calculate how fully a circuit is being utilized, make a list of all of the electric devices that run on the circuit and then add up their total wattage. (The wattage for appliances and tools is listed on their nameplates. If the rating is given in amps, multiply the amperage by the voltage—either 120 or 240—to get the watts.)

Here, for example, is the calculation for a typical 15-amp circuit.

Device	Wattage
Room light	150 (two 75-watt bulbs)
Table lamp	60
Television	200
VCR	55
Stereo	300
Sewing machine	75
Total	840 watts

Since a 15-amp, 120-volt circuit has a total of 1800 watts available (15 amps × 120 volts = 1800 watts), we can see that this particular circuit has a lot of excess capacity. In fact, with everything in use, it would only draw 7 amps (840 watts ÷ 120 volts = 7 amps).

But if we add a hypothetical room air conditioner to the equation—rated at, say, 900 watts—the same circuit quickly approaches an overloaded condition, drawing 1740 watts (14.5 amps).

By combining the totals from the branch circuits, you can calculate wattage and amps for the entire electrical system and thereby determine how close it is to capacity. This information is key in avoiding overloaded branch and main circuits and in deciding whether or not you need an electrical upgrade.

Breakers and Fuses

CAUTION: Before you open the service panel, protect yourself with thick rubber gloves and remember to work with only one hand at a time. For more safety tips, read "Electrical Safety Tips" on page 102.

There are various types of circuit breakers and fuses, as shown in *Typical Electrical Service Equipment* on page 100. A breaker is an electro-mechanical safety switch that "reads" current moving through the circuit and automatically flips off when there is an overload or short circuit.

Fuses provide the same function in a different way, directing current through a small wire that breaks or vaporizes if there's an overload or short circuit. Unlike a circuit breaker, which is a permanent, resettable fixture, fuses must be discarded and replaced once they're blown.

Resetting a Circuit Breaker

An overload or short circuit on a branch circuit will cause the breaker protecting that circuit to "trip" or switch itself to a center position, halfway between *OFF* and *ON,* as shown in *Tripped Breakers and Blown Fuses*.

After you've diagnosed and corrected the problem that caused the breaker to trip (see "Troubleshooting Circuit Breakers and Fuses" on page 101), the affected breaker has to be reset in order to restore power to the circuit. This is done by switching the breaker from its center or tripped position to its OFF position, and then back to its ON position. If the main house breaker has also tripped, it will need to be reset as well. (See "Understanding Your Electrical System" on page 6 and "No Electric Power" on page 109.)

Replacing a Fuse

A plug-style (screw-in) fuse shows that it has failed in one of two ways. If the circuit was overloaded, the thin metal strip inside the fuse will show a clean break. If there was a short circuit, the glass will usually be blackened as well.

Once you've diagnosed and fixed the problem that caused the fuse to blow (see "Troubleshooting

TRIPPED BREAKERS AND BLOWN FUSES

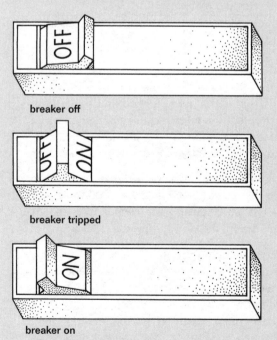

breaker off

breaker tripped

breaker on

A breaker switch has three possible positions: off, tripped, or on.

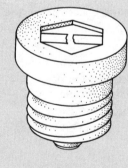

The metallic strip will show a clean break if there's been an overload.

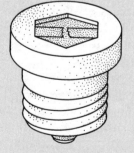

With a short circuit, the glass will be darkened as well.

Circuit Breakers and Fuses" on page 101), simply unscrew the failed fuse (counterclockwise) and replace it with a fuse of exactly the same amperage.

Cartridge-style fuses, some of which have protruding blades on either end, usually don't show any sign of failure. But since cartridge fuses are always "dedicated" to protecting the main power circuit and/or a single major appliance, it's an easy matter to figure out which one has failed—provided, of course, the circuits inside the panel are clearly labeled. (See "Adding Up the Amps" on page 104.)

If you can't tell which cartridge fuse has blown, remove them—one at a time—and touch either end with the probes of a continuity tester, as shown in *Testing a Cartridge Fuse*. (A good fuse will conduct current through it.) Plug-style fuses can be tested in the same way, touching one probe to the center contact on the tip and the other to the metal shell. If you don't have a continuity tester, you can address the problem blindly by replacing all of the cartridge fuses.

TESTING A CARTRIDGE FUSE

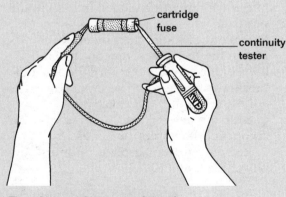

cartridge fuse

continuity tester

Touch a probe to each end of the disconnected fuse. If the fuse is good, the continuity tester will light.

CAUTION: Be careful to avoid shock when removing cartridge fuses from the service panel. If the metal tips of the fuse are exposed to view, which is typical in older electrical systems, use an insulated fuse puller to remove and replace the fuse, as shown in *Pulling Fuses*. In newer installa-

tions, cartridge fuses are housed in a pull-out compartment that automatically cuts power to the fuses when it's removed.

Once you've identified the failed fuse—and corrected the problem that caused it—replace it with a fuse of exactly the same amperage rating.

PULLING FUSES

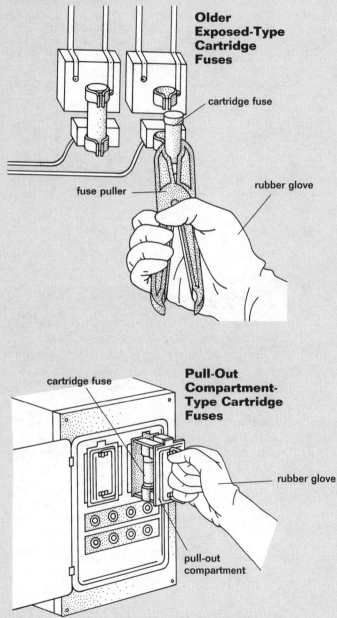

Older Exposed-Type Cartridge Fuses

cartridge fuse

rubber glove

fuse puller

cartridge fuse

Pull-Out Compartment-Type Cartridge Fuses

rubber glove

pull-out compartment

When working with fuses, your hands are close to electrical contacts, so take special care to follow the applicable points in "Electrical Safety Tips" on page 102.

INSIDE A SERVICE PANEL

With the power off, the cover plate can be removed to reveal circuit breakers and wiring.

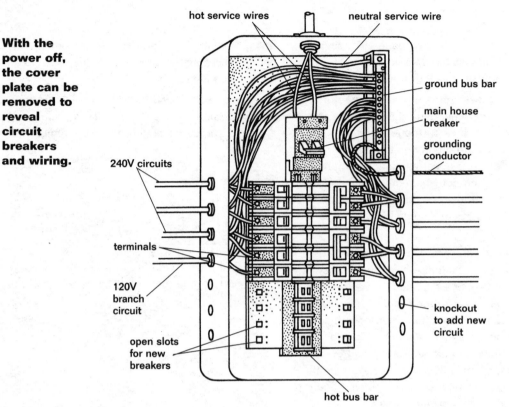

hot service wires

neutral service wire

ground bus bar

main house breaker

grounding conductor

240V circuits

terminals

120V branch circuit

open slots for new breakers

knockout to add new circuit

hot bus bar

Jangled Nerves?

If you are inexperienced or nervous working with electricity, hire an electrician. The expense of hiring a pro is much preferred to frying your fingers. ●

make sure it's dead. This is done by touching one of the volt-ohm meter's probes to the breaker's terminal and the other to any of the white wires attached to the ground bus bar.

5. Once you're sure the power is off, loosen the terminal screw on the faulty breaker, disconnect the wire (double-pole breakers will have two screws and two wires), and pull the breaker out.

6. Slide the new breaker into position, and reconnect the wire(s) as it was.

7. Remount the cover plate, and turn the power back on.

No Electric Power

Be sure to keep a flashlight handy for after-dark power outages. Don't touch your service panel if you suspect it has been damaged by lightning.

Quick Response

1. Call neighbors to see if they've lost power and if they already reported problem.

2. Turn off electrical devices that were running.

3. If yours is only home affected, read "Troubleshooting a Power Outage" on this page.

4. If outage was caused by lightning, see "Lightning Strikes!" on page 180.

3
ELECTRICAL EMERGENCIES

TROUBLESHOOTING A POWER OUTAGE

If your house is without power (but the neighbors' houses are unaffected), here are four possible reasons.

The main house breaker has tripped or the main fuse has blown in response to an overloaded or short circuit. A whole-house overload occurs when the branch circuits, taken together, are drawing more than the rated amperage of the main breaker or fuse. The problem is corrected simply by unplugging or turning off electrical devices on one or more of the branch circuits and then resetting the main breaker or replacing the main fuse. If the prob-

Hazards

● Do not attempt to reset breakers or replace fuses if the main service panel has been damaged by lightning or if there is water inside the panel or on the floor. *Leave such repairs to a utility emergency team or electrician.*

● During a prolonged power outage—usually associated with a hurricane or blizzard—refrigerated and frozen foods begin to spoil. If an extended outage seems possible, open the refrigerator and freezer doors as seldom as possible. Don't eat frozen foods that have thawed unless you're absolutely sure they're safe.

Survival Pantry

Prepare for natural emergencies by stocking a "survival pantry" with canned food, batteries, first-aid gear, and other crucial supplies. (See "Preparing for an Emergency" on page 10.) ●

lem occurs often, it's a signal that your electrical system needs upgrading.

Sometimes the main house breaker will trip or the main fuse will blow even when the overload or short circuit was limited to a single branch circuit. This is because breakers and fuses, being mechanical devices, don't always perform as they're designed to. In other words, an overload or a short circuit on a single branch circuit can trip the main circuit breaker or blow the main fuse without disturbing the smaller breaker or fuse that protects the affected branch circuit.

It's also possible that an overload or short circuit in a branch circuit will trip *both* the branch *and* the main circuit breaker or both fuses, as the case may be.

For more information on how to diagnose an overload or short circuit, see "Overloaded Circuit" on page 101 and "Short Circuit" on page 102.

Power is lost due to a problem with the utility transformer or line that feeds your house. If there's no problem evident with your main house breaker or fuse, call the electric utility and report the problem.

NOTE: In some service panels, the main house circuit is protected by cartridge-style fuses, which don't usually show any external sign of failure. One way to find out if a cartridge fuse has failed is to remove it and test it with a continuity tester. (See "Breakers and Fuses" on page 106.) Or you can replace the suspect fuse with a fuse that you *know* is good and see if that corrects the problem.

CAUTION: For safety's sake, the replacement fuse must be of the exact same amperage as the original.

The main circuit breaker has failed. Like other mechanical devices, circuit breakers occasionally fail. Unfortunately, such failures can be hard to diagnose, since the breaker may fail in its *ON* position without any external sign of failure.

Try switching the main circuit breaker on and off a few times to see if power is restored. If that doesn't work, have your electric utility check to make sure your service panel is receiving electricity. If it is, call an electrician—do not attempt to replace the main breaker yourself.

You forgot to pay your electric bill. Utilities issue repeated warnings and provide a grace period of several weeks—or even months—to delinquent customers before they finally pull the plug.

Spikes, Brownouts, and Blips

Flickering or dimming lights are a sure sign of power fluctuations that can potentially damage electronic equipment like computers and televisions.

DEFINING ELECTRICAL TERMS

Beyond a total disruption of your electrical service, there are a number of other phenomena that can cause trouble. These include spikes, brownouts, and blips.

Spikes are high-voltage surges of current that can damage your electric service panel, wiring, and appliances—especially computers and other sensitive electronic gear. Although primarily caused by lightning (see "Lightning Strikes!" on page 180), spikes can also occur when your utility company switches from one

Quick Response

1. If main service panel is undamaged following spike, turn off main breaker or remove main fuse. Call utility's emergency line. (See "Understanding Your Electrical System" on page 6.)

2. In event of brownout, turn off electrical devices to see if voltage returns to normal. (See "Overloaded Circuit" on page 101.) If it doesn't, report problem to utility.

3. If lights flicker, expect power outage.

Hazards

● If there's any sign of smoke or fire after a high-voltage surge, call your fire department at once. (See "Fire!" on page 244.)

● Do not work inside the main service panel if it's wet or damaged. Call an electrician or utility emergency team. (See "Electrical Safety Tips" on page 102.)

generator to another or when motorized household appliances (for example, hair dryer, vacuum cleaner, or dishwasher) or power tools are switched on.

Brownouts occur when the voltage in your lines drops below a certain point. This can cause incandescent lightbulbs to dim and appliances to underperform. A brownout may be a signal that one or more of your electric circuits is close to full capacity. Or it may mean that your utility company is having difficulty supplying enough power to meet the demand.

Blips are momentary power outages that cause lights and appliances to flick on and off at quick intervals. They often happen just before the power fails completely. Prepare flashlights, propane lanterns, candles, batteries, and other emergency supplies for a complete outage.

BLOCKING SPIKES

Though electric utilities strive to keep line voltage within carefully defined parameters, both high- and low-voltage conditions do occur. A high-voltage surge may be only a few volts above normal or—in the case of a lightning strike—millions.

Many pieces of electronic equipment, such as computers, VCRs, microwaves, and televisions, are sensitive to even small increases in voltage and should be protected by a surge suppressor, an electronic device that senses the spike in voltage and shunts it to ground. While there are dozens of different brand names and configurations available—ranging in price from $10 to $300—surge suppressors fall into two broad categories, *primary* and *secondary*.

The *primary* type, as shown in *Hard-Wired Surge Protection* on this page, is installed as a permanent fixture near the main service panel, where it protects all of the home's branch circuits. The installation should be done by a licensed electrician.

Secondary surge suppressors can be installed or plugged into any grounded (three-prong) outlet. (See *Secondary Surge Suppressors* on the opposite page.) These devices will protect any electrical equipment that is powered from that outlet. Some models have multiple outlets and built-in phone jacks to protect modems, telephones, and fax machines. Others incorpo-

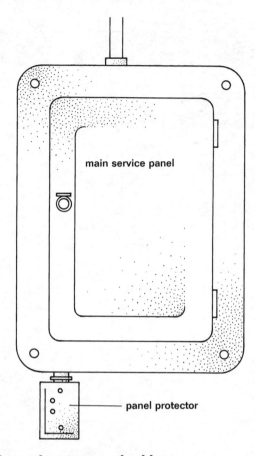

main service panel

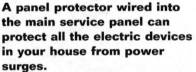

panel protector

A panel protector wired into the main service panel can protect all the electric devices in your house from power surges.

rate a low-voltage monitor to protect your equipment against brownouts. (See "Avoiding Brownouts" on the opposite page.)

Regardless of the features you choose, secondary surge suppressors are easy to install and can be readily moved from one receptacle to another. They are especially recommended for sensitive electronic equipment, including computers, microwaves, electric pianos, TVs, stereos, and VCRs.

The best way to select a secondary surge suppressor is to call the dealer or manufacturer of the device you want to protect and ask them what they recommend. If the device you want to protect is connected to phone lines or cable TV, call the phone or cable company and ask their advice as well. And be sure that any surge suppressor you buy is certified by Underwriters Laboratories (UL) or other qualified testing agency.

SECONDARY SURGE SUPPRESSORS

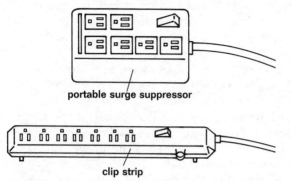

portable surge suppressor

clip strip

Portable secondary surge suppressors should be used to protect individual appliances.

Equipping your house with primary and secondary surge suppressors will prevent or mitigate damage from most voltage spikes. A direct lightning strike, however, is a different story. See "Lightning Strikes!" on page 180 for further details on protecting your home from that kind of emergency.

AVOIDING BROWNOUTS

A low-voltage condition can occur in several ways. If your household circuits are close to their full capacity, the resulting voltage drop can cause lightbulbs to dim and your television picture to shrink and may trip a circuit breaker or blow a fuse. (See "Overloaded Circuit" on page 101 and "Adding Up the Amps" on page 104.)

Low-voltage problems and overloads are often caused by the thoughtless addition of new appliances. Even a single new appliance can cause problems if it's a big energy user (such as a point-of-use [tankless] water heater or an electric ceramic kiln). That's why it's smart to consult an electrician and/or your utility company *before* you add a large appliance to your electrical load.

Another possibility is that the voltage being supplied by the utility is less than normal parameters. This occurs when electric demand in the utility's service area is heavy and the generating and distribution system is operating near full capacity. The resulting voltage drop, which can affect large areas, is called a *brownout*.

To avoid brownouts and blackouts, utilities use radio, TV, and other media to advise customers that the system is facing peak demand and to encourage them to conserve electricity.

Sometimes, low voltage is limited to an isolated utility line. Imagine, for example, a house situated at or near the end of a long, rural electric line, as shown in *Time to Upgrade the Power Lines* on this page. Perhaps the voltage to the house was ade-

TIME TO UPGRADE THE POWER LINES

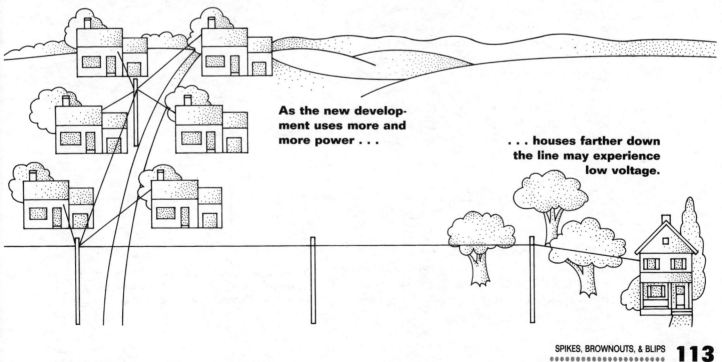

As the new development uses more and more power . . .

. . . houses farther down the line may experience low voltage.

quate until a number of new houses were built along the line—each drawing additional voltage. As the line's capacity becomes strained, the houses it serves will suffer a drop in voltage. The only real solution to this problem is for the utility to invest in the equipment needed to upgrade the line.

If you suspect that you're getting low voltage from the utility, call them and ask them to come check. Make sure that their voltage tests encompass the morning rush hour, dinner hour, and other periods of peak use, during the season when the problems are most acute.

If the utility is slow to act or uncooperative, you can conduct your own test. Buy an inexpensive voltage monitor (about $13 from Radio Shack), and simply plug it into a receptacle. It will provide you with a continual readout of the available voltage. To establish a benchmark for your test, call the public utility commission to find out what the parameters are for residential voltage. Then keep track of the actual voltage at different times of day for about a week. Be sure to run the test during the season when the problems are most severe, as the voltage may vary dramatically from season to season. Spring and fall are usually the seasons of the lowest electrical use, while electrical use increases in winter and summer as heaters and air conditioners are turned on. If your test confirms that you're receiving low voltage, report the results to your utility.

DEALING WITH BLIPS

When your electricity blinks on and off at short intervals, it usually indicates that there's a short circuit somewhere in the utility line or transformer serving your house. (See *Line*

Troubles on this page.) This can be caused by a tree branch that's fallen or leaning against a power line, ice, high wind, a leak in the transformer—even a squirrel gnawing through a utility line.

The resulting blinks in your electric service occur when a utility safety switch—called a *recloser*—senses the short circuit and momentarily cuts power off. If the short persists, the switch, after two or three "looks" (blinks), will shut the power off to protect the circuit.

If the lights do go out, call your neighbors to determine whether the failure is related

LINE TROUBLES

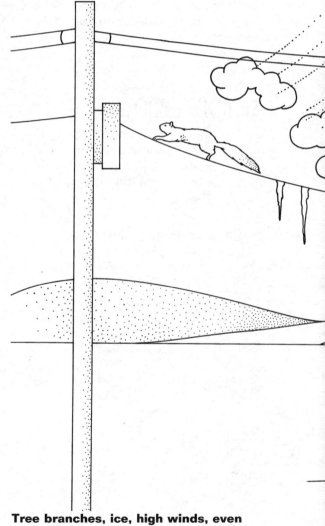

Tree branches, ice, high winds, even squirrels and other critters can play havoc with your electric lines.

directly to your system or is more widespread and to find out if they've already notified the utility. (See "No Electric Power" on page 109.)

FOLLOWING UP
ON OTHER ODDITIES

If your lightbulbs are behaving strangely—oscillating from dim to bright—and appliances are performing erratically, it's a good bet that the neutral wire in the line between your house and the utility pole is disconnected.

If one of the two 120-volt "hot" wires in the line is cut, you could end up with power in some parts of your house and a blackout in others.

Irregular or intermittent service can also result if moisture gets inside the service panel, corroding the contacts between the bus circuits and the breakers.

All three of these circumstances require professional service. Call a licensed electrician to check out the problems.

Heating & Cooling Emergencies

4

HEATING & COOLING EMERGENCIES

Gas Leak

Quick Response

1. Evacuate house, leaving doors open.

2. Turn gas valve off at main meter or tank.

3. Use neighbor's phone to call fire department, then gas company.

4. If odor is faint, check to see if pilot light has gone out. If so, ventilate area until smell dissipates, and relight pilot. If odor persists, evacuate.

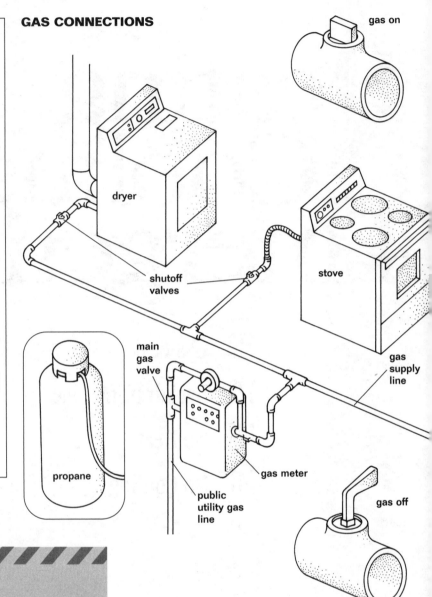

GAS CONNECTIONS

gas on

dryer

shutoff valves

stove

gas supply line

main gas valve

propane

gas meter

public utility gas line

gas off

Hazards

● If the gas or propane valve does not turn easily when you try to shut it off, *don't force it*. Leave the valve open and call for help from a neighbor's house.

● *Do not* work electrical switches, telephones, or flashlights during a gas emergency. The spark may set off an explosion.

● *Do not* try to relight a pilot if there is a persistent smell of gas. When in doubt, get out!

● After you've evacuated the house, make sure that no one goes back in to retrieve personal items or pets.

● Gas or propane leaking from an underground line can lose its odor as it filters up through the soil. If you suspect there's a leak but can't smell it, call your supplier. (See "Tool Strikes Buried Cable or Pipe" on page 259.)

SNIFFING OUT THE PROBLEM

The distinctive rotten-egg odor that's given to natural gas and propane during the production process is put there exclusively for your safety. Otherwise, natural gas and propane would be odorless.

If you or someone else in your family smells natural gas or propane, assume that a pipe, fitting, valve, or appliance is leaking

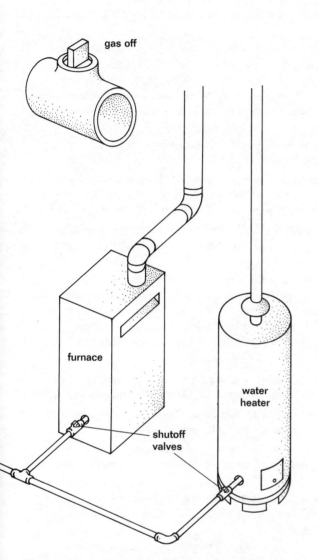

gas off

furnace

water heater

shutoff valves

The gas for the house can be shut off at the gas meter or propane tank, while gas to individual appliances can be shut off at nearby valves. One type of valve requires pliers; the other type can be turned by hand.

and immediately evacuate the house. (See "Quick Response" on the opposite page.)

Keep in mind that most modern gas furnaces and appliances do *not* have a pilot light, which was a frequent source of gas smells in years gone by. Electronic ignitions are now the norm. Those appliances that do have pilot lights—mainly water heaters—are equipped with a thermocouple, a safety device that automatically shuts off the gas if the pilot light goes out. Thus, unless you

Shutting Off the Gas or Propane

As shown in *Gas Connections* on the opposite page, each gas or propane appliance in your house is equipped with a valve that controls the fuel supply to that particular appliance.

To cut off the fuel to one of these appliances, simply turn the handle or valve stem until it's perpendicular to the supply pipe. (If there's no handle, grip the stem with a pair of pliers.)

To shut off natural gas to the *entire* house, find the main gas meter, which is usually located outside, close to the foundation wall. (See *Your Gas System* on page 8.) Using an adjustable wrench, turn the main shutoff valve a quarter turn until it's perpendicular to the supply pipe, as shown in *How to Shut Off the Main Natural Gas Valve*.

HOW TO SHUT OFF THE MAIN NATURAL GAS VALVE

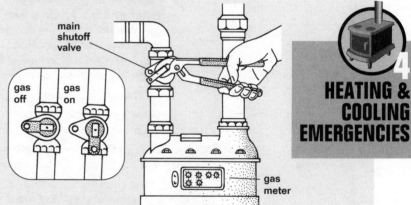

main shutoff valve

gas off

gas on

gas meter

To turn off the gas, turn the valve perpendicular to the supply line.

CAUTION: The shutoff valve on your gas meter may not have a stop for the *OFF* position—that is, the valve can be turned past *OFF*, opening up the flow of gas again. Take care to turn the valve a quarter turn only, so that it sits perpendicular to the pipe.

To shut off the propane supply to the *entire* house, locate the tank (always outside), lift the tank cover (if there is one), and turn the shutoff valve clockwise until it's fully closed, as shown in *How to Shut Off a Propane Tank Valve*.

CAUTION: If either valve is stuck, don't force it. Leave it open and call for help from the neighbor's house.

HOW TO SHUT OFF A PROPANE TANK VALVE

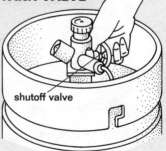

shutoff valve

Turn valve clockwise to close.

8 Reasons You Might Smell Gas

1. A false alarm. Sewer gas backing up from a municipal sewer or private septic system is sometimes mistaken for natural gas or propane, even though the smell is quite distinct.

What you can do: Sewer gas bubbling back through a toilet or other fixture suggests that the main plumbing vent is clogged (call a plumber) or perhaps the water in one or more drain traps has evaporated or been siphoned dry (pour in a bucket of water into the sink to refill the trap). Odors outdoors suggest a broken sewer pipe or problems with the septic tank or drain field, requiring professional service.

2. The pilot light has gone out on a gas furnace or appliance. (See the discussion on pilot lights on pages 80 and 119.)

What you can do: Ventilate the area and wait five minutes. If there's no gas smell remaining, relight the pilot light according to the instructions in the manual or those appearing on the appliance itself. (Also see "Gas Furnaces" on page 132.)

3. The pilot light or burner is poorly adjusted. If the air-to-gas mixture is too rich, uncombusted natural gas and carbon monoxide are released. (See **8. Backdraft** on this page.)

What you can do: On a pilot light, adjust the small screw that controls the air-to-gas mixture. If the fuel is natural gas, the pilot flame should be blue, with only a trace of yellow at the tip. If the fuel is propane, adjust for a blue-green inner flame, with just a fleck of yellow at the tip. Adjusting the main burners on a furnace, water heater, stove, or clothes dryer is a job that's best left to a professional.

4. The pilot assembly is leaking around the orifice.

What you can do: Turn off the supply valve to that particular appliance, ventilate the area, and call the gas company's service department or a heating contractor.

5. A pipe, valve, or fitting leaks due to old age. Pipes and fittings usually rust out around the threads while old valves typically leak around the stem.

What you can do: Do *not* attempt to find and repair the leak yourself. Evacuate the house and call the fire department, then the gas company's emergency line, from a neighbor's house.

6. A pipe, valve, or fitting is accidentally damaged. This can occur due to impact, earthquake, house settling, or careless excavation. (See "Tool Strikes Buried Cable or Pipe" on page 259.)

What you can do: If the damage is clearly isolated to one appliance, turn off the supply valve to that appliance, ventilate the area, and call the gas company's service department or a heating contractor. Otherwise, evacuate the house and call the fire department, then the gas company's emergency line from a neighbor's house.

7. The propane tank is leaking. Tanks can wear out or rust to the point where they leak, usually around the valve. Other times they leak because they're accidentally hit by a car or lawn tractor.

What you can do: Evacuate the house and a large area around the leaking tank. Don't let anyone enter the area. Call the fire department, then the propane company's emergency line from a neighbor's house.

8. Backdraft. Toxic combustion gases that are normally vented outside the house "spill" back into the living area.

What you can do: Open windows and doors. Turn off combustion appliances and exhaust fans. If smoke or combustion odors persist, evacuate the house. Seek professional help. (See "Backdrafting Flue" on page 122.)

Gas Hotline

Most gas utilities man a 24-hour, seven-day-a-week hotline to handle emergencies. Find out what that number is and post it near your telephone. ●

own an aged range or clothes dryer, an extinguished pilot light is *not* likely to produce any smell.

Also bear in mind that while natural gas and propane have similar odors, their properties are quite different. Leaking natural gas will diffuse quickly through the house, reaching your nose in short order. Propane, being much heavier, tends to pool on the floor and diffuse (along with its smell) more slowly.

Thus, the best place to sniff out a propane leak is at floor level (or ground level if you're outside), where the odor will be stronger and easier to detect.

Whether you use natural gas or propane and regardless of the circumstances, *always* err on the side of caution. Gas and propane companies as well as many fire departments are equipped with combustible gas detectors that are much more sensitive than your nose.

If you or someone in your house has lost the sense of smell, ask the safety officer at your local gas utility about installing a gas detector that can sound an alarm or flash lights if there's a leak.

For a list of manufacturers who make UL-approved gas detectors, write Underwriters Laboratories, Inc., 333 Pfingsten Road, Northbrook, IL 60062.

Backdrafting Flue

Quick Response

1. Open windows and doors.

2. Turn off combustion appliances and exhaust fans.

3. If smoke or combustion odors persist, evacuate house.

4. Get immediate professional help in finding and eliminating source of backdraft. *Do not reoccupy house—especially overnight—until problem is resolved.*

Even an innocent-looking woodstove like this can release poisonous fumes into your living space. Make sure the stove, stovepipes, and chimney are well sealed.

Hazards

● If you or another family member exhibits symptoms of carbon monoxide poisoning, leave the house and see a doctor immediately. (See "Identifying Carbon-Monoxide Poisoning" on the opposite page.)

● Furnaces, woodstoves, fireplaces, or appliances that are backdrafting smoke and toxic gases may also present a serious fire hazard.

AVOIDING GAS SPILL-BACK

A backdraft occurs when combustion gases that are normally vented outside the house "spill" back into the living area—with potentially dangerous results. The problem can occur with any vented combustion appliance, including a furnace, boiler, woodstove, fireplace, space heater, water heater, or clothes dryer, as shown in *Possible Sources of Carbon Monoxide* on page 124.

The gases produced during combustion vary with the type of fuel, the appliance, and the condition of the appliance. Carbon monoxide

(CO), nitrogen dioxide (NO_2), and sulfur dioxide (SO_2) are three common by-products of combustion, with carbon monoxide being far and away the most dangerous. According to the American Medical Association, there are more than 400 carbon-monoxide–related deaths in the United States each year and an estimated 5,000 incidents in which people require emergency hospital treatment.

UNDERSTANDING BACKDRAFTS

To operate safely, combustion appliances must have an ample supply of "make-up" air in the combustion chamber and an exhaust vent that's properly installed and maintained. If either or both of these conditions are not met, it sets the stage for backdraft.

State-of-the-art combustion appliances are designed to draw their make-up air from outdoors—through a dedicated vent—so there's little chance that the burner will be starved for air. (If the air intake vent is obstructed for some reason, the appliance automatically shuts itself off.)

Older-style combustion appliances, which draw their make-up air from indoors, must be guaranteed an ample supply of air. If such appliances are located in a utility room, closet, or other tight space, adequate vents or ducts into the space must be provided—as specified by the manufacturer and national fire codes (available at your local fire department or municipal building department)—to ensure proper combustion.

Keep in mind that all of your combustion appliances—and exhaust fans as well—are in a sense "competing" for indoor air. Thus, when you install a new clothes dryer, fireplace, or exhaust fan in your home—that is, anything that exhausts or blows to the outside—you're placing additional demand on the available supply of indoor air. At some point, as demand overcomes supply, the house is depressurized to the point where combustion gases flow back down the chimney or exhaust vent into the living space.

Unexpected backdraft problems can also occur in houses that undergo extensive weather tightening. When the cracks around windows and doors are weather-stripped and caulked, the natural flow of air from outdoors

Identifying Carbon-Monoxide Poisoning

Carbon monoxide (CO), a by-product of incomplete combustion, is an odorless, colorless, tasteless gas that's extremely dangerous. Once inhaled, it's readily absorbed into the blood, slowly depriving the victim of oxygen.

Low-level carbon-monoxide poisoning produces flulike symptoms, including the following:

● Headache

● Dizziness, faintness, or confusion

● Nausea

● Fatigue

● Chest pains

● Heart palpitations (especially in people with heart disease)

Higher concentrations of CO in the blood can lead to the following conditions:

● Unconsciousness

● Damage or death to the fetus in pregnant women

● Brain damage

● Coma

● Death

If you are experiencing some of the symptoms noted above but can't tell whether it's the flu or carbon-monoxide poisoning, *don't take any chances*. Leave the house immediately and get some fresh air. If it's carbon-monoxide poisoning, exposure to fresh air should quickly alleviate the symptoms.

Two additional measures are strongly recommended. First, ask your doctor to test your blood's carboxylhemoglobin level—it's the only way that carbon-monoxide poisoning can be medically confirmed.

Second, call your fire department or fuel supplier and ask them to probe your house with a carbon-monoxide detector.

Under no circumstances should you reoccupy your house without confirming that it's free of carbon monoxide.

4

HEATING & COOLING EMERGENCIES

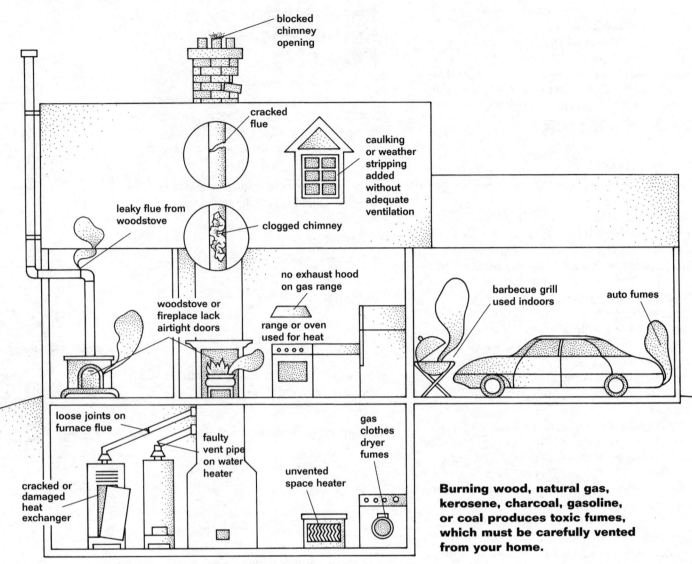

blocked chimney opening

cracked flue

caulking or weather stripping added without adequate ventilation

leaky flue from woodstove

clogged chimney

no exhaust hood on gas range

barbecue grill used indoors

auto fumes

woodstove or fireplace lack airtight doors

range or oven used for heat

loose joints on furnace flue

faulty vent pipe on water heater

gas clothes dryer fumes

unvented space heater

cracked or damaged heat exchanger

Burning wood, natural gas, kerosene, charcoal, gasoline, or coal produces toxic fumes, which must be carefully vented from your home.

to indoors can be substantially reduced—hence, there's less make-up air available for combustion appliances. The answer to this problem, contrary to popular wisdom, isn't to "loosen up the house" so it can "breathe" but to provide the house with an adequate, controllable ventilation system and/or to provide individual combustion appliances, including fireplaces, with a dedicated air supply.

The second key element in preventing backdrafts is to make sure that each combustion appliance in your home exhausts into an adequate-size chimney or vent that's been properly installed and maintained. It's especially hazardous to tie a new combustion appliance into a chimney or exhaust vent that's already in use without having a professional check the installation.

PREVENTING BACKDRAFTS IN 6 SURE STEPS

1. Make sure that all of your combustion appliances are properly installed, maintained, and vented to the outside.
2. All chimneys and exhaust vents should be inspected annually for damage or blockage. If you burn wood or coal, sweep the chimney at least once a year, before the heating season begins.
3. If you build a cosmetic or sound-proofing enclosure for your furnace, water heater, or other combustion appliance, equip the space with an adequate air duct to the outside or otherwise make sure that the appli-

ance gets plenty of make-up air. Check with your local code authorities before you start.

4. Equip your fireplace with airtight doors and a duct to bring in combustion air from outside. (These changes will make the fireplace burn a lot more efficiently, too.) Never close the damper on the fireplace—even part way—until the fire is completely out.

5. If you are weather-tightening your house or adding a new appliance that's equipped with a burner or exhaust fan, have a qualified heating technician re-evaluate your home's ventilation needs.

6. When shopping for a new furnace, water heater, or other combustion appliance, consider a direct-vent model that brings outside air into the combustion chamber through a special duct.

Put a Detector in Your Life

A dozen or more manufacturers now sell UL-approved carbon-monoxide detectors for under $100. The units, which are plugged into an ordinary electrical outlet or powered by batteries, are mounted on the ceiling or high on the wall in or near your bedrooms. If carbon monoxide in the air reaches a dangerous level, the detector sounds an ear-splitting alarm.

CO detectors are especially recommended in homes that have fuel-fired space heaters, woodstoves, or fireplaces. Specially designed models are available for garages, attics, and recreational vehicles.

Like smoke detectors, a carbon-monoxide detector requires careful installation and maintenance. Once in place, it should be tested weekly or monthly, depending on the type. The sensor may periodically require recalibration or replacement, according to the manufacturer's maintenance recommendations.

Before you buy a detector, check the label to make sure it's been tested and approved by Underwriters Laboratories, Inc. Or you can get a list of approved manufacturers by writing to Underwriters Laboratories, 333 Pfingsten Road, Northbrook, IL 60062. Underwriters also publishes an informative pamphlet on the subject titled "Questions and Answers about Carbon Monoxide and CO Detectors."

Preventing Carbon-Monoxide Poisoning at Home

Common sense and good maintenance practices can go a long way toward preventing carbon-monoxide poisoning in your home. Here are some important tips to remember.

● Gas-fired appliances should be cleaned and inspected every two years. Oil-fired appliances need to be serviced annually. The technician should clean and adjust all burners and pilots, make sure the heat exchanger on the furnace is sound, and inspect each chimney and exhaust vent. If you've added a new combustion appliance or exhaust fan or tightened up your home, ask the technician to run a combustion safety test to make sure there's no danger of backdraft.

● Chimneys connected to wood- or coal-burning stoves should be swept and inspected annually. If the door gaskets on your stove are worn out and leaking, replace them.

(CAUTION: Some old gaskets are made of asbestos. Consult with the manufacturer or local dealer before you replace them. Two booklets from the U.S. Environmental Protection Agency that may help are "Asbestos in Your Home" and "What You Should Know about Combustion Appliances and Indoor Air Pollu-tion." Write IAQ INFO, P.O. Box 37133, Washington, DC 20013-7133, or call 1-800-438-4318.)

● Do not use unvented gas or kerosene space heaters inside your house, even if the manufacturer claims it's safe to do so.

● Never use gas or charcoal grills indoors.

● If you have a gas oven or range top, equip it with an exhaust fan and use it whenever you're cooking. Don't use the oven or range for heat.

● Do not idle your car, truck, or other vehicles inside your garage. The carbon monoxide from the exhaust will work its way into your house.

● When shopping for new combustion appliances, consider models that have electronic ignitions (no pilot light) and closed combustion.

● Keep alert to the telltale signs of carbon monoxide. These might include smoky, gaseous, or sulfurous smells in the house, soot deposits around the combustion chamber or flue on a furnace or appliance, and high indoor humidity.

No Heat

Quick Response

1. Check thermostat to make sure it's in correct mode, and raise set point.

2. Check heating system's on/off switch.

3. Use fireplace, woodstove, or space heater for emergency heat while trouble-shooting main system.

THERMOSTAT TYPES

Standard Round Model

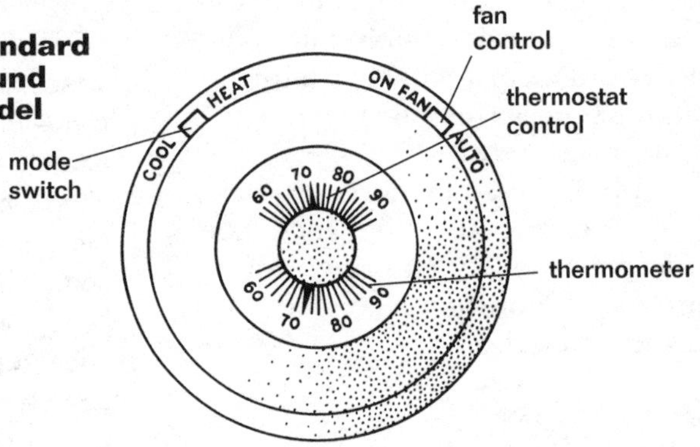

mode switch

COOL HEAT ON FAN AUTO

fan control

thermostat control

thermometer

60 70 80 90

60 70 80 90

Electronic Model

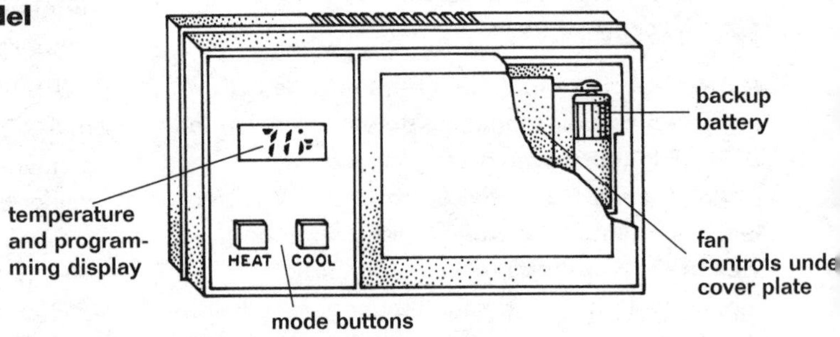

temperature and programming display

71°

HEAT COOL

mode buttons

backup battery

fan controls under cover plate

Thermostats come in many different shapes and sizes. Some use simple mechanical controls while others use programmable electronic controls.

Hazards

● Do *not* use a gas oven, unvented kerosene heater, or outdoor cooker for emergency heat.

● Make sure the electricity is off and the floor is dry before you do any repair work. Wear rubber-soled shoes and rubber gloves as an added precaution against shock. (See "Electrical Safety Tips" on page 102.)

● Use your nose! If you smell gas or fumes, open windows and doors to ventilate the house. If the smell persists, get everyone out and call for help from a neighbor's house. (See "Gas Leak" on page 118 and "Backdrafting Flue" on page 122.)

● Don't work on the system until you're properly dressed. Wear shoes (never work barefooted or in house slippers) and tight-fitting clothes (a loose robe belt or unbuttoned sleeve can snag on a fan or other moving part).

● Do not smoke.

PROCEEDING SYSTEMATICALLY

A very large percentage of heating system failures can be fixed—at least temporarily—through simple adjustments and repairs. Starting at the thermostat, work your way one by one through the checkpoints outlined in the following pages. After each point, wait a few minutes to see if the system responds. If it doesn't, move on to the next.

Remember that even if you succeed in getting the system started, you should consider having it professionally serviced as soon as possible.

The repair measures spelled out here are meant to address emergencies in which the heating and cooling systems even more convenient, we have added timers, displays, and a myriad of controls that may make some of us long for simpler times. The thermostat is in essence your heating system's brain—just don't let it give you a nervous breakdown.

Wrong mode: Make sure the mode switch is set on *HEAT.* (See *Thermostat Types* on the opposite page.) Move the set point well above the room temperature (80°F or more) to make sure that the thermostat is calling for heat. If there's still no response, move the thermostat setting all the way down, wait 30 seconds, and move it back up again.

Out of level: Thermostats equipped with mercury switches must be level to operate properly. If the thermostat has been twisted or knocked out of level, loosen the adjusting screw and reposition it. *NOTE:* Most digital thermostats don't have a mercury switch and aren't susceptible to this problem.

Dead battery (digital models only): Some thermostats are completely battery-powered; others use a battery to hold their setback program if there's a power failure. If the digital readout on your thermostat is absent or weak or if there's an indicator reading *LOW BAT,* replace the battery. If the display is still weak or absent after a fresh battery is installed, the furnace (or boiler) has probably shut down or experienced a transformer failure.

Ambient factors: Check the space around the thermostat for anything that might be producing heat. A newly installed television set or space heater, lit candles, even a wall mirror reflecting sunlight onto the thermostat, can "mislead" it into "thinking" there's plenty of heat.

Dirty switch contacts: Modern thermostats, which have sealed contacts, usually aren't affected by household dust and grime. But if you have an older or inexpensive thermostat, the exposed contacts may have become grimy enough that the metal isn't making contact.

To clean the contacts, first turn off the power to the heating system at the main electric service panel. (See *Your Electrical System* on page 6.) Then unscrew or unclip the thermostat's cover and loosen the screws that hold the thermostat's body to its mounting plate. (Be careful not to remove any screws that secure components or wires.)

Slip an index card, business card, or other clean, firm paper between the thermostat contacts, then push the contacts together, and

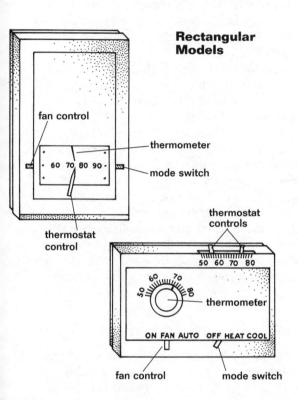

Rectangular Models

fan control

thermometer

mode switch

thermostat control

thermostat controls

thermometer

ON FAN AUTO OFF HEAT COOL

fan control

mode switch

heating system delivers *no* heat at all. If your system is merely underperforming, read the maintenance recommendations in "Understanding Your Heating and Cooling System" on page 8.

ADDRESSING UNIVERSAL PROBLEMS

All heating systems have thermostats and certain other elements in common. That's where you should start your troubleshooting.

THERMOSTAT PROBLEMS

When our predecessors wanted more heat, they threw another log on the fire. We have the convenience of twisting a knob on a thermostat. However, in an attempt to make our

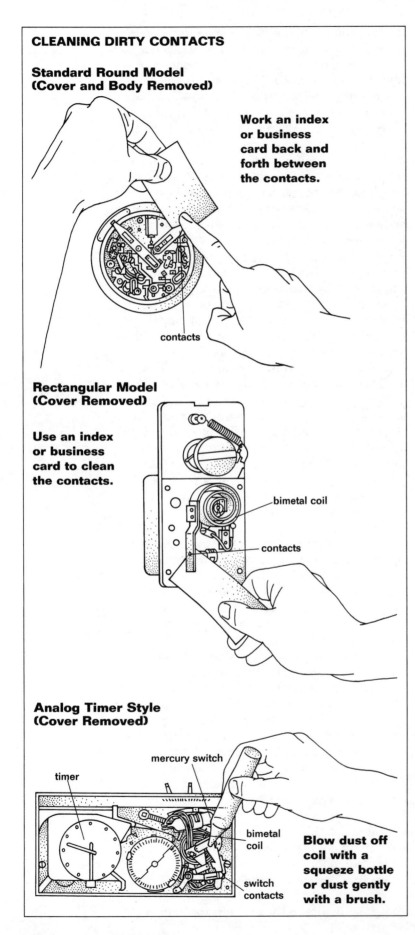

CLEANING DIRTY CONTACTS

Standard Round Model (Cover and Body Removed)

Work an index or business card back and forth between the contacts.

contacts

Rectangular Model (Cover Removed)

Use an index or business card to clean the contacts.

bimetal coil

contacts

Analog Timer Style (Cover Removed)

timer

mercury switch

bimetal coil

switch contacts

Blow dust off coil with a squeeze bottle or dust gently with a brush.

draw the card slowly through them. (See *Cleaning Dirty Contacts* on this page.)

As long as you have the thermostat disassembled, take a minute more to blow the dust off the bimetal coil. As shown in *Cleaning Dirty Contacts*, the bimetal coil is the spiral-shaped spring that's attached to the mercury switch. Use a plastic squeeze bottle or a soft brush to gently blow off the dust. Do *not* use a vacuum cleaner, as it may damage the delicate coil.

After the thermostat is cleaned, reassemble it and set it on *HEAT*. Give the system a few minutes to respond. If it doesn't, move on to the next checkpoint.

CAUTION: Make doubly sure that the power is off before cleaning the thermostat on an electric baseboard system. These run on 120-volt line current (versus 24 volts in other thermostats) and present a *serious* risk of shock. After switching the power off at the main service panel, test the main electrical wires coming into the thermostat (these are the heaviest wires that are connected to terminals) with a volt-ohm meter as an added precaution.

NO ELECTRICITY

It is fairly obvious that if you have electric baseboard heaters, they will stop heating up if you lose electrical power. But furnaces and boilers also depend on electricity even though they're fueled with gas or oil.

Utility outage: Contact the utility to see how long they expect the outage to last and make plans accordingly. (See "No Electric Power" on page 109.) If your water pipes are in danger of freezing, open each faucet enough to allow a thin but continuous stream of water to flow out.

Tripped circuit breaker or blown fuse: Reset the breaker or replace the fuse. (See "Circuit Breaker Trips or Fuse Blows" on page 100.) If it immediately trips or blows again, keep the power off and call a heating technician.

NOTE: For heat pump owners, if the power is off for more than an hour and the temperature outdoors is below 50 degrees, switch your thermostat's mode setting to *EMERGENCY HEAT* or *AUXILIARY* and leave it that way for six hours. This gives the heating element inside the compressor time to warm the lubricant, avoiding valve damage when it starts up again.

NO FUEL

Did you forget to pay your fuel bill last month, or did the weather produce a harsh cold spell? A missed payment can result in your fuel supply being cut off or not delivered. Extreme cold can drain propane and fuel oil tanks quickly.

Natural gas: Confirm the outage by checking your gas stove, water heater, or other gas appliances. Call the gas utility's 24-hour emergency response line to report the problem.

Propane: Confirm the outage by checking other propane-fired appliances. Make sure the valve is open on the propane tank. Call your supplier.

Fuel oil: If the tank is indoors, check the fuel gauge to confirm that you've run out of fuel. Outdoor tanks have to be measured with a metered dip stick, as shown in *Checking the Oil Supply* on this page. Most tanks are effectively empty when there's about 3 inches of oil left in the bottom.

If the tank is empty, call your supplier to see if you can get an emergency delivery. If that's not possible, and you're desperate for heat, you can buy diesel fuel from a local gas station and haul it to your house. You'll need some 5-gallon fuel cans and a funnel to do the job. *CAUTION:* Never put kerosene, gasoline, or other fuels into the oil tank.

If the furnace or boiler doesn't fire after you've fueled the tank and reset the primary control, the fuel pump has probably lost its prime and you will have to prime it.

As shown in *Priming the Fuel Pump* on this page, the fuel pump is part of the burner assembly, coupled to the motor. To prime it, follow these steps.

1. Locate the bleeder valve nut—a short, tube-shaped fixture—on the underside of the pump housing.
2. Place a catch pan underneath it.
3. Reset the primary control, which will start the burner and pump.
4. Using a wrench or allen wrench (typically ⅜ inch), loosen the bleeder valve nut a half turn and leave it open until a clear stream of oil shoots out.
5. Retighten the bleeder valve nut.

If the burner doesn't fire within about 45 seconds, the primary control will shut it off. If

PRIMING THE FUEL PUMP

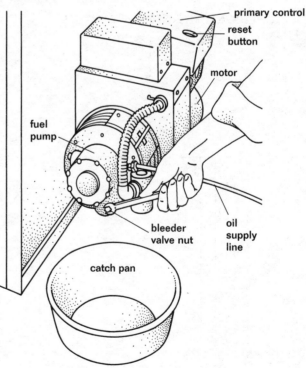

To prime the pump, loosen
the bleeder valve nut until
an even stream of oil runs
out. Then, retighten it.

CHECKING THE OIL SUPPLY

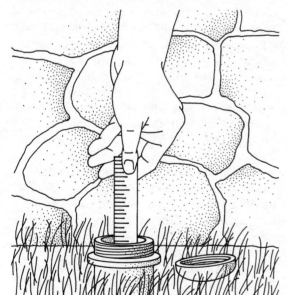

Dip a long stick into
the oil tank to check the oil
level. A long measuring stick
would work well.

that happens, simply close the bleeder valve nut, reset the primary control, and try it again. (For more information on resetting the furnace, see "Oil Furnaces" on page 133.)

ON/OFF SWITCH

Most furnaces and boilers are equipped with their own on/off switch. It's typically located on the side of the heating unit, on a nearby post, or perhaps at the top of the basement stairs. Some switches are marked with a special red cover plate. (See *Checking the On/Off Switch* on this page.)

Though it seems simplistic, make sure that the on/off switch is *ON*. Heating contractors have dozens of stories about cats and kids and careless elbows—even a broom falling in the night—that accidentally switched the heat off.

Also, some types of on/off switches are separately fused. If you have that type (you'll have to take the cover plate off to find out), turn off the power at the main service panel, remove the switch cover, and check the fuse inside.

CHECKING THE ON/OFF SWITCH

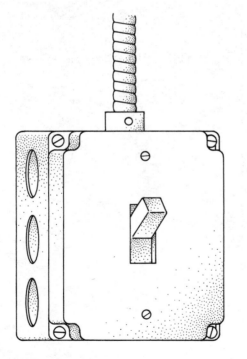

If you have no heat, check to see if the furnace or boiler on/off switch is turned on.

TROUBLESHOOTING FORCED-AIR HEATING SYSTEMS

NOTE: The problems discussed in this section apply only to forced-air heating systems, which have a central furnace and use a fan to distribute warm air through a system of ducts and registers. If you have a hot-water heating system, which has a central boiler and uses a circulator pump to distribute hot water through pipes and radiators, jump ahead to "Troubleshooting Hot-Water Heating Systems" on page 134.

Troubleshooting a forced-air system begins with the four checkpoints under "Addressing Universal Problems" on page 127. If none of these elements are to blame for your lack of heat, consider the following possibilities, which are specific to forced-air heating systems.

PROBLEMS COMMON TO BOTH GAS AND OIL FURNACES

Blower compartment door ajar: In order to work efficiently, air heated by a gas or oil furnace must be distributed evenly throughout the house by an electric-powered blower. If the blower shuts down, so does the furnace's ability to heat the house. Refer to *Blower Compartment Problems* on the opposite page as you address blower compartment problems.

CAUTION: Before you open the blower compartment, turn off the furnace switch and cut power at the main electric service panel.

Modern gas and oil furnaces have an interlock safety switch that automatically turns the system off if the blower compartment door is removed or left ajar. This is to prevent the furnace from backdrafting into the room and to keep curious kids and cats from crawling into the path of a moving fan. If you find the door removed or ajar, secure it. Turn the power back on. The furnace should restart.

Blower jammed: If you find that the air filter or a piece of metal framing has come loose and jammed the blower, free it up and restore power to the system.

Belt and pulley problems: If you have a belt-driven blower, here's a checklist of possible problems that can cause the furnace to shut down.

● *Broken belt:* If the belt breaks, the furnace will overheat and trigger the high-limit cutout switch. You can fashion a makeshift belt out of pantyhose to keep the fan working

BLOWER COMPARTMENT PROBLEMS

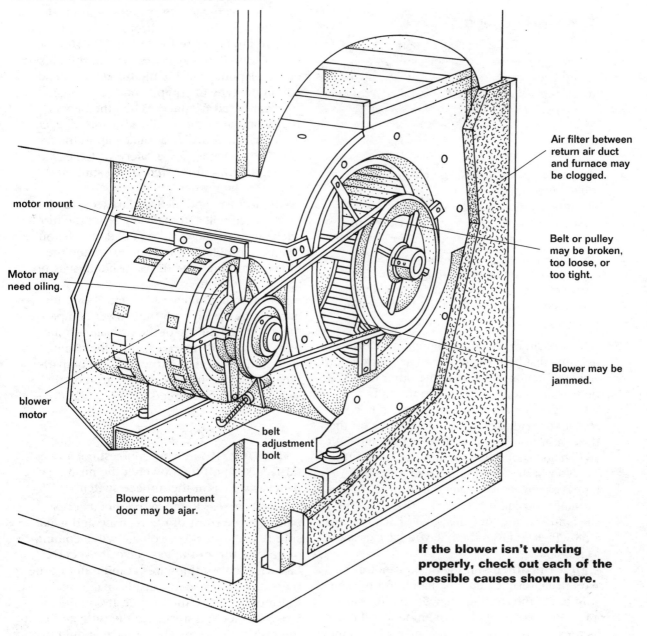

motor mount

Motor may need oiling.

blower motor

belt adjustment bolt

Blower compartment door may be ajar.

Air filter between return air duct and furnace may be clogged.

Belt or pulley may be broken, too loose, or too tight.

Blower may be jammed.

If the blower isn't working properly, check out each of the possible causes shown here.

until you can buy a replacement belt. Any vendor of plumbing and heating supplies should have a new belt in stock. For nighttime or weekend emergencies, you might be able to find one in a well-stocked gas station. Once you have the new belt, loosen the adjustment bolt(s) on the motor mount (as described below) and install the belt.

● *Belt too loose or too tight:* If the belt is too loose, it won't drive the blower. To tighten the belt, locate the belt adjustment bolt(s) on the motor, loosen the locknuts, and adjust the bolt(s) or mount to increase the tension on the belt. When the belt is

tightened to the point where there's only about 1 inch of slack when pushed, tighten the locknuts.

If the belt is too tight, it may have overloaded the motor and caused it to cut out or blow a fuse. To loosen the belt, follow the procedure described above, adjusting the bolt(s) or motor mount until the belt has about 1 inch of slack.

If the belt has jumped off the pulleys, wrap it back around the small pulley on the motor first, then around the larger blower pulley. Rotate the blower pulley as you gently pressure the belt into the groove, until it slips into place. Adjust the tension as described above.

When you restore power at the service panel and switch the system back on, the blower motor will automatically reset itself.

● *Loose pulley:* If one of the pulleys has come loose on its shaft, retighten it. The setscrew on the motor pulley typically takes an allen or hex wrench; the blower pulley may be set with a simple bolt.

If the pulleys are out of alignment, loosen the nuts that hold the motor to its bracket and slide the motor one way or the other until the pulleys are lined up. Retighten the nuts.

Clogged air filter: An air filter can become so choked with dirt that it finally shuts off the flow of heat. It may even trigger the high-limit switch and shut down the furnace. If you find the filter in that condition, wash it (some types) or replace it. To get the furnace up and running, you can just remove the filter, reset the controls, and turn the power back on. Get a new filter or clean the one you have as soon as possible.

Motor problems: If the blower motor won't run, turn it a little by hand. If it doesn't spin easily, the bearings may be dry. By putting a few drops of light oil in the motor's oil ports, as prescribed in your owner's manual, you may be able to free the bearings.

Direct-drive motors (no belt) may or may not have oil ports. (Some are permanently sealed and lubricated.) If your blower has a direct-drive motor with oil ports, you may have to disassemble the blower housing to reach the motor's inner port.

Giving a stalled motor a couple of turns by hand also serves to move it off a "dead spot," which can prevent it from starting.

If the blower motor does subsequently start when you restore power, set the system controls so that the blower runs continuously, thereby avoiding further problems. On systems that have air conditioning, this is done simply by switching the thermostat fan setting from *AUTOMATIC* to *ON.* On systems without air conditioning, the fan control switch at the furnace has to be set to the *ON* or *SUMMER* position. The switch may be located on the outside of the plenum or inside the furnace, depending on the type of equipment.

Overheated furnace: When the blower isn't working or the air filter is badly clogged, as described above, heat builds up in the furnace. If it gets too hot, a safety switch called the *high-limit cutout switch* will shut off power to the burner.

On most gas- and oil-fired furnaces, the high-limit switch will automatically refire the furnace once it's had time to cool down. If you've fixed the problem (for example, gotten the blower working), the furnace should start up and work just fine.

However, if you have a "counterflow" furnace—that is, one with the blower compartment situated on top of the furnace—you'll have to manually reset a second high-limit switch that's located in the blower compartment above the furnace. The button on the switch should be marked *RESET.*

GAS FURNACES

CAUTION: Before you troubleshoot a gas furnace, turn off the power at the main service panel as well as at the furnace switch.

Loose wires: Remove the metal access panel on the front of the furnace and make sure that the two low-voltage wires coming out of the top of the gas valve are secure. Likewise, check the wires coming out of the transformer. These four leads enable the thermostat to fire the burner. If you find a loose connection, resecure the wire and turn the power back on. The furnace should fire normally.

Pilot light out: If the pilot light has gone out, consult your owner's manual or read the instruction label mounted on the controls. If you have neither a manual nor a label to work from, take a look at *Relighting the Pilot* on the opposite page and follow these steps.

1. Turn off power to the furnace (or boiler).

2. Turn the manual control knob (usually red) to *OFF.*

3. Let the furnace (or boiler) sit for five minutes. In the meantime, get a fireplace match or a gas grill lighter ready, or tape an ordinary wooden match to the end of a stiff wire

RELIGHTING THE PILOT

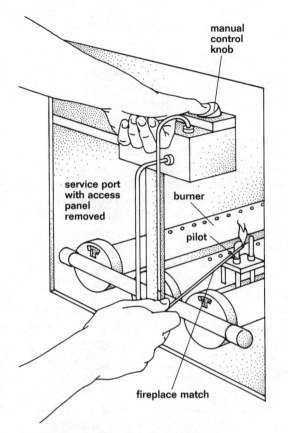

manual control knob

service port with access panel removed

burner

pilot

fireplace match

A sudden draft or a disruption in the gas flow can quickly snuff out a pilot light, but you should be able to relight it quickly by following the directions starting on the opposite page.

that's long enough to reach the pilot. If you smell gas (or propane) after five minutes, don't attempt to relight the pilot. Call a service technician or your gas supplier immediately.

4. Turn the manual control knob to *PILOT* and press it down. You should hear gas hissing out of the pilot.

5. Using the match or grill lighter, light the pilot. Continue to hold the knob down for about a minute, then release it.

6. If the pilot stays lit, turn the knob to *ON.* Restore power, and the burner should fire.

Pilot won't stay lit: If the pilot won't stay lit or has a dirty, lazy flame (white and wavy), turn the system back off as described above. Find a length of ¼-inch plastic or rubber tubing and a screwdriver. Direct one end of the tubing across the pilot orifice (tip) and blow on

the other. Tap the pilot *gently* with the screwdriver to dislodge any grit or gunk that's jammed in the orifice, then blow on it again. Repeat the pilot lighting sequence outlined on the opposite page.

If the pilot still won't light, the odds are that the thermocouple has failed, requiring a new part and professional service.

Electronic ignition problems: Many modern gas furnaces (and boilers) have an electronic ignition instead of a pilot. Some of these come with a safety device called a *lock-out module,* which shuts off power to the burners if combustion isn't established within a few seconds after the fuel valve opens. Occasionally, a module may cut power for no reason, which is known in the trade as a nuisance lockout. If this happens, you can reset the ignition simply by turning the power off for a few seconds and then back on.

Of course, even if you get the furnace (or boiler) started this way, it doesn't necessarily mean you've solved the problem. A service call may still be advisable.

CAUTION: If your furnace (or boiler) has an electronic ignition, do not try to light it with a match or gas grill lighter. In addition to the danger from high voltage, the flame could flash back at you.

Blocked vent: Some state-of-the-art furnaces and boilers are equipped with a special duct that brings combustion air into the unit from outdoors (rather than drawing air from the surrounding room). These so-called *direct-vent heaters* are designed to shut themselves down if anything blocks the flow of incoming combustion air or outflowing exhaust.

Before you call for service, go outside and check the intake and exhaust vents. (They typically run sideways through a wall, although the exhaust vent may tie into a chimney or go up through the roof.) If either the intake or exhaust vent is clogged with ice or snow, leaves, or other debris, clean it out and restart your furnace.

Other problems: Numerous other problems, including a failed high-limit switch, burned-out transformer, and bad gas valve can cause a no-heat emergency. These require replacement parts and professional service.

OIL FURNACES

Modern oil furnaces have a photocell on the primary control that "looks" into the combustion chamber. If there's no flame established within 15 to 45 seconds, the safety function automatically shuts the furnace down. This is to keep unburned oil from flooding the combustion chamber. When the primary control shuts the system down, the reset button on top of the burner kicks out. (See *Oil Furnace Ignition Problems* on this page.)

The primary control on older furnaces (pre-1970) is linked to a stack sensor on the flue rather than a photocell. The sensor's heat-sensitive probe extends from the relay box into the vent pipe. If the probe doesn't heat up in the proper amount of time, confirming that combustion is taking place, the stack sensor turns off the fuel pump and igniters. On this type of primary control, the reset button is located on the front of the stack sensor.

Ignition problems: Locate the fuel supply line that runs into the furnace (or boiler) and give it a gentle tap or two with the screwdriver. If dirty electrodes are the problem, you may succeed in knocking enough gunk off them to get the burner started. After you've tapped on the line, push the reset button that's on top of the primary control or on the front of the stack sensor.

If the burner just hums, turn off the power and look for a second reset button (usually red) on the end or side of the pump motor. Manually, give the motor shaft a quarter turn (to move it off a possible dead spot), then push the reset button and turn the power back on. If the motor still doesn't turn and trips the reset button, don't try to reset it a second time, as it probably has an internal short, which carries some risk of an electrical fire.

CAUTION: Keep your face away from the the inspection door while you're working. Oil furnaces and boilers sometimes experience a very loud and hot ignition, called a *puffback*.

If the furnace doesn't light, try pushing the primary control reset button one last time.

If it still doesn't light, the best course is to wait for professional service. Resetting the primary control more than twice runs the risk of filling the combustion chamber with oil.

Blocked vent: See entry under "Gas Furnaces" on page 133.

Other problems: Various other problems, such as a failed fuel pump motor, broken coupling, and burned out transformer, can result in a no-heat emergency. These, however, require replacement parts and professional service.

OIL FURNACE IGNITION PROBLEMS

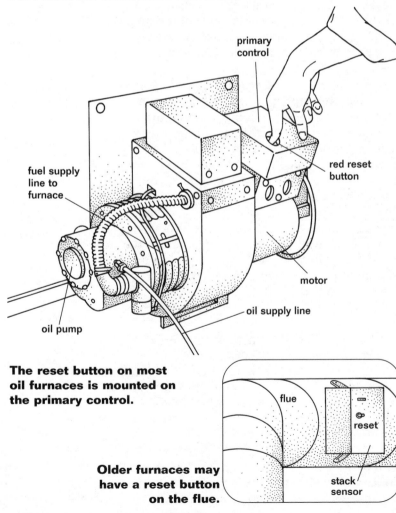

primary control

red reset button

fuel supply line to furnace

motor

oil supply line

oil pump

The reset button on most oil furnaces is mounted on the primary control.

flue

reset

Older furnaces may have a reset button on the flue.

stack sensor

TROUBLESHOOTING HOT-WATER HEATING SYSTEMS

Hot-water heating systems rely on a central boiler to produce heat. (See *Components of a Hot-Water Heating System* on the opposite page.) While most residential boilers are gas- or oil-fired, some use propane, wood, electricity, or coal as fuel. Hot water produced in the boiler is pumped through distribution pipes to the radiators, which release their heat to the rooms. The heating cycle is completed when the water has given up its heat in the radiators and returns to the boiler.

PROBLEMS COMMON TO BOTH GAS- AND OIL-FIRED BOILERS

Troubleshooting a hot-water system begins with the four checkpoints under "Addressing Universal Problems" on page 127. If none of these elements are to blame for your lack of heat, consider the following possibilities, which are specific to hot-water heating systems.

Aquastat set too low: Apart from the thermostat, hot-water heating systems have a second control device, called an *aquastat,* which tells the boiler, within an adjustable range, how hot to heat the water. If the aquastat is set too low, you might not get much heat.

To check the setting, simply locate the aquastat—a small, box-shaped control on or near the boiler—and open the door. Inside, you'll find the adjustable temperature dials that dictate the boiler's operating range. During cold weather, a reasonable setting might be 180° to 200°F for the high limit and 140° to 160°F for the low limit, assuming the boiler is also producing domestic hot water. If hot water is produced by a separate water heater, the low-limit dial (if there is one) may be set as low as 110°F.

Frozen pipes: Heating pipes are less likely to freeze than water pipes because the water (usually warm) is constantly circulating. Still, it can and does happen.

A frozen heating pipe will typically leave you with heat in some radiator zones and no heat in others. As with water pipes, heating pipes are most likely to freeze where they pass through a crawl space or poorly insulated wall. To locate the point of the freeze and thaw out the pipe, first shut the system down and open up all the valves, including all radiator valves. Then refer to "Thawing Frozen Pipes" on page 58.

Blocked vent (direct-vent boilers only): See entry under "Gas Furnaces" on page 133.

Aquastat shuts the boiler down: The aquastat contains a high-limit control switch, a safety device that senses the boiler's water temperature and shuts the system down if it gets too hot.

This might occur, for example, if the circulator pump, which pumps water through the pipes, quits.

Circulator pump seizes: To check this, turn off the power to the system and examine the circulator pump. If the coupling between the motor and circulator pump is broken or if you have a water-lubricated circulator (no coupling), there's nothing you can do but call for service.

But if the coupling is sound, it could be that the circulator's bearings are dry. Try turning the shaft by hand. If it's stuck, soak it with

COMPONENTS OF A HOT-WATER HEATING SYSTEM

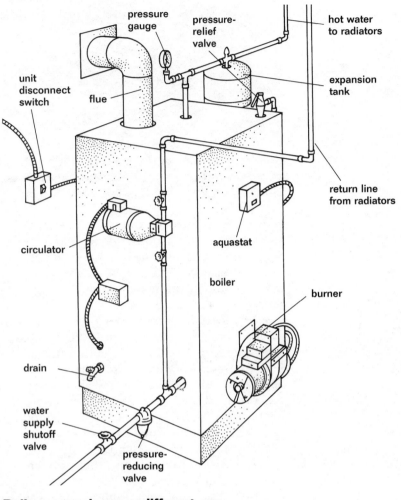

Boilers come in many different configurations, but all of the above components will be included.

motor oil and try turning it again. If you succeed in loosening it up, apply more oil, until it's turning freely. Then restart the system.

You'll need to keep a close eye on the circulator pump until it can be professionally serviced. With a little oil, you may be able to nurse it along for a while.

Other problems: Various other problems, such as a failed pump motor, broken coupling, and burned-out transformer, can result in a no-heat emergency. These, however, require replacement parts and professional service.

GAS-FIRED BOILERS

Some gas-fired boilers have standing pilot lights that ignite the natural gas (or propane) as it comes out of the burner ports. If the

Phone Help

If you've put in a call for service, but it's going to be hours or even days before someone can come, ask the service company if they're willing to give you some simple diagnostic help over the phone. ●

boiler's not firing, and you've already worked your way through the troubleshooting points above, it's a good bet that you have an ignition problem.

Pilot light out: With the heating system turned off, open the burner door and check the pilot light. If it's gone out, see pilot light entries on pages 132 and 133.

Electronic ignition problems: See the entry on page 133.

Safety switch shuts boiler down: Atmospheric gas boilers—that is, boilers that draw their combustion air from the surrounding room—have a safety switch that will sense any backdrafting in the flue and shut the system down. Though it's possible to reset or override the "spill" switch, it's not a safe practice. A backdrafting flue can be deadly. (See "Backdrafting Flue" on page 122.)

Other problems: Various other problems, such as a faulty gas valve, failed thermocouple, or bad aquastat, can result in a no-heat emergency. These require professional service.

OIL-FIRED BOILERS

For safety's sake, oil-fired boilers are equipped with either a photocell (newer models) or a stack sensor (older models) that will shut the system down if the oil spraying into the combustion chamber isn't ignited within a certain time. (These safety switches are described in detail in "Oil Furnaces," starting on page 133.)

Safety switch shut-off: If the safety switch has shut the unit down, try resetting it. Details on how to do this are found under **Ignition problems** on page 134.

CAUTION: Do not reset the burner more than twice; otherwise, you may flood the combustion chamber with uncombusted fuel oil. The same twice-only rule applies to the

Buying a New Furnace or Boiler

It just figures that an unreliable furnace or boiler will fail in the coldest part of winter when it's under the most strain. Not only can this leave your family in the cold but it can also leave your pipes vulnerable to freezing. If your furnace or boiler is more than 15 years old and suffers frequent breakdowns, it's probably time to think about buying a new one.

Evaluating New Equipment

One of the best ways to evaluate new heating equipment is by its efficiency—that is, how much usable energy the furnace or boiler delivers from each unit of fuel it burns. This is described by its Annual Fuel Utilization Efficiency (AFUE), which is printed right on the model's label. (AFUEs are derived from performance tests conducted under the auspices of the U.S. Department of Energy.)

The AFUEs on new furnaces range from 78 percent efficiency on the low end all the way up to the high 90s. New boilers have AFUEs running from 80 on the low end to about 90 percent on the high end.

NOTE: The efficiency of heat pumps is rated on a different performance scale, which is described in "Buying a New Air Conditioning System" on page 144.

High-efficiency furnaces and boilers are equipped with a secondary heat exchanger that extracts additional heat from the hot combustion gas before it's allowed to escape out the flue. In fact, the hot gas cools to the point where water vapor condenses out of it—hence the name, *condensing* furnace or boiler. Such systems are fitted with a drain to remove the slightly acidic condensation.

Because the flue gas temperature on condensing furnaces and boilers is so low—around 100°F—you may be able to use an inexpensive plastic flue pipe instead of a metal flue or metal-lined masonry chimney.

Check with your dealer and local building-code officials to see what's permitted.

Generally speaking, if you have severe winters and relatively high fuel prices, a high-efficiency furnace or boiler is a good investment and will pay for itself in a few short years. Conversely, such equipment may not be worth the extra money if you have mild winters and low fuel costs.

Becoming an Educated Consumer

Here are some other timely tips to consider before you buy new heating equipment.

● Make sure the heating contractor does a thorough heat loss calculation on your house and that the furnace or boiler you select is sized to meet your load—not exceed it. (If the contractor says he wants to size the new unit off the old unit's BTU rating without doing a heat loss calculation, you'd probably be wise to find another contractor.)

● Never install a new furnace or boiler without having a reputable contractor inspect your existing flue. Modifications may be needed to make it safe for the new equipment. An inadequate flue could be a fire hazard, and a crack or leaking flue could pose a serious health threat. (See "Backdrafting Flue" on page 122.)

● Consider buying a furnace or boiler that draws its combustion air from outdoors. Such models tend to be safer, more economical, and longer lived.

● Be aware that installing a new furnace or boiler can affect the performance of water heaters, fireplaces, and other combustion appliances in your home. Ask your heating contractor to evaluate your home's overall ventilation needs before you make any final decision about your new furnace or boiler. Improper ventilation can also pose a serious health threat. (See "Backdrafting Flue" on page 122.)

● If you're shopping for a new furnace, consider a system with a variable-speed blower. Constant-speed blowers often bang or clatter when engaged. A variable-speed motor enables the fan to come on slowly and quietly and adjust its speed according to the demand.

● Another worthwhile feature on a new furnace is a built-in humidifier, which will alleviate throat and nasal irritations, static electricity, peeling paint, and other problems associated with dry winter air. A saturated pad or steam-type humidifier (with no reservoir) is recommended.

● If possible, design the new installation so that it meets both your space heating and water heating needs with one efficient heater.

On hot-water heating systems, this is done by installing a pumped, hot-water loop that proceeds out of the boiler, through a heat exchanger inside a superinsulated water storage tank, and back again to the boiler.

An integrated or "combo" system is also possible, though less commonly done, on forced-air heating systems. In this case, a high-capacity water heater is the source of heat. When there's a call for heat, hot water is pumped out of the water heater, through a serpentine coil inside the plenum, and back again to the water heater. Air blowing across the coil is heated and routed into the house through conventional air ducts and registers.

● Check to see if your local gas or electric utility is offering any kind of rebates for installing a high-efficiency heating system in your home.

● Last but not least, make sure that you hire an experienced and reputable contractor, preferably one who has a full 24-hour service division. He should be ready, willing, and able to stand behind the equipment's warranty, which should cover at least 1 year on parts and 20 years or more on the heat exchanger.

reset button on the fuel pump motor because there's a risk of an electrical fire.

Other problems: Various other problems, such as dirty electrodes, a dead pump motor, or a failed aquastat, can result in a no-heat emergency. These require professional service.

TROUBLESHOOTING HEAT PUMPS

Because heat pumps are almost always paired with backup electric heating, the chances of having a no-heat emergency are slim. It could happen, however, if there were a power outage, since both the heat pump and the backup heating depend on electricity, or if the thermostat failed in a way that shut everything down.

Thermostat breakdowns: Unlike ordinary furnace thermostats, heat-pump thermostats work in two stages. The first stage turns on the compressor, which starts the refrigerant cycle and brings heat into the house via the heat pump's indoor coil.

The thermostat's second stage is set a couple degrees below the first, so that if the heat pump can't produce enough heat and the indoor temperature drops, the backup electric heat is turned on. The backup electric coils are situated in the plenum or adjoining ductwork, downstream from the heat pump coils.

If you're in a low-heat or no-heat situation, set the thermostat way up so that you're sure it's calling for heat. This will activate both the heat pump and the electric backup.

Tripped breakers or blown fuses: After checking the thermostat, check the breaker or fuse, as shown in *How Heat Pumps Are Fused* on this page. The heat pump's electric circuit is

HOW HEAT PUMPS ARE FUSED

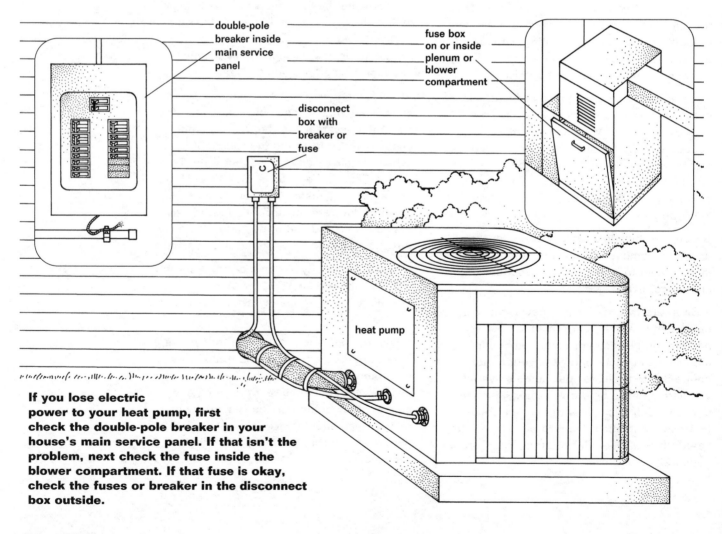

double-pole breaker inside main service panel

fuse box on or inside plenum or blower compartment

disconnect box with breaker or fuse

heat pump

If you lose electric power to your heat pump, first check the double-pole breaker in your house's main service panel. If that isn't the problem, next check the fuse inside the blower compartment. If that fuse is okay, check the fuses or breaker in the disconnect box outside.

New Brains for an Old Body

Before you plunk down several thousand dollars for a new furnace or boiler, consider the possibility that the system's brain—that is, the thermostat—could be the source of your heating woes.

For less than $200, you can buy a state-of-the-art programmable thermostat that will automatically raise or lower the indoor temperature to fit your schedule. Without making any sacrifices in comfort, you'll enjoy a 10 to 30 percent savings on your annual heating bill—simply because you're not heating the house when you're not home.

Be advised, however, that some programmable thermostats are so hard to program that not even a *child* can do it. So try a few different models at the dealer's showroom—if you can—or make sure you can return the thermostat if it ends up frustrating you.

Some other worthwhile features to look for in a programmable thermostat include: easy changeover from heating to cooling mode, low-battery indicator, and manual override that lets you override the current temperature set point without reprogramming the thermostat.

typically protected by a 240-volt double-pole circuit breaker or a cartridge fuse located inside the main service panel. (See "No Electricity" on page 128.)

However, even if the breaker or fuse in the main panel is OK, you could have fuse problems further down the line. Heat pumps are different from other heating systems in that they have additional fuses mounted on or inside the plenum or blower compartment (to protect the electric resistance heater) and in a unit disconnect box outside the house (to protect the compressor).

If the breaker or fuses in the main service panel aren't the problem, turn the power *off* by throwing the breaker or removing the fuses. Proceed to the blower compartment and locate the secondary fuses. If they're not found on the side of the plenum or blower compartment, remove the front service panel(s). Then remove the control box cover and locate the cartridge fuses inside. Use a fuse puller to remove the fuses to test or replace them. (See "Replacing a Fuse" on page 106.)

Put the control box cover and panel back on, then restore power to the system. If the fuse blows again, call for professional service.

If the fuses inside the plenum control box aren't the problem, go outside and locate the heat pump's unit disconnect switch. It's typically inside a metal box mounted on the house close to the heat pump's outdoor unit.

Shut off the power at the main service panel, then open the box. Inside, you'll find the circuit breaker or cartridge fuses that protect the heat pump's compressor. (On some boxes, you may have to unscrew a cover plate to access the fuses.)

Reset the circuit breaker or replace the fuses, if necessary. If they trip or blow again once you restore power, leave the system off and call for professional service.

NOTE: On a few heat pump models, the controls and unit disconnect switch are located *inside* the house.

Auxiliary heat on, but heat pump won't run: Your thermostat may have an indicator light that signals when the heat pump isn't running but the backup heat is on. Even if it doesn't, you may notice that the fan on the outdoor unit isn't running, that there's no noise coming from the compressor, or that the heat pump isn't going through its usual defrost cycle, which should produce some noise and steam from the outdoor unit every 30 to 40 minutes in cold weather.

There are a few simple things you can try to get the heat pump going again, which will keep your electric bill from skyrocketing and might even forestall a service call.

Spike in electricity trips the compressor: The heat pump's outdoor unit has a lockout module that protects the compressor from too much current. It may, on occasion, shut the unit down due to a temporary flux in current or some other anomaly.

To automatically reset the compressor, simply turn the thermostat off.

While it's resetting, walk outside and check to make sure that the fan blade on the outdoor unit isn't jammed with ice or other foreign matter. If it is, slip a ⅜-inch dowel through the grill and *gently* knock the obstruction off the fan blades.

CAUTION: Take care not to damage the fan or any of the delicate tubing around it.

Finally, give the fan a little nudge with your dowel, enough to move it an inch or so, in case the motor is stalled on a dead spot.

Now go back inside and turn the thermostat back on. If an overload was the problem, the compressor will have automatically reset itself and the system should start.

Stuck reversing valve: During cold weather, the heat pump is designed to reverse its function every 30 to 40 minutes to melt the ice off the outdoors coils. This defrost cycle, which lasts about 10 minutes, in effect switches the heat pump into its air-conditioning mode, expelling heat through the outdoor coil.

If the system's reversing valve sticks, the heat pump can't defrost itself and will eventually shut down.

To remedy this, try reversing the heat pump manually by switching the thermostat mode to *COOL* or *AC*. Leave it that way for 30 minutes, then reset the thermostat mode to *HEAT*. If that doesn't work, switch the thermostat to *EMERGENCY HEAT* and call for professional help.

Other problems: Other problems, such as a failed compressor and low refrigerant, can cause a no-heat emergency. These repairs are a bit advanced for a do-it-yourselfer and require professional parts and service.

No Cooling

CLEANING THE CONDENSER

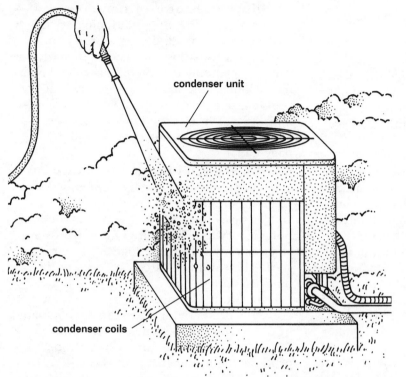

condenser unit

condenser coils

Dust, grass clippings, and airborne seeds can clog a central air conditioner condenser. To clean the condenser, spray the coils with a garden hose held at about a 15-degree angle.

Quick Response

1. Check thermostat to make sure that it's on *AC* or *COOLING* mode, and lower set point.

2. Use alternative cooling methods prescribed in "Cool as a Cucumber— Naturally" on page 145.

4

HEATING & COOLING EMERGENCIES

KEEPING YOUR COOL

For some reason, air conditioners and heat pumps always seem to fail right when they're needed most—that is, in the middle of a scorching heat wave, when service people are as scarce as hen's teeth.

With that in mind, some simple measures follow that may help you get the system up and running. The checkpoints are presented in logical sequence—if one fails, move on to the next.

Remember that even if you succeed in getting the system to work, the fact that you had trouble in the first place may signal the need for professional service.

Hazard

Make sure the electricity is off, the floor is dry, and that you're safely dressed before attempting repairs. (See "Electrical Safety Tips" on 102.)

TROUBLESHOOTING A CENTRAL AIR CONDITIONER

When it comes to efficiency, central air conditioners win hands down over window air conditioners. But, when a central air conditioning system fails, it means your whole house is affected.

THERMOSTAT PROBLEMS

Start by making sure that the thermostat is mounted level and equipped with good batteries. These points are discussed in more detail in "No Heat" on page 126.

Next, be sure that the thermostat mode switch is on *AC* or *COOLING*. Lower the temperature setting to 60°F (or cooler) to make sure that the controls are calling for air conditioning. Give the system about ten minutes to respond, since it may have a built-in delay circuit. If the system doesn't respond after ten minutes, turn the thermostat off, wait a couple minutes, and turn it back on again.

NOTE: Dirty switch contacts and ambient factors, which are discussed in "No Heat" on page 126, are unlikely to affect an air conditioning thermostat.

ON/OFF SWITCH

If your air-conditioning system is teamed up with a furnace or boiler, be sure to check the on/off switch that runs the heating side of the system. If it's accidentally turned off, it may shut the air conditioner down as well. (See "Checking the On/Off Switch" on page 130.)

BY-PASS DAMPERS

Some air-conditioning systems have a by-pass damper inside the plenum that needs to be seasonally adjusted for heating or cooling. If the damper is left open—that is, in the heating position—it will reduce the flow of cool air to the registers and may cause the coils to ice up.

If you have this type of system, open the plenum and double-check the by-pass damper to make sure it's closed.

A second type of damper, which routes conditioned air through or around an in-duct humidifier, can also affect cooling performance. If you have an in-duct humidifier, make sure that it's set on *SUMMER* mode so that cool air is ducted around rather than through it.

NO ELECTRICITY

Electrical problems come in several forms that can affect your central air conditioner in different ways.

Utility outage or brownout: During a power outage, the air-conditioning system won't respond at all; during a brownout (a low-voltage situation), it may try to start, but it may repeatedly trip the breaker or blow a fuse. Contact the utility to see how long the problem might last and make plans accordingly. (See "No Electric Power" on page 109 and "Spikes, Brownouts, and Blips" on page 111.)

Tripped circuit breaker or blown fuse: Your air-conditioning system probably has three different sets of circuit breakers and/or fuses to protect its wiring and components. Two of these are in the main service panel, which is the logical place to start. The third is located outdoors in the unit disconnect box.

Typically, the compressor (located outdoors) is protected in the main service panel by a 240-volt double-pole breaker or a cartridge fuse. A second circuit breaker or fuse protects the motor that runs the indoor blower. (This second breaker or fuse could be wired at either 120 volts as a single breaker or ordinary fuse or 240 volts as a double breaker or cartridge fuse.)

Don't reset the breakers or replace the fuses in the main service panel until you've checked the compressor circuit in the outdoor unit.

Tripped compressor circuit: If the breaker or fuse protecting the compressor has tripped or blown, walk outside and inspect the outdoor unit. Make sure there are no sticks or other foreign matter jamming the compressor fan. If so, remove any you see.

Dandelions and cottonwood trees, with their prolific airborne seeds, are notorious for clogging the outdoor coils, which can raise the system's pressure enough to blow a fuse. To clean fuzz, dirt, or other foreign matter out of the condenser, spray it from the top with a garden hose, held at about a 15-degree vertical angle, as shown in *Cleaning the Condenser* on page 141. (Do not spray water into the condenser straight on, as this will only force the gunk further back into the condenser.)

Once you've cleaned away any foreign matter, reset the breaker or replace the fuse (with an exact duplicate) and restart the system. (See "Circuit Breaker Trips or Fuse Blows" on page 100.) If the breaker or fuse goes a second time, leave the system off until you can get professional service.

Tripped or blown blower circuit: If you find that the breaker or fuse protecting the blower motor has tripped or blown, open up the blower compartment and inspect the motor-blower assembly. See the detailed troubleshooting checklist under "Troubleshooting Forced-Air Heating Systems" on page 130.

After you've corrected any problems inside the blower compartment, reset the breaker or replace the fuse with an exact duplicate. (See "Circuit Breaker Trips or Fuse Blows" on page 100.) If it trips or blows a second time, leave it off until a pro can check it out.

Tripped or blown outdoor disconnect switch: If there's no problem with the breakers or fuses in the main service panel, check the outdoor disconnect box. It's typically a metal box mounted against the side of the house in proximity to the air conditioner's compressor unit.

With the power turned off at the main service panel, open the box. Inside, you'll find the circuit breaker or cartridge fuses that protect the compressor. (On some boxes, you may have to unscrew a cover plate to access the fuses.)

Reset the circuit breaker or replace these fuses, if necessary. (See "Circuit Breaker

Trips or Fuse Blows" on page 100.) If they trip or blow again once you restore power, leave the system off and call for professional service.

NOTE: On some air conditioning systems, the unit disconnect switch is located *inside* the house.

BLOWER COMPARTMENT PROBLEMS

The blower assembly and air filter on air conditioning systems are quite similar to those used on forced-air heating systems. You'll find troubleshooting details under "Problems Common to Both Gas and Oil Furnaces" on page 130.

SYSTEM ICED UP

When ice forms anywhere in the system, it's a sure sign of trouble. Anything that slows or restricts the flow of air over the evaporator (the inside coil) can cause icing. This could be due to a dirty air filter or to some sort of obstruction (for example, a rug or piece of furniture) blocking the return air grille. Icing will also occur if the refrigerant level in the system is too low.

Ice typically forms in the evaporator first but may be visible on the sheet metal around the plenum or on the insulated copper tubing that conducts the refrigerant back and forth between the outdoor and indoor coils.

If ice is apparent, turn the thermostat off but set the fan switch to *ON*. This will help melt the ice off the evaporator by circulating warm air through it.

Leave the system shut down, with the blower running, for four hours. Be forewarned that the melting ice may be more than the condensate drain can handle, so be prepared to sponge or mop up the overflow.

While the system is off, check to make sure the air filter is clean. (See **Clogged air filter**

Buying a New Air Conditioning System

Even if the service technician just pronounced last rites over your old air conditioner, there's no cause for panic (though a little mourning might be in order).

Since the last thing you want to do is rush out in a sweat and buy a very expensive mistake, this is a good time for clear thoughts and solid calculations.

If the problem was diagnosed as a dead compressor, yet your system is relatively new—say, seven years old or less—consider replacing the compressor only, since there's probably quite a bit of life left in the other components.

On an older system, by contrast, it might be smarter to junk the whole thing and install a new system. This judgment call between repairing the old and buying new is a delicate one, with many shades of gray. That's why it pays to have an experienced and trustworthy technician in your corner.

Be a Savvy Consumer

If you do decide to install a new system, here are some additional tips:

● The hotter your climate, the more it pays to have high-efficiency equipment. Central air conditioners and heat pumps are tested and given a Seasonal Energy Efficiency Rating (SEER) to indicate their cooling efficiency. SEERs range from 10 on the low end to about 17 on the high end.

Because heat pumps reverse their function to provide wintertime heating, they're assigned a second rating—Heating Season Performance Factor (HSPF)—to reflect their heating efficiency. HSPFs range from 6.8 up to 10, depending on the heat pump's make and capacity.

The colder your climate, the more emphasis you should put on buying a heat pump with a high HSPF rating.

● Make sure the contractor does a heat-gain calculation on your house to find out how many BTUs per hour your new air conditioning equipment needs to provide. Guesswork won't do! Bigger is *not* always better. An oversize air conditioner delivers less comfort at higher costs and will probably die young.

● Don't try to save a few bucks by keeping the old indoor coil. Replace it along with the rest of the system so that the indoor and outdoor coils are precisely matched.

● Ask your contractor how a new air conditioning system might provide your home with better ventilation and/or cleaner air. Also give careful thought to what kind of thermostat you want and whether or not zoning would be a worthwhile benefit. Zoning can provide more comfort for less money because it delivers cool air only to the rooms that need it.

● Give thought to where the new equipment is placed, both indoors and out. It needs to be as quiet and accessible as possible.

● An air-to-air heat pump, which uses ambient air as a heat source, is probably not the wisest choice for heating in a colder climate, unless the heat pump is to be used to supplement a furnace. A ground-coupled heat pump, which uses the earth or groundwater as a heat source, *is* suitable for cold climates.

● Check with your electric company to see if there are any subsidies or rebates available for installing high-efficiency cooling equipment. Gas-fired heat pumps, which are just now coming to market, are one possibility.

● Shop for a strong warranty. Many air conditioning systems come with a one-year warranty on parts and labor. But it's worthwhile insurance to get one that has a five-year warranty (or better) on the compressor and all condenser components.

on page 132.) After four hours, restart the system in the usual way.

OTHER PROBLEMS

Various other problems can leave you without any air conditioning. These include a failed compressor or condenser, a faulty blower motor, a broken expansion valve, a dead capacitor, or a leak in one of the refrigerant lines. All of these problems require new parts and professional service.

TROUBLESHOOTING A HEAT PUMP

A heat pump operates essentially the same way that a central air conditioner does, with one very important distinction—it can reverse operation to provide wintertime heat.

All of the troubleshooting advice prescribed above applies to a heat pump as well as to a central air conditioner. However, there are small but important differences in a heat pump's thermostat and possibly in the way the system is fused. To learn more about these, read "Troubleshooting Heat Pumps" on page 138. (You can ignore the sections on auxiliary heat and a stuck reversing valve, as these pertain to the heat pump's heating cycle only.)

TROUBLESHOOTING A ROOM AIR CONDITIONER

Here's a simple troubleshooting guide for a room air conditioner. If these steps don't work, you probably have a component failure or loss of refrigerant, requiring professional service.

1. If the air conditioner is running, but cooling poorly, remove the indoor grille (some snap or slide off; others unscrew) and check the air filter, as shown in *Servicing the Filter* on page 146. If the filter is really grungy, it will block the flow of cool air and cause ice to form on the evaporator coil.

2. If the air conditioner doesn't run at all, check to make sure the unit is plugged in.

3. Carefully check the cord and plug for wear or damage. If you find a problem, leave the system unplugged until repairs are made.

4. If there's no problem with the cord or plug, turn the thermostat setting to maximum cool to make sure the control is calling for air conditioning.

5. If the system doesn't respond, try setting the controls in various positions. While a switch may have a dead contact or be shorted out in one position, it could work in another.

6. Check the main service panel to see if the circuit breaker (or fuse) protecting the air conditioner's circuit has tripped (or blown). Try resetting the breaker or replacing the fuse. If it trips or blows again, leave the

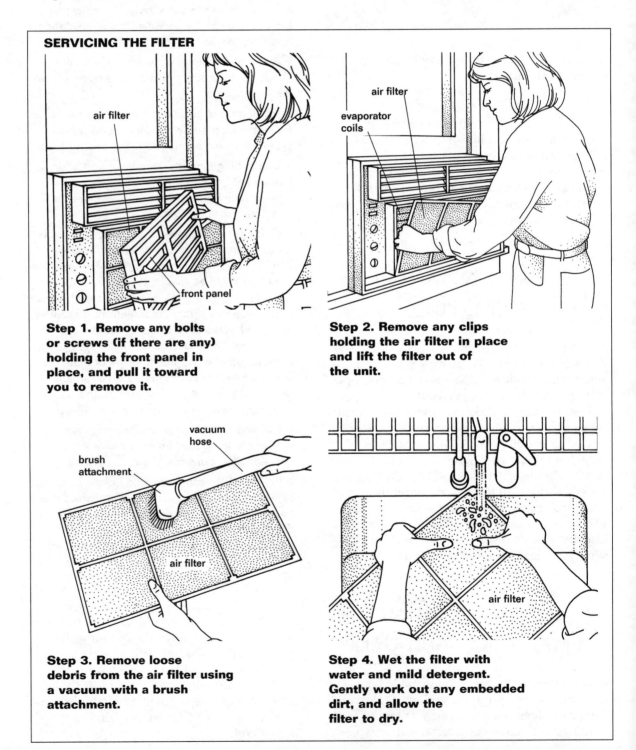

SERVICING THE FILTER

Step 1. Remove any bolts or screws (if there are any) holding the front panel in place, and pull it toward you to remove it.

Step 2. Remove any clips holding the air filter in place and lift the filter out of the unit.

Step 3. Remove loose debris from the air filter using a vacuum with a brush attachment.

Step 4. Wet the filter with water and mild detergent. Gently work out any embedded dirt, and allow the filter to dry.

power off and call for service. *NOTE:* Plugging even a small room air conditioner into an ordinary 15-amp circuit will likely overload it. Because room air conditioners pull a lot of amperage (12 amps or more for a larger capacity model), it's wise to plug them into a dedicated circuit. It may also be advisable to protect the circuit with a time-delay fuse or breaker, which enables the air conditioner to get through its power-hungry start-up cycle without tripping the breaker

or blowing the fuse. Ask an electrician for advice on these points.

If necessary, replace or wash the filter, let the air conditioner sit for a few hours (until the ice has melted off the coils), and then restart it.

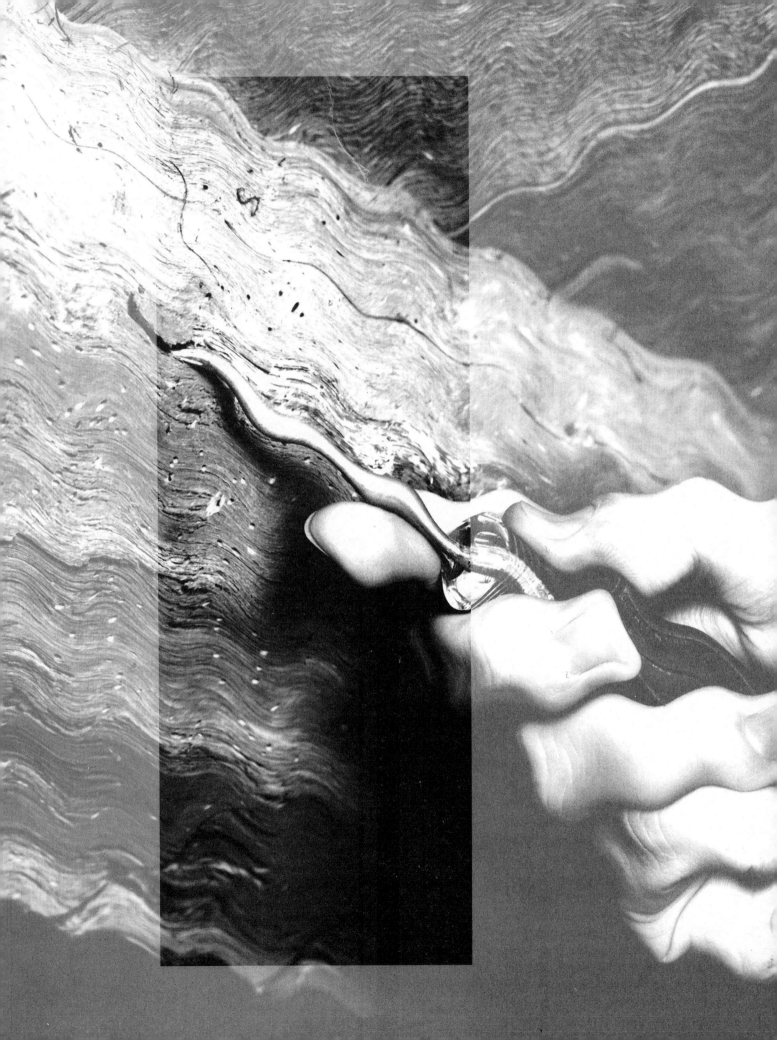

Structural Emergencies

**5
STRUCTURAL
EMERGENCIES**

Damaged Siding

Quick Response

Drape plastic sheeting over damaged area to temporarily protect it from water damage. Tuck plastic sheeting under overhanging panel or clapboard and secure with tape or furring strips and nails.

A hammer, tape measure, and nail puller are common tools for siding repair of all types. The zip tool (*upper right*) and a utility knife will help with the repairs to vinyl siding shown here.

Hazards

● Wear work gloves to avoid splinters or metal cuts.

● If the repairs require ladder work, always put safety first. (See "12 Steps to Ladder Safety" on page 35.)

● If the damage is extensive and above easy reach, rent a scaffold. Not only is scaffolding safer than working from a ladder, but it will also save you time and frustration.

TIME, TIDE, AND UNCLE HARRY

Whether it happens overnight or over many years, nature takes its toll on even the most durable siding. Fallen branches, rot, woodpeckers, and ultraviolet light are the most common sources of damage. But there are also self-inflicted wounds, such as when Uncle Harry sideswipes the house with the lawn tractor or Junior smashes a baseball into the vinyl siding.

Deciding whether to patch or replace a damaged section of siding is the key starting place. Don't waste your time and money on patchwork if the section is badly rotted or seriously damaged—go ahead and replace the whole length.

Whether you do the repairs yourself or hire a pro, the trickiest part will be getting a good cosmetic match between new materials and old. In most cases, a perfect match is unattainable, even for a pro.

REPAIRING WOOD SIDING

Vinyl and aluminum siding look good from a few feet away, but there is no substitute for the look and feel of real wood clapboards up close. So, if you've got wood siding, it's probably worth the extra effort to repair and maintain it.

REPAIRING A SPLIT

A split in a solid wood clapboard can be repaired by following the simple steps shown in *Repairing a Split Clapboard* on this page. First, insert a screwdriver or chisel into the crack to wedge it open a little. Then fill the entire length of the crack with a generous bead of waterproof exterior glue, and remove the screwdriver or chisel.

Finally, drive a few finishing nails up under the butt of the damaged clapboard, angled so they force the glued seam closed. Leave the nail heads raised so they can be easily removed once the glue has dried.

If permanent nails are needed to secure the clapboard, drill pilot holes first to keep from resplitting the board. Use galvanized finishing nails, then countersink and putty them.

PATCHING A SMALL HOLE

A small area of rotted or damaged wood siding can be effectively patched with epoxy putty. Use a stiff wire brush or chisel to remove any splintered or punk wood so that the sound wood underneath is exposed. Then brush the exposed wood with Cuprinol and let it dry.

Once the preservative has dried, use a putty knife to fill the hole with epoxy putty. The patch doesn't have to be cosmetically perfect; it can be chiseled, planed, sanded, and painted *after* the epoxy has cured.

CAUTION: Be sure to follow the manufacturer's instructions and precautions in mixing and applying epoxy. (See "Hazards" on page

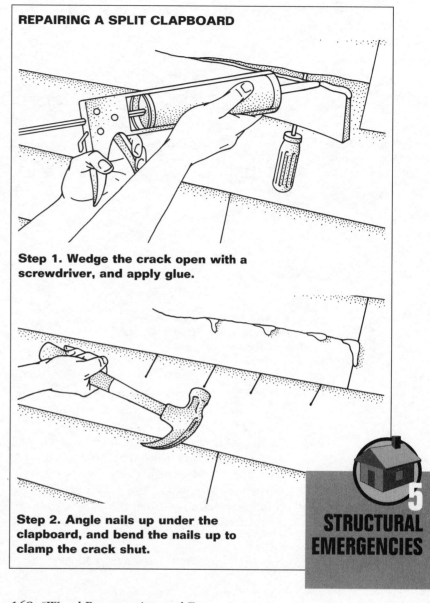

REPAIRING A SPLIT CLAPBOARD

Step 1. Wedge the crack open with a screwdriver, and apply glue.

Step 2. Angle nails up under the clapboard, and bend the nails up to clamp the crack shut.

5

STRUCTURAL EMERGENCIES

168, "Wood Preservative and Epoxy Suppliers" on page 174, and "Epoxy Repairs" on page 176.)

REPLACING A DAMAGED CLAPBOARD

A damaged section of clapboard can be replaced with some careful cutting. First, use a carpenter's square and pencil to draw a straight, vertical line on either end of the section that's to be replaced. Then, tap wooden shims up underneath the damaged board, just enough to nudge it out (wood shingles work nicely), as shown in *Shimming the Clapboard* on page 152. The shims serve a double purpose, protecting the clapboard underneath as you make your saw cuts and raising the damaged clapboard just enough so you can pull the nails out.

SHIMMING THE CLAPBOARD

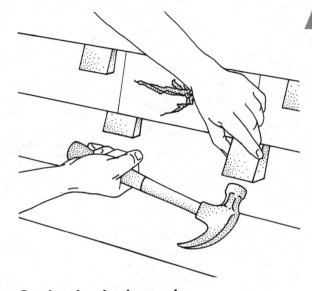

Gently raise the damaged clapboard by driving shims underneath it.

Next, cut the clapboard at either end with a backsaw, using downstrokes only, so the board above isn't damaged. Note how *Cutting Out the Damaged Section* on this page shows a shim positioned underneath the saw blade to protect the clapboard below it.

Once you've sawn through the board at either end, shim up the overhanging clapboard above the saw cuts so you can insert a hack-

CUTTING OUT THE DAMAGED SECTION

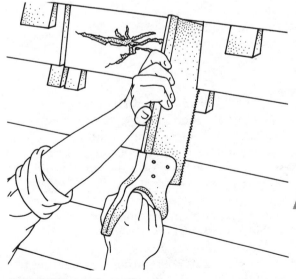

Carefully cut through the clapboard with a backsaw.

Don't Tear the Tarpaper

Try not to tear the tarpaper (or other membrane) underneath the siding. If you do, patch it with more tarpaper and roofing cement. ●

saw blade, and complete the cut, as shown in *Completing the Cut* on this page. Wrap the end of the hacksaw blade with masking tape to provide a safe grip. Or buy a special mini-handle for the job.

COMPLETING THE CUT

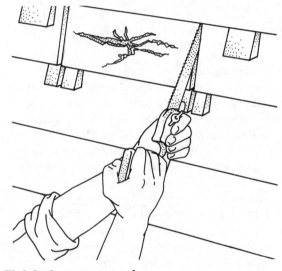

Finish the cut up under the clapboard above with a hacksaw blade.

Next, use a pry bar or hammer to remove any nails that hold the damaged section in place. Avoid digging into the undamaged siding. Use a power drill to drill the heads off difficult nails, then set the shank with a sharpened nailset. (A ⅛-inch drill bit works nicely

Weathering Wood

A new section of redwood or cedar clapboard can be "aged" to match the surrounding boards by brushing it with several coats of household bleach. Commercial products are also available to give new siding a weathered look. ●

on a #7 box nail.) If there are nails concealed up under the overhanging clapboard, use a hacksaw blade (wrapped with tape to form a handle) to cut them off.

If there's no replacement clapboard around the house, buy one at a local lumberyard or salvage yard. Cut the new section to the right length and coat it with Cuprinol (especially the end grain). Insert a piece of tarpaper or aluminum flashing behind the butt joint and then nail the clapboard into place with #7 galvanized box nails.

The abutting clapboards may also need to be nailed. Countersink the nail heads and putty the holes before you apply stain or primer. When driving a new nail into an old nail hole, angle the shaft slightly so that it can bite into new wood underneath.

REPAIRING VINYL SIDING

Vinyl siding has become extremely popular in the last decade. In fact, homeowners now choose it twice as often as any other siding product. It's easy to install and durable, and it never needs painting.

Repair work on vinyl siding is best scheduled for warm weather, when the siding is relatively pliant. The older the vinyl, the more brittle and difficult it becomes to work with, especially in cold weather.

To remove a damaged section of vinyl siding, you'll need to buy a siding replacement tool—sometimes called a *zip tool*—available for about $5 from a building supply center or siding contractor. As shown in *Using a Zip Tool* on this page, the tool slips up into the joint

USING A ZIP TOOL

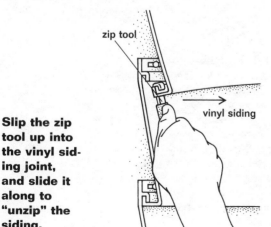

Slip the zip tool up into the vinyl siding joint, and slide it along to "unzip" the siding.

Vinyl Transplant

If you're concerned about appearances, you can move a new or repaired panel to a less visible spot (for example, under the deck), removing an undamaged panel to take its place. ●

that holds the panel in place, top and bottom, and unlocks the joint. The exposed nails are then removed with a pry bar.

When removing a panel, unlock the top joint first and pry out the nails. Then unlock the bottom joint. To install a panel, the sequence is reversed.

Once you've removed the damaged panel, you can either patch it or replace it.

PATCHING A SMALL HOLE

For small holes and cracks, a patch will work just fine, if you're not too fussy about the looks.

Just remove the panel, as described above, turn it over, and glue a piece of scrap vinyl, finished side down, over the damaged area, as shown in *Making a Vinyl Patch* on this page. Pipe fitting (PVC) cement makes a good adhesive.

MAKING A VINYL PATCH

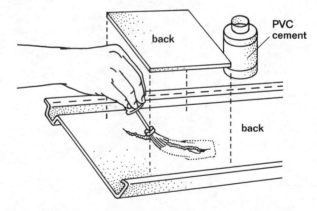

Cement the patch face down to the back of the siding.

Use aluminum ring shank nails to resecure the panel, leaving the nail heads slightly raised so the panel can expand and contract.

For more serious wounds, you're better off installing a new panel. Since vinyl siding

Repairing a Damaged Corner Post

Whether vinyl or aluminum, the outer face of the damaged corner post must be cut away so that a new corner post, modified to fit, can take its place. Follow the steps shown in *Cutting Away the Old Post, Cutting Off the Flanges, Applying the Sealant,* and *Fastening the New Post.*

CUTTING AWAY THE OLD POST

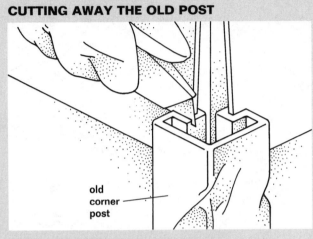

Step 1. Cut the damaged face off the old post by scoring it with a sharp utility knife, as shown above. The old nailing flanges are left in place. If you're working with aluminum, bend the metal back and forth (after scoring) until it breaks free.

CUTTING OFF THE FLANGES

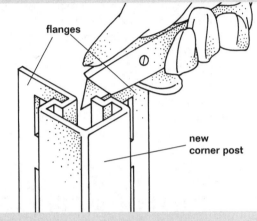

Step 2. Using the cutting techniques described in Step 1, modify the new post by cutting the nailing flanges off, as shown above.

APPLYING THE SEALANT

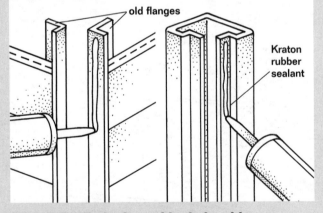

Step 3. Caulk the face of both the old and new flanges, as shown above, using Kraton rubber sealant. (Neutral cure silicon is acceptable for aluminum, but not for vinyl.)

FASTENING THE NEW POST

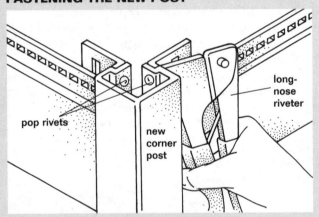

Step 4. Fit the new (modified) corner post into place over the old nailing flanges. You'll have to spread the new corner piece a bit to slip it onto the old flanges. After the new post is in place, secure it with pop rivets on both sides. Since the flange is hard to get to, you'll need an awl or a right-angle drill to make the holes (typically $\frac{1}{8}$-inch diameter) and a long-nose riveter to set the rivets, as shown above.

fades or grays in the sun over time, the color of the new vinyl section won't perfectly match the old.

Damaged corner posts are somewhat trickier to repair, as you have to make precision cuts with a utility knife on both the damaged post and the replacement post. See "Repairing a Damaged Corner Post" on the opposite page for details.

REPAIRING ALUMINUM SIDING

The siding of choice in the '70s, aluminum, has been largely supplanted by vinyl. But because of its former popularity, aluminum is still fairly common and is frequently in need of repair.

REPAIRING A DENT

Drill several, evenly spaced, $\frac{1}{8}$-inch diameter holes through the deepest part of the dent. Turn sheet metal screws into the holes, leaving the screw heads raised so that you can get a pair of pliers on them. Gently tug on the screw heads, one after the other, to gradually lift the dented metal back level with the undented aluminum.

Remove the screws and fill the holes and any remaining depressions with Liquid Steel, which is available in toothpaste-size tubes at auto supply stores. It can be sanded and painted once it dries.

REPLACING DAMAGED ALUMINUM SIDING

Using a straightedge and a sharp utility knife, score the panel horizontally, just above the damaged area, from one end to the other, as shown in Step 1 of *Replacing the Damaged Section* on this page. Bend the damaged section back and forth along the score until it breaks. Then remove and recycle the damaged section.

Cut the top lock off the new panel, end to end, by scoring and bending it, as shown in Step 2 of *Replacing the Damaged Section* on this page.

Push the new panel up into the old lock to see if it will slip into place. If not, use a putty knife to pry the lock open a bit, where necessary.

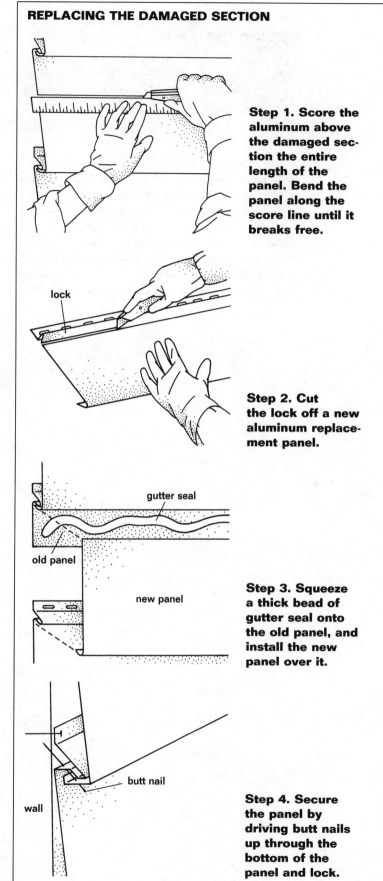

REPLACING THE DAMAGED SECTION

Step 1. Score the aluminum above the damaged section the entire length of the panel. Bend the panel along the score line until it breaks free.

lock

Step 2. Cut the lock off a new aluminum replacement panel.

gutter seal

old panel

new panel

Step 3. Squeeze a thick bead of gutter seal onto the old panel, and install the new panel over it.

butt nail

wall

Step 4. Secure the panel by driving butt nails up through the bottom of the panel and lock.

Once you're satisfied that the new panel will slide easily up into the old lock, apply a thick, even bead of gutter seal along the old panel from one end to the other. Carefully install the new panel over the gutter seal, as shown in Step 3 of *Replacing the Damaged Section*. Lock the top and bottom of the new panel into place and press it with your hand end to end so that the gutter seal bonds firmly between the old panel and the new. Further secure the panel with two headless butt nails, nailed up into the panel at an angle, as shown in Step 4 of the illustration. Tap the nails in with a punch.

REPAIRING WOOD SHAKES, BRICK, AND STUCCO

Damaged shakes can be repaired or replaced using the same techniques outlined for wood shingles in "Leaky Roof" on page 24. Repairs for damaged brick and stucco are discussed in "Cracks in Concrete, Masonry, and Stucco" on the opposite page.

Cracks in Concrete, Masonry, and Stucco

Ignoring exterior cracks invites serious trouble as wind-driven rain or groundwater will get into the crack, causing further damage and creating interior water problems.

Quick Response

1. Seal cracks in exterior walls to keep water and termites out.

2. Cracks due to earthquakes, flood erosion, or other sudden changes in soil around foundation should be checked by professional.

5

STRUCTURAL EMERGENCIES

ANALYZING WHY CRACKS HAPPEN

Cracks in poured concrete, masonry, or stucco walls are an eyesore to be sure. But they can also be a troublesome source of leaks and may signal the onset of serious structural problems.

All cracks are the result of movement in the wall (or slab), which is caused by one or more of the following conditions:

Hazards

● Protect your eyes with safety goggles when chipping away old mortar.

● The lime in wet mortar can cause serious skin burns. Wear gloves and protective clothing. Avoid skin contact.

● When using caulks, sealants, or epoxy, follow the manufacturer's precautions regarding proper ventilation, eye protection, and clothing.

● Exterior cracks in a brick or stone chimney may signal that the flue has been damaged. Have a pro inspect it to make sure there's no fire hazard.

● Repointing chimneys is dangerous and best left to a pro.

Normal drying and settling: Once a new house is finished, the concrete or masonry used in the foundation and walls continues to dry and shrink. Also, the ground underneath and around the house—though well compacted during construction—may experience some additional settling. Small hairline cracks will develop in most new houses—especially during the first year—and are usually nothing to worry about. It is only when such cracks begin to widen or shift or when new cracks develop later on, that concern is warranted.

Failed construction materials or techniques: Cracks in poured concrete walls and slabs sometimes result from inadequate preparation of the ground under and around the foundation, poorly placed or missing expansion and control joints, or careless backfilling techniques.

In masonry walls, cracks may result from defective bricks or blocks, improperly mixed mortar, or inadequate tooling of the mortar joints.

Failing to control surface water through proper site grading and rain gutters and the lack of effective waterproofing on the outside of the foundation wall can also lead to cracks and leaks.

Water pressure: Some soils swell as they become saturated with water and later shrink as they dry out. Soils rich in clay or silt are especially prone to expand and contract with changes in moisture content.

When the soil around a foundation wall becomes laden with water, the pressure may increase enough to bow or crack the wall. Likewise, wet soil expanding underneath the foundation may actually heave the footings up out of place or buckle the slab, producing serious cracks.

Uncontrolled surface water and plumbing leaks are the two most common sources of problem water around and under house foundations. Both can be prevented or controlled, as explained in "Broken Pipes" on page 56, "Leaky Basement" on page 61, and "Tool Strikes Buried Cable or Pipe" on page 259.

Frost: When frost penetrates below one or more of the footings, it can cause the soil to shift or heave erratically as it freezes, producing cracks in the foundation walls. Thus, an especially severe winter may produce cracks where none occurred before.

Drought: As the soil around and under the house dries out, it contracts, reducing the bearing surface for the foundation. Thus, a prolonged drought may cause the walls and slab to settle and crack.

Root pressure: It usually takes a sizable tree in close proximity to the foundation to exert enough root pressure to produce a crack in poured concrete. Block walls are more vulnerable, especially if the mortar joints are weak.

Vibrations: Poured concrete and masonry can crack under the heavy, constant vibrations produced by a nearby highway or railroad, subway, or heavy construction, including blasting, pile driving, and the movement of heavy equipment. The biggest crack maker of them all, of course, is an earthquake.

SIZING UP A CRACK

As mentioned above, hairline cracks are common in almost all concrete and masonry work and are usually nothing to worry about. Even larger cracks, up to about ⅛ inch wide, are apt to be structurally insignificant. (Even so, exterior cracks that are ⅛ inch wide or wider should be sealed to keep damaging water from penetrating the wall or slab. See the various techniques described in "Making Repairs" on page 160.)

In other cases, however, a crack may be a warning signal of serious structural problems. Here are some checkpoints to watch.

● If a crack is active or moving over time (versus stabilized or dormant), it's a sign that the force or forces that moved the wall or slab in the first place are still at work and probably inflicting further damage. Active cracks may open and close with changes in moisture and temperature, and their alignment may shift.

You can determine if the crack is growing wider or longer simply by marking it in a few places with an indelible marker, as shown in *Monitoring a Crack* on this page, and returning every few days to measure and note any changes.

If you end up hiring a professional, these carefully dated measurements will help the pro to correctly diagnose and fix the problem.

• A vertical crack in the foundation that is wider than ⅛ inch is usually a sign that the foundation is settling or heaving. A settling foundation will usually display matching vertical cracks on either end of the portion of the wall that is moving downward. A heaving foundation usually creates a single vertical crack that is wider at the top than at the bottom.

• A slab that heaves up will usually lift support columns and fireplaces as it rises, producing noticeable cracks and serious distortions in the wood framing above it.

• A diagonal crack indicates lateral movement in the foundation wall, often due to soil pressure.

• The appearance of new cracks is evidence of a current, ongoing problem that needs to be addressed. You can recognize new cracks because they tend to be relatively clean, without paint, dirt, or algae. If new cracks are related to earthquakes, flood erosion, or other external events (see **Vibrations** on the opposite page), call in a pro to evaluate the damage.

• A horizontal crack in a foundation wall is a sure sign of trouble, especially if there's any bulging or bowing in the wall.

• When masonry cracks vertically or diagonally *through* the brick, block, or stone rather than along the mortar lines, it could be due to drying and shrinkage (during the first year or two following construction) or evidence of structural failure.

If you're experiencing one or more of these problems, have a professional inspection done. This would preferably be carried out by a home inspector or geotechnical engineer who has no vested interests in making any repairs that might be needed. (To get a referral to a qualified home inspector in your area, contact one or more of the national associations listed in "Hiring a Pest Control Professional" on page 238.)

Checking Cracks for Movement

To determine if a crack is dormant (stationary) or active (moving), draw a straight line across it at two or three spots along its length. The lines should be perpendicular to the crack so that any changes in the crack's alignment becomes obvious. (See *Monitoring a Crack*.)

Make the lines of equal length—say, 6 inches long—with hashmarks at either end—so any changes in the width of the crack can be easily measured. If the ends of the cracks are visible, mark those with hash marks as well to find out if the crack is growing longer.

If your lines are going to be exposed to rain or leaking water, be sure to use an indelible marker.

Return every few days to remeasure the crack and keep a clear record of any changes.

MONITORING A CRACK

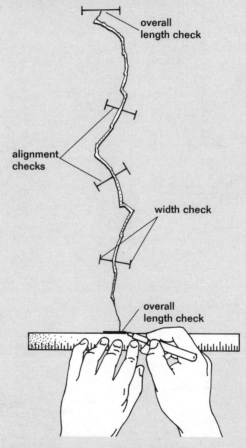

overall length check

alignment checks

width check

overall length check

Mark the crack with indelible ink. Measure every few days, and record the changes.

USING PROFESSIONAL TECHNIQUES

Professionals who specialize in repairing structural failures in poured concrete and masonry employ a variety of techniques. In every case, their first priority is to discover the underlying cause of the failure and to either eliminate it or compensate for it in the repairs.

A foundation that has settled and cracked can be raised again through a technique known as *mudjacking* or *slabjacking,* in which a special grout—made from water, cement, soil, and sand—is pumped in under the settled section at high pressure.

As shown in *Underpinning* on this page, another technique, called *underpinning* or

UNDERPINNING

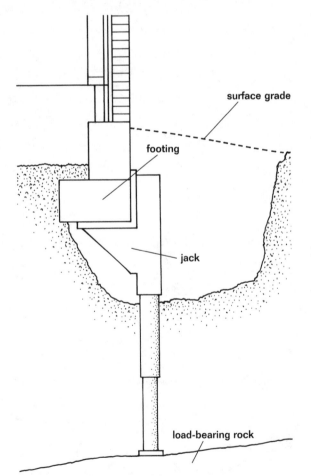

surface grade

footing

jack

load-bearing rock

The soil is removed to expose the underside of the footing and is refilled after underpinning.

Exterior Repairs

Cracks in foundation walls are best repaired from the outside. Excavate the crack all the way down to the footing, if necessary, then clean it and let it dry before starting repairs. If exterior excavation would ruin expensive landscaping, patios, sidewalks, or other structures, patch the crack from the inside. ●

permajacking, lifts the foundation by pinning it to a steel pipe that's been driven into the bedrock below. Once the shaft is in place, the structure is hydraulically jacked to its proper elevation and permanently pinned.

These techniques are generally successful in raising the structure enough to close existing cracks, straighten door frames, and correct other cosmetic distortions.

Various techniques also exist to repair cracks and bows in masonry walls. This usually entails reinforcing the wall, internally or externally, with steel rods or columns (pilasters). As with all repairs, the key to lasting success is to first remove or compensate for the forces that caused the problem in the first place.

MAKING REPAIRS

Cracks that are dormant—that is, not moving much—can be repaired by a do-it-yourselfer. If you discover that the crack has opened significantly after you've patched it, you've discovered the hard way that it was actually an active crack.

CRACKS IN POURED CONCRETE WALLS

Hairline cracks can generally be ignored, since they present no structural threat and won't admit significant amounts of water. However, for larger cracks, here are three repair options.

● *Make a mortar patch.* Bevel (undercut) the crack with a cold chisel, clean it out with a stiff wire brush, and press foam backing rod into the crack, as shown in *Preparing the Crack* on the opposite page.

PREPARING THE CRACK

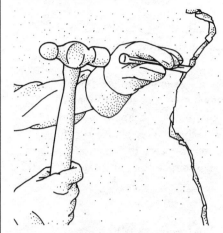

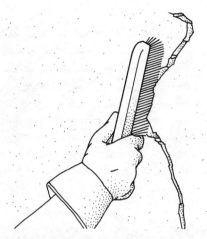

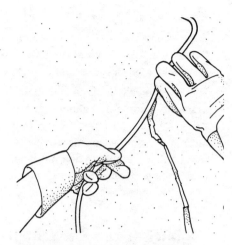

Step 1. Undercut the edges of the crack slightly with a cold chisel. (See Step 1 in *Patching Cracks and Holes* on page 62 for a sample of an ideal undercut.)

Step 2. Clean debris from the crack with a wire brush.

Step 3. Insert foam backing rod into the crack to support the caulk.

Then, mix up some mortar and fill the crack. A mortar patch will quickly fail if there's movement in the crack. Under that condition, either of the following two options is preferred.

● *Make a polyurethane patch.* Prepare the crack, as in the previous option. Apply polyurethane caulk (*not* to be confused with polyurethane foam) to the crack with a caulking gun, and work the caulk deeply into the crack with a putty knife, as shown in *Caulking the Crack with Polyurethane* on this page. (See "Caulk Suppliers" on this page.)

Caulk Suppliers

A complete line of caulks, sealants, and adhesives is available from these companies.

Macklanburg-Duncan
4041 North Santa Fe
Oklahoma City, OK 73118
(405) 528-4411

Ohio Sealants
7405 Production Drive
Mentor, OH 44060
(216) 255-8900

CAULKING THE CRACK WITH POLYURETHANE

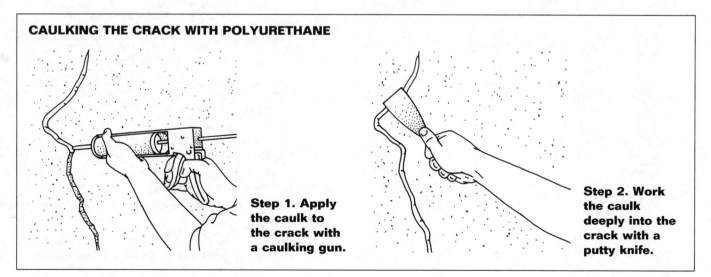

Step 1. Apply the caulk to the crack with a caulking gun.

Step 2. Work the caulk deeply into the crack with a putty knife.

Epoxying a Crack

Easy-to-use epoxy kits designed for concrete repair (and wood rot) are available through the manufacturers listed in "Epoxy Repairs" on page 174 and at some building supply and concrete repair outlets. Epoxy will work on cracks in poured concrete, brick, or solid block but *not* on hollow block.

The kits typically include cartridges, injection ports, and surface seal epoxy. The one I tested (from E-Poxy Industries) contained enough epoxy to inject 8 linear feet of crack (up to ¼ inch wide) at a cost of about $70. While this is a lot more expensive than sealing a crack with mortar or polyurethane caulk, the epoxy is much stronger—using it almost welds the two faces together. These kits typically have a throwaway plastic cartridge that contains the resin and hardener in separate reservoirs. These elements are mixed inside the cartridge, just prior to use, by depressing a plunger, which breaks the seal between the two reservoirs, and then rotating the plunger to mix the elements.

Repairing the Crack Step-by-Step

1. A crack can be injected on the interior *or* exterior side, depending on which is more accessible. Use a wire brush to knock any loose concrete, rubble, or old paint out of the crack and off surfaces on either side to about 1 inch. Use a vacuum cleaner to remove dust. Do not use water, detergents, or acids to clean the crack.

2. Read the instructions and precautions on the epoxy carefully. *CAUTION: Wear rubber gloves and safety goggles. Apply barrier cream to exposed skin. Provide plenty of ventilation and avoid inhaling fumes.*

3. Place the injection ports along the crack at intervals equal to the wall's thickness—typically 8 to 12 inches, as shown in *Placing the Ports*. They are held in place by applying surface seal epoxy around their flanges. *NOTE:* It's crucial to mix and apply the epoxy in *small* batches, as it sets up very quickly and becomes unworkable.

4. Cap the rest of the crack with a layer of surface seal epoxy, as shown in *Capping the Crack*. Massage the gel over the crack, using enough pressure to get good contact between the concrete and gel. The cap should be at least 1 inch wide and ⅛ inch deep to keep the injection epoxy from leaking out. Let the surface seal epoxy cure, as recommended.

CAPPING THE CRACK

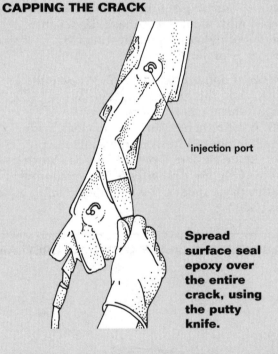

injection port

Spread surface seal epoxy over the entire crack, using the putty knife.

NOTE: If the other side of the wall is accessible and the crack goes all the way through, cap the crack on the other side, too. This will prevent epoxy from dribbling out the back side of the wall.

5. Thoroughly mix the epoxy in its cartridge, as specified in the directions.

6. Inject the bottom port first, until epoxy just begins to ooze out of the port above, as shown in *Injecting the*

PLACING THE PORTS

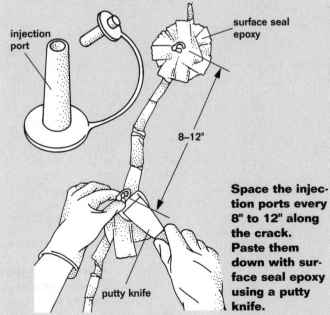

injection port

surface seal epoxy

8–12"

putty knife

Space the injection ports every 8" to 12" along the crack. Paste them down with surface seal epoxy using a putty knife.

Epoxy. Then, crimp or cap both ports. Move your caulk gun up to the third port and inject it until the fourth port begins to ooze, and cap them both. Continue on to the top in this leapfrogging manner.

INJECTING THE EPOXY

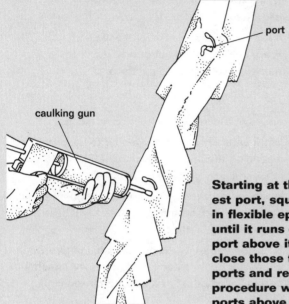

port

caulking gun

Starting at the lowest port, squeeze in flexible epoxy until it runs out the port above it. Then, close those two ports and repeat the procedure with the ports above them.

If, after a healthy injection, the epoxy doesn't ooze out of the port above, it's probably dribbling out the back side of the crack. If you can access the back side, cap the crack with surface seal epoxy. (See Step 4.) If not, the epoxy should be injected in stages, allowing some curing time at each port before moving up. (Read the directions on the package for details.)

If there's water in the crack, the epoxy oozing out of the port above will have a milky appearance. Manufacturers recommend that you continue to inject until the oozing epoxy turns clear, indicating that the water has been purged.

7. After the epoxy has cured, you can snip the tips off the injection ports and grind, sand, and paint the surface as desired. Since curing times vary with different formulations as well as with the temperature and moisture conditions during application, check the directions to determine the recommended curing time.

8. Properly dispose of used cartridges, wipes, and gloves. Once the epoxy is mixed and cured, these are not considered to be hazardous wastes.

Better Left Alone?

From an aesthetic standpoint, hairline cracks in masonry walls might best be left alone, as any patchwork is likely to be more noticeable than the cracks themselves. Block walls are sometimes coated with latex-based paint or brushed with a surface grout (cement and water) to fill fine cracks. As long as the entire wall is covered, the cosmetic results should be good. ●

● *Make an epoxy patch.* Inject the crack with epoxy, as described in "Epoxying a Crack" on the opposite page. Using epoxy is a lot more expensive and somewhat more difficult than using mortar or polyurethane caulk, but it results in the strongest and most permanent repair. Epoxies come in different formulations that determine their viscosity, their ability to flex (once cured), and their suitability for moist and cold weather applications. Give the dealer or manufacturer plenty of details about your particular job so they can specify the right formulation.

CRACKS IN MASONRY WALLS

If the crack follows the mortar joints, chip out the old mortar with a plugging chisel and repoint the joints, as shown in "Repointing Brick, Block, or Stone" on page 164. If the crack runs *through* the brick or block, you can patch it using mortar, polyurethane caulk, or epoxy. (See the three options under "Cracks in Poured Concrete Walls" on page 160.) Or, you can remove and replace a cracked brick, as shown in "Replacing a Brick" on page 166. This last option usually results in the best-looking repair.

NOTE: Epoxy is *not* recommended for patching cracks in hollow blocks. Polyurethane caulk can be used, provided the crack is filled with foam backing rod to keep the caulk from oozing into the hollow.

CRACKS IN STUCCO

Do-it-yourself attempts to patch damaged stucco are likely to produce an ugly and leaky patch. If the stucco is badly cracked and/or you desire a good cosmetic finish, I
(*continued on page 167*)

Repointing Brick, Block, or Stone

Over time, the mortar joints in masonry deteriorate due to moisture, vibration, air pollution, poor workmanship, and other causes. When the mortar becomes loose or crumbly or shows sizable cracks, the masonry should be repointed as soon as the weather permits. Otherwise, water will get further into the joints and cause additional damage. If the cause of the deterioration can be diagnosed—say, a settling foundation or leaky rain gutters—the problem should be remedied.

CAUTION: If bricks are cracked in a load-bearing section of a wall (for example, above a window or door), consult a mason before you attempt to repair them.

Masonry joints are repointed by chipping out old mortar between bricks, blocks, or stones and tucking new mortar into the joints. *NOTE:* Only joints that are actually worn out or cracked should be repointed. Original joints in good condition are *always* preferable to patchwork.

Repointing Step-by-Step

1. Prepare the joints, preferably on a dry, warm day—70°F is ideal. Don't work in cold weather, as it will weaken the mortar. Spread a plastic tarp to catch the mess. For high-altitude work, use scaffolding rather than a ladder, or call in a pro.

2. Clean out the old mortar. Using a 2-pound hand sledge and a chisel, cut the damaged mortar joints back far enough to reach sound mortar (usually ½ to 1 inch), as shown in *Chiseling the Joints.* Any masonry chisel that fits into the joint will do the job, but a plugging chisel (also called a joint chisel or tuck-pointer's chisel) is best. Its specially tapered blade is less likely to chip the

CHISELING THE JOINTS

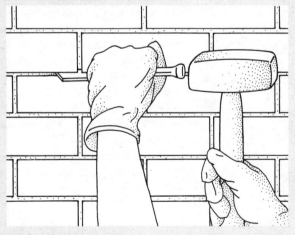

Chisel out any old, crumbly mortar.

edges of the surrounding brick or block.

Work carefully (no power tools!) to keep from damaging the brick or block. *CAUTION:* Be sure to wear safety goggles and gloves.

Make the grooves as square as possible (rather than V-shaped) so the new mortar will have a good bearing surface.

3. Clean the joints, using a brush, compressed air, or a vacuum cleaner with a blower attachment to remove any dust or loose mortar remaining in the joints.

4. Using a dry, ready-mix mortar, add just enough water to blend the ingredients together. (You should be able to press a handful into a ball that retains its shape.) Let the damp mixture set for 30 minutes. This will preshrink the mortar, so to speak, so that it won't crack later on. After 30 minutes, slowly add more water, until you have a workable consistency like cottage cheese.

NOTE: Ready-mix mortar is too strong and hard for use in restoration work on older masonry, with its soft bricks and lime-based mortar, and may crack the edge of the bricks. To properly match the physical properties, texture, and color of the old mortar, contact someone in your local preservation society or a mason who specializes in restoration work.

5. Pack the joints with mortar. Start at the top and work your way down. Dampen the joints (but don't drench them) with a spray bottle just before you pack the mortar in. Misting is especially important in hot weather.

Use a mason's hawk and a small pointing trowel to do the work, as shown in *Packing the Joints.* (If you don't have a hawk, you can build one simply by nailing a handle on to an 8 × 8-inch piece of plywood.)

Place a small pile of mortar on the hawk, slice off a ribbon with the trowel, and pack it tightly into the joint. Do the vertical joints first.

Don't try to fill the joints in one pass. Apply the mortar in ¼-inch layers. Let each layer dry, until it will hold the impression of your thumb when pressed, then mist it lightly and add another layer. Each layer should be packed tightly and make solid contact with the masonry around it. Take care not to get mortar on the bricks or blocks—if you do, wipe it off quickly.

The last layer of mortar should overfill the joints slightly and then be tooled into shape. (See Step 6.)

Don't try to cover too much area at one time. The pros typically pack and tool about 4 square feet at a time.

PACKING THE JOINTS

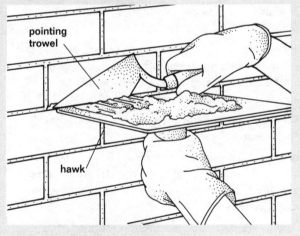

Push a ribbon of mortar off the mason's hawk and into the joint with a pointing trowel.

6. Once the final layer of mortar is thumbprint dry, *strike* the joints with the appropriately

shaped tool so that they match the old joints, as shown in *Striking the Joints.* The mortar should be firmly compacted against the adjoining bricks or blocks.

Masonry supply houses sell professional jointing tools used to strike square, convex, or concave joints, or you can use common tools and household items. For example, you can use the tip of your trowel to strike a V-shaped joint, a piece of small diameter pipe or dowel to strike a U-shaped joint, or a small piece of lumber, the width of which exactly matches the width of the joint, to strike a square joint.

Whatever tool you use, wet it continually as you work. Strike the joints in the same order that you filled them—vertical joints first.

STRIKING THE JOINTS

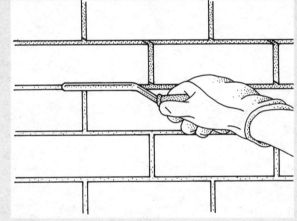

Strike the joints with a jointing tool. Strike the vertical joints first and finish by doing the horizontals.

7. Scrape any excess mortar off the masonry before it has time to dry, and clean your tools. To keep the new mortar from drying too fast, mist it every 12 hours with your spray bottle, for about four days.

After a week, you can scrub the surface of the wall with a dry stiff brush, if necessary to remove any mortar residue.

Replacing a Brick

Bricks that are cracked through the body (rather than along mortar joints) can be repaired by beveling the crack with a chisel and filling it with mortar (see *Preparing the Crack* on page 161) or by injecting it with epoxy (see "Epoxying a Crack" on page 162). These methods produce a temporary cure and the problem will probably reappear in the future.

Replacing the broken bricks, however, will result in a stronger and better-looking repair. This is done in nine steps, as follows:

Replacing a Brick Step-by-Step

1. Use a cold chisel or plugging chisel and 2-pound sledge to break up and remove the damaged brick, as shown in *Removing the Damaged Brick*. Be careful not to damage any surrounding bricks. If some of the bricks are loose, but whole, save them for reuse. Wear safety goggles and gloves to protect yourself.

REMOVING THE DAMAGED BRICK

Carefully chisel out the damaged brick.

2. Try to salvage and reuse any of the bricks you can. If you need new bricks, buy them from a local masonry supply or salvage yard. If you have trouble matching the old brick, perhaps you can cannibalize some from another part of your property.

3. Carefully chisel out any old mortar left in the cavity, as shown in *Chipping Away Mortar.* Use a brush, compressed air, or a vacuum cleaner with a blower attachment to clean mortar dust and particles out of the cavity.

CHIPPING AWAY MORTAR

With the brick removed, chisel out any old mortar that surrounded it.

4. Mix the mortar, as detailed in Step 4 under "Repointing Brick, Block, or Stone" on page 164.

5. Lightly dampen the walls of the cavity with a spray bottle. Use a trowel to apply a smooth ¾-inch bed of mortar to the bottom and sides of the cavity, as shown in *Applying Mortar and Inserting the Brick.*

6. Coat the top and ends of the replacement brick with mortar (but not the back or front).

7. Press the brick firmly into the hole. Tap it gently until it's aligned and flush with adjacent bricks. Some mortar should squeeze out of the joints. Pack more mortar into the joints if necessary.

8. Tool the joints, as described in Step 6 under "Repointing Brick, Block, or Stone" on page 165.

9. Clean up the mess and let the mortar dry, as detailed in Step 7 under "Repointing Brick, Block, or Stone" on page 165.

APPLYING MORTAR AND INSERTING THE BRICK

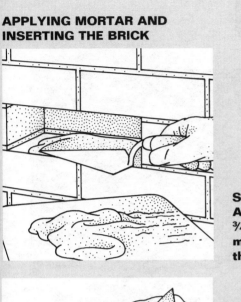

Step 1. Apply a ¾" bed of mortar to the cavity.

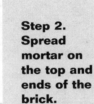

Step 2. Spread mortar on the top and ends of the brick.

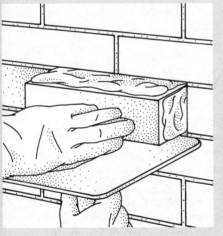

Step 3. Press the brick into the hole.

recommend you hire a pro. But be forewarned that even experienced stucco workers can't be expected to match the color and texture of the patch to the existing stucco precisely and often recommend painting the entire surface after the repairs are completed. That's when things start to get expensive.

If the crack is ¼ inch wide or less and you're not overly fussy about the aesthetic appearance of the patch, you can do a simple and inexpensive repair yourself using acrylic latex or rubber-based (butyl) caulk. First, select a caulk to match the color of your stucco. Since there are hundreds of different colors available, you should be able to get a good match. (See "Caulk Suppliers" on page 161.)

Don't widen the crack. As shown in *Patching a Crack in Stucco* on this page, place strips of masking tape over the entire length of the crack, then use a utility knife to slit the tape. Inject the caulk by running the nozzle over the slit, forcing the caulk through the tape and into the crack. The tape will help keep the caulk from oozing back out.

Take care not to overfill the joint or smear any excess caulk on the adjoining stucco. Strip off the tape before the caulk completely sets.

PATCHING A CRACK IN STUCCO

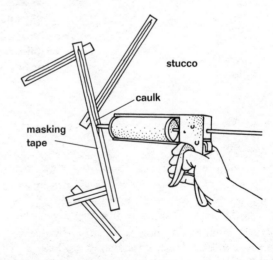

stucco

caulk

masking tape

The masking tape helps prevent the caulk from oozing out of the crack.

Rotting Wood

Quick Response

1. Eliminate source of water or water vapor on which rot fungus depends.

2. Remove (or treat) rotted wood, and replace or brace it, as necessary.

You can check the wood beams, joists, and rafters in your house for rot by probing with an ice pick, awl, or small screwdriver. Rotted wood crumbles easily and breaks away.

Hazards

● When using Bora-Care (sodium borate), Cuprinol (copper or zinc naphthenate), or other wood preservatives, protect yourself with gloves, safety goggles, and a dust mask. Read and follow the safety precautions detailed on the product label.

● Wear a dust mask when cutting pressure-treated wood to avoid inhaling toxic sawdust. Wash your hands well when the work is finished. Do not use pressure-treated wood where infants or pets are likely to lick or gnaw it. Do not burn pressure-treated wood scraps.

● Inhaling the spores from rot fungus can cause allergic reactions and respiratory problems, especially in hypersensitive people. When cutting away or treating rotten wood, wear a dust mask—or better yet, a respirator.

STOPPING THE SLOW FIRE

Wood rot is sometimes characterized as a "slow fire" or "slow-motion emergency." But once the decay fungus has established itself in a house and it has a steady supply of water, it can do an amazing amount of damage in a relatively short time. One case, documented in Maine, found a four-year-old house so badly rotted that it had to be demolished down to the foundation and rebuilt.

The serious and widespread nature of wood rot reveals itself in a single statistic: Americans spend more than $2 billion each year to replace wood that has been destroyed by rot or termites.

UNDERSTANDING THE ENEMY

Wood rot (along with yeasts, molds, mildews, smuts, and mushrooms) belongs to a group of primitive plants known as *fungi*. Their seeds, called *spores,* are carried on the wind and are abundant everywhere, waiting for the proper conditions to germinate. The various fungi that produce wood rot have only four simple needs—moisture, oxygen, suitable temperature (40° to 100°F), and a ready source of wood.

As the spores germinate and the decay fungus grows, it secretes an enzyme that breaks down the wood. The cellulose and lignin that make up the wood cells are converted into glucose, which the fungus uses as food.

Wood rot is usually invisible in the early stages of the attack because the fungus's threadlike filaments, called *hyphae,* penetrate the wood on a microscopic level. Eventually, the hyphae become so numerous that they form white or gray sheets on the surface of the wood that are called *mycelia.*

If the source of moisture dries up or the temperature falls much below 40°F, the fungus will become dormant, waiting to resume the attack whenever the conditions become favorable again.

Brown and white rot are the two most common types of wood decay. A third type, soft rot, is rarely found in houses, except occasionally on wood-shake roofs.

Both brown and white rot are difficult to detect in their early stages. The first sign of attack is usually a change in the wood's color, accompanied by a musty odor that's similar to the smell of mushrooms.

Brown rot, which primarily attacks softwoods (for example, framing lumber, windows, siding), turns wood dark brown as it progresses. The wood splits across the grain, developing cubical checks, giving the wood a charred appearance. An advanced infestation will have one or more fruiting bodies, shaped like pancakes, producing new spores by the zillion.

Some (happily rare) types of brown rot have the insidious ability to pipe water into other parts of the house, thereby supporting a distant attack on seemingly dry wood. The water is conducted through special rootlike hyphae called *rhizomorphs,* which can grow in diameter to the size of a pencil. Rhizomorphs can pass over brick, stone, or metal to deliver

In Pursuit of Rot

Make an annual inspection for rot, concentrating on those dark, damp, hard-to-get-to places. (See *Hot Spots for Rot* on page 170.) Be sure to revisit areas that were previously treated to make sure the decay fungus hasn't returned.

water to an advancing body of decay that's at a considerable distance from the original attack. Hence the term *dry rot* is sometimes used to describe it. This term is a misnomer, however, since decay fungus, whatever the variety, *always* requires water.

White rot, which is much less common than brown rot, usually attacks hardwoods (for example, oak beams and flooring). The fungus turns the surface of the wood gray-white or yellow-white, giving it a bleached-out look. In its advanced stages, white rot produces cottony masses of hyphae (mycelia) and fruiting bodies that eject new spores. A thin black line on the wood's surface often marks the leading edge of the rot's attack.

In some cases, both brown and white rot will show up in the same infestation.

DETECTING ROT EARLY

Obviously, the best time to spot and treat rot is before it's discolored the wood and turned it punky. To make that early discovery, see *Hot Spots for Rot* on page 170 and check your house once a year with a sharp eye out for the following telltale symptoms:

● The presence of mold, mildew, algae, lichens, or moss inside the house or out is a signal that the moisture and temperature conditions are right for wood rot. (See "Mold and Mildew" on page 213.)
● Peeling or blistering paint suggests the presence of moisture, especially if the wood underneath is discolored.
● Water stains on rafters, joists, or other framing members or sheathing reveal a water problem. Whatever the source of water (roof leak, plumbing leak, or condensation from excessive indoor humidity), the stage is set for rot.

(continued on page 172)

STRUCTURAL EMERGENCIES

5

Hot Spots for Rot

Rot can attack almost any part of your house, but some parts are more susceptible than others. One thing is certain: Any part of your house that is constantly damp is an open invitation to rot.

Likely Trouble Spot	Water Source	Solution
FLOOR JOISTS AND SILL OVER CRAWL SPACE (A)	Water vapor rising from soil or blown in through open vents condenses on joists, subfloor, and sill. Leaking heat duct adds more warm, moist air.	Cover bare soil with 6-mil plastic vapor barrier. (See "Moisture-Proofing a Crawl Space" on page 173.) Seal and insulate heating and cooling ducts. Keep crawl space vents closed during summer.
UNTREATED SILL (B)	Water wicks up through concrete, masonry, or bare soil on which sill sits.	Treatment with boron rods and brush-on wood preservatives will slow onset of rot. Replacing sill with pressure-treated lumber may be necessary. If so, metal shield should be installed between foundation and wood as moisture barrier.
STUDS (C)	Water vapor migrating through wall condenses on wood.	Take steps to lower indoor humidity and seal cracks or holes in wall that allow warm, moist air into wall cavity. (See "Controlling Indoor Humidity" on page 217.)
BATHROOM FLOOR (D)	Leaky wax ring under toilet, crack in shower pan, or broken tub tiles leak water into space between flooring and subfloor. Water vapor condenses against toilet and pools on floor.	Repair, caulk, or regrout leaking fixtures, tile, or flooring. Lower humidity in bathroom by using exhaust fan and other measures. (See "Controlling Indoor Humidity" on page 217.)

LIKELY TROUBLE SPOT	WATER SOURCE	SOLUTION
KITCHEN FLOOR (E)	Leaks and splashes create moist environment under kitchen sink.	Make sure faucets, pipe, and trap are watertight. Caulk sink so that water can't migrate into cabinet and flooring below.
WINDOWS (F)	Water vapor condenses on glass, sashes, and sill. Outside, lack of drip cap (top-edge flashing) lets rainwater seep into framing around window.	Take steps to lower indoor humidity. (See "Controlling Indoor Humidity" on page 217.) Keep windows, inside and out, in good repair. Install or repair drip cap over window.
WOOD SIDING (G)	Improper grading leaves siding in contact with soil. Open downspout splashes water onto siding. Leaking gutters let rainwater cascade down side of house. Dense vegetation hugs and shades siding, retaining moisture.	Make sure that siding is at least 6 inches above grade (12 inches is preferable). Keep gutters and downspouts in good repair, directing water away from house. (See "Clogged Rain Gutter" on page 33 and "Damaged Rain Gutter" on page 37.) Keep siding well painted. Trim foundation plantings back 8 inches from siding.
FASCIA AND SOFFIT BOARDS (H)	Through capillary action, rainwater and snow melt wick their way into wood through joints.	Install drip edge flashing (see "Leaky Roof" on page 24) and keep rain gutters in good repair (see "Clogged Rain Gutter" on page 33 and "Damaged Rain Gutter" on page 37). Keep fascia and soffit boards well painted. Take steps to prevent ice dams. (See "Avoiding Ice Dams" on page 41.)
RAFTERS, TRUSSES, AND SHEATHING (I)	Leaky roof exposes framing and sheathing to rainwater. (See "Leaky Roof" on page 24.) Water vapor migrating up from rooms below condenses on wood.	Fix roof leaks promptly. Take steps to lower indoor humidity and seal cracks and holes in ceiling through which warm, moist air rises into attic. (See "Controlling Indoor Humidity" on page 217.) Make sure that attic has adequate ventilation. (See "Avoiding Ice Dams" on page 41.)
DECKS, FENCE POSTS, LATTICE WORK, AND EXTERIOR STEPS (J)	Wherever wood is in direct contact with ground, water will wick up from soil into wood. Water will also migrate through concrete footings into deck and porch posts.	Posts and step stringers should rest on poured concrete base at least 6 inches above grade. Treat with boron rods and brush-on preservatives to slow the onset of rot. Keep wooden surfaces that are above grade (e.g., decking) well painted. Replace rotten members with pressure-treated wood.
PLANTER BOXES (K)	Water runs down wall behind box, where it's trapped, promoting rot.	Planter boxes should be made of pressure-treated lumber, well drained, and flashed on back side to protect siding. Better yet, take them off wall and turn them into stand-alone planters.
WOODEN FENCE RAILS OR SCREED BOARDS ABUTTING HOUSE (L)	Moisture and wood decay move through rails or boards to attack wood siding or untreated sill.	Avoid nailing fence rails to house or flash them so there's barrier against moisture and rot. Screed boards should be cut off 2 inches from house and space filled with concrete.
CELLULOSE DEBRIS (M)	Rotting tree stumps, old form boards (left in place after foundation was poured), and wood scraps left under crawl space or deck provide fertile ground for rot and termites to get started.	Remove rotten stumps and other cellulose debris that are in proximity to house.
SEAMS OR CRACKS IN SLAB AND FOUNDATION (N)	Water (and termites) enter basement from soil abutting foundation wall or from under slab.	Fill voids, cracks, and expansion joints in concrete or masonry with mortar, polyurethane caulk, or epoxy. (See "Cracks in Concrete, Masonry, and Stucco" on page 157.)

● Condensation forming on windows and interior walls indicates high indoor humidity. This suggests that condensation is also forming *inside* the walls and attic, inviting rot.
● Humps or sags in the floor within 3 feet of an outside wall are a sign that the sill and/or floor joists may be weakened by rot.
● Curling at the corners or along the edges of bathroom floor tiles suggests that water has become trapped between the vinyl and subfloor. If the floor feels soft or sags under your weight, rot may have already caused structural weakening.
● A pronounced sag in the roof may be a clue that sheathing, rafters, or beams have rotted. In fact, a badly rotted roof will sag—or even collapse!—under your feet as you walk across it. (*NOTE:* Roofs sometimes sag or "creep" near the middle of their rafters as a symptom of old age, not rot. The sag is caused by the gradual bending of structural members under their own weight and the roofing materials as well as from the cumulative effect of wind, rain, snow, and ice.)

Wood decay is always linked directly to the sustained presence of moisture. Among the most common areas to find rot in the home are the bathroom floor, windowsills, roof sheathing and rafters, soffit and fascia boards, exterior corner trim, the untreated wood in decks and fence posts, and the sill plate.

Sometimes, a fine-looking veneer of paint hides a serious rot problem. The best way to probe a suspect area is to jab an ice pick into the wood at an angle. When you pry the point up, sound wood will produce a sharp crack and a long splinter, typically still attached at one end, as shown in *Probing for Rot* on this page. Rotten wood, on the other hand, tends to break quietly over the ice pick, with both ends of the splinter still attached to the wood, as shown in *Probing for Rot*. If the ice pick sinks easily and deeply into the wood, it indicates advanced rot or, if the center of wood is badly tunneled, insects. (See "Termites, Beetles, and Carpenter Ants" on page 231.)

ASSESSING THE DAMAGE

Having spotted wood rot in your house, the first priority is to identify and cut off the source(s) of moisture that feeds it. This will stop any further spread of the fungus. (See *Hot Spots for Rot* on page 170 and "Moisture-Proofing a Crawl Space" on the opposite page.)

Once the rotted area has thoroughly dried, perform exploratory surgery. Use a wood chisel and stiff wire brush to cut away the rotted wood, probing with an ice pick for sound wood underneath.

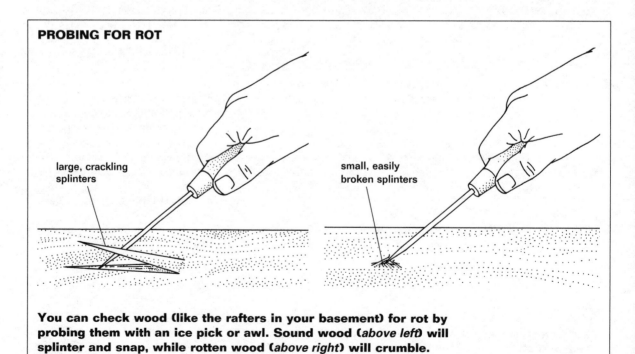

PROBING FOR ROT

large, crackling splinters

small, easily broken splinters

You can check wood (like the rafters in your basement) for rot by probing them with an ice pick or awl. Sound wood (*above left*) will splinter and snap, while rotten wood (*above right*) will crumble.

Moisture-Proofing a Crawl Space

An effective way to dry out a damp crawl space is to cover the bare ground with thick (6-mil) plastic sheeting. As shown in *Sealing a Crawl Space,* the sheets should be overlapped 12 inches and lapped up the side of the foundation wall. A liberal, unbroken bead of butyl caulk is used to seal the laps. *NOTE:* It's important to seal the seams tightly and not leave any rips or punctures in the plastic.

If the foundation wall is too irregular to get a good bearing surface for the plastic sheet—a problem common with stone foundations—the plastic can be lapped up to the sill plate and secured there.

If the plastic membrane is properly installed, it will also reduce the migration of radon gas from the soil into the floor above. For houses that have a radon reading only slightly above the "action level" of 4 picocuries per liter, the membrane alone may be enough to bring the radon level below 4. (See "Radon" on page 205.)

SEALING A CRAWL SPACE

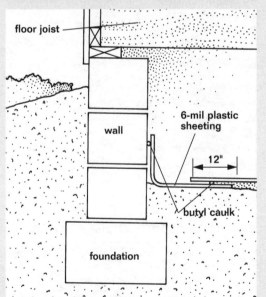

Run a bead of butyl caulk along the wall of the crawl space and push the edge of the plastic against it to form a seal. Seal subsequent sheets of plastic together in the same way.

If the rot is limited to a relatively small area and doesn't threaten the structural integrity of your house, you can likely repair it yourself. (See "Doing the Simple Repairs Yourself" on this page.)

However, if you discover that the sill plate, floor or ceiling joists, carrying beams, roof rafters, or other structural elements are heavily rotted, you should hire a pro. (See "Hiring a Pest Control Professional" on page 238.) Deciding whether to repair or replace rotted structural elements and how to go about it are judgment calls that require real expertise. Likewise, the safe use of hydraulic and screw jacks, which are used to support the weight of the house while the underlying structural lumber is replaced or repaired, is not something that's learned overnight. Jacking up a house without a sure knowledge of what you're doing can cause serious structural and cosmetic damage.

A professional is also recommended if you discover the presence of rhizomorphs. These tubelike extensions, which transport water from one patch of rot to another, can penetrate the mortar joints in masonry and tiny cracks in concrete or plaster and can bridge metal and other nonwood surfaces. They signal the presence of an especially pernicious form of brown rot, which is best treated by a professional.

DOING THE SIMPLE REPAIRS YOURSELF

Before you tear your house down and rebuild it from scratch, consider shoring up the solid wood around the rot, replacing a few rotted boards, and/or treating the rot with preservatives, as discussed below.

EXTERIOR POSTS AND STEPS

Deck posts, fence posts, and step stringers are especially prone to rot at the point where they rest on concrete footings or, worse yet, sit in direct contact with the ground. If the rot isn't too severe—that is, the post or stringer is still structurally sound—use a chisel and wire brush to cut away the rot until you've uncovered sound wood.

Further decay can be stopped by drilling small holes in and around the affected area and then treating the area with sodium borate. The borate is inserted in the form of rods (Impel rods) or injected as a gel (ITF gel) with a syringelike applicator. (See "Wood Preservative and Epoxy Suppliers" on this page.)

The profile of the post or stringer can be restored and strengthened by filling the cavity with WoodEpox or other epoxy putty. To fill a larger cavity, chisel out the hole to accommodate a block-shaped filling made out of pressure-treated wood, then use the epoxy putty to bind and finish the repair. (See "Epoxy Repairs" on page 176.) The finished surface, which can be rasped or sanded flat, can be further treated with Cuprinol (copper or zinc naphthenate) or paint.

JOISTS

A joist with a small amount of rot on the bottom or end doesn't necessarily have to be replaced. Chisel away the rotten wood and scour the surface with a stiff wire brush until you've exposed sound wood. If the joist is protected from the weather, coat the cavity and surrounding wood with two coats of Bora-Care (sodium borate), a water-soluble preservative and fungicide that has good penetrating ability. (See "Wood Preservative and Epoxy Suppliers" on this page for sources.) If the joist is exposed to the weather (for example, under an open porch or deck), treat it with two coats of Cuprinol instead. Inspect the spot frequently to make sure that decay doesn't reappear.

If the joist is rotted where it butts up against the sill, rim joist, or ledger board, consider bracing the underside of the joist with a pressure-treated ledger, as shown in *Supporting Joist with a Ledger* on this page.

SUPPORTING JOIST WITH A LEDGER

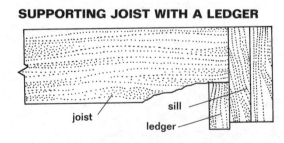

Cut the rot away on the end of the joist and then nail a ledger below it. If rot extends into the sill, treat it with borate rods or gel.

If the rot extends a little way into the sill, rim joist, or ledger board, treat it with borate rods or gel, as described in "Exterior Posts and Steps" on page 173.

DECKING

Before you replace rotten decking, consider the condition of the underlying joists and posts (see "Joists" on the opposite page), then make a thoughtful assessment of how best to repair or replace the structure and whether or not you can do it yourself.

Provided the posts and joists are sound, replace any rotten deck boards with planks of the same dimension, using galvanized nails to secure them. Redwood, cedar, or pressure-treated lumber are the best choices because they resist rot. If you must use ordinary pine or fir decking, coat the top and bottom with Cuprinol before you nail the lumber in place. Be sure to cut and drill the board *before* you brush on the preservative. The end grains are best treated by letting each end of each board soak for a few minutes in a bucket filled with 2 or 3 inches of Cuprinol.

Once you've installed the new decking, paint or stain it to match the original.

RAILINGS, BALUSTERS, AND COLUMNS

Decks, porches, and balconies become progressively more dangerous as rot attacks wooden hand railings, balusters, and columns. Again, carefully assess the entire structure before you decide exactly what to repair or replace.

A lathe-turned hand railing or baluster can sometimes be repaired using wood block patches and epoxy, provided the rot isn't too far advanced beyond the block ends. The beautiful thing about epoxy for this type of repair (also for columns, cornices, and moldings) is that once the epoxy has

Get the Rot Out

As you make repairs, move the decayed wood and debris well away from your house. This reduces the number of fungus spores in the air and eliminates a potential food source for termites and carpenter ants. ●

Replacing Tongue and Groove

If you're replacing an area of rotted tongue-and-grove deck boards, stagger the end cuts over several framing members so that the new boards mesh well with the old. In order to fit the last board in place, trim off the bottom lip along the grooved edge so that it can fit down on the tongue of the original deck board. ●

hardened, it can be rasped and sanded to match the original profile. (See "Epoxy Repairs" on page 176.)

Rebuilding a rail or baluster with epoxy isn't quick or cheap, but it's usually faster and a lot less expensive than hiring a woodworker to turn new pieces for you or trying to order duplicates through a specialty catalog.

Once the wood is repaired, prepare both the original part and the patch for painting. Use a good primer and outdoor finish coat to complete the job.

A simple, straight hand railing or baluster should be replaced with redwood, cedar, or pressure-treated wood to resist rot. If those options aren't workable, use kiln-dried wood coated with Cuprinol and covered with a good exterior paint or stain. (See "Decking" on this page for details.)

WINDOWS

Renovation contractors who spot a little rot on your windows may urge you to replace them—after all, there's more profit in selling you new windows than in repairing the old ones.

But if the rot isn't too far advanced—that is, if the windows are still structurally sound—you can save a lot of money by repairing them yourself. This is especially true if replacement windows would have to be custom-made.

Start your restoration work by cutting away the decayed wood with a chisel and stiff wire brush. Once you're down to healthy wood, coat the cavity with two coats of Bora-Care, with time allotted between coats for penetration and drying.

Fill the hole with WoodEpox or other epoxy putty. Once the patch has hardened, sand it until it's flush with the original wood, then paint or stain it to match the surrounding finish. (See "Epoxy Repairs" on page 176.) If nec-

Costly Coverups

Whatever you do, don't try to cover up rot with a fresh coat of paint or other cosmetic measures. Like a cancer, decay fungus has to be cut out before it can spread any further. ●

essary, the corners of an old window can be reinforced with steel or brass L-brackets.

The wooden components of the window won't suffer further decay if you keep them dry and well painted. Installing storm windows and lowering the indoor humidity are two key steps in reducing the formation of condensation on the glass and wood. (See "Controlling Indoor Humidity" on page 217.) Also, make sure that there is cap flashing above the drip cap on the top of the window outside, as shown in *Proper Cap Flashing* on this page. The flashing diverts rainwater and snow melt away from the window. If there isn't flashing above the drip cap, install it or have it professionally installed.

PROPER CAP FLASHING

Flashed drip caps over windows and doors prevent rot.

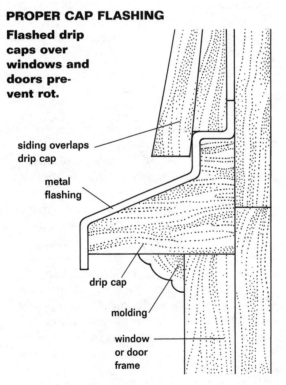

siding overlaps drip cap

metal flashing

drip cap

molding

window or door frame

Epoxy Repairs

Using an epoxy kit, a homeowner can effectively patch a small area of rotted wood. Though the repair shown on this page is to a rotted windowsill, a similar technique can be applied to other window and door components, decks, porches, wood components under sinks, and bathroom baseboards.

Two-part epoxy systems are mixed just prior to use by combining the resin with the hardener. The consistency of the epoxy varies with the use, ranging from waterlike to pastelike. Make sure the components you're using are thoroughly mixed and that you don't make too much epoxy at one time.

CAUTION: Read and follow the manufacturer's instructions, especially regarding skin, eye, and respiratory protection.

Follow the steps illustrated in *Cutting Away Punky Wood, Drilling Holes, Applying Liquid Epoxy, Filling the Cavity,* and *Finishing the Surface* to patch a rotted windowsill using epoxy.

CUTTING AWAY PUNKY WOOD

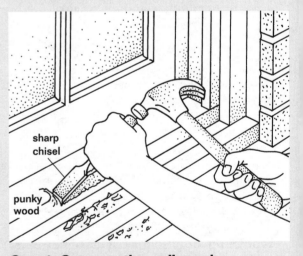

sharp chisel

punky wood

Step 1. Cut away the really punky wood to reveal sound wood, as shown above.

DRILLING HOLES

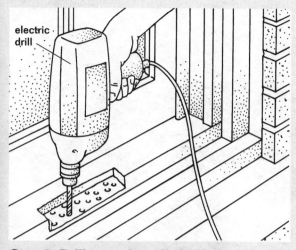

electric drill

Step 2. Drill a number of small holes into and around the decayed area, as shown above. (On more absorbent surfaces, you can simply brush or pour on the liquid epoxy.)

APPLYING LIQUID EPOXY

LiquidWood

Step 3. Inject LiquidWood (or other liquid epoxy) into the holes using a squeeze bottle, as shown above. The liquid epoxy impregnates the wood fibers and hardens into a strong, water-resistant mass.

FILLING THE CAVITY

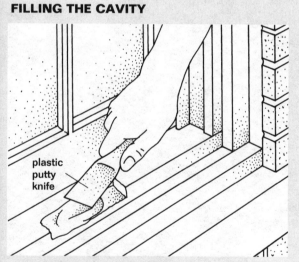

plastic putty knife

Step 4. Fill the cavity with WoodEpox (or other epoxy paste), using a plastic putty knife, as shown above.

FINISHING THE SURFACE

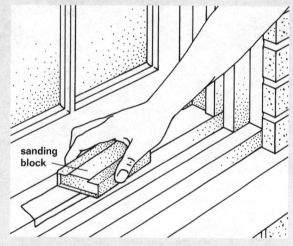

sanding block

Step 5. Once the epoxy has cured, chisel and sand the surface until it's flush with the surrounding wood, as shown above. (The patch can also be planed, rasped, or drilled.) Apply a primer and top coat of paint, and the wood is almost as good as new.

Natural Emergencies

6 NATURAL EMERGENCIES

Lightning Strikes!

Quick Response

1. Get *everybody* out and call fire department or 911 from neighbor's house. Even if there's no evidence of damage, electrical fire may be smoldering behind walls.

2. If someone has been shocked and quits breathing, start CPR immediately. Call 911 or other emergency help. (See "Electrical Safety Tips" on page 102.)

Lightning is inevitable, and chances are a strong storm will be headed your way in the next year. So consider taking some precautions now to protect your home and family.

Hazards

● A lightning strike can damage your house wiring and service panel *without* leaving any visible signs. Have an electrician run a thorough check on the panel, circuits, and receptacles.

● Installing lightning rods is *not* a do-it-yourself project. Small mistakes can turn a lightning protection system into a lightning *electrocution* system!

ASSESSING YOUR RISK

During an average year, lightning causes about 90 deaths, 2,000 injuries, and $400 million in property damage in the United States. About 18,000 homes are struck on the average. (See "Where the Thunderstorms Roam" on the opposite page.)

While lightning presents some degree of hazard to every house, a number of variables work to increase or decrease the risk. For example, if your house is situated alone, at the top of a hill, or in a region of frequent thunderstorms, it runs a dramatically higher risk of being struck than a house in a densely populated, low-lying area where thunderstorms are rare. The type of construction materials used in your roof, the soil type, and

Where the Thunderstorms Roam

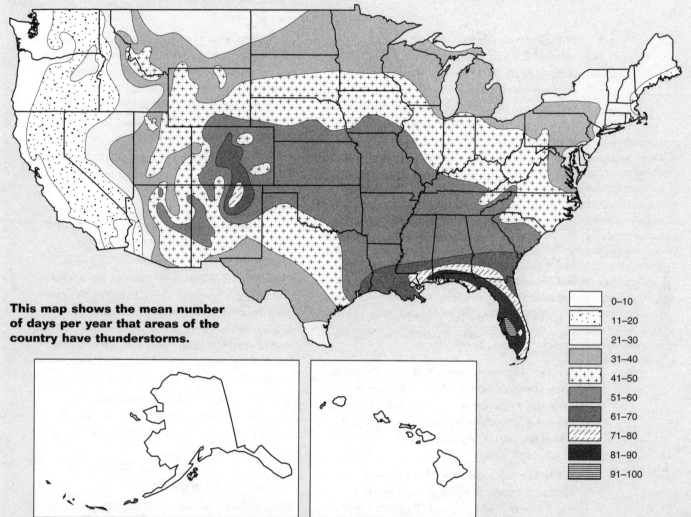

This map shows the mean number of days per year that areas of the country have thunderstorms.

	0–10
	11–20
	21–30
	31–40
+++	41–50
	51–60
	61–70
///	71–80
	81–90
	91–100

This isokeraunic map shows the mean annual days of thunderstorm activity in various parts of the United States.

While the average number of stormy days is 40, the extremes range from just 1 in southern Alaska to 100 or more such days in south-central Florida.

You can estimate the number of lightning strikes that will hit close to your house each year by figuring one or two strokes per thunderstorm. If, for example, your area has 50 days with thunderstorms each year, you can expect 50 to 100 lightning bolts to hit within a half mile of your house each year.

6
NATURAL EMERGENCIES

Redrawn from the photograph/map, *Mean Annual Number of Days with Thunderstorms,* provided by the National Oceanic and Atmospheric Administration/National Weather Service, Silver Spring, Maryland

the home's proximity to water also affect the degree of risk.

The National Fire Protection Association (NFPA) has developed a Lightning Risk Assessment Guide that can help you weigh the risks to your house more precisely. The guide is available free of charge by sending a self-addressed, stamped envelope to the Lightning Protection Institute, 3365 North Arlington Heights Road, Suite J, Arlington Heights, IL 60004. The institute also has free copies of a brochure titled "Lightning Protection for Home, Family, and Property."

For some additional tips on staying safe in a thunderstorm, see "Thunderstorm Safety Tips" on page 184.

Zapped!

With storm clouds threatening, Terry Lasky ushered his dinner guests in off the porch and closed the door. It wasn't the first time that summer that he'd had to batten down the hatches—in fact, tiny Chatham, New York, was beginning to get something of a reputation for stormy weather in 1994.

That and the fact that his new $600,000 house was situated on a knoll, in the middle of an open field, had prompted Terry to have the house equipped with lightning rods. In fact, the installation crew had started work that very afternoon and was scheduled to return Monday to complete the job.

But Monday, as things turned out, would be too late.

A split second after Terry and his guests left the porch, there was a flash of lightning and an ear-splitting *CRACK*.

"I looked out on the patio and saw chunks of brick scattered about," Terry remembers. "I rushed out into the breezeway and looked up. The top of the chimney was blown away. At the end of the roof, I could see smoke pouring out of the ridge vent."

While Terry dashed to get his children— Malcolm, 3, and Phoebe, 2—out of their second-floor beds, his wife, Patricia, tried to call the fire department.

"Our computerized central phone system had been fried to a crisp," he says, "but we managed to patch an extra phone into the fax machine, and get a call through to the fire department."

Once Patricia, the kids, and the dogs were safely out—hustled away with the dinner guests to a neighbor's house—Terry grabbed a fire extinguisher and headed back upstairs.

"Smoke was pouring out of the top of the laundry chute," he recalls. "But the fire was buried deep inside the walls where I couldn't get to it with the extinguisher."

Though he was in a state of panic and near shock by the time the fire department arrived, Terry had the presence of mind to answer their questions clearly, which enabled them to put out the fire without much collateral damage from axes and water. Still, when the final toll was taken, there was $45,000 in damage.

"Lightning is a strange and unpredictable beast," says Terry. "The bolt hit the chimney, destroying the flue, then arced along the metal heating duct that runs through the attic. Near the master bedroom, it jumped from the ductwork to the metal laundry chute, where it ignited the studs and rafters.

"Virtually all of the electronics in the house were fried," Terry relates, "including the phone system, computer modem, intercom, TV, and stereo. In the upstairs hall, lightning arced from nail to nail, shooting them out of the drywall like bullets. In my son's room, the intercom exploded out of the wall and flew 20 feet."

Oddly, the main house wiring and breakers were spared, probably because of the primary surge protector that was installed in the main service panel.

Terry can't help but scratch his head over the uncanny timing of the hit.

"Another 48 hours and the lightning rods would have been completely installed and grounded," he laments. "We might have gone on with dinner and never even noticed."

To add insult to injury, Terry's house was struck by lightning again the following Monday, just as the installation crew finished grounding the last lightning rod. Though one of the installers was knocked down, no one was seriously hurt. And there was no additional damage.

"So much for the old adage that lightning never strikes twice in the same place," says Terry. And he adds, with a seasoned smile, "If it strikes us a third time, we're about as ready as we can be."

ADOPTING LIGHTNING PROTECTION

A nearby lightning strike can cause a high-voltage surge or spike in your home's wiring. Such a surge can cause considerable damage to any electrical equipment (especially that containing sophisticated electronics, like computers, microwave ovens, and televisions) that happens to be plugged in at the time. Your best defense against these voltage spikes is to have adequate lightning rods installed on your house and to protect your wiring and equipment with devices known as surge suppressors.

LIGHTNING RODS

The simple principle behind lightning rods, as Benjamin Franklin discovered, is to create a pathway for lightning that will let it flow to ground with the least amount of resistance.

As shown in *Lightning Rod Protection* on this page, this is done by installing copper

LIGHTNING ROD PROTECTION

A lightning rod system is a great way to protect your home from lightning, but it must be installed professionally as detailed here. Your system should include a minimum of two groundings, set at least 10 feet deep.

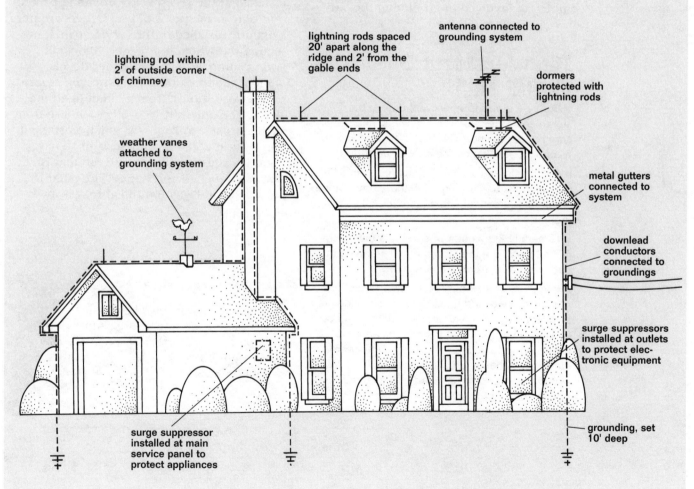

lightning rod within 2' of outside corner of chimney

lightning rods spaced 20' apart along the ridge and 2' from the gable ends

antenna connected to grounding system

dormers protected with lightning rods

weather vanes attached to grounding system

metal gutters connected to system

downlead conductors connected to groundings

surge suppressors installed at outlets to protect electronic equipment

surge suppressor installed at main service panel to protect appliances

grounding, set 10' deep

Pull the Plug

A sure-fire way to protect your valuable electronic equipment from lightning damage is to leave it unplugged, especially if you're going to be away from home for an extended period of time. ●

or aluminum rods along the topmost lines of the house. Lightning is conducted through the rod into a metal cable that conducts the stroke quickly and harmlessly to ground. All of the home's metal-based systems, including its electrical wiring, phone lines, plumbing, gas lines, and heating ducts must be properly tied to the grounding cables.

The installed cost of a lightning rod system depends on the size of the house and the complexity involved in grounding the various household systems. To retrofit an average house, the bill might run from $1,500 to $5,000. In new construction, lightning protection is roughly estimated at 1.5 percent of the construction cost.

CAUTION: Installing lightning rods is *not* a do-it-yourself project.

To avoid hucksters and incompetents, seek out a professional who's been certified through Underwriters Laboratories or the Lightning Protection Institute. If you'd like a reference to someone in your area, call the United Lightning Protection Association at (800) 668-8572.

SURGE SUPPRESSORS

Surge suppressors are electrical devices that sense voltage spikes and shunt the excess current to the ground, before it can do any damage. Some of these units are installed at the receptacle, providing protection only at the point of use. Others are permanently installed in the service panel, protecting the whole house. See "Blocking Spikes" on page 112 for further details.

Surge suppressors alone, however, *cannot* protect your house from a direct lightning strike. The only way to protect a house from such awesome voltage—as much as 100 million volts at 200,000 amperes!—is to have lightning rods installed. And even that isn't always enough. See "Zapped!" on page 182 for a first-hand account of lightning's awesome power.

Thunderstorm Safety Tips

● Before a storm front arrives, unplug the TV, stereo and other electronic devices, and the garage door opener. *CAUTION: Do not attempt to unplug anything if it's already lightning.*

● Avoid using telephones, appliances, and plumbing fixtures during a thunderstorm. These are often the conduits that lightning takes to ground.

● Generally, the center of a room is the safest place to wait out the storm. Avoid standing in doorways or in front of a fireplace.

● If you are caught out in the open, avoid high ground and isolated trees. Seek a low-lying area away from water. If you feel your hair stand on end—an indication that lightning is about to strike—drop to your knees and bend forward, putting your hands on your knees. *CAUTION: Do not lie flat on the ground or place your hands on the ground.*

Protect the Pump

If you have a water well, ask your electrician to install an additional surge suppressor in the pump's subpanel to protect the motor from lightning. If you're going to buy a new well pump, get one with built-in lightning protection. ●

Contaminated Drinking Water

Simple, in-line water filters like the one shown here are fine for removing some contaminants. More effective—and costly—options are discussed starting on page 190.

Quick Response

1. If you're suspicious about quality of your water, stop using it for drinking and cooking.

2. If you rely on municipal system or private water company, report problem immediately.

3. If you have your own well, have water tested by qualified, independent laboratory as soon as possible.

6 NATURAL EMERGENCIES

LOOKING FOR CLEAN, COOL WATER

While drinking water in the United States is remarkably pure compared to that of the rest of the world, the incidence of contamination is rising. This is due both to ongoing pollution and to pollution that occurred prior to the passage of the 1972 Clean Water Act and other federal environmental laws.

Hazards

● Contaminated water can cause serious health problems, especially for young children. If you're at all doubtful about the quality of your water, have it tested. Switch to good quality bottled water while you await the results. (See "What's in the Bottle?" on page 190.)

● An in-home water purification system that is poorly maintained may do more harm than good.

Some water-quality problems are short term in nature, arising from specific incidents, such as floods or broken supply pipes, that temporarily contaminate the distribution system or overload the water treatment plant.

If you use municipal water, you would be notified of any such short-term problems and given timely advice on how to proceed. For example, you might be advised to boil the water before you drink it or to use the water for only bathing and cleaning until the source of the contamination has been eliminated.

In other instances, contamination may be long term in nature, such as when hazardous chemicals are leaching into a municipal or private well. This type of contamination usually compels a homeowner to make a permanent switch to another water source or to install one of the in-home water purification systems discussed on page 190.

BEING ALERT TO CHANGES IN YOUR WATER

Any sudden change in the taste, color, or smell of your drinking water should send off a quick alarm. So, too, should any illness in your family that seems linked to your drinking water. Also, be alert to any complaints or problems voiced by your neighbors, since they are likely to be drawing their drinking water from the same source as you are.

Generally speaking, your sense of taste, smell, and sight *won't* be able to tell you if a contaminant in your water is harmful. As the table "Unpleasant but Not Poisonous" on the opposite page shows, a number of substances—most of them naturally occurring— can give water an unpleasant taste, color, or

Chill the Chlorine

If water from your municipal system is healthy but lacking in the taste department, try refrigerating it in an open container overnight. Municipal water is often purified with chlorine, which can impart a strong flavor to the water. The overnight break allows much of this chlorine to evaporate, thereby improving the flavor. ●

smell without presenting a health hazard.

Unfortunately, the inverse is also true: Water containing lead, radon, volatile organic compounds, protozoa, and other harmful contaminants may look and taste just fine.

So don't rely on your senses alone. Turn to your local water company, state and local health officials, and/or a qualified testing laboratory to provide definitive answers.

ASSESSING MUNICIPAL WATER

If you're part of the 85 percent of Americans who get their water from a municipal system and you're worried about its overall quality, call the city and ask them for a copy of their annual water quality report. The report, based on tests done over the course of the year, will tell you the *average* level of various contaminants as well as their *peak* levels. To help you interpret the results, the report should also list the U.S. Environmental Protection Agency's (EPA) standards for each type of contaminant.

If one or more of the contaminants in your water exceeds the maximum safe level established by the EPA, you should consider installing an in-home water purification system or making a permanent switch to bottled drinking water. This is especially true if the report reveals a prolonged or recurring pattern of EPA violations and the city is not moving aggressively to address the problem.

If the municipal water report doesn't list EPA standards, ask for them. If you still have trouble understanding the report and there's no one at the water department willing or able to give you a candid interpretation, get help from your local or state health officials. You can also get some answers by calling the EPA's drinking water hotline at (800) 426-4791.

Of course, a good report from the municipal water department isn't an absolute guarantee that your drinking water is safe. Contaminants can get into the water *after* it's left the treatment plant, originating in the distribution system or in your own plumbing.

Lead, a dangerous contaminant that leaches out of solder, brass fittings, and lead pipes, is the most common example. If you suspect that your house has lead water pipes, it'd be smart to have the water tested by a reputable lab. (See "What to Do about Lead?" on page 188.)

UNPLEASANT BUT NOT POISONOUS

Not all water contaminants are health-threatening, but bad taste or odors and strange colors in your water can be bothersome. You should be able to alleviate these aesthetic problems by following the advice below.

PROBLEM	SOURCE	SOLUTION
CHLORINE TASTE	Chlorine commonly added to water as disinfectant*	Use activated carbon filter
ROTTEN EGG ODOR	Hydrogen sulfide naturally occurring in groundwater	Use oxidizing filter or chlorination and activated carbon filter
WATER IS REDDISH BROWN AND HAS METALLIC TASTE	Naturally occurring iron or rust from old pipes	Use water softener or iron filter; replace old steel pipes or rusty water heater
WATER IS GRAY OR BLACK; SMELLS	Manganese in groundwater	Use zeolite-ion exchange filter or iron manganese filter
WATER IS MUDDY OR SANDY	Mud or sand drawn up from bottom of well	Repair sediment screen at well bottom; install particle filter
WATER IS CLOUDY; SCALY DEPOSITS ON TOILET, TUB	Dissolved calcium, magnesium, and other minerals	Use water softener or reverse osmosis unit
SALTY TASTE	Chloride or sodium from road salting or saltwater	Flush well; use activated carbon filter

*Chlorine itself is harmless, but a group of chlorine by-products called trihalomethanes may present a health hazard in drinking water. The U.S. Environmental Protection Agency has mandated changes in the way chlorine is used in water treatment to reduce the incidence of trihalomethanes.

ASSESSING WELL WATER

Since private wells are usually not subjected to frequent testing and continuous treatment, they're more likely to contain a hazardous pollutant than a public water system. This is especially true of shallow, unsealed wells, which are easily polluted by algae, decaying plant matter, insects, and animal wastes, all of which contribute to high levels of microorganisms. Wells are also susceptible to contamination from septic systems, particularly when the well is located down slope from a nearby drain field, as shown in *Contamination from a Septic System* on page 188.

In some parts of the United States, radioactive contaminants such as radon, uranium, and radium-228 occur naturally in ground-

water. (See *Radioactivity in the Water* on page 189.) Generally speaking, private wells are much more likely to contain dangerous concentrations of these contaminants than public water supplies.

If you use drinking water from a private well, you can protect your health by following these key recommendations.

● Have the well water tested by a reputable laboratory at least every two years, including a test for radioactive contaminants and synthetic organic chemicals. You may want the water tested more often if well contamination is a frequent problem in your area.

● If the well is open, have it properly sealed (and treated, if necessary) to prevent the invasion of microorganisms.

What to Do about Lead?

Lead is a tasteless, colorless, and odorless metal that leaches out of lead pipes, soldered joints, and brass fittings and can contaminate your water. According to the U.S. Environmental Protection Agency (EPA), it presents a potential health hazard to some 40 million Americans, children being the most vulnerable.

The symptoms of lead poisoning are many and varied, including loss of appetite, fatigue, insomnia, constipation or diarrhea, and pain in the joints or abdomen.

Since lead pipes and lead-based solder were banned nationwide in 1986, newer houses don't usually present as high a risk as older ones do. But the water in houses built prior to 1986—especially those built between 1910 and 1940 when lead pipes were commonly used—should be carefully checked for lead contamination.

Lead pipe is easily distinguished from copper by its softness and dark gray color (copper is harder and reddish gold or brown) and from galvanized steel by its lack of magnetism (a magnet will be attracted to steel or iron pipe but not to lead). Similarly, lead-based solder is much softer and darker than tin-based solder.

The presence of lead pipe or solder does not necessarily mean that the concentration of lead in your water is more than 15 parts per billion—the level at which the EPA recommends remedial action. Other variables, such as the acidity of the water and the extent to which the lead has become covered with a protective coating of mineral deposits, can greatly affect how much lead actually leaches into the water.

Nonetheless, if you have lead pipes or solder, it's prudent to take the following precautions:

● Have your water tested at a reputable lab. (See "Testing Your Water" on this page.)

● Avoid drinking or cooking with water that has been standing in the pipes for a long time. After returning from vacation or a weekend away, open the tap and let it run for a full minute to flush out the stagnant, lead-bearing water.

● When cooking, use water from the cold tap, not the hot. Since cold water is less corrosive than hot, its lead content will likely be lower.

CONTAMINATION FROM A SEPTIC SYSTEM

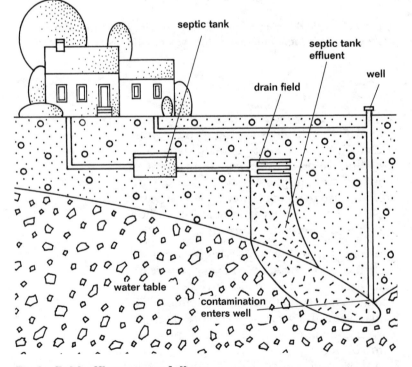

septic tank

septic tank effluent

well

drain field

water table

contamination enters well

Drain field effluent may follow the water table to the well.

TESTING YOUR WATER

One good way to select a quality laboratory is to call your state health department and ask them for a recommendation. Another is to contact ACIL, a nonprofit group that will provide (free of charge) a list of reputable labs in your area. (ACIL's address and phone are listed in "For More Information" on page 193.)

Since test prices vary quite a bit from one commercial lab to the next, you may want to contact several for price quotes before you proceed. And *always* double-check to make sure that the lab is EPA-certified to do the specific tests that you're requesting.

Contaminants can be categorized into five groups, as follows:

● **Additives,** including chlorine (trihalomethanes), fluoride, and flocculents, which are sometimes used to purify municipal drinking water
● **Microorganisms,** including bacteria, protozoa, and viruses
● **Organic chemicals,** found in industrial wastes, pesticides, gasoline, cleaning fluids,

RADIOACTIVITY IN THE WATER

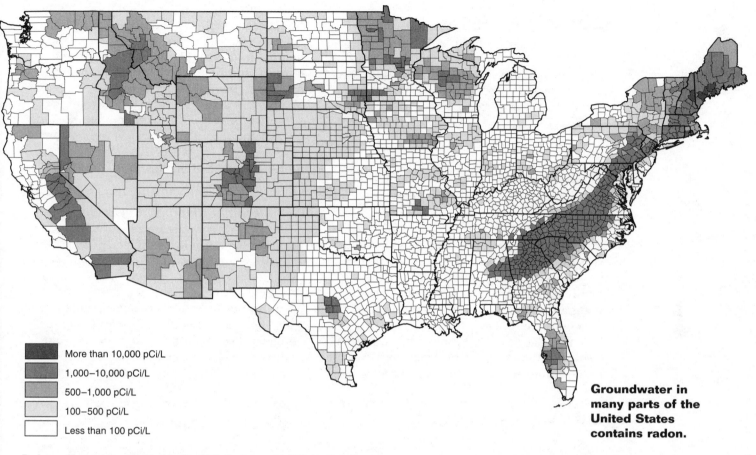

More than 10,000 pCi/L

1,000–10,000 pCi/L

500–1,000 pCi/L

100–500 pCi/L

Less than 100 pCi/L

Groundwater in many parts of the United States contains radon.

Redrawn from a map provided by the U.S. Environmental Protection Agency

paint thinners, and so forth
- **Radioactive substances,** including radon, uranium, and radium-228
- **Toxic metals and minerals,** including arsenic, lead, mercury, silver, fluoride, and nitrate

Since it would be enormously expensive to test your water for *all* of the possible contaminants in these groups, the best strategy—unless you have a precise idea of what you're looking for—is to use three indicator tests.

Radon in Your Well?

If you have a private well, ask your local or state health department if there's been any incidence of radon contamination in area wells. If so, it'd be prudent to have the water tested for radon. (See "Radon" on page 205.) ●

The first of these—for coliform bacteria—costs $12 to $40. Though coliform itself is not dangerous, it signals the presence of other harmful bacteria.

The second indicator test is for total organic halides—sometimes called a TOX test—which costs $45 to $90. While a TOX test won't identify specific organic pollutants, it can alert you to the need for additional testing. However, a TOX test is *not* recommended if your water is chlorinated (most municipal water is), since the chlorine interferes with the test results.

The third indicator test, which costs $25 to $55, is for total organic carbon (TOC). A TOC test measures the water's total organic pollution, whether manmade or natural, and can signal the need for additional tests.

It's critical that you follow the lab's instructions on how to take the water sample, package it, and mail it. If the test results are positive, it's wise to run the test a second time—to confirm the results—before taking any remedial action.

SELECTING IN-HOME WATER PURIFICATION SYSTEMS

Whether you're treating water for aesthetic reasons, such as taste or hardness, or need to address a genuine health concern, it's vitally important that you select a reputable company to install *and* service the purification equipment. Look for an established business that has a good reputation, permanent location, and a stable relationship with one or more reputable manufacturers.

The water treatment equipment you buy should meet the standards established by the National Sanitation Foundation or the Water Quality Association. Both are independent, not-for-profit organizations that test products to see if they remove the specific contaminants that their manufacturers claim. (See "For More Information" on page 193.)

Three types of systems are commonly used for in-home treatment. Since each has its specific strengths and weaknesses, they're sometimes used in combination.

ACTIVATED CARBON FILTERS

Line pressure forces water through one or more canisters packed with activated carbon granules, which trap and hold contaminants. (See *How Activated Carbon Filters Work* on this page.) Carbon filters can remove bad odors and tastes, chlorine, and organic chemicals. Some are effective in treating radon and lead. Installed retail prices range from about $50 for a simple countertop model up to $450 for a high-volume, under-the-sink model. The high-volume systems require replacement filters every 1,000 gallons, at a cost of $15 to $75.

DISTILLATION

Water is electrically heated inside a vessel to make steam, which is then condensed in a coil to produce distilled water. (See *How Distillation Works* on the opposite page.) Distillation will remove most dissolved solids, including salts and heavy metals, such as lead, but it is not effective in removing volatile organic compounds, such as gasoline and cleaning fluids. Distillation requires a lot of electricity and releases appreciable amounts of heat into the room, a plus in the winter but a negative in the summer. An installed system costs from $250 to $1,000. Most models need to be cleaned periodically to remove scaly mineral deposits.

HOW ACTIVATED CARBON FILTERS WORK

water in

water out

activated carbon

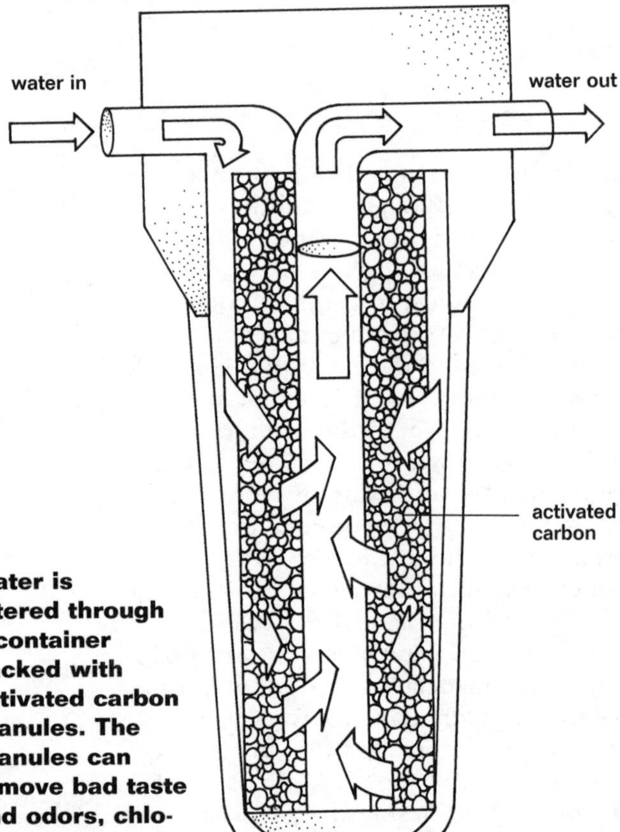

Water is filtered through a container packed with activated carbon granules. The granules can remove bad taste and odors, chlorine, and organic chemicals.

What's in the Bottle?

If you're switching to bottled water for aesthetic or health reasons, remember this: All bottled water is *not* created equal. Apart from distinct differences in taste, there can be important differences in purity and price.

To ensure that you're getting a truly healthy product (and your money's worth), follow these tips.

● Look for the words *DRINKING WATER* or *PURIFIED WATER* on the label. These denote that the water has been carefully filtered and treated. *DISTILLED WATER* is also a healthy choice but usually flunks the taste test.

● Check the label to make sure that the manufacturer is a member of the International Bottled Water Association (IBWA). IBWA members test their products for over 200 contaminants and submit to an annual plant inspection conducted by an independent third party.

● If you have doubts about whether a particular bottler is an IBWA member or not, write or call the International Bottled Water Association, 113 N. Henry Street, Alexandria, VA 22314-2973; (703) 683-5213.

● Write the company and ask them for a laboratory report on their water. The report will carry more weight if it's done by an independent lab rather than the company itself.

● Make sure bottles are sealed properly. Store bottled drinking water in a cool place away from solvents that could degrade the plastic.

● Compare prices. High transportation costs (from remote suppliers), fancy labels, and expensive advertising campaigns can boost the price of a bottled water without delivering any added quality.

HOW DISTILLATION WORKS

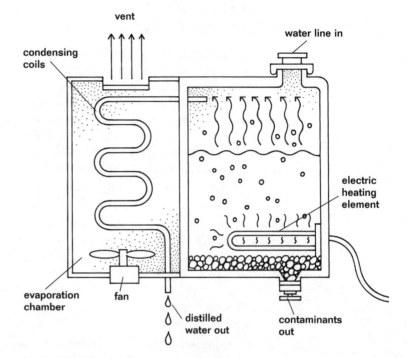

Water heated to steam condenses in a coil and is collected. Distillation removes salt and heavy metals.

HOW REVERSE OSMOSIS UNITS WORK

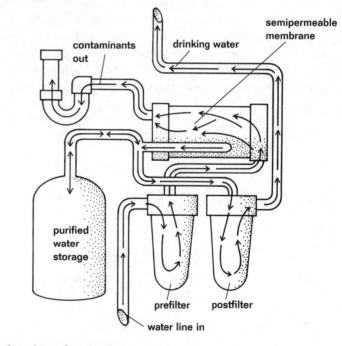

Molecules of pure water are forced through a membrane. Purified water is collected in a storage tank.

REVERSE OSMOSIS UNITS

(See *How Reverse Osmosis Units Work* on this page.) Line pressure forces molecules of pure water through a thin semipermeable membrane. Purified water is slowly collected in a storage tank while dissolved contaminants, unable to pass through the membrane, are drained away. Reverse osmosis (RO) will remove 90 to 99 percent of the impurities in water, including lead and other toxic metals, nitrates, and organic contaminants. But RO units waste 3 to 5 gallons of water for every

Considering Water Softeners

Water that contains a lot of calcium, magnesium, and other minerals is sometimes described as "hard." Though hard water doesn't present any known health hazards, it can make the water cloudy and cause scaly deposits to build up on toilets and tubs. Hard water also makes it more difficult to rinse the soap off your skin when you shower and to rinse the soap out of your clothes when you do the laundry.

Water-softening equipment is typically installed at the point where the main water line enters the house and usually requires an electrical hook-up to power the system's regeneration cycle (see below). The equipment is designed to treat the water supply for the whole house.

The system works on water line pressure, which pushes hard water through a canister filled with resin and salt. Through a process called *ion exchange,* the "hard" calcium and magnesium ions dissolved in the water are exchanged for "soft" sodium ions affixed to the resin.

When the resin becomes saturated with calcium and magnesium—typically after about 2,000 gallons of processing—the system automatically regenerates itself by flushing the resin with salt water from a companion tank that's filled with brine. From time to time—the interval depends on the unit's

ANATOMY OF A WATER SOFTENER

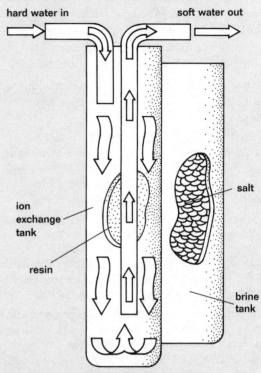

A water softener exchanges the "hard" calcium and magnesium ions in the water for "soft" sodium ions affixed to the resin.

design and how much it's used—the brine tank has to be reloaded with salt.

The installed retail price for a water softener ranges from about $750 to $2,200.

gallon that's purified. The installed retail price runs from $450 to $1,000. Replacement filters cost from $150 to $300 each.

INSTALLING AND MAINTAINING A SYSTEM

Since less than 1 percent of the water used in the average home is for cooking and drinking, it's usually not necessary to treat all of the incoming water. Instead, treatment equipment is installed only at the point of use—that is, in

proximity to faucets from which drinking and cooking water is drawn.

Sometimes, however, it's necessary or desirable to install a point-of-entry treatment system that processes *all* of the home's water. This is usually recommended when there are elevated levels of radon or volatile organic compounds in the water.

As you shop for a reputable firm to install water treatment equipment, keep this in mind: *The equipment will quickly become useless— possibly even dangerous—if not properly maintained.* (The jury is still out on if the microorganisms that can multiply inside a poorly maintained system present a health haz-

For More Information

If you want to find out more about the quality of your drinking water, water filtration, bottled water, or water softening, the organizations listed below provide excellent resources.

ACIL
Suite 400
1629 K Street NW
Washington, DC 20006
(202) 887-5872

International Bottled Water Association
113 N. Henry Street
Alexandria, VA 22314-2973
(703) 683-5213

National Sanitation Foundation
P.O. Box 1468
3475 Plymouth Road
Ann Arbor, MI 48105
(313) 769-8010

U.S. Environmental Protection Agency
Office of Drinking Water (WH5500)
401 M Street SW
Washington, DC 20460
(800) 426-4791

Water Quality Association
4151 Naperville Road
Lisle, IL 60532
(708) 505-0160

ard.) So, obtaining good follow-up service (perhaps in the form of a service contract) should be a top priority in making your decision.

Also bear in mind that the lifetime operating and maintenance costs of water treatment systems can be several times their original purchase price, especially when the costs of wasted water (in a reverse osmosis unit) and electricity (in a distillation unit) are factored in.

Polluted Indoor Air

Quick Response

1. Reduce or eliminate source of pollution.

2. Increase ventilation to dilute pollutant.

3. If necessary, add air filtration device to remove pollutant from air.

When working with hazardous chemicals or fuels, use a work mask or respirator designed to filter out those hazards. The masks and respirators like the ones shown here are available at home centers.

Hazards

● Each type of indoor pollutant has different potential health effects. (See the individual entries in this chapter.)

● The concentration of the pollutant, the length of exposure, and your sensitivity determine how a certain pollutant will affect your health.

● In some cases, indoor air pollutants have a cumulative effect on human health, such as when two or more substances work together to push an individual past his level of tolerance, or when the presence of cigarette smoke increases the health risks associated with radon.

FINDING CLUES TO POLLUTED AIR

The symptoms associated with polluted indoor air—watering eyes, sore throats, headaches, upper respiratory problems, nausea, vomiting, fatigue, and rashes—may be mistaken for flu or cold symptoms.

So how can you tell the difference?

First of all, there's an unpleasant odor associated with some pollutants, especially volatile organic compounds (cleaning agents, formaldehyde, pesticides, solvents), combustion by-products, and mold (allergenic spores).

Second, some pollutants are actually visible to the naked eye, such as when asbestos fibers, flecks of lead paint, or particles of fiberglass become airborne. Likewise, you can usually spot mold growing in a dank corner (though the airborne spores are too small to see).

Finally, you can distinguish the symptoms of indoor air pollution from a cold or flu because your "illness" doesn't get better and because in most cases, when you leave the house, your symptoms will mysteriously abate or disappear.

Be forewarned, however, that two very dangerous pollutants—radon and carbon monoxide—are *not* detectable through the senses and won't give you any early-warning symptoms.

IDENTIFYING POLLUTANT TYPES

In order to combat indoor air pollution, you need to know what you're looking for. *Sources of Indoor Air Pollution* on page 196 shows common causes of pollution in the home, and the categories that follow spell out the details.

AIRBORNE PARTICLES

The health problems associated with inhaled asbestos fibers (asbestosis and lung cancer) and lead dust (blood, kidney, neurological, and reproductive disorders) are well documented.

While the use of asbestos and lead-based paint was banned in residential construction in the late 1970s, the materials still abound in many middle-aged and older houses. Asbestos, a white or grayish fibrous material, was widely used to insulate boilers and pipes and as a component in floor and ceiling tiles. Lead-based paint was applied to both indoor and outdoor surfaces.

Generally speaking, asbestos and lead-based paint don't present a hazard as long as they're left in place. It's only after they're damaged or disintegrated and subsequently picked up by moving air that hazardous particles find their way into human lungs. *NOTE:* Lead is also toxic when swallowed, as when it's present in drinking water. (See "What to Do about Lead?" on page 188.)

Asbestos Check

If you suspect you have asbestos in your house, you can have a sample piece checked at a lab for about $50. Paint can be checked with a do-it-yourself test kit (available for around $10 at home centers) to find out if it contains lead. ●

Air currents moving in through an open window—especially when propelled by a window fan—can lift flecks of lead paint and dust off the windowsill and distribute them throughout the house.

Leaky heating and air conditioning ducts can also draw hazardous particles into the air and propel them through the house. (See "The HVAC Connection" on page 218.)

If you discover that your house contains asbestos, but it's not damaged or disintegrating, your best strategy is probably to leave it right where it is. However, if it's crumbling or flaking or coming out of the heating registers, contact an asbestos abatement contractor who's been certified by your state environmental agency.

Lead-based paint that's in good shape can be covered by a fresh coat of nonpolluting paint. (This is especially important if children might touch or lick the lead paint.) If lead-based paint is chipping or peeling or otherwise needs to be removed, use a nontoxic liquid paint stripper or a low-temperature heat gun.

CAUTION: Do not use a propane torch, high-temperature heat gun, sandpaper, or sandblasting to remove lead-based paint, as these methods will fill the air with lead dust.

6
NATURAL EMERGENCIES

Airborne Fiberglass

Bits of fiberglass or cellulose insulation sucked into broken ductwork in the attic, basement, or crawl space are fairly common as sources of indoor air pollution. While these particles can irritate the nose, throat, and lungs, there's no evidence that they cause serious health problems. Nonetheless, quick steps should be taken to repair the broken duct. ●

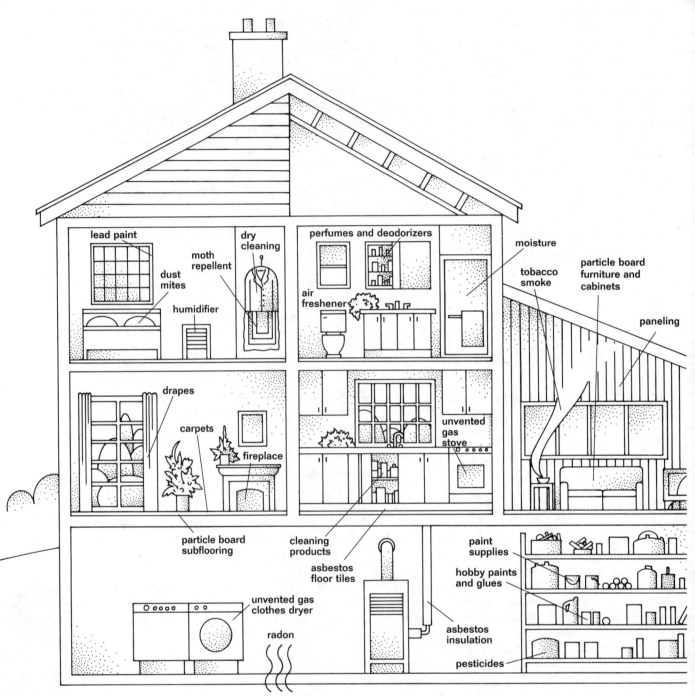

lead paint

dry cleaning

moth repellent

dust mites

humidifier

perfumes and deodorizers

air freshener

moisture

tobacco smoke

particle board furniture and cabinets

paneling

drapes

carpets

fireplace

unvented gas stove

particle board subflooring

cleaning products

asbestos floor tiles

paint supplies

hobby paints and glues

unvented gas clothes dryer

radon

asbestos insulation

pesticides

Keep It Dry

The single most effective way to limit indoor air contamination from biological pollutants is to eliminate standing water in and around your home and to keep the relative humidity indoors between 35 and 50 percent. For pointers on how to accomplish this, see "Controlling Indoor Humidity" on page 217. ●

BIOLOGICAL TYPES

These include plant pollens and mold spores, dust mites (as shown in *Microscopic Monster* on page 198), bacteria, and various insect and pet allergens. Their health effects encompass a variety of allergic reactions and respiratory problems, including asthma.

Plant pollens and mold spores are among the most common indoor pollutants. Sometimes they originate outdoors and find their

Paint Roundup

Take an inventory of old and leftover paint cans. Any remaining paint that contains lead or phenylmercuric acetate (which can outgas mercury vapor) should be treated as a hazardous waste. See **Hazardous chemicals and fuels** on page 198. ●

Water, whether in liquid or vapor form, is the key element that enables microorganisms and insects to thrive. A bathroom carpet that remains damp and warm day in and day out may play host to as many as 10 million microorganisms and mold spores per square foot.

Other breeding grounds include basements, crawl spaces, and wet attics; reservoir-type humidifiers; heating and cooling ducts; dirty air filters; and the pans and drains on heating and cooling equipment. (See "Mold and Mildew" on page 213.)

COMBUSTION BY-PRODUCTS

Furnaces, boilers, fireplaces, woodstoves, gas water heaters, and other combustion appliances require plenty of make-up air and a well-maintained vent or chimney to operate safely. When these safeguards are missing, carbon monoxide, nitrogen dioxide, and other combustion by-products can backdraft into the house with potentially deadly results. (See "Backdrafting Flue" on page 122.)

CONSUMER PRODUCTS

Many consumer and personal care products—especially those that come in aerosol cans—contribute to indoor air pollution. Without proper ventilation, the vapors they emit can linger in a room for hours. Some

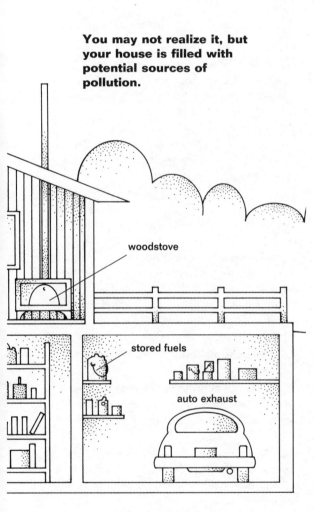

You may not realize it, but your house is filled with potential sources of pollution.

woodstove

stored fuels

auto exhaust

way inside through open windows, doors, and ducts. Other times they're spawned from houseplants or fungi (mold and mildew) growing *inside* the house.

House dust allergens derived from cockroaches, dust mites, fleas, and furniture that contains animal products (like feather-stuffed cushions) also contribute to indoor air pollution and the health problems described above.

Dust Mite Dilemma

If someone in your family has dust mite allergy problems, consider ceramic tiles, a hardwood floor, or vinyl flooring instead of wall-to-wall carpeting. In any case, *don't* carpet the bathroom. The combination of carpet and almost continuous moisture creates a virtual paradise for dust mites and microorganisms. ●

MICROSCOPIC MONSTER (DUST MITE)

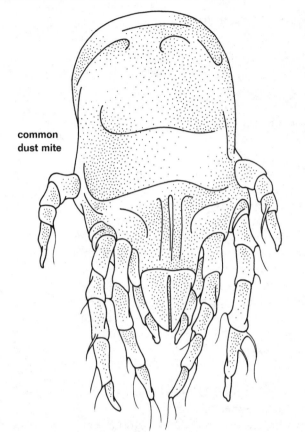

common dust mite

You can't see them, but dust mites are your permanent—and prolific—house guests.

10 Ways to Alleviate Your Allergy Problems

1. If pollen is the source of your allergy problems, avoid going outdoors in the morning when the pollen count is typically highest.

2. Get away to the seashore (or other low-pollen destination) during the height of the pollen season.

3. Use an air conditioner inside the house or car. It can help prevent pollen and mold allergens from entering.

4. Frequently change or wash the air filters on your heating and cooling equipment. (See "Filtering the Air" on page 202.)

5. Eliminate any sources of moisture in and around your home that might generate mold. (See "Mold and Mildew" on page 213.)

6. If you own a forced-air heating or air conditioning system, have the duct work cleaned out periodically. (See "The HVAC Connection" on page 218.)

7. If you're allergic to dust (dust mites), wash your clothes, bed linens, and curtains in 130°F (or hotter) water. Dust the house often, using a damp cloth or oiled mop. Consider removing wall-to-wall carpets and soft furnishing, especially down-filled blankets and feather pillows, which make dust control almost impossible. Encase your mattress in a zippered plastic bag.

8. Consider buying a room air cleaner to remove dust and pollen. (See "Filtering the Air" on page 202.)

9. If you are allergic to the cat (and can't bear to part with it), bathe and comb it frequently to reduce the airborne allergens it releases.

10. Avoid unnecessary exposure to aerosols, tobacco smoke, fresh paint, and other chemical irritants that can aggravate your allergy.

contain volatile organic compounds (for example, benzene, toluene, and xylene), which may have short- and long-term health effects. (See "VOCs" on page 200.)

Among the more than 200 aerosol products on the market are carpet "fresheners," flea killers, hair-styling sprays, kitchen and bathroom cleaners, oven cleaners, pesticides, room deodorizers, spot removers, and spray paints.

Generally speaking, these products are safe to use, provided you *read* and *follow* the instructions. It's always prudent, however, to use aerosols as sparingly as possible and to flood the area with fresh air during and after their use. Whenever possible, aerosols should be used outdoors.

HAZARDOUS CHEMICALS AND FUELS

The average home contains a startling number of hazardous materials, including pesticides, weed killers, gasoline, camping fuel,

glues, lacquers, paint removers, wood stains, varnishes, shellacs, and wood preservatives.

It's essential that hazardous chemicals and fuels be stored in a safe place in a safe container when they're not in use. (See "An Ounce of Prevention" on page 256.) When they're in use, follow the instructions on the label, *flood* the area with fresh air, and protect yourself with proper clothing and a mask or respirator. Don't be deceived into thinking

Migrating Fumes

Don't forget that toxic fumes released in your workshop or garage will migrate into other parts of the house, even when the door is closed. This is especially true if you have heating and cooling ducts interconnecting various parts of the house. See "The HVAC Connection" on page 218. ●

that an ordinary dust mask, which is designed to trap large-diameter, nontoxic particles, will protect you from toxic fumes. See "Work Masks and Respirators" on this page for information on respirators.

As a final precaution, get rid of any hazardous chemicals or fuels that are polluted, outdated, or no longer needed. Since they are too dangerous to be simply flushed down the drain or hauled away in a garbage truck, contact your municipality or local recycling center for instructions on how to handle them.

POLLUTANTS FROM OUTDOORS

Sometimes the original source of indoor pollution is located *outside* the home.

Pesticides or herbicides used on surrounding lawns or fields can be drawn into your house through a furnace intake, clothes dryer vent, or through the cracks around windows and doors. A nearby plant, factory, or business can also be a serious source of pollution, such as when an underground storage tank leaks at a nearby gas station.

If you suspect that your indoor air is being polluted by a neighbor, be it a residence or business, see if you can enlist their friendly cooperation in trying to track down and eliminate the source of the pollution *before* you contact municipal, state, or federal authorities. But if friendly persuasion doesn't get results, give your state or federal environmental protection office a call.

RADON

This odorless, invisible, radioactive gas is formed in the soil by the gradual decay of uranium. Unlike other uranium "daughters," which generally remain trapped in the ground, radon can percolate up through the soil as a free gas. It can also contaminate groundwater, presenting problems for homeowners who rely on artesian wells.

When released outdoors, radon poses no threat. But when it builds up indoors and

Work Masks and Respirators

Shop workers, beware! Flooding your shop with fresh air through open windows and doors may not protect you from toxic vapors.

For about $25, you can equip yourself with a good half-face organic vapor respirator that uses replaceable charcoal cartridges and particle filters. This type of mask provides a safe and inexpensive defense against most, though not all, organic vapors. (Methylene chloride, the solvent used in paint strippers, and methyl alcohol, used in lacquer thinner, paint remover, shellac, and aniline-based wood stains, are two notable exceptions.) The mask can be used for spray painting, applying wood preservatives, and other hazardous chores around the home, so it's well worth the money.

The Cabot Safety Corporation, 3M, and North Safety Products are three prominent manufacturers of respirators that you'll find in hardware stores. Be sure to choose a model that's right for the job, comfortable, and snug-fitting. Look for the prefix *TC* on the mask's certification number and the emblem of the National Institute for Occupational Safety and Health.

Remember that if the mask doesn't fit you well, if its exhaust ports are blocked, or if you don't change cartridges and filters frequently enough, it ceases to be effective. If you smell fumes inside the mask, that's a sign that your protection has broken down.

Also keep in mind that the fumes of some hazardous chemicals—again, methylene chloride and methyl alcohol are two good examples—can be absorbed through the skin, even when there's no direct contact. Thus, superabundant ventilation and proper clothing become doubly important. In fact, if it's at all possible, work with these products outdoors.

makes its way into human lungs, radon becomes a powerful carcinogen. The U.S. Environmental Protection Agency (EPA) estimates that radon causes up to 30,000 lung cancer deaths a year in the United States.

Because radon is such a prevalent and serious problem (as many as one out of every five homes may have health-threatening levels), I have devoted an entire chapter to the subject. See "Radon" on page 205.

TOBACCO SMOKE

Studies show that cigarette smoke is a major source of indoor air pollution. Many of the 4,000 plus chemicals contained in mainstream tobacco smoke are known to be toxic or carcinogenic. Moreover, there's mounting evidence that breathing secondhand tobacco smoke causes lung cancer in nonsmoking adults and increases the risk of asthma, bronchitis, and pneumonia in children. As noted above, tobacco smoke can compound or aggravate the effects of other pollutants, particularly radon.

VOCS

Volatile organic compounds, or VOCs, include a variety of chemicals, such as benzene, formaldehyde, perchloroethylene, toluene, and xylene, that are emitted as gases from thousands of solid and liquid products, including the following:

● *Certain household furnishings and office equipment:* cabinets, pressed wood furniture, subflooring, carpets, drapes, copiers, and photographic solutions
● *Construction materials:* fiberboard, paneling, plywood, and urea-formaldehyde insulation (now banned)
● *Household products:* oven cleaners, rug "fresheners," etc. (See "Consumer Products" on page 197.)
● *Woodworking products:* adhesives, finishes, glues, lacquers, paints and paint removers, and wood preservatives

Symptoms of exposure to VOCs include eye and upper respiratory irritation, fatigue, headache, and rash. Formaldehyde has been classified as a probable human carcinogen. Benzene is known to cause leukemia.

Some of the construction materials and products that outgas VOCs carry warning labels detailing the risks and outlining procedures for safe use; others don't. In some cases, it may be

Formaldehyde Detection

A passive formaldehyde monitor is available for homeowners through Air Quality Research, Inc., 4310 Miami Boulevard, Durham, NC 27703 for $77.50. The price includes two test monitors, laboratory analysis, and shipping and handling. ●

feasible to replace outgassing building materials or furnishings with alternative products.

When you use a spray- or brush-on product that contains VOCs (if you're not alerted by the product label, you can usually tell by the smell), flood the work area with fresh air and make sure that you store or dispose of the container safely once you're finished.

FINDING REMEDIES

As outlined in "Quick Response" on page 194, indoor air pollution problems can be addressed in three ways: removing the source, ventilating the area, and filtering the air.

Most air-quality experts view removing the source of the pollutant and ventilating the area as the two key elements in addressing indoor air problems. Using filtration is often a complementary or supporting tactic.

REMOVING THE SOURCE

Once you've identified the source of the pollution, which may require the help of a professional, how you reduce or eliminate it varies.

If the pollution is coming from a consumer product or household chemical, the solution may be as simple as discarding the substance or storing it in a different place or container.

You can usually reduce or eliminate biological pollutants by cutting off the source of water that enabled the organisms to thrive and then sanitizing the affected area. In many cases, the infested material will have to be discarded. (See "Mold and Mildew" on page 213.)

The physical removal of hazardous construction materials, like lead paint and asbestos, is sometimes necessary, *and best left to professionals*. Other times, the offending material can be left in place or encapsulated with paint, plywood, or polyurethane.

Buying New Carpet?

First, here's the bad news: Carpets, padding, and the adhesives sometimes used to install them emit volatile organic compounds (VOCs), which contribute to indoor air quality problems. (See "VOCs" on the opposite page.)

Now for the good news: In recent years, carpet manufacturers have voluntarily altered their materials and production techniques to eliminate or lower VOC emissions. Nonetheless, I recommend that you check the back of carpet samples for a certification label that confirms the carpet has been tested and rated *LOW VOC*, as shown in *Air Quality Label*.

If possible, let your new carpet and padding air out for a few days in your garage before it's installed. And try to schedule the installation during warm weather when windows and doors can be left open to ventilate the house.

Once installed, the carpet should be thoroughly vacuumed at least once a week, with touch-ups in between. Vacuuming removes the organic materials (soil, skin, and hair) that dust mites and microorganisms feed on. And since dirt is abrasive, a clean carpet will also last longer.

Keep in mind that some vacuum cleaners have very porous collection bags that let a lot of dust escape back into the house. To keep the dust where it belongs, equip your vacuum cleaner with a micron filter bag.

Avoid using carpet fresheners, especially those that contain formaldehyde. It's much better to smell the dog than to inhale the formaldehyde.

Finally, have your carpet steam-cleaned by a professional every year or two.

AIR QUALITY LABEL

INDOOR AIR QUALITY CARPET TESTING PROGRAM

product type:

FOR MORE INFORMATION
The Carpet and Rug Institute
1 - 800 / 882-8846

Check the back of carpeting for this label, which certifies that it has been tested and rated *LOW VOC* (volatile organic compound).

Reproduced with permission from the Carpet and Rug Institute, Dalton, Georgia

VENTILATING THE AREA

By introducing plenty of fresh air into your house, through natural and/or mechanical means, you obtain these powerful benefits.

● Ventilation dilutes indoor air pollutants and helps flush them out of the house.

(Ventilation alone, however, usually won't solve a serious radon, formaldehyde, or moisture problem.)

● Ventilation helps lower indoor humidity and reduce condensation, which cuts off the water that microorganisms need to flourish. Lower humidity will also slow the rate at which formaldehyde outgasses from construction materials.

● Ventilation helps to keep the air pressure indoors and outside in equilibrium. (If the air pressure inside the house is lower than outside—a condition that's common in winter—moisture, radon gas, and other pollutants can be sucked up into your basement, crawl space, or ground floor.)

● Ventilation ensures that your combustion appliances have plenty of make-up air, reducing the chances of backdraft. (See

Read the Label

Watch what you bring into your house! Read the labels, especially any warnings or precautions. Whenever possible, opt for nontoxic alternatives. If you have to buy a toxic product, buy the smallest quantity possible. ●

Filters and Air Flow

Since upgrading to a more efficient filter may alter the air flow in your forced-air heating or air conditioning system, it may be necessary to adjust the blower speed or make other modifications. A more efficient filter may also need to be washed or replaced more frequently than the old one. In any case, consult a professional heating and air conditioning technician *before* you change to a different type of filter. ●

"Backdrafting Flue" on page 122.)
● Ventilation provides natural cooling in the summer, reducing the need for expensive air conditioning.

While opening windows and doors may provide adequate ventilation part of the year, most houses require some type of mechanical ventilation. This could include one or more of the following options:

● Attic fan
● Bathroom and kitchen exhaust fans
● Central air conditioning with fresh-air cycle (for ventilation only)
● Ducted central exhaust fan with pressure-activated wall ports to admit fresh air
● Ducted ventilation system with heat recovery (air-to-air heat exchanger)
● Room air conditioner with fresh-air cycle (for ventilation only)
● Window fan

Since it is beyond the scope of this book to examine each of these ventilation options in depth, I recommend that you talk with a competent professional who can assess your home's ventilation needs and make a wise recommendation.

I encourage you to write for a free copy of *The Home Ventilating Guide,* available from the Home Ventilating Institute, 30 West University Drive, Arlington Heights, IL 60004. (See "For More Information" on the opposite page.)

FILTERING THE AIR

Indoor air can be filtered in one of two ways: by placing a filter in the plenum or duct on a forced-air heating and cooling system or by using a stand-alone (usually portable) room model.

While air filtration offers definite benefits in improving indoor air quality, reducing or eliminating the source of the pollution should be tried first.

If you own a forced-air heating or air conditioning system, the air moving through it is probably filtered by a disposable or washable filter made out of woven fiberglass. This simple, inexpensive filter, situated in the blower compartment or plenum, can remove spores, pollen, and large dust particles from the air. Its main purpose is to keep the furnace's heat exchanger, air conditioning coils, and ductwork clean.

You can improve your indoor air quality (and better protect the equipment) by installing a more efficient air filter. See the table "Filter Efficiency" on page 204 for some filter options and the percentage of pollutants they remove from the air.

An upgrade to a media air filter is worthwhile in most cases, even for people who don't perceive any problem with their indoor air quality.

Installing an electronic air cleaner or HEPA is a much more expensive proposition. And both require careful, ongoing maintenance to remain effective.

Before you consider a complex and expensive air filtration system, every effort should be made to reduce the source of the pollution and increase the ventilation rate.

Stand-alone or room air cleaners can be effective in removing dust, cigarette smoke, and pollen. They are rated according to their Clean Air Delivery Rate, which is certified by the Association of Home Appliance Manufacturers (AHAM).

For a listing of certified manufacturers and a free pamphlet titled *Consumer Guide for*

Faulty Filters

Beware of exaggerated claims from some manufacturers of room air cleaners. While a certain model may be able to remove a high percentage of the pollutants that come in contact with its filter, the volume of air moving through the unit may be too small to make much of a difference. Conversely, other room air cleaners may be able to filter a large volume of air, but not very effectively. ●

For More Information

If you know where to look, there is lots of reliable information available on indoor air quality. Unless otherwise noted, individual copies of the following publications are free.

Air Conditioning and Refrigeration Institute
4301 N. Fairfax Drive
Suite 425
Arlington, VA 22203

● *Air Conditioning and Refrigeration Equipment: General Maintenance Guidelines for Improving Indoor Air Environment*

● *Breathing Clean: How Air Filters Provide Cleaner Living*

● *How to Humidify Your Home or Business*

● *Indoor Air Quality Briefing Paper*

American Lung Association
1740 Broadway
New York, NY 10019
1-800-LUNG-USA

● *Air Pollution in Your Home?*

● *Everything You Should Know about Carbon Monoxide, Propane Gas, Natural Gas, Smoke, and Fire*

● Fact sheets: *Asbestos; Biological Pollutants; Carpet; Combustion Pollutants; Formaldehyde; Household Products; Radon; Secondhand Smoke*

Association of Home Appliance Manufacturers
20 N. Wacker Drive
Chicago, IL 60606

● *Consumers Guide for Room Air Cleaners* ($2)

● *Product Directory: Dehumidifiers* ($5)

● *Product Directory: Humidifiers* ($5)

Carpet and Rug Institute
P.O. Box 2048
Dalton, GA 30722
(800) 882-8846

● *Carpet Care and Maintenance for Maximum Performance*

● *Indoor Air Quality and New Carpet*

● *CRI Labeling Program*

Environmental Hazards Management Institute
10 Newmarket Road
P.O. Box 932
Durham, NH 03824
(603) 868-1496

The Household Hazardous Waste Wheel (Inquire about price)

Home Ventilating Institute
30 W. University Drive
Arlington Heights, IL 60004
(703) 394-0150

● *Certified Products Directory*

● *The Home Ventilating Guide*

National Institute of Allergy and Infectious Diseases
Office of Communication
Building 31, Room 7A50
9000 Rockville Pike
Bethesda, MD 20892
(301) 496-5717

Something in the Air: Airborne Allergens

U.S. Environmental Protection Agency
Public Information Center
401 M Street SW
Washington, DC 20460
(800) 438-4318
(800) SOS-RADON

● *Asbestos in Your Home*

● *Biological Pollutants in Your Home*

● *The Inside Story: A Guide to Indoor Air Quality*

● Fact sheets: *Carpet and Indoor Air Quality; Residential Air Cleaners; Secondhand Smoke; Use and Care of Home Humidifiers*

● *What You Should Know about Combustion Appliances and Indoor Air Pollution*

Room Air Cleaners, write to AHAM, 20 North Wacker Drive, Chicago, IL 60606.

Because a detailed discussion of air filtration technology is beyond the scope of this chapter, consult a competent professional before making any decisions. Using the resources in "For More Information" on this page will also help you to make wise choices.

FILTER EFFICIENCY

Filters differ in the amount of particulates they remove from the air that passes through them. The Maximum Efficiency below represents the percentage of particulates removed by each filter listed. The Efficiency Value is based on the air filter's cleaning efficiency in relationship to cost.

FILTER TYPE	EFFICIENCY VALUE	MAXIMUM EFFICIENCY (%)
DUST LINT FILTER	Poor	5
SELF-CHARGING MECHANICAL FILTER	Fair	8
MEDIA AIR FILTER	Good	35
ELECTRONIC AIR CLEANER	Excellent	95
HIGH EFFICIENCY PARTICLE ARRESTING (HEPA) FILTER	Excellent	99

Adapted from American Society of Heating, Refrigerating, and Air Conditioning Engineers (ASHRAE), Atmospheric Dust Spot Efficiency Test

Radon

If you are wondering about radon, you can buy inexpensive long- or short-term detectors like the ones shown above.

UNDERSTANDING THE RADON THREAT

Radon—an invisible, odorless, radioactive gas—is formed in the soil by the gradual decay of uranium. While the other by-products of uranium generally remain trapped in the soil, radon gas migrates to the surface and escapes into the air. This poses no threat as long as the gas is released outdoors, where it dissipates. But when radon builds up *inside* a house and is subsequently inhaled, it becomes a serious health risk.

The U.S. Environmental Protection Agency (EPA) estimates that radon causes between

Quick Response

1. If test results show indoor radon levels above 4 picocuries per liter, conduct second test to confirm results.

2. Leave windows and doors on lower levels of house open to provide ventilation.

3. Spend less time in basement, where radon is usually concentrated.

4. Seal cracks and holes below grade, cover sump pump hole with tight lid, and seal bare soil with plastic sheeting.

6
NATURAL
EMERGENCIES

Hazards

● Smoking compounds the risks associated with radon. You'll dramatically lower your risks by creating a smoke-free home.

● Avoid salespeople or telephone solicitors who try to pressure you into fast decisions. Deal exclusively with people who are listed through the U.S. Environmental Protection Agency's Radon Proficiency Measurement Program and Radon Contractors' Proficiency Program.

7,000 and 30,000 lung cancer deaths a year in the United States, which makes it the second leading cause of lung cancer deaths *after* smoking. (See the *Radon Zones in the United States* on this page.)

Fortunately, almost any house can be cured of radon problems, sometimes with fairly simple and inexpensive measures. And studies show that real estate values aren't negatively affected once the radon problem has been confronted and fixed.

In most cases, radon gas enters the house through open cracks and joints in the foun-

dation or seeps into the first floor above a closed crawl space. (See *Radon Entry Routes* on the opposite page.) Sump pump holes and the gaps around utility wires and pipes that enter the house below grade can also provide entry routes.

Radon seepage into a basement or crawl space is accelerated if the air pressure inside the house is lower than the air pressure on the soil around the foundation.

One source of depressurization is the so-called *stack effect*—that is, the upward movement of warm house air when the

RADON ZONES IN THE UNITED STATES

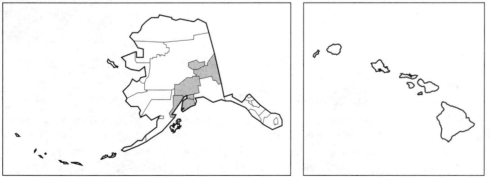

■ Zone 1
▨ Zone 2
☐ Zone 3

The dark areas on this map show the highest percentage of detected radon while the white areas show the lowest levels of detected radon. However, homes with elevated levels of radon have been found in all three zones. Thus, all homes should be tested regardless of their geographic location. This map is used to assist national, state, and local organizations in targeting their resources and in implementing radon-resistant building codes.

Redrawn from a map provided by the U.S. Environmental Protection Agency

weather is cold. As warm air leaks out the upper part of the house, cooler air (and radon gas) are drawn into the lower levels to compensate.

Exhaust fans, combustion appliances, and forced-air heating and cooling systems that have leaky ductwork can further depressurize a house and increase the rate at which radon is drawn up out of the soil. (See "The HVAC Connection" on page 218.)

Radon can also become an indoor air problem when it's found at high levels in well water. But problems stemming from contaminated water are relatively rare, accounting for less than 5 percent of all residential radon problems.

The incidence of uranium deposits in the area is a fair indicator of the frequency of radon problems in houses. But numerous other variables—including the design of the house, construction quality, and how porous the soil is—complicate the picture. Because of radon's fickle nature, broad generalizations rarely hold true. Tests have revealed dangerously high levels in one house while a home of similar design situated right across the street showed no problem whatsoever. Thus, each house needs to be individually tested.

TESTING FOR RADON

As with all things radioactive, there's a certain stigma attached to radon. Sometimes homeowners are afraid to test, fearing that it might lead to enormous expense, undercut the value of their property, or open the door to future lawsuits long after they've sold their property.

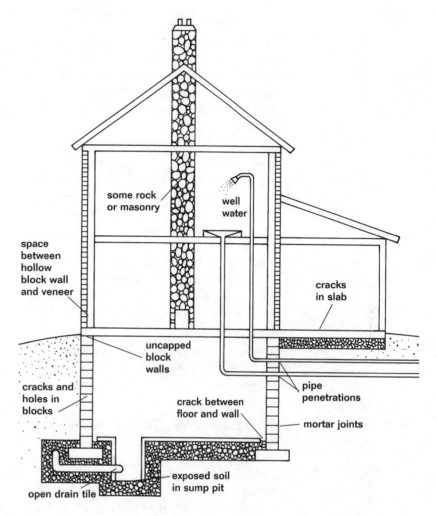

Radon percolating up through the soil can enter your house in various ways, as identified above.

Protect Yourself

Hire an independent EPA-listed firm to test a house you plan to sell or a house you are considering buying. Make sure the firm takes measures to ensure that there is no tampering by placing tamper-resistant seals on doors and windows and by placing tamper-resistant paper under the detector itself. Don't disturb the detector or seals, or you could be liable in court. ●

Of course, the very opposite is true—it's when you play ostrich and ignore the potential problems that you put your health and wealth at risk.

Essentially, homeowners should treat a radon problem the same way they would treat a leaky roof. Determine the extent of the problem (if, in fact, there is one) and have it fixed by a trustworthy professional. There's no reason for panic or paranoia.

Unless you're in the middle of a real estate transaction, where an independent test is

The Real Estate Link

If you are buying or selling a house, it's smart to have the structure tested for radon *before* the deal goes through. This is true even if the house is located in an area that has never been identified with radon problems.

While it's true that many states now have some type of real estate disclosure law, a prospective buyer cannot count on these laws for protection. To begin with, most disclosure laws aren't mandatory and carry little or no penalty for sellers who don't comply. Moreover, the laws typically refer to disclosing "known defects" that adversely affect the property. Well, that begs a couple of serious questions: Is radon, in the eyes of the law, actually a defect? And how can the seller be expected to know about it if a test was never done?

Since the laws are vague and the courts have not gone very far in clarifying them, *caveat emptor*—let the buyer beware—remains in full force.

Radon tests, including a well water test if the house is served by a private artesian well, are normally done at the buyer's expense and conducted by an independent EPA-listed testing firm. If the house does show problems, the seller might be expected to pay the costs of the mitigation work or perhaps lower his asking price to compensate the buyer for handling the problem.

Interestingly, most realtors and lawyers are advising sellers to do a radon test *prior* to placing their homes on the market. The theory is that it's better for the seller to discover a radon problem—and deal with it beforehand—than to have a prospective buyer uncover it in the middle of negotiations.

In any event, trying to hide a radon problem from a potential buyer is the worst mistake a seller can make, for it leaves him liable to all sorts of legal claims, including the future medical costs of anyone living in the house who might be stricken with cancer.

Some of the radon-related worries associated with real estate deals may eventually be calmed by better and cheaper technology. Scientists are working on ways to analyze the soil characteristics of undeveloped lots so that home builders can anticipate radon problems before they break ground and modify their construction plans accordingly.

Even without some indication of the radon potential of a site, it is a wise precaution to build a new house with radon-resistant construction. Details of this can be obtained from the EPA and from state radon offices. (See "For More Information" on the opposite page.)

---

usually desirable, there's no reason to pay a private firm to do the initial testing for you. Do-it-yourself test kits containing charcoal canisters, vials, or pouches are available from hardware stores, home centers, and some state and local health departments for $10 to $15 apiece. (See "For More Information" on the opposite page.)

The open test kit is placed in the lowest *lived-in* level of your house for two to four days with the windows and doors left closed as much as possible. The key is to closely follow the instructions that come with the kit, and mail the sampler back to the lab in a timely fashion. The postage, lab analysis, and report are usually included in the kit's price, but check beforehand to make sure.

Other types of radon test kits are available that don't use charcoal as the test medium. As long as they are EPA-listed, you can use them with confidence.

EVALUATING THE RESULTS

The higher the initial test results (above the EPA's 4-picocurie action level), the more urgency there is to conduct a second test.

If, for example, the first test revealed radon levels of 8 picocuries or more, it would be prudent to conduct another short-term test using charcoal canisters, vials, or pouches as soon as possible. If the average from the two tests is above 4, you've confirmed the need to have mitigation work done. The higher the average, the more urgency there is to have the problem fixed.

If, on the other hand, your first test shows radon levels only slightly above 4, say, in the 4 to 7 picocurie range, you may want to conduct a longer-term, more accurate type of test.

This can be done with an alpha track detector, which is left in place for weeks or even months. Alpha track detectors contain a small piece of polycarbonate plastic that picks up the track of radon decay products as they strike the material. These invisible imperfections are revealed and counted when the device is returned to the lab.

At $20 to $50 each, alpha track detectors are more expensive than charcoal devices, but they can determine the yearly *average* of radon levels in your home. This long-term average is an important assessment tool, since radon levels may vary radically from week to week and season to season.

Homes with a yearly average radon concentration above 4 picocuries should have mitigation work done to lower the level below 4. At levels of 20 picocuries or more, the EPA recommends "quick" action, commensurate with the higher risk.

Finally, if tests indicate that radon levels in the upper part of your house are two or three times higher than those in the lower part, it may be a signal that radon is being released from your water. *NOTE:* Such contamination is possible only if you draw your water from an artesian (drilled) well, not from a lake, river, reservoir, or shallow well.

Radon-contaminated well water presents a double threat. When the water is agitated, as when a clothes washer or shower is on, the radon becomes airborne and is subsequently inhaled. Radon is also hazardous when it remains in the water and is swallowed.

If you suspect your water is contaminated, have your state environmental lab or an EPA-listed private lab test the water specifically for radon. The test, which costs about $15, requires that the homeowner follow a strict protocol in gathering the water sample and mailing it to the lab on time.

The fee includes the laboratory analysis and a printed report, which you receive by return mail.

For More Information

Contact either of the following organizations for the radon information listed.

The National Safety Council
P.O. Box 33435
Washington, DC 20077-2854
(800) 557-2366
Offers homeowners an EPA-listed radon detection kit for $9.95.

U.S. Environmental
Protection Agency
Public Information Center
401 M Street SW
Washington, DC 20460
(800) SOS-RADON
● *A Citizen's Guide to Radon*
● *Consumer's Guide to Radon Reduction*
● *Home Buyer's and Seller's Guide to Radon*

REDUCING RADON LEVELS

Since running follow-on tests and having repairs done may take months to accomplish, it's important that you take interim steps to reduce your health risks. Follow the measures described in "Quick Response" and "Hazards" on page 205, especially with regard to ventilation and smoking.

In selecting a radon mitigation firm, stick with candidates that are listed with the EPA's Radon Contractors' Proficiency Program. You can obtain a list of these companies from your state or local health department or from a regional EPA office. Technicians working for EPA-listed companies carry a photo ID attesting to the fact, a safeguard that's been instituted to help keep hucksters and incompetents out of the industry.

Your contract with the mitigation firm should be as detailed as possible, establishing work start and finish dates, a payment schedule, and written details about warranties. If the contractor promises to reduce the indoor radon level below 4 picocuries, specify in the

A Pennsylvania Story

Joe MacAniff's house, located in Doylestown, Pennsylvania, was under contract to be sold when the radon test came back and stymied the deal.

"It wasn't the test results that upset me," Joe says. "The radon levels in the house weren't that high. What upset me was the reaction of the buyers. They just walked away."

Since Joe is in the real estate business, he decided to turn the situation into a professional learning experience. He invited three mitigation contractors to the house, watched them as they made their inspections, and then compared their proposals and prices.

In the end, he chose Buffalo Homes of Pennsylvania, whose president, Bill Brodhead, is an experienced radon contractor.

"They guaranteed that the radon level would remain under 4 picocuries for a year, which was important to me in trying to sell the house," Joe explains.

Bill Brodhead and his co-workers used a three-pronged strategy to deal with the radon.

First, cracks, joints, and other places where radon might enter the basement were caulked or otherwise sealed.

Second, the oil furnace was equipped with an independent air supply from outside so that its draw wouldn't reduce the air pressure inside the basement and pull more radon up from the soil.

Finally, a sub-slab depressurization system was installed. Five 4-inch-diameter pipes were sunk through the slab at strategic points, connected overhead, and vented through the roof. An electric exhaust fan situated in the pipe pulls radon up from under the slab and exhausts it outside before it can seep into the house. The whole project cost $1,600.

When a follow-up test was done, the radon level inside the house had fallen from 27 picocuries to less than 1. (The EPA's recommended threshold for safety is 4.)

"The story has a happy ending," says Joe MacAniff. "New buyers looked at the post-mitigation test results and were completely satisfied. I ended up getting a higher price for the home than I would have under the first contract."

contract that follow-on tests are to be conducted to verify the results. At least one of the follow-on tests should be conducted during the winter, when the house is buttoned up tight and radon levels are generally at their peak.

Mitigation work generally starts with a thorough inspection of the house and additional testing. Some firms use continuous radon monitors, which provide a "real time" reading on radon levels, and "grab sampling" equipment, which can pinpoint the spots where

radon is entering the house. Technicians may bore one or more small test holes in the slab so they can check how porous the soil is underneath.

A technique called *sub-slab suction* is the most commonly used strategy for mitigation. As shown in *Sub-Slab Suction* on the opposite page, a 3- or 4-inch-diameter plastic pipe is seated tightly through a hole in the slab. The pipe runs up through the roof or out a side wall with an in-line electric fan that draws radon gas up from beneath the slab and exhausts it harmlessly outside. The fan, typically rated at 100 cfm (cubic feet per minute), runs continuously, drawing about the same amount of electricity as a 100-watt lightbulb. A light or other warning device alerts the homeowner in the event the fan should fail. (In new construction, when a layer of porous gravel and a plastic radon barrier are positioned underneath the slab to facilitate the flow of radon gas to the outdoors, the electric fan may not be necessary.)

Because of the many variables involved in retrofitting a house with sub-slab suction, the price can range from $500 to five times that much.

Other techniques used to reduce radon, often in combination with sub-slab suction, are as follows:

● *Balancing indoor-outdoor air pressure:* Furnaces, water heaters, clothes dryers, and other appliances that normally draw their air from inside, thereby depressurizing the house, are equipped with ducts that bring in outdoor air. Eliminating the depressurizing effect of appliances reduces the amount of radon gas that is drawn up from the underlying soil.

● *Installing drain tile suction:* Existing drain tile around the foundation is equipped with a vertical pipe and electric fan to suck radon from the soil before it can enter the house.

● *Installing heat recovery ventilation:* A special ventilating unit brings in fresh air and exhausts radon-laden air. In winter, heat is reclaimed from the exhaust to save energy.

● *Sealing cracks:* Caulk, mortar, and other sealants are used to fill open joints and cracks in the foundation, gaps around utility pipes, and the voids in concrete blocks.

● *Sealing exposed earth:* The exposed

Talk to the Experts

Be sure to talk with your state radon office about your test results. They can help you interpret the data and give you the names of EPA-listed mitigation firms. ●

SUB-SLAB SUCTION

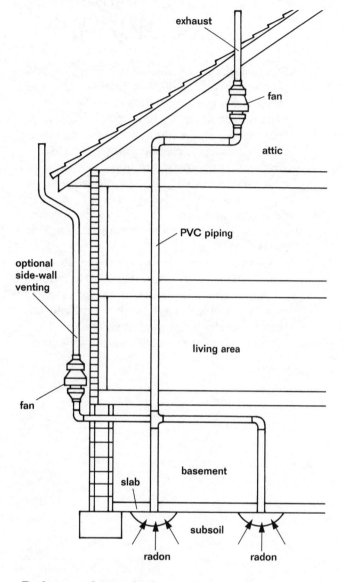

exhaust

fan

attic

PVC piping

optional side-wall venting

living area

fan

slab

basement

subsoil

radon   radon

Radon can be sucked from below the concrete slab and vented safely outdoors.

earth found in crawl spaces, cold rooms, and unfinished basements is surfaced with concrete or covered with 6-mil plastic sheeting. (See "Moisture-Proofing a Crawl Space" on page 173.) Sump pump pits are fitted with airtight covers.

● *Ventilating block walls:* Using pipes or sheet metal baseboards as channeling systems, radon is drawn by fan from spaces within block walls before entering the house.

TREATING RADON-CONTAMINATED WATER

When well water is the source of your radon problem, two remedies are feasible. The less expensive approach, which costs $800 to $1,000, is to install a high-capacity activated charcoal filter. The filter and adjoining storage tanks are placed near the point where your well water line enters the house. However, the charcoal filters must be meticulously maintained to do their job and there is some concern that the filters themselves may present a handling or disposal risk as they accumulate radioactive material.

A second approach to treating radon-contaminated water is to install an aeration chamber. These appliance-like devices use bubbles or jets of air to agitate the contaminated water, thereby stripping out the radon. The radon gas is vented safely outside while the purified water is pumped into a holding tank. While the most effective aeration systems can remove 99 percent of the radon from well water, they cost from $2,000 to $4,000.

LIVING HAPPILY EVER AFTER

Once the mitigation work is complete, your contractor will conduct follow-on tests to make sure the results are satisfactory. As previously noted, at least some of the verifying tests should be done in winter, when seasonal soil and house conditions tend to generate the highest radon levels.

Once the contracting firm has succeeded in lowering the radon level, it's still wise to periodically retest your home. Ask your contractor what kind of follow-up test device and timetable is recommended.

Mold and Mildew

Cleaning mold and mildew from surfaces is only one part of the battle. Without preventive measures, the growth will quickly return.

Quick Response

1. To kill mold and mildew fungi, sponge with solution of chlorine bleach and water or commercial mildewcide.

2. Open windows and use fan to ventilate and dry out area.

MINDING YOUR MOLD AND MILDEW

Molds and mildews are part of the fungus family, a large, primitive group of plants that also includes mushrooms, smuts, wood rot, and yeasts. (For the purposes of this discussion, molds and mildews will be referred to collectively as mildew, since the biology and treatment for the two problems are essentially the same.)

Mildew grows both indoors and out, usually feeding on wood, fabric, leather, or other organic materials. (A few types of mildew can grow on inorganic vinyl or aluminum siding,

Hazards

● The spores (seeds) from molds and mildews are a major cause of allergic reactions (seasonal allergic rhinitis). Though rare, the inhalation of spores can also cause more serious lung disease, including asthma, hypersensitivity pneumonitis, and allergic bronchopulmonary aspergillosis.

● Use homemade and commercial mildew removers with care, protecting yourself with rubber gloves, safety goggles, and plenty of ventilation. Do not mix household chemicals (for example, ammonia with chlorine bleach), as they can interact and produce harmful by-products.

● When using commercial mildewcides, always read and follow the instructions carefully.

6
NATURAL EMERGENCIES

feeding on airborne organic matter and using dew and rain for water.)

Mildew usually appears as shadowy spots or webbing on the surface. While black is the most usual color, mildews can also be blue, brown, white, red, orange—even pink.

Mildew needs a few simple elements to thrive: oxygen, organic matter, moisture (relative humidity above 50 percent), and temperatures above 70°F (for most strains). The shadier the spot, the better mildew likes it. These conditions are met outdoors in rotting stumps and logs, fallen leaves, compost piles, shady gardens, and some living grasses and weeds.

On the exterior of your house, mildew tends to form on unheated surfaces, such as fascia and soffit boards, crawl-space timbers, porch ceilings, and the underside of decks, especially if shaded and frequently collect dew.

Inside your home, mildew's favorite breeding grounds include damp basements and attics, unventilated bathrooms, closets, condensate drains on heating and cooling equipment, humidifiers, and ductwork interiors—in other words, all the areas that are prone to high humidity, poor ventilation, and no to low light.

Like other members of the fungus family, mildew reproduces by ejecting millions of spores, which give rise to new growth. As noted above, these spores are a prime cause of allergies and other respiratory ailments.

While spores are omnipresent, they tend to be most abundant in the humid summer months when mildew thrives. Mildew can grow indoors year-round—as long as the moisture and temperature conditions are right—producing allergy attacks even in the middle of January.

Apart from its health effects, mildew is also unsightly and gives off an unpleasant, musty odor. When you see the evidence, it should be taken as a warning sign that moisture and temperature conditions are also suitable for wood rot, termites, and other more serious pests. (See "Rotting Wood" on page 168 and "Termites, Beetles, and Carpenter Ants" on page 231.)

REMOVING MILDEW

To kill surface mildew, brush, sponge, or spray the surface with a 1-to-3-part mixture of household bleach (containing sodium

Test the Solution

When removing mildew, test the bleach solution (or commercial mildewcide) on a *small* area first. If the test surface shows too much discoloration, add another part of water to the bleach solution and try it again. If the discoloration is still unacceptable, try another product or resign yourself to repainting the surface once the mildew is removed. ●

hypochlorite) and water, as shown in *Removing Mildew* on the opposite page. Or use a commercial mildewcide. In either case, be sure to wear rubber gloves and eye protection. To remove tough black stains from the grout between ceramic tiles, try scrubbing it with a toothbrush and denture cleaning cream.

After applying the bleach solution or commercial mildewcide to a wall or ceiling, rinse the surface with clean water and let it dry. Then gently scrape a small test area of the surface with a sharp knife—if mildew shows up underneath, treat the surface a second time, rinse, and let dry as before.

If you have to repaint or recoat the treated surface for cosmetic reasons, make sure that the new coating contains a mildewcide. (See "Using Preventive Coatings and Treatments" on page 216.)

If mildew has penetrated into a wood surface, it may be possible to remove the discoloration by lightly sanding or planing the wood before refinishing it.

When mildew has spread over a large area, such as roofing or siding, it can be killed by spraying the surface with the bleach-and-water solution described above or a commercial mildewcide. (See "Products and Suppliers" on the opposite page.)

PREVENTING MILDEW

Since mildew thrives in damp, shady conditions, the best way to prevent it from forming (or reforming after it's been removed) is to eliminate its sources of moisture and, if possible, introduce natural or artificial light to the area.

REMOVING MILDEW

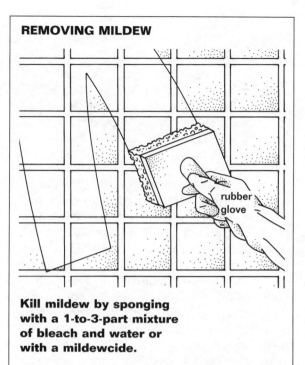

Kill mildew by sponging with a 1-to-3-part mixture of bleach and water or with a mildewcide.

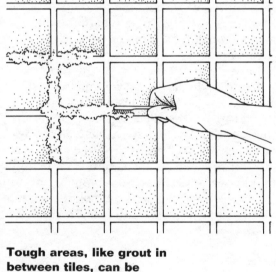

Tough areas, like grout in between tiles, can be scrubbed with an old toothbrush and denture cleaning cream.

"Controlling Indoor Humidity" on page 217 suggests various ways to reduce relative humidity inside your home. The goal is to reduce condensation on windows, walls, and ceilings.

Of course, mildew can also draw its water, directly or indirectly, from other sources, including leaky roofs, leaky plumbing, and leaky basements. For more details, read "Leaky Roof" on page 24, "Broken Pipes" on page 56, "Troubleshooting Guide to Wet Basements" on page 66, and "Hot Spots for Rot" on page 170.

TREATING CLOSETS AND CORNERS

A dark, damp closet is one of the most common and stubborn breeding grounds for mildew. The best way to treat it is to remove everything—clothes, shoes, old tennis rackets—so they can be washed, dry cleaned, or thrown away.

Products and Suppliers

If your paint store doesn't stock what you need to remove mildew and prevent its return, you can order products directly from the manufacturers. Here are a few reputable products and suppliers to consider.

B501 Water Sealant with Mildewcide
Use: Brush-on clear coat
Source: Bethel Products, P.O. Box 176, New Carlisle, OH 45344; (513) 845-2380

Gone Plus Mildew Wash and Cleaner
Use: Removes surface mold and mildew
Source: Enviro-Chem, 4 West Rees, Walla Walla, WA 99362; (800) 247-9011

Mildew Check
Use: Spray-on mildewcide for exterior use only
Source: PPG Architectural Finishes, 1 PPG Place, Dept. 37, Pittsburgh, PA 15272; (800) 441-9695

Stay-Clean I/E Mildewcide Paint Additive
Use: Blends into interior or exterior paints (latex or oil-based) or into wallpaper paste
Source: Enviro-Chem, 4 West Rees, Walla Walla, WA 99362; (800) 247-9011

Z-Stop Moss and Fungus Inhibitor
Use: The zinc strip is installed along both sides of the ridge cap. When wetted by rain, the strip releases zinc carbonate onto the roof, inhibiting the growth of mildew and moss.
Source: Wespac Enterprises, P.O. Box 46337, Seattle, WA 98146; (800) 845-5863

Once the closet is empty, wash surfaces with the bleach-and-water solution described on page 214 or with a commercial mildewcide. To circulate more air through the space, replace the solid door with a louvered one and use wire storage racks instead of solid shelves. If possible, install a low-wattage lightbulb, which can be burned intermittently or continually, to illuminate the closet and raise the temperature. (Raising the air temperature lowers the relative humidity.) Make sure the lightbulb is a safe distance from anything that's combustible.

Another common spot for mildew inside the house is where an exterior wall meets the ceiling, as shown in *Insulating a Cold*

No Quick Cover-Up

Never apply fresh paint, stain, or clear coats over a mildewed surface without killing the mildew first. Otherwise, the mildew will grow up through the coating and quickly ruin it. ●

Spot on this page. The problem is often due to a gap in the attic insulation above, which lets the surface below get relatively cold, producing added condensation. Such gaps have two origins: Either the attic insulation wasn't properly installed in the first place or it's been gradually nudged out of place by air currents blowing in through the soffit vents. This latter possibility is especially common with cellulose and other types of loose-fill insulation.

After you've cleaned the mildew off the surface below, inspect the attic insulation—especially at the corners where framing meets and along the lower edge of the roof (near the eaves)—to make sure that the insulation extends all the way to the top plate.

Ready-made baffles or vent guards are available to keep attic insulation in its proper place. Installed between the rafters, the baffles allow you to insulate all the way to the eaves (top plate) or into a tight corner but prevent the insulation from being blown out of place or from bulging out onto the eaves, where it would block the flow of air up into the soffit vents. (See *Insulating a Cold Spot.*)

INSULATING A COLD SPOT

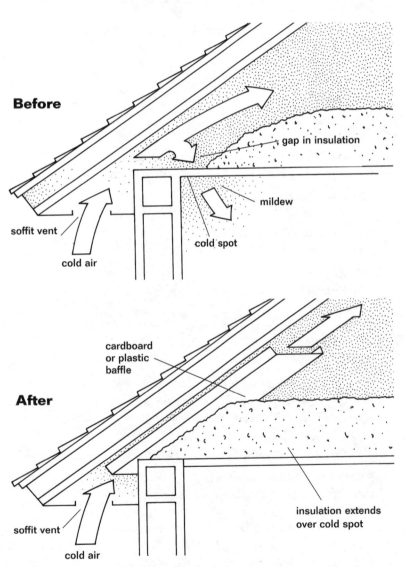

Before

gap in insulation

mildew

soffit vent

cold spot

cold air

cardboard or plastic baffle

After

insulation extends over cold spot

soffit vent

cold air

Cardboard or plastic baffles make it possible to insulate cold corners where midew is apt to grow without blocking soffit vents.

USING PREVENTIVE COATINGS AND TREATMENTS

Many paint stores carry paints, stains, and clear sealants that already contain a fungicide or mildewcide. Or you can buy the mildewcide in a separate packet or bottle and mix it with the coating later. Some fungicides are suitable for indoor or outdoor use; others are restricted because of their toxicity to outdoor use only. *So make sure you know what you're buying and how to use it safely.*

Controlling Indoor Humidity

When the relative humidity indoors climbs much above 50 percent (optimum), molds, mildews, and bacteria begin to proliferate. Not only does water vapor condense on walls, ceilings, carpets, and other visible surfaces, but it also condenses in the hidden cavities behind the walls and above the ceilings.

Most houses experience some condensation, of course, but windows and walls constantly bleeding with moisture signal a real problem.

MEASURING HUMIDITY

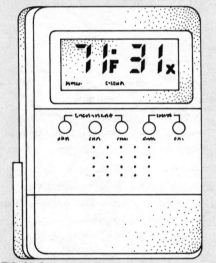

Digital hygrometer

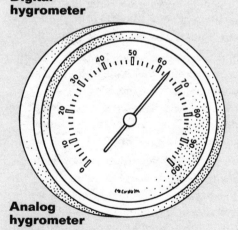

Analog hygrometer

There was a time when weather monitors—usually an analog thermometer, barometer, and hygrometer—were popular in homes. Today you can also buy a digital hygrometer and thermometer combination.

The appearance of mold and mildew, which flourish when the relative humidity exceeds 70 percent, is another harbinger of trouble. Rot and insect pests won't be far behind.

To measure indoor humidity, you can borrow or buy a hygrometer, as shown in *Measuring Humidity*. Radio Shack sells a wall-mounted unit for about $30 that measures and displays both the relative humidity and indoor temperature. More precise and expensive instruments—called *sling psychrometers*—are also available to measure humidity.

If your observations or measurements confirm that the indoor humidity is habitually high, consider some of the following steps to lower it:

● Increase natural ventilation by opening windows and doors (but only if the humidity outdoors is lower than inside).

● Use more mechanical ventilation. This might include (installed singly or in combination) a bathroom exhaust fan, a power vent over the range, a window fan, a whole house fan, an exhaust-only ventilation system, or an air-to-air heat exchanger.

● Install central or unit air conditioning. Air conditioners dehumidify the air as they cool it. Some air conditioners have a ventilation-only cycle that helps control indoor humidity and saves you money on cooling costs.

● Don't let cooking pots boil needlessly or showers run any longer than necessary.

● Don't store green firewood inside the house.

● Reduce the number of houseplants and don't overwater the ones that remain.

● Make sure your clothes dryer and all exhaust fans are properly vented to the outside—never into conditioned space or into an attic, basement, or crawl space.

● Check all combustion appliances to make sure they're properly vented. High indoor humidity is sometimes linked to a backdrafting furnace or appliance. (See "Backdrafting Flue" on page 122.)

● As a last resort, use a mechanical dehumidifier to dry out a wet basement or damp area.

The HVAC Connection

If you have heating, ventilation, or air conditioning (HVAC) ducts in your home, it's important to know that without careful maintenance they can become a dangerous source of moisture problems and contamination.

Moisture and/or contaminants can be drawn into the ductwork through unsealed seams (where two lengths of duct are joined) or through open intake vents. Imagine, for example, a leaky duct or open intake sucking moist air out of a damp basement or crawl space and circulating it all over the house. No wonder there's mildew everywhere! (See *Leaky Ducts.*)

Leaky ductwork can also suck in and distribute nearby contaminants, including bits of cellulose or fiberglass (from attic insulation), toxic fumes (from open shop containers or automobile exhaust), insecticides (sprayed under the crawl space or around the foundation to control pests), and fungi spores (from a damp basement or crawl space).

When too much moisture gets into the ductwork—combined with household dust and other organic material—the duct itself can become a lush breeding ground for fungi and bacteria.

Here are some pointers to help you keep moisture and contaminants out of the ductwork.

● Make sure all heating and cooling ducts—especially those outside the conditioned space—are tightly sealed and properly insulated. The best course is to hire a pro to test and reseal the ductwork for you. You can do the insulation work yourself.

● If the return side of the system has a common intake (no ducts), equip the grille with a good filter and make sure there are no potential contaminants around it.

● Regularly change or clean the air filter on your forced-air system. Consider upgrading to a more efficient filter. (See "No Heat" on page 126 and "Polluted Indoor Air" on page 194.)

● If there's a humidifier built into your heating system, make sure that it's carefully maintained and adjusted. Otherwise, mold, mildew, and bacteria can proliferate inside the humidifier and ductwork. (See "For More Information" on page 203.)

● Consider having the inside of your ducts professionally cleaned every few years. (See "High-Tech Helpers" on the opposite page.) This is an especially good idea if a lot of moisture and contaminants have been introduced into the ductwork through leaks, breaks, or poor filter maintenance. To locate a professional duct cleaner in your area, contact the National Air Duct Cleaners Association, 1518 K Street NW, Suite 503, Washington, DC 20005; (202) 737-2926.

LEAKY DUCTS

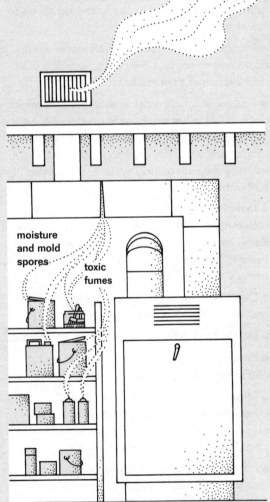

moisture and mold spores

toxic fumes

Leaky ductwork can suck in moisture, spores, and toxins, spreading contaminants into the ductwork and other parts of the house.

High-Tech Helpers

Contractors who specialize in cleaning dirty heating and air conditioning ducts use a variety of high-tech tools, including robots and sophisticated optical devices, as shown in these photographs.

The tread-driven Duct Walker, equipped here with a stiff rotary brush, can inspect, clean, or apply coatings to the interior surface of ductwork. It's used mainly in commercial and industrial settings.

Indoor Environmental Solutions

Instrument Technology

To inspect and photograph the inside of a duct without tearing it apart, contractors use an optical device called a borescope. The probe, equipped with a special lens and integral light, is inserted into the duct through a small drilled hole. The view inside can be photographed or videotaped.

Vac System Industries

A motorized brush, attached to the end of a rigid rod or flexible cable, is used to clean residential ductwork.

The Super Trac robot, designed to clean the ductwork in large homes and commercial buildings, carries its own light source and video camera. Its motorized arm can be equipped with a power brush, spray attachment, or air broom (pictured here).

Wildlife Pests

PESTS?

Pests come in all shapes and sizes. But even the cute and furry kind can damage your house and property.

Quick Response

1. If wild animal is loose inside house, get kids and pets out of area.

2. Leave animal clear path of escape.

3. Remain calm and move slowly so animal doesn't feel threatened.

4. Give animal plenty of time and space to retreat back out where it came in.

5. Do *not* handle animal.

Hazards

● Virtually all wild animals can bite or scratch. Some, like squirrels, can make their bite felt through thick leather gloves. Others, like raccoons and skunks, may carry rabies. (See "Rabies" on the opposite page.)

● If you elect to use legal repellents or poisons to get rid of a pest, follow instructions carefully and make sure that children and pets can't get to the bait or repellent.

● If you must move a dead animal, do so with gloves on. Wildlife and the ticks and fleas that live on them may carry disease, including rabies, Lyme disease, and Hanta virus.

LIVING WITH WILDLIFE

As Americans move further and further out into what was once sparsely populated country, the opportunities for contact and problems with wildlife increase. In other cases, it's the animals that are doing the moving. Raccoons, skunks—even foxes—are moving back into suburban and, in some cases, urban areas to live.

In Boston, for example, the raccoons are so city smart that they've learned how to use sewers as subterranean highways. In Los Angeles, it's not unusual for a coyote to swoop down out of the hills, slip into a person's backyard, and eat the cat's food (or

PREVENTING AN INVASION

Despite the reputation that wild animals have for being independent, there are many species that *like* being subsidized by humans. When pet food, open garbage cans, and drops off your fruit trees are left in the yard, it's like hanging up a *FREE FOOD* sign to every critter within a country mile. And once wild animals get a taste of your goodies, they'll be back for more—probably with their friends in tow.

Likewise, if your house has an open crawl space, cracks or holes in the foundation, or unscreened soffit and gable vents, you may as well hang out a *VISITORS WELCOME* sign to wild birds, bats, and animals that are prospecting for a new home.

Keep in mind that bats, mice, and snakes can get into your house through holes less than ½ inch in diameter. An open chimney top—as seen from a raccoon's, squirrel's, or wren's point of view—looks like a ready-made penthouse.

maybe the cat itself!) for dinner.

Luckily, you don't have to be from a rural background or familiar with animals to resolve a wildlife problem safely. As described below, the solution is usually a matter of recognizing the elements that attract the animal and eliminating them from the scene. It's only when these simple exclusion and prevention measures don't solve the problem that repellents, traps, or poisons become necessary. At that point, you should consider calling in a pro.

In every circumstance, put your health and safety first. Even if the animal appears beautiful and friendly, your first thought should be: "This is a wild animal that I know nothing about."

Rabies

Bats, raccoons, skunks, and other warm-blooded wildlife can carry rabies, which is transmitted to humans through the infected animal's saliva. While a bite is the most common means by which rabies are transmitted to humans, it can also be transmitted if the infected animal's saliva gets into a person's eye, nose, mouth, or an open wound. The rabies virus attacks the central nervous system and is invariably fatal if not treated.

An animal that is rabid may act unusually lethargic or aggressive and may "foam" at the mouth.

If someone has been bitten by a wild animal, wash the affected area thoroughly with soap and water. Capture the animal, without damaging its head, and seek immediate medical attention. If you can't capture the animal, keep an eye on it until health or wildlife authorities can arrive to help. By quickly getting the victim and the animal to health authorities, you may be able to avoid the uncomfortable and expensive ($1,000 or more) series of prophylactic shots.

6
NATURAL EMERGENCIES

The most effective way to discourage wildlife pests is to remove their food supply and seal up the holes and cracks in your house so that they have no point of entry. See *Critter-Proofing Your Home* on the opposite page for the key household elements that merit your attention.

USING REPELLENTS

With a few notable exceptions, commercial repellents for wildlife pests are either not available or not effective. (See "A Brief Guide to Critter Control" on page 224.) Some, like the "ultrasonic" devices that are supposed to repel or frighten pests with high-frequency sound waves, are particularly long on advertising claims and short on results.

Some folks say that placing a radio in the garden broadcasting loud music will discourage varmints. But a friend in upstate New York reports seeing a trio of deer contentedly munching the tops off his lettuce while a nearby radio blared out the loudest rock music imaginable. (Maybe he should have tried rap music?!)

If you do choose to use a repellent, it should be only *after* you've done everything possible to curtail the critter's food and shelter opportunities.

Consider trying the following old-fashioned remedies that may also qualify as repellents:

Mothballs (naphthalene) will repel some forms of wildlife, including bats, but quickly lose their potency. By filling mesh bags with mothballs and hanging them from the rafters in an unoccupied attic or floor joists in a crawl space, you may be able to force the pest out long enough to seal up the holes and cracks that gave the animal entry in the first place.

CAUTION: Mothballs are not to be used in this fashion inside occupied living areas. Take precautions to make sure that kids and pets can't get near them.

Ammonia is an off-the-shelf "repellent" that can help keep pests out of your garbage because of its strong odor.

If you place your garbage out on the curb in plastic bags (without the benefit of cans with tight-fitting lids to protect them), raccoons and other marauding critters can have a party. If they persist in ripping open the bags, even when they're tightly bound, pour a cup of ammonia in with the garbage before you cinch up the bag. One good sniff of that should put the marauders to flight and eventually break them of their habit.

If you use metal or plastic trash cans, regularly wash them out with an ammonia-based cleaner to remove the scent of food. The lingering smell of the ammonia will also act as a repellent.

Ammonia can also be used to flush a raccoon or squirrel up out of your chimney. Wait till the fireplace is cool, then set a large flat pan full of ammonia inside the hearth or in the ash bin so that the fumes can waft into the chimney. Once you're absolutely sure the critter and any offspring are out of the flue (check top and bottom with a flashlight to make sure), install a tight-fitting weather cap over the chimney to prevent reentry.

Family pets may also be employed in the battle. Tying up or penning the family dog near the garden to discourage a vegetable raider or near the chicken coop to frustrate a hungry fox or coyote is a practical, time-honored tactic. Maybe you can even figure out a way to stimulate the cat (don't ask me how) to get up off her duff and take care of the mice.

TRAPPING AND RELOCATING THE PEST

Companies like Havahart Traps and Tomahawk Live Traps, Inc., build metal box traps to catch just about any size animal.

Again, make sure that you've done *all* you can to cut off the animal's food supply and exclude it from your property before you resort to any kind of trap.

Live trapping requires the right trap, the right bait (see "A Brief Guide to Critter Control" on page 224), the proper placement of the trap, good timing, and a truckload of patience. Even with all that on your side, you may still fail. While some animals, like raccoons, are relatively easy to trap live, others, like groundhogs, may test your sanity.

Before you start, call one or more of the professional organizations listed under "Tapping a Pro" on page 228. They'll be able *(continued on page 226)*

CRITTER-PROOFING YOUR HOME

There are two types of backyards, those that serve as an open invitation to pests and those that are less pest friendly. To transform yours into the latter, follow this advice.

1. Thin or remove ivy and other dense vegetation, branches overhanging the roof, dead trees, stumps, and rotten landscaping ties. Pick up dropped fruit and nuts. Eliminate any conditions that allow standing water or moisture to accumulate.

2. Cover garbage cans with tight lids and place them in a rack where they can't be turned over, or keep them inside the garage. Clean the cans regularly, especially in hot weather.

3. Keep compost heap well turned, covered, and free of sweets and meats.

4. Stack firewood up off the ground (on rails) and well away from the house and outbuildings.

5. Install a chimney cap that meets the building code and National Fire Protection Association (NFPA) specifications.

6. Don't leave pet food out.

7. Screen soffit, gable, and crawl-space vents and any construction gaps that invite insect or critter nests.

8. Use caulk, sheet metal, steel wool, or cement to seal cracks and holes in foundation, siding, and roof. Weather-strip all windows and doors.

9. Put a plastic shield over window wells to keep water and animals out.

10. Make sure basement windows and doors are tight and well maintained.

11. Equip bird feeder with a baffle to keep unwanted critters from feeding.

12. Keep outbuildings closed up tightly.

A Brief Guide to Critter Control

Critter	Problems	What You Can Do
BAT	May carry rabies; may bite or scratch; excrement can create mess or odor problem	See "Snag That Bat!" on page 227.
BIRDS (FRUIT-EATING)	May bite or scratch; excrement can create mess or odor problem; may raid fruit trees; makes noise	Eliminate food and shelter opportunities; post guard dog; protect fruit trees or bushes with nets; use sonic or visual repellents
BIRDS (MIGRATORY)	May bite or scratch; excrement can create mess or odor problem; may damage siding, shingles, or other wooden elements; may raid garden; may raid fruit trees; may raid bird feeders; makes noise; may damage lawn	Eliminate food and shelter opportunities; post guard dog; wait for flock to move on; use sonic or visual repellents
CHIPMUNK	May bite or scratch; may raid bird feeder; makes noise; may damage lawn	Eliminate food and shelter opportunities; post guard dog; use live trap baited with peanut butter; use lethal trap
COYOTE	May carry rabies; has serious bite; may be threat to chickens, livestock, or pets; may raid trash; makes noise	Eliminate food and shelter opportunities; post guard dog; use sonic or visual repellents; use lethal trap; hire professional pest control firm
FOX	May carry rabies; has serious bite; may be threat to chickens, livestock, or pets	Eliminate food and shelter opportunities; post guard dog; use sonic or visual repellents; use lethal trap; hire professional pest control firm
GOPHER	May bite or scratch; may raid garden; will chew telephone and power cables; may damage lawn; may damage trees	Eliminate food and shelter opportunities; use lethal trap; hire professional pest control firm
MICE	May bite or scratch; may damage siding, shingles, or other wooden elements; carries fleas and related diseases; may raid trash; makes noise; will chew telephone and power cables	Eliminate food and shelter opportunities; use Ro-pel (repellent); use lethal trap; use Talon or Decon (poisons); hire professional pest control firm
MOLE	May bite or scratch; may damage lawn	Use lethal trap
OPOSSUM	Has serious bite; may be threat to chickens, livestock, or pets; may raid trash; may raid fruit trees; may raid bird feeders	Eliminate food and shelter opportunities; post guard dog; use live trap baited with sardines; hire professional pest control firm
RABBIT	May bite or scratch; may raid garden; may damage tree	Eliminate food and shelter opportunities; post guard dog; use live trap baited with cob corn or dried apples; use rabbit repellent

CRITTER	PROBLEMS	WHAT YOU CAN DO
RACCOON	May carry rabies; has serious bite; may be threat to chickens, livestock, or pets; may damage siding, shingles, or other wooden elements; carries fleas and related diseases; may raid trash; may raid garden; may raid fruit trees; may raid bird feeders	Eliminate food and shelter opportunities; post guard dog; use live trap baited with sardines; hire professional pest control firm
RAT	Has serious bite; may be threat to chickens, livestock, or pets; may damage siding, shingles, or other wooden elements; carries fleas and related diseases; may raid trash; makes noise; will chew telephone and power cables	Eliminate food and shelter opportunities; use Ro-pel (repellent); use lethal trap; use Talon or Decon (poisons); hire professional pest control firm
SKUNK	May carry rabies; may bite or scratch; may raid trash; has obnoxious smell; may damage lawn	Eliminate food and shelter opportunities; use live trap baited with catfood or fish; hire professional pest control firm
SNAKE (NONVENOMOUS)	May bite; may be threat to chickens, livestock, or pets	Eliminate food and shelter opportunities; capture by hand and remove—can be picked up and safely removed by grabbing just behind head or covering with towel; hire professional pest control firm
SNAKE (VENOMOUS)	Has serious bite; may be threat to chickens, livestock, or pets	Eliminate food and shelter opportunities; hire professional pest control firm
SQUIRREL	Has serious bite; may raid bird feeders; makes noise; will chew telephone and power cables	Eliminate food and shelter opportunities; post guard dog; use live trap baited with peanut butter; hire professional pest control firm
TOAD OR LIZARD	—	Capture by hand and remove.
TURTLE	May bite or scratch	Eliminate food and shelter opportunities; capture by hand and remove
WOODCHUCK (GROUNDHOG)	May carry rabies; may bite or scratch; may raid garden	Eliminate food and shelter opportunities; post guard dog; put up fence; use live trap baited with apples and carrots
WOODPECKER	May damage siding, shingles, or other wooden elements; makes noise; may damage trees	See "Woodpecker Pests" on page 226.

to tell you if you need a permit to trap and transport the animal and whether or not the species you're trapping has any history of rabies. They may also suggest a place to release the trapped animal where it will have a good chance of surviving and won't become an immediate nuisance to someone else. In some cases, county and state game agents may be willing to loan you a trap and otherwise provide direct assistance.

CAUTION: A trapped animal may be excited and irritable, which makes it more prone to bite or scratch than usual. Be sure to work out a game plan for handling, transporting, and releasing the animal *before* you set the trap.

USING LETHAL METHODS

When you stop to consider how beneficial birds and animals are, it's natural to want to preserve them. Did you know, for example, that bats rarely bite humans, but that a single bat will gobble a thousand or more mosquitoes on a typical summer night? And that snakes, despite their sordid reputation, are instrumental in keeping the world from being overrun with rodents, insects, and amphibians?

Any of the nonlethal methods for dealing with a wildlife pest are preferable to killing it, except, perhaps, if you're dealing with field

Woodpecker Pests

Woodpeckers can be noisy and persistent pests, and sometimes inflict serious damage on wooden siding, deck posts, and other wooden structures. When woodpeckers hammer on wood, they're trying to pry out cluster flies and other insect food. When they rattle on a metal TV antenna or aluminum rain gutter, they're trying to establish their territory and lure a mate by making as much noise as possible. (See *Northern Three-Toed Woodpecker.*)

Since woodpeckers are protected by the Federal Migratory Bird Treaty Act, it's illegal to kill them. However, you may be able to "persuade" the woodpecker to move elsewhere or at least limit the damage to your house. Here are a few measures worth trying.

● The best time to scare a woodpecker away from your house is when it first shows up—that is, before it nests. Try banging on a garbage can lid or firing a blank gun.

● String 6-foot strands of flash tape from the soffit, just underneath the rain gutters, to the siding below. As the shiny tape twists in the light, it effectively scares woodpeckers away. Your county cooperative extension agent or a representative from the Animal Damage Control office can provide more specific instructions.

● By filling the gaps and cracks in wood siding with caulk, you eliminate the holes where insects hide and breed, thereby eliminating the food that lures woodpeckers.

● Smear a sticky bird repellent (such as Roost-No-More, 4-the-Birds, or Tanglefoot) on the wooden surface that's under attack. Woodpeckers dislike the tacky goop and tend to stay away. (*CAUTION:* Woodpecker repellents may stain some surfaces, so read the instructions carefully before you apply it.)

● If all else fails, try feeding your enemy. Woodpeckers are especially fond of suet. If you set up a feeder, they may forget all about your siding.

NOTE: If you live in an area with perennial woodpecker problems and are going to install new siding, consider vinyl or choose a wood siding with as few knots and checks as possible.

NORTHERN THREE-TOED WOODPECKER

These beautiful birds can be very noisy and can seriously damage wood siding.

Snag That Bat!

Bats sometimes bumble into our homes through an open window or door and have a hard time finding their way back out. Other times, when bats are roosting in the attic, one will crawl down through the wall to escape the attic heat and come out through an opening for pipes or electric wires in a room below. (See *Little Brown Bat*.)

While it's true that bats can carry rabies, human deaths related to rabid bat bites are extremely rare. Only 19 such deaths have been documented in the last 25 years.

On balance, bats are powerful helpers in controlling mosquitoes and other insect pests, which they munch by the thousands. In Europe, and increasingly in the United States, it's not uncommon for a homeowner to erect a bat house in the yard to attract these beneficial mammals. (See "Sources" on this page.)

A bat that has blundered into your house will usually find its way out if you confine it to one room and leave the windows and doors open. Dimming the lights may help, since bright light may confuse the bat and prompt it to seek shelter in a curtain or under furniture.

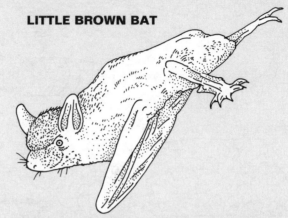

LITTLE BROWN BAT

Though despised in myths and legend, many bat species, like this little brown bat, benefit humans by eating hundreds of soft-bodied insects and beetles each night.

If the bat doesn't find its way out, don't try to swat it with a newspaper or tennis racket. Instead, put on your gardening or work gloves and wait for the bat to land. When it does, slip an empty coffee can over it and a piece of cardboard in under the can to close the opening. Carry the bat outside, away from people, and release it. If you haven't got an empty coffee can, a fisherman's landing net will do nicely.

If bats are roosting in your attic, the best ploy is to wait until they fly out around dusk and then seal up the openings through which they enter. Bear in mind that a bat can crawl through a crack that's only ½ inch wide.

In the North, the best time to bat-proof your attic is during the winter or early spring, before migrating bats return from the South. In southern climates, where bats roost year-round, you may be able to flush the bats out of the attic by hanging mesh bags full of mothballs from the rafters. While the bats are out of the roost, seal up the holes and cracks that permitted entry.

Sources

Bat house plans and other information are available in *The Bat House Builders Handbook* ($6.95), published by Bat Conservation International. The group also offers a free brochure titled *Dealing with Unwanted Guests*. Contact Bat Conservation International, P.O. Box 162603, Austin, TX 78716; (800) 538-BATS. (See also "The Bat Lady of Mineral Wells" on page 229.)

mice or rats, which generally can't be controlled otherwise. (See "A Brief Guide to Critter Control" on page 224.)

Though migratory birds and some animal species are protected by state and federal law, it is within your rights as a homeowner to kill an animal—even a protected species—if it comes inside your house. This "right to kill" may not apply, however, to protected birds or animals that are merely in your yard or on surrounding land, so it's smart to call your county extension agent or other wildlife professional *before* you take any action. It's possible, for example, that you'll need to get a permit from the state (before or after the fact) to legally kill the animal.

IDENTIFYING POISONOUS SNAKES

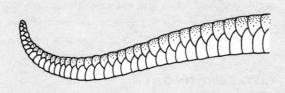

Harmless snakes have divided scales under the tail.

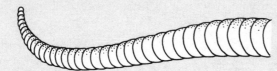

Poisonous snakes have undivided scales under the tail.

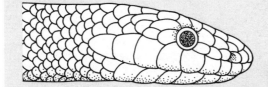

round nose

Harmless snakes have round eyes and a round nose.

stub nose

Poisonous snakes have elliptical, catlike pupils, a stub nose, and pits behind the nostrils.

Look 'Em in the Eye

Though the vast majority of snakes are nonvenomous and beneficial to us, it's worthwhile to know the poisonous species. In the United States, these include copperheads, coral snakes, cottonmouths, and rattlesnakes. Except for the coral snake, which is smooth and wormlike with a glossy black head, all poisonous snakes are husky and have heads that are much wider than their necks. Poisonous snakes have elliptical pupils, as shown in *Identifying Poisonous Snakes,* while harmless snakes have round pupils.

Guns, killing traps or poisons are the lethal alternatives when there's no other practical solution.

Guns generally aren't a safe or legal option in urban and suburban settings, where a stray bullet can end in tragedy. But guns still find use in the country, when a woodchuck defies capture or a coyote makes one raid too many on the chicken coop.

Killing traps, which are used mostly on gophers, moles, mice, and rats, are designed to spear, snare, or squeeze the animal to death. When set properly, they are quick and efficient.

Poisons, while effective, present some serious drawbacks. First, a poisoned animal may die—and subsequently begin to smell—inside a wall cavity or other place where you can't easily find or remove it. Second, poisons have to be placed and protected with utmost caution lest they end up killing a child or pet.

TAPPING A PRO

Here's a list of professionals, ranging from local to federal, who can give you information and advice—perhaps even direct help—in dealing with a wildlife pest.

- County cooperative extension agent
- State Fish and Game Department agent
- State Agricultural Department agent

Who's the Pest?

Not all commercial pest control firms are competent or ethical. Ask someone at the State Fish and Game Department or Animal Damage Control to recommend two or three good firms or individuals. ●

The Bat Lady of Mineral Wells

Amanda Lollar's first encounter with a live bat—back in 1987—wasn't exactly a pleasant one.

"To tell you the truth, I was disgusted by the sight of it," she remembers. "But I could see that its wing was hurt, and that it was suffering, and . . . well, I've got this soft spot for critters."

Aware that she shouldn't touch the injured bat, Amanda used a newspaper to scoop it up off the hot sidewalk and take it inside. She placed the bat in a little box with a little bowl of water and used cotton swabs to maneuver it around so that it could drink.

"The more I watched her, the more I realized what a gentle creature she was," Amanda says. "She wasn't trying to bite me. In fact, she was a lot more afraid of me that I was of her. I decided to keep her and try to heal her wing. I named her Sunshine."

Mike Chamberlain

Amanda Lollar relaxes with Sunshine.

Amanda made a trip to the library that day—the first of many—to learn about bats. It marked the beginning of a studious love affair with bats that continues to this day.

"Almost everything I *thought* I knew about bats turned out to be wrong," she relates. "They aren't blind. And they're not aggressive—in fact, they're very timid. Contrary to popular belief, fewer than ½ of 1 percent of all bats get rabies, and when they do, they almost always die quietly by themselves. People also don't realize that bats are one of mankind's most powerful weapons in controlling insects. In short, they're one of the most lovely and gentle creatures on earth."

As her studies progressed, Amanda's reputation as an authority on bats began to grow. When local homeowners or businesses had a bat "problem," it was Amanda Lollar who got the call and went riding to the rescue.

"I agreed to help local businesses get the bats out of their buildings—under the condition that they put up suitable bat houses outside."

Amanda herself designed the new roosts; her father, Luther Lollar, volunteered to build them.

"We now have 45 official bat houses in downtown Mineral Wells," she reports, "including one atop the police station and another one on the city's largest bank. These businesses are so proud of their bat roosts that many of them have put their logos up on the bat houses."

As part of her educational efforts, Amanda gives "bat chats" in the local schools and writes in her spare time. Her first effort with the pen, published in 1992, was called *The Bat in My Pocket: A Memorable Friendship* (Capra Press, Santa Barbara, California). The book details her relationship with Sunshine, who survived the injury and lived on in the Lollar home for more than a year. Amanda has also written and published a ground-breaking manual on bat rehabilitation and captive care.

In 1995, Amanda left the family furniture business behind and opened Bat World, a nonprofit museum and sanctuary that features, along with other attractions, 12 different species of bats living in their natural habitats.

So what's next for "The Bat Lady of Mineral Wells," as the locals call her?

"Well," she speculates, "there's lots of talk now about organizing a community festival to honor the bats—an annual 'Bat Day', so to speak. It seems like everyone from the mayor on down wants to get on the bat wagon."

Bat World is located at 217 N. Oak Avenue, Mineral Wells, TX 76067; (817) 325-3404. In exchange for a donation to Bat World, you'll receive plans for Sunshine's bat house.

Trapping Mice

The best strategy for getting rid of mice is to plan a Saturday night massacre using a large number of traps baited with peanut butter, which has a powerful aroma and sticks nicely to the trigger.

The peanut butter works best when pressed onto the *underside* of the trigger, which prevents the mice from licking and running.

Place the baited traps flush against a wall or post, with the trigger end next to the wall, as shown in *Trap Placement*.

If you're trapping rats, sprinkle the trigger end of the trap with a little fish oil to cover your scent. Use gloves when you remove dead mice from the traps and flush them down the toilet. Rats can be buried.

TRAP PLACEMENT

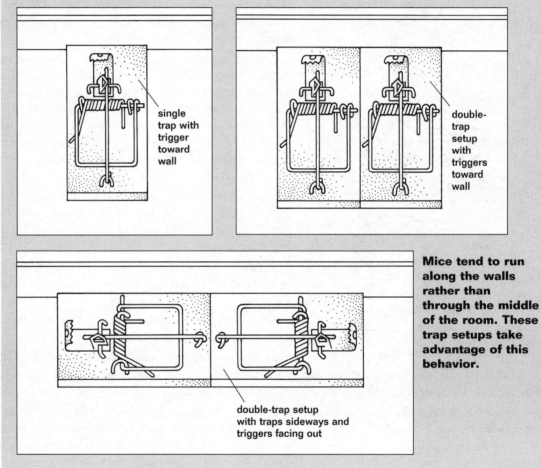

single trap with trigger toward wall

double-trap setup with triggers toward wall

Mice tend to run along the walls rather than through the middle of the room. These trap setups take advantage of this behavior.

double-trap setup with traps sideways and triggers facing out

- State Health Department agent (for rabies questions)
- State Department of Natural Resources agent
- State Department of Environmental Control agent
- Animal Damage Control agent (a branch of the U.S. Department of Agriculture)
- Commercial trappers and pest control professionals

If you want to hire a professional pest control firm to solve your critter problem, expect to pay $75 to $200, depending on how many visits are needed. Some firms, like Critter Control, Inc., will also contract to do the patching, sealing, and other home and yard alterations necessary to keep the pest from returning. (See "Hiring a Pest Control Professional" on page 238.)

Termites, Beetles, and Carpenter Ants

SUBTERRANEAN TERMITES

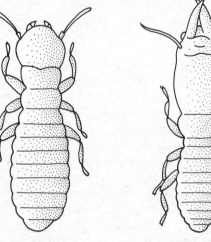

Worker   **Soldier**

Subterranean termites are found in the two distinct forms shown here. In addition to workers and soldiers, a colony would also include a queen, king, nymphs, and winged alates.

TRACKING THOSE MONEY-EATING INSECTS

Americans spend an estimated $1.5 billion annually to treat, repair, and replace wood that's been damaged by insects. The biggest culprit by far is the subterranean termite (see *Subterranean Termites* on this page), which accounts for a whopping two-thirds of the damage. The less common types of termites—drywood and dampwood termites—and wood-boring beetles account for the rest.

While carpenter ants look menacing and can certainly be a nuisance, they don't decimate wood the way that termites and beetle larvae do. Carpenter ants are mostly interested in wood (preferably when it's damp and rotting) as a place to nest.

Quick Response

1. If you find termite tubes in crawl space or around foundation, break them up and examine adjoining wood for damage.

2. If you discover exit holes made by wood-boring beetles, make sure they're *active* before you call pro.

3. Track carpenter ants to nest and destroy it with spray-on insecticide.

6 NATURAL EMERGENCIES

Hazards

● Do not apply termite poisons yourself. If you have old cans of chlordane (now banned) or other termiticides in storage, call your state environmental protection office for advice on how to dispose of them safely.

● If someone becomes ill due to a misapplication, spill, or accidental exposure to insecticides, seek medical attention immediately and report the incident to the state agency that licenses pest control contractors.

● When applying ant killer or other topical insecticides, read the instructions and safety precautions carefully.

Discovering termites, beetles, or carpenter ants in your home can be an unnerving experience. It's easy to imagine the roof caving in or the floor falling through unless something is done right away.

But there's no real cause for panic. Even a well-established termite colony of 60,000 workers eats only ⅕ of an ounce of wood a day. With that in mind, you can take your time locating two or three licensed pest control contractors and evaluating their respective strategies and prices. In most cases, a delay of a few weeks, or even a few months, is of little consequence. (See the exception described in "Illegal Aliens" on this page.)

The urgency in treating wood-boring beetles and carpenter ants is even less pronounced—in fact, with a little patience you may be able to solve the problem yourself.

Generally speaking, wood-destroying insects focus their attacks on damp wood, especially around the foundation and under the crawl space. *NOTE: The single most important step you can take to prevent or combat an infestation is to cut off the insects' source of water.* (See "Troubleshooting Guide to Wet Basements" on page 66 and *Hot Spots for Termites* on page 235.)

UNDERSTANDING SUBTERRANEAN TERMITES

The United States has varying degrees of termite infestation with the largest populations in the warm South, tapering off to few or no termites in the cooler North, as shown in *Termite Territory* on the opposite page. Three types of termites make up this population: subterranean, drywood, and dampwood.

Subterranean termites live throughout the United States, with the exception of the white areas on the map, dampwood termites live mainly in the southern United States from California to Florida, and drywood termites live from the western states down to the Gulf coast of Texas.

The subterranean variety is easily the most prevalent and damaging. As the name implies, subterranean termites build their colony underground and forage for cellulose. Wood, in the form of stumps, firewood, and building materials, is their usual diet, but they'll also munch

Illegal Aliens

An infestation of Formosan termites should be treated with more urgency (but still no panic, mind you!) than other types of termites. These relative newcomers, limited to a few areas in the South, are the most voracious termites in the United States. A medium-size colony of 3 million Formosan termites can eat the equivalent of 6 inches of a 2 × 4 a day! Miami, Charleston, New Orleans, and Houston are among southern cities that have reported infestations. ●

books, clothing, paper, and leather goods, if the opportunity presents itself.

Subterranean termites hate sunlight and cold and must stay in contact with the moist earth. The colony usually forms 5 to 10 feet underground and is active year-round.

Subterranean termites love to find wood that's in direct contact with soil—say, a deck post or stair step sitting directly on the ground—so they can chew right into it without ever being exposed to sunlight, air, or predators. As they bore through the wood, creating tunnels and galleries, worker termites are careful not to break the surface of the wood, exposing themselves to sunlight and drying air. Thus the wood may look perfectly healthy on the outside, with a thin shell of wood or paint intact, while the termites are eating out the center and hauling the wood back to the colony.

When subterranean termites can't find wood in direct contact with the earth, they look for seams or cracks in concrete or masonry where they can pass protected and undetected to reach the wood above. A crack as small as ⅟32 of an inch can provide them entry.

Termites also like to find exterior foam board insulation or stucco veneer that's abutting the ground. To reach the wood above, they burrow up behind or through the insulation or wind their way up through voids left between the stucco veneer and the foundation.

Subterranean termites may also build shelter tubes made from excrement, mud, and saliva. These hollow, brown-colored tubes—up to ½ inch thick—enable the termites to bridge over concrete footings, pressure-treated sill plates, termite shields, and other obstacles so they can reach a vulnerable source of wood.

TERMITE TERRITORY

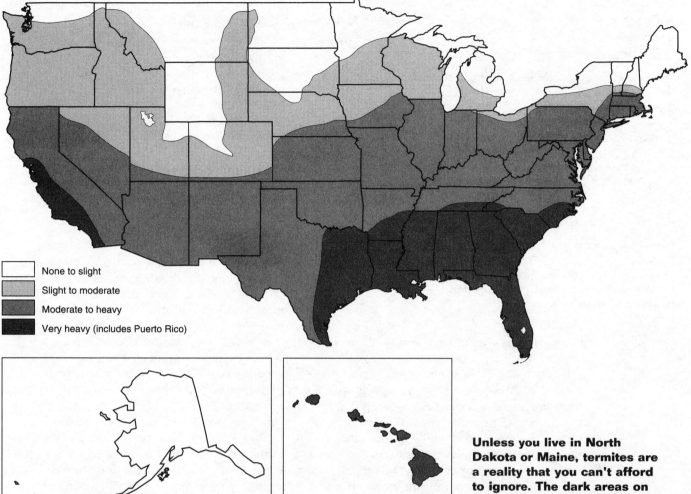

None to slight

Slight to moderate

Moderate to heavy

Very heavy (includes Puerto Rico)

Unless you live in North Dakota or Maine, termites are a reality that you can't afford to ignore. The dark areas on the map indicate the heaviest termite infestation while the white areas in the North have no termites at all.

Redrawn from a map published in the National Institute of Building Sciences' "Wood Protection Guidelines" (November 1993)

Termite tubes are sometimes found on plumbing and electrical conduits in contact with the ground. Other times, they wind their way up the side of a pier or foundation wall. In crawl spaces, they sometimes shoot straight up to reach the wooden floor joists or subfloor above. (See *Termite Tubes* on page 234.)

SPOTTING THE ENEMY

It's wise to set aside one day a year to inspect your home for subterranean termites, or hire a professional to do it for you. In warm, humid parts of the country where termites are especially active, a twice-a-year inspection is probably smart.

A termite inspection can be conveniently combined with an inspection for wood rot, since both of these pests tend to attack unprotected wood around the foundation and need moisture to survive. (See *Hot Spots for Rot* on page 170 and *Hot Spots for Termites* on page 235.)

Start the inspection by putting on your grubbiest old work clothes. Then arm yourself with a good flashlight and the determination to do a really thorough job.

Examine the outside of the foundation first, looking for termite tubes or signs of punk wood. Look carefully behind any shrubs or vines that may be camouflaging the enemy. The crack between the foundation and precast concrete steps is a favorite point of entry. Don't be shy about crawling under the porch, deck, or crawl space to check the sill, posts, floor joists, subfloor, and the underside of

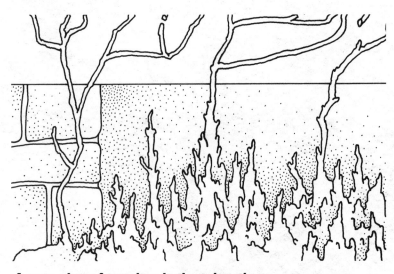

A sure sign of termites is the tubes they sometimes build to reach the wooden structure of your house.

Just Say No

Avoid pest control contractors who show up at your door claiming to see signs of insect infestation, who don't have a listed phone number, or who claim to have a "secret" formula. (See "Hiring a Pest Control Professional" on page 238.) ●

wooden steps—that's exactly where termites and wood rot are most likely to be found.

If you spot termite tubes, break them open and see if any small, gray-white insects—they look almost like grains of rice—emerge. If not, the tubes may be abandoned. Perhaps the colony has moved on. But break the tubes down anyway, in the event that termites return. (If a later inspection reveals that the tubes have been rebuilt, it's proof positive that you have an active infestation.)

Once you've broken the tubes down, the termites in the wood above will quickly die from lack of moisture, while workers from the main colony underground will start to rebuild.

The absence of termite tubes does *not* mean your house is free of termites. Termites prefer to enter your house through wood that's in direct contact with soil or through cracks in the foundation.

As you make your inspection, keep an eye out for termite pellets (excrement) or shed wings. The pellets, which are dark, sand-size particles, are sometimes visible beneath an area of infested wood. The presence of shed termite wings indicates a mature colony—at least several years old—that has sent out winged reproductive termites to form new colonies.

If your timing is just right, you may spot swarming (flying) termites in the spring. This is the only time when subterranean termites expose themselves to sunlight and dry air. Of course, only those assigned to reproduction emerge for the annual swarm—the rest remain underground, in the tubes, or in the galleries and tunnels that they've hollowed out in the wood.

It's easy to mistake winged ants for swarming termites. But the differences in the shape of their bodies and antennae are easy to distinguish, as shown in *Ants versus Termites* on page 236.

As you inspect your home, look for spots where the paint has peeled or the wood is discolored. Probe any suspect areas with an ice pick to make sure they're sound. (See *Probing for Rot* on page 172.) Pay special attention to sill plates, joists, and hardwood flooring.

If the ice pick turns up tunnels and galleries in the center of the wood—filled with a siltlike mixture of excrement, soil, and chewed wood—you've probably got an active infestation of termites. The discovery of any live insects removes all doubt.

TREATING SUBTERRANEAN TERMITES

For decades, the standard practice in termite control was to inject powerful, long-lived termiticides, such as chlordane or heptachlor, into the soil under and around the foundation.

Go for Broke

A "partial" inspection for termites or rot may be worse than no inspection at all, since it gives you a false sense of security. The best course is to ask for a whole-house inspection that covers the foundation, substructure, siding, living areas, attic, and roof. Ask the inspector to probe hidden and hard-to-access spots, such as the wood behind stucco siding, inset rain gutters, and painted window sashes. ●

HOT SPOTS FOR TERMITES

As illustrated here, subterranean termites are always on the hunt for untreated wood that's in direct contact with the ground or for cracks in the foundation that provide them with a dark, moist passageway inside. Drywood termites, which enter through an unscreened gable or soffit vent, will sometimes set up shop in the attic.

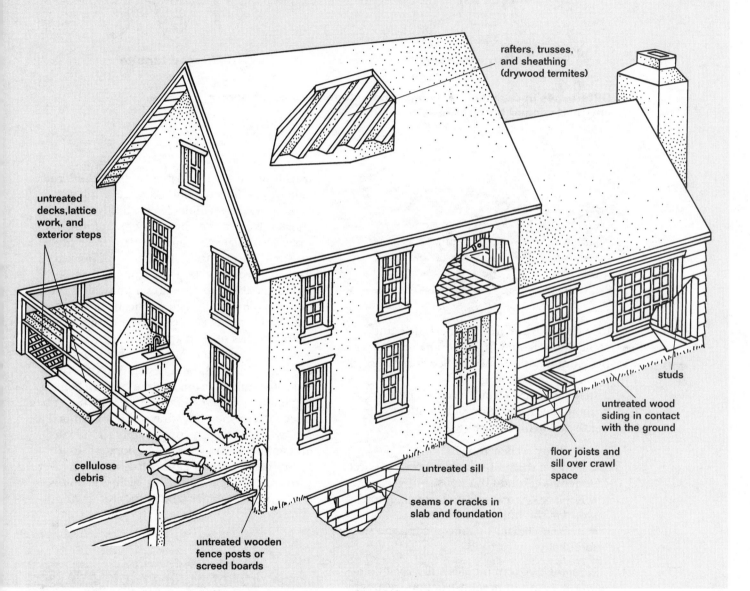

rafters, trusses, and sheathing (drywood termites)

untreated decks, lattice work, and exterior steps

cellulose debris

untreated wooden fence posts or screed boards

untreated sill

seams or cracks in slab and foundation

studs

untreated wood siding in contact with the ground

floor joists and sill over crawl space

One application of these termiticides could effectively protect a house for decades.

But during the late 1980s, investigators discovered that the same qualities that make these poisons so effective against termites—that is, high toxicity and longevity in the environment—also present serious environmental hazards to humans and animals. Chlordane,

heptachlor, and a number of other old-time termiticides were subsequently banned and new tactics for fighting termites began to emerge.

Today, the first step in getting rid of subterranean termites (and preventing their return) is to alter the environment under and around the house and make structural modifications (for example, removing cellu-

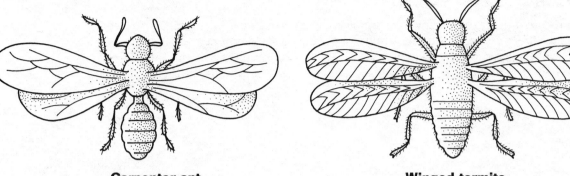

ANTS VERSUS TERMITES

Carpenter ant   Winged termite

Differences in body shape, wings, and antennae make carpenter ants and winged termites easy to distinguish.

Hire a Sleuth

Termites can be very difficult to spot in houses that have slab-on-grade foundations and/or stucco veneers. I recommend that you get a professional inspection. ●

lose debris from around the house and replacing infested or vulnerable wood with pressure-treated lumber). See *Hot Spots for Termites* on page 235.

In some cases, termites can be held at bay without any application of termiticides, by taking the following measures:

● Tear down their tubes.
● Deprive them of wood and water sources under and around the house.
● Replace or treat infested or vulnerable wood in the house's substructure.
● Remain vigilant by reinspecting the sites frequently.

Nonetheless, termiticides still play a common role, both in preconstruction treatment and in treating existing houses. Typically, the termiticide is injected into the ground around the foundation, creating a poisonous perimeter defense that termites can't cross. Sometimes, poison is also applied underneath the house. If there's a crawl space, the termiticide can be injected directly into the ground underneath it. In slab-on-grade construction, holes are bored through the concrete slab,

usually along the foundation wall, so the termiticide can be injected into the underlying soil.

Happily, the termiticides currently in use are shorter-lived in the environment and much less toxic to humans and animals than their predecessors. For example, Dursban, a popular termiticide produced by Dow Chemical, is biodegradable and has shown no evidence of being carcinogenic. The downside is that Dursban loses its effectiveness after about five years and has to be reapplied.

Many researchers and pest control operators are enthusiastic about a new group of termiticides formulated from sodium borate (hence the name *boracides*). Boracides, which can be injected, brushed on, sprayed on, or applied as a powder, have very low toxicity to humans and animals—in fact, sodium borate is less toxic than common table salt—but have proven to be quite effective against termites, wood-boring beetles, and carpenter ants.

Seal Ducts against Insecticide

If insecticides are to be applied in an attic or crawl space that contains heating and cooling ducts, make sure that the ducts are tightly sealed before the application begins. Otherwise, fumes from the insecticide can be drawn into the rest of the house through the ductwork. (See "The HVAC Connection" on page 218.) ●

If you hire a professional pest control operator to do an inspection or if necessary, a treatment, take the time to choose a good one. And ask for details about how the work is going to be done, as described in "Hiring a Pest Control Professional" on page 238. When dealing with termite control, don't look for a bargain. Poor or ineffectual treatment now may hurt your home's resale value later.

Termite Screening

If you live in an area where drywood termites are a threat, make sure soffit, gable, and other vents into the attic are tightly screened. This prevents the airborne queen from entering and setting up house—in *your* house! ●

UNDERSTANDING DRYWOOD AND DAMPWOOD TERMITES

Two other species of termites are found in the United States—drywood and dampwood—both of which are much rarer than the subterranean type.

Whereas subterranean termites build their colonies deep underground, drywood and dampwood termites live aboveground, building nests in the wood itself. As the names imply, drywood termites tend to infest dry, healthy wood—especially oak and redwood—while dampwood termites need moist, decaying wood to thrive. Otherwise, the two species are very similar.

Timely Departure

Try to schedule a trip or vacation away while your house is being treated for termites. If you do remain at home, keep children and pets away from the foundation and crawl space. Ask your pest control contractor for *specific* safety advice. ●

SPOTTING THE ENEMY

Drywood and dampwood termites can be hard to spot. Their nests typically remain small—a few thousand insects—and damage to the wood develops slowly. Look for small holes (¹⁄₁₆ inch) in the wood and a pile of hard, barrel-shaped pellets (excrement) underneath. Chinks and cracks are sometimes visible on the wood's surface. Probe suspect wood with an ice pick, as described in *Probing for Rot* on page 172, to see if there are termite tunnels underneath.

TREATING DRYWOOD AND DAMPWOOD TERMITES

When an infestation of drywood termites is limited to a small area, it's sometimes possible to get rid of them simply by replacing the infested wood with pressure-treated lumber. If the wood can't be replaced (and if it isn't coated), a brushed or sprayed-on application of boracide may do the trick. Boracide, being water-soluble, can penetrate deeply into the wood and poison the termites. If the wood is coated, small holes are sometimes drilled so that a termiticide can be injected.

Serious infestations of drywood termites are sometimes treated by a technique called *tent fumigation,* in which the whole house is treated with Vicane or other gaseous termiticide. Unfortunately, tent fumigation is expensive and it leaves no residual protection, so the termites are at liberty to return.

Dampwood termites can usually be evicted simply by eliminating the source of water—say, a roof or plumbing leak—and removing the damp, rotting wood in which they make their nest.

UNDERSTANDING WOOD-BORING BEETLES

Among the many, many varieties of wood-boring beetles found in American homes, the four most common are the deathwatch beetle, furniture beetle, old-house borer, and powderpost beetle. While each has its distinct appearance, as shown in *The Beetles* on page 239, all lay their eggs in or on wood. When the larvae emerge from the eggs, they bore through the wood, ingesting the cellulose and leaving tunnels full of powdery excrement called *frass.*

Hiring a Pest Control Professional

The customary time to have a house inspected for termites or rot is when the property is put up for sale. In fact, the mortgage banker will probably insist on a professional pest inspection before approving the loan.

But even if you're not buying or selling, it makes good sense to have your house inspected by a professional every few years. This is especially true if you live in a warm, humid part of the country where termites and rot fungus are especially active. (See *Termite Territory* on page 233.)

While an annual do-it-yourself inspection for termites and rot is a great idea, a homeowner may overlook subtle evidence of termites or rot that a pro could readily spot. (See "Detecting Rot Early" on page 169 and "Spotting the Enemy" on page 233.) For example, an infestation hidden behind stucco, brick, or stone veneer could easily escape a layman's eye.

The wisest strategy for hiring pest control professionals is to separate the inspection work from the mitigation and repair work. This avoids conflict of interest that might bias the inspection. The firms or individuals you select should meet the following criteria:

● They should be properly licensed or certified by the state.

● They should be fully insured. The contractor's policy should warrant termite (or wood decay) protection for five to seven years, provide general liability coverage, and include a "repair" bond to cover future repair work should termites (or decay fungus) reappear.

● They should be a well-established business and have a good reputation. Check references.

● They should have a clean record with the Better Business Bureau.

● They should be a member in good standing with one or more of the professional associations listed in "Finding a Pro" on this page.

If the inspection reveals an infestation of termites or rot fungus, have a second inspection and report done by a different firm. Keep in mind that it's difficult even for an honest and experienced inspector to assess the full extent of the damage until the repair work actually begins. Thus, a second inspection gives you the benefit of another (hopefully seasoned) opinion before you hire someone to do pest treatment and repair work.

It's prudent to get at least two bids on the treatment and repair work so that you can compare prices and strategies. But remember that two different contractors—both honest and competent—may recommend different strategies. Both approaches may be perfectly acceptable, reflecting differences in the contractors' training, experience, and personal work preferences. Ask each of the bidders to explain the pros and cons behind their recommended strategies—especially regarding any termiticides they plan to use—then you make the final choice.

Be sure that the contract for treatment and repairs is clear and detailed, especially regarding any guarantees the contractor is making.

Once the repairs are done, have your independent inspector return to inspect and certify the work.

Should problems develop during inspection, treatment, or repairs, try to resolve the problem in a direct and congenial discussion with the inspector or contractor.

If that fails, you can pursue the matter through the state licensing board or by filing a civil lawsuit. Provided the statute of limitations hasn't run out, the inspector and/or contractor can be held legally responsible for failing to detect an infestation or properly treat it. If the state board or court finds the contractor liable, he will be made to pay for repairs and treatment at no additional charge to you.

Finding a Pro

To find reputable pest control professionals in your area, check with your county cooperative extension agent or a local Realtor, or call or write any of the following organizations:

American Inspectors Association
P.O. Box 64309
Lubbock, TX 79464
(806) 794-1190

American Society of Home Inspectors
85 W. Algonquin Road
Suite 360
Arlington Heights, IL 60005
(708) 290-1919

National Association of Home Inspectors
5775 Wayzata Boulevard
Suite 860
Minneapolis, MN 55416
(800) 448-3942

National Pest Control Association
8100 Oak Street
Dunn Loring, VA 22027
(703) 573-8330

THE BEETLES

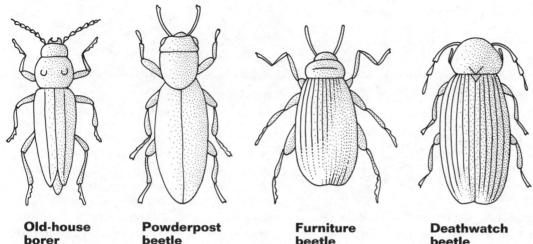

Old-house
borer

Powderpost
beetle

Furniture
beetle

Deathwatch
beetle

All of these beetles find a perfect nursery for their young in the wood in and around your house.

The larvae burrow through the wood for a year or more before emerging as adult beetles. The adults lay new eggs, reinfesting the wood.

SPOTTING THE ENEMY

Wood-boring beetles inflict their damage slowly but surely, with no visible signs to read until the adult comes forth, leaving a small exit hole in the wood. The holes vary in size from about ¹⁄₁₆ inch (powderpost beetle) to ³⁄₈ inch (old-house borer). Particles of frass will silt out of the holes and accumulate on the surface below, providing another telltale sign.

If you probe the wood with an ice pick and find narrow, frass-filled galleries running along and across the grain, you've confirmed that beetle larvae have been at work. But the question remains: Is the infestation still active, or have the beetles moved on?

Ask for Living Proof

Before you pay a pest control operator to exterminate beetles, ask him to show you a *living* larva or other solid evidence that the infestation is active. ●

Protective Coating

After the beetles and larvae have been killed, wood can be protected from reinfestation by coating it with paint, polyurethane, or other film-forming coatings, which deny the adult beetles a place to lay their eggs. ●

To find out, vacuum the old frass up and lay down some clean white paper beneath the suspect wood. If new frass (bright and cream-colored) collects on the paper, it's good evidence that there are live beetles at work. Another way to verify an active infestation is to circle a number of exit holes with a crayon, mark the number of exit holes inside, then return later to see if the number of exit holes inside the circle increased.

TREATING WOOD-BORING BEETLES

Most types of beetle infestations tend to die out naturally. Other times, when the infestation is limited to a single board or two, the problem is solved simply by replacing the infested boards with pressure-treated lumber.

If those solutions don't apply, the infested wood can be treated with a boracide, which is brushed or sprayed on the surface of uncoated wood or injected into drilled holes in coated wood.

As a last resort, tent fumigation is sometimes used to exterminate beetles, but it's expensive, won't kill the beetles' eggs, and has no residual effect, so a reinfestation is possible.

UNDERSTANDING CARPENTER ANTS

Carpenter ants, as shown in *The Carpenter Ant Family* on this page, aren't nearly as destructive to wood as their size (up to ⅞ inch long) and fierce-looking mandibles might suggest. They like to build their nest in wood that is already moist and rotting, whether inside the house or out. While they may munch on damp wood, they're more apt to go foraging for kitchen scraps or other nonwood food outside the nest.

Some of their favorite nesting spots are fascia boards that abut a leaking roof or rain gutter, joists and girders underneath a leaking sink or tub, and deck or porch posts that are starting to rot. If rotten wood isn't available,

THE CARPENTER ANT FAMILY

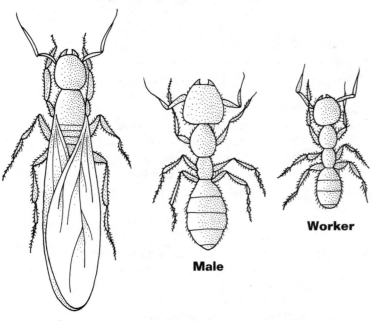

Queen

Male

Worker

Only queens and males have wings, which they shed before nesting.

carpenter ants will sometimes chew their way into foam insulation and set up quarters there.

Like termites, winged carpenter ants emerge in the spring to swarm and establish new colonies. But distinct differences in their anatomy make them easy to distinguish from termites. (See *Ants versus Termites* on page 236.)

SPOTTING THE ENEMY

Because carpenter ants forage boldly across thresholds and along baseboards, they're usually easy to spot. If ants appear only in small numbers and vanish in the winter, the nest is probably outside. If they appear in large numbers and are active year-round, their nest is probably inside the house.

TREATING CARPENTER ANTS

If the nest is outside the house and ants appear sporadically, it may not be necessary to find and destroy the nest. These few simple preventive measures may be enough to discourage the marauders.

- Weather-strip windows or doors that are points of entry.
- Caulk exterior cracks that serve as passage points.
- Place ant traps at strategic spots.
- Sweep up crumbs and other edibles.
- Trim back tree branches that touch the roof or walls.

If the nest is inside and ants are appearing in large numbers, the only solution is to track down the nest and destroy it. And the only way to find it is to watch the ant trails and track the ants back to their nest.

Carpenter ants sometimes leave a telltale pile of "sawdust" and excrement beside or below their nest, which can help in locating it. It may also be possible to hear them—in the quiet of the night—"skritching" around behind a wall. (Professional exterminators sometimes use a stethoscope to pinpoint an ant nest that's hidden behind a wall.)

Once you've located the nest and are ready to destroy it, make sure that kids and pets are clear of the area and that there's plenty of fresh air ventilation to clean out the fumes from the insecticide.

Move quickly when you raid the nest. Tear away the rotten wood or other veneer that protects the nest and spray the exposed galleries with an insecticide that's *specifically made for ants*.

At the first sign of an intruder, the ants will scatter, carrying away as many eggs as they can. So spray the poison around the perimeter of the nest first, then work your way toward the middle. Use enough to do the job, but no more.

Keep kids and pets away from the destroyed nest until you've had time to clean up the mess. Wear gloves to protect yourself from contact with the insecticide.

Remember that the key to preventing a reinfestation of carpenter ants is to eliminate the source of moisture that rotted the wood that attracted them in the first place. (See "Troubleshooting Guide to Wet Basements" on page 61 and *Hot Spots for Termites* on page 235.)

Self-Inflicted Emergencies

SELF-INFLICTED EMERGENCIES

Fire!

Quick Response

1. Get everyone out of house.

2. Alert fire department.

3. If fire is small and contained—and you have *clear* escape route to your rear— use properly rated fire extinguisher to put out fire.

USING AN EXTINGUISHER

To operate an extinguisher, pull the pin to free the handle (shown in inset), then stand 6 to 10 feet from the fire, and direct the spray at the base of the fire, sweeping from side to side. Always stand between the fire and a clear escape route.

Hazards

● Don't pour water on an electrical, chemical, or grease fire.

● Using an extinguisher that's not properly rated can put you at further risk from electric shock or splattered grease. (See "Preparing for an Emergency" on page 10 and "NFPA Fire Extinguisher Logos" on the opposite page.)

● If the extinguisher empties before the fire is out, the flames spread, or smoke obstructs your vision, leave the house at once, closing the doors behind you.

● Once the house is evacuated, make sure no one goes back inside for pets or other possessions.

USING A FIRE EXTINGUISHER

If you don't know how to use a fire extinguisher, it won't do you much good in fighting a fire. So take the time to learn now—before you need to use one. Run a drill including all adult members of your household to familiarize yourself with these steps.

1. Pull the pin. (Some models require releasing a lock latch or other first step.)
2. Position yourself 6 to 10 feet from the fire with a *clear* escape route to your rear.

3. Aim the nozzle at the *base* of the fire and squeeze the handle.
4. Sweep the nozzle from side to side, spraying until the fire appears out.
5. Watch for flashback or rekindling of the flames.
6. Have the fire department check the house.

FIGHTING KITCHEN FIRES

Kitchen fires are very common and are easy to deal with if you keep your head. Follow these steps and refer to *Extinguishing Kitchen Fires* on this page. *CAUTION:* Never use water on a grease fire. Splashed grease can ignite other materials nearby.

STOVE-TOP FIRES

1. Use an oven mitt to protect your hand.
2. Turn off the burner and hood fan.
3. *Leave the pan where it is.* Do not try to carry it to the sink or outdoors.
4. Carefully slide a lid or large pan over the

NFPA Fire Extinguisher Logos

Ordinary **A** Combustibles — Trash ● Wood ● Paper

Flammable **B** Liquids — Liquids ● Grease

Electrical **C** Equipment — Electrical Equipment

Extinguishers are labeled with letters that identify the type of fire they can handle, as shown here.

At the very least, keep an ABC-rated fire extinguisher in your kitchen. A red slash through any of the fire-classification symbols tells you that an extinguisher can be dangerous if it is used on that type of fire.

fire. If flaming oil has splashed outside the pan, toss baking soda on it or snuff it out with a properly rated fire extinguisher.
5. Leave the lid in place until the oil and burner have cooled.

OVEN FIRE

1. Leave the oven door closed.
2. Turn off the heat. (Microwaves and toaster ovens should be turned off at the main service panel.)
3. Allow the fire to die from lack of oxygen.

EXTINGUISHING KITCHEN FIRES

Smother flames in the pan with a lid. Wear an oven mitt to protect your hand.

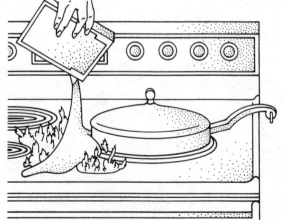

Smother the fire on a stove surface by pouring on a generous amount of baking soda or salt.

SELF-INFLICTED EMERGENCIES

A Recipe for *Really* Hot Potatoes

Deep-fried Indonesian potato balls are among Anna Lisa Yoder's most memorable recipes—*not* because of their scrumptious taste or exotic origin, mind you, but because they almost burned her apartment down.

Anna Lisa first decided to fix the recipe during the winter of 1994, when she and husband Rob shared an apartment in Coopersburg, Pennsylvania. As she rounded up the ingredients and did the prep work, it brought back delicious memories from the Far East, where she and Rob had lived some years before. What better way to warm up a cold Pennsylvania night, she figured, than by serving a hot Indonesian dish?

But when Anna Lisa dropped that first innocent-looking potato ball into the pan, the hot oil suddenly foamed and spilled over onto the burner. In a flash, the whole pan burst into flames that shot almost to the ceiling.

Rob, who was setting the table at the time, had a real-life chance to play hero. He rushed to the stove, turned off the burner, and plopped a large pan lid over the flaming oil. Without any oxygen to feed it, the fire quickly died.

"Up to that point, I was a bona-fide hero," says Rob. "I'd done everything just right."

Unfortunately, Rob couldn't resist the temptation to take a peak under the pan lid to examine the damage. (*Could it be that the potato ball had survived the conflagration?*)

When Rob lifted the lid, exposing the still-hot cooking element and oil to fresh oxygen—*POOF!*—the flames reignited and burned Rob's hand in the process.

Fortunately, Bob Gehman, a friend and neighbor, chanced upon the hectic scene, grabbed a box of table salt, and poured it liberally over the burner and flaming oil.

This time the fire was extinguished for good, with only a little smoke damage and some ruined potato balls.

Though Rob Yoder's moment in the limelight was brief and quickly tarnished, he still comes out a hero after all.

"The fire showed me how vulnerable we were in that apartment, with neither a smoke detector nor a fire extinguisher on hand," he says. "When Anna Lisa and I moved into our new house a short time later, I made sure that we had both."

Anna Lisa's subsequent attempts to make Indonesian potato balls, we're happy to report, haven't required any heroics at all.

Spills

There's nothing worse than grape juice spilled on a light-colored carpet, but lots of water and fast action can save the day.

Quick Response

1. Blot up spills quickly before they can dry.

2. If water is leaking from broken pipe or fixture, shut off main water valve.

3. Roll back carpets and move furnishings.

4. Circulate fresh air to dry out area and dissipate fumes.

MOVING FAST

Fast action is the key to limiting the damage from a spill. Ninety percent of the spots on carpet and upholstery can be removed completely if they are absorbed, blotted, and flushed immediately (within two or three minutes) with plain water or a mild detergent solution.

Use white towels or rags to blot up as much as you can, rotating the cloth to use a fresh surface with each wipe. (White lets you see what you're removing and it won't bleed.) Work from the outside of the spill toward the center without scrubbing, which can spread the stain and damage the surface.

Hazards

● Don't enter an area where standing water has come in contact with appliances, outlets, or extension cords. If you can do it safely, go to the main circuit box and switch off the breaker or fuse that serves the flooded area.

● If the cleanup work involves using a wet-dry vac or other electrical devices, plug them into an outlet or extension cord protected by a ground fault circuit interrupter (GFCI).

● Water that's stagnant or contaminated with sewage presents a *serious* risk of bacterial infection, especially to people with asthma and other respiratory ailments.

● Never use a gasoline-powered water pump indoors—the fumes can be deadly.

● A chemical spill may present a triple hazard: toxic fumes, fire danger, and the possibility of skin burns. (See "Cleaning Up Chemical and Oil Spills" on page 254.)

● Do not concoct household cleaning remedies other than ones in the table on page 250. Mixing chemicals, such as chlorine bleach and ammonia, can produce toxic fumes.

7
SELF-INFLICTED EMERGENCIES

On substances that glob (for example, wax, grease, chewing gun, dried spaghetti sauce, etc.), scrape the surface with a spoon to remove what you can before resorting to other cleaning techniques. Applying ice to a glob of wax or chewing gum makes it easier to chip and remove.

"A Guide to Household Spills" on page 250 provides cleanup tips for common household spills. Work though the procedures one at a time, in the order they're presented. Be patient, giving each cleaning agent several minutes to work. If the first agent listed fails to eliminate the spot or stain, move on to the second, and so forth. Remember that more is not necessarily better; use as little cleaning agent as possible to accomplish the job. Avoid soaking the upholstery or carpet.

You can buy professional spot removal kits like the one shown here from carpet and furniture stores.

Cure or Curse?

Always test a cleaner or spot remover on an inconspicuous part of the furniture or carpet to make sure it's not going to damage or fade the material. When you do treat the spot, apply the cleaner gently. If sponging or light rubbing doesn't remove the spot, don't try to scrub it out. ●

If chlorine bleach is used, be sure to test fabric dyes in an inconspicuous area. After the spot is removed, rinse the area thoroughly with water—otherwise, the chlorine residue may degrade or discolor the material.

Finally, be sure to dry the affected area with an absorbent towel or hair dryer.

If the cleaning techniques in the table don't succeed, or if you prefer to try a commercial product, here are some top performers you can try.

● *Upholstery and carpet cleaner:* Blue Coral Dri-Clean Upholstery and Carpet Cleaner
● *Spray-on cleaners for hard surfaces:* Lysol Direct; Fantastic Lemon Scent
● *Pourable cleaners for floors and other hard surfaces:* Real Pine; Spic and Span Pine; Texize Pine Power
● *Deodorizers:* For pet urine, vomit, sewage, or spoiled food odors, try Exod or Outright, available from AquaTerra, Biochemical Corporation of America,

1803 Howard Road, Waxahachie, TX 75165; (800) 527-9919. Another effective deodorizer is Bac-Attac, from Nisus Corporation, 215 Dunazant Street, Rockford, TN 37853; (800) 264-0870.
● *Decontamination:* Lysol

Commercial spot removal kits, like the one shown in the photograph on this page, are available through retail carpet and furniture stores or from professional cleaners. For stains that are especially stubborn or when the underlying material is expensive, your best course is to call a professional. They may even be willing to give you free advice over the phone. (See "How to Find a Pro" on the opposite page.)

CLEANING UP AFTER A FLOOD

While there's no magic available to clean up a mess of standing water, a wet-dry vac, as shown in *Using a Wet/Dry Vacuum* on the opposite page, is the next best thing. Be careful to keep both the vacuum and its cord a healthy distance from any standing water and to use an outlet or extension cord that's protected with a GFCI, if one is available.

If you don't have a wet/dry vacuum, there's always the old mop-and-bucket method. The work will go faster if you use

USING A WET/DRY VACUUM

When using a wet/dry vacuum, keep the tank and electric cord away from the spill.

rags or towels to confine the water to the smallest possible area.

If you have a Noah-size flood on your hands, in which there is overall wetting or more than 2 inches of standing water, your best bet is to call in a professional who can effectively dry out and disinfect the flooded area. Otherwise, mold, mildew, decay fungus, and other microorganisms can flourish, presenting long-term health and maintenance problems. (See "How to Find a Pro" on this page.)

If you can't get a pro to come right away or you've decided to clean up the mess yourself, rent an electric- or gasoline-powered pump to remove the water, as shown in *Using a Trash Pump* on this page. Different models, ranging from a submersible electric sump pump to a high-capacity gasoline-powered "trash" pump, are available from tool rental shops on a day-fee basis. Read through the instructions and learn how to work the pump safely *before* you take it home.

The pump will cease to work once the water level falls below 1 inch (depending on the model) because the intake will start to pull air. At that point, you'll have to finish up with a wet/dry vac or mop.

Once the water is cleaned up, ventilation becomes the key to preventing further damage and keeping mold and mildew from growing. Open windows and doors to pro-

How to Find a Pro

The Institute of Inspection, Cleaning, and Restoration Certification in Vancouver, Washington, maintains a nationwide list of professionals who specialize in carpet and upholstery cleaning, water damage restoration, fire and smoke restoration, and odor control. You can call the Institute toll-free at (800) 835-4624 to get the names of certified professionals working in your area. Or write to the Institute of Inspection, Cleaning, and Restoration Certification, 2715 East Mill Plain Boulevard, Vancouver, WA 98661.

vide a crosscurrent of fresh outdoor air (unless it's raining or the humidity is excessively high). Use window, ceiling, and floor fans to circulate air through the area. If you have an electric dehumidifier or air conditioner, use it to dry out and cool the area—mold and mildew can't thrive when the humidity is 50 percent or less and the indoor temperature is under 70°F.

Take wet throw rugs and other movable items outside and hang them over a clothes line or sawhorse so they can air out.

(continued on page 252)

USING A TRASH PUMP

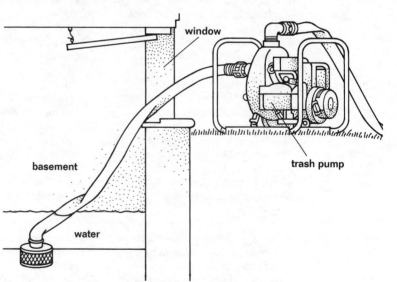

Gasoline-powered trash pumps like the one shown above are commonly used by builders to pump out basements or excavations. Just remember to keep the pump and its exhaust fumes outside your house.

A Guide to Household Spills

Try each procedure in the order listed, giving each several minutes to work. Dry cleaning fluid and other cleaning products may be flammable or harmful to breathe. Follow the precautions on the label. Keep traffic off the treated area until completely dry.

SPILL

WHAT YOU CAN DO

	Upholstery	Carpet	Resilient Flooring (Vinyl)
Ballpoint Ink	• Use rubbing alcohol or alcohol-based stain remover	• Use rubbing alcohol or alcohol-based stain remover • Sponge with mixture of 1 tbs. ammonia in 1 c. cool water (test for colorfastness)	• Use rubbing alcohol or alcohol-based stain remover • Rub gently with solution of 1 part household chlorine bleach to 9 parts water (test for colorfastness); rinse
Blood or Egg	• Blot with clean cloth, then sponge with water • Sponge with mixture of 1 tbs. ammonia in 1 c. cool water (test for colorfastness) • Blot, then sponge with solution of 2 tsp. mild liquid detergent (nonbleach) to 2 c. water; rinse and blot dry with white towels • Sponge in few drops of 10 volume (3%) hydrogen peroxide (test for colorfastness) • Use Perky Spotter* or other commercial stain remover	• Blot with clean cloth, then sponge with water • Sponge with mixture of 1 tbs. ammonia in 1 c. cool water (test for colorfastness) • Blot, then sponge with solution of 2 tsp. mild liquid detergent (nonbleach) to 2 c. water; rinse and blot dry with white towels • Sponge in few drops of 10 volume (3%) hydrogen peroxide (test for colorfastness) • Use Perky Spotter* or other commercial stain remover	• Blot with clean cloth, then sponge with water • Blot, then sponge with solution of 2 tsp. mild liquid detergent (nonbleach) to 2 c. water; rinse and blot dry with white towels • Rub gently with solution of 1 part household chlorine bleach to 9 parts water (test for colorfastness); rinse
Coffee, Tea, Fruit Juice, or Soda	• Blot with clean cloth, then sponge with water • Sponge with solution of 1 part white vinegar to 2 parts water • Blot, then sponge with solution of 2 tsp. mild liquid detergent (nonbleach) to 2 c. water; rinse and blot dry with white towels • Use Perky Spotter* or other commercial stain remover	• Blot with clean cloth, then sponge with water • Sponge with solution of 1 part white vinegar to 2 parts water • Blot, then sponge with solution of 2 tsp. mild liquid detergent (nonbleach) to 2 c. water; rinse and blot dry with white towels • Use Perky Spotter* or other commercial stain remover	• Blot with clean cloth, then sponge with water • Blot, then sponge with solution of 2 tsp. mild liquid detergent (nonbleach) to 2 c. water; rinse and blot dry with white towels • Rub gently with solution of 1 part household chlorine bleach to 9 parts water (test for colorfastness); rinse
Chocolate	• Sponge with mixture of 1 tbs. ammonia in 1 c. cool water (test for colorfastness) • Blot, then sponge with solution of 2 tsp. mild liquid detergent (nonbleach) to 2 c. water; rinse and blot dry with white towels • Use Perky Spotter* or other commercial stain remover	• Sponge with mixture of 1 tbs. ammonia in 1 c. cool water (test for colorfastness) • Blot, then sponge with solution of 2 tsp. mild liquid detergent (nonbleach) to 2 c. water; rinse and blot dry with white towels • Use Perky Spotter* or other commercial stain remover	• Blot with clean cloth, then sponge with water • Blot, then sponge with solution of 2 tsp. mild liquid detergent (nonbleach) to 2 c. water; rinse and blot dry with white towels • Rub gently with solution of 1 part household chlorine bleach to 9 parts water (test for colorfastness); rinse
Glue	• Use dry cleaning fluid, such as Energene or K2R, with plenty of ventilation • Apply nail polish remover with amyl acetate; don't use on upholstery if contains acetone	• Use dry cleaning fluid, such as Energene or K2R, with plenty of ventilation • Apply nail polish remover with amyl acetate; don't use on upholstery if contains acetone	• Blot with clean cloth, then sponge with water • Use dry cleaning fluid, such as Energene or K2R, with plenty of ventilation

*Perky Spotter is available from Groom Industries (800) 397-3759.

SPILL

WHAT YOU CAN DO

	UPHOLSTERY	CARPET	RESILIENT FLOORING (VINYL)
GREASE OR OIL	• Use dry cleaning fluid, such as Energene or K2R, with plenty of ventilation • Use Perky Spotter* or other commercial stain remover	• Use dry cleaning fluid, such as Energene or K2R, with plenty of ventilation • Use Perky Spotter* or other commercial stain remover	• Blot with clean cloth, then sponge with water • Sponge with mixture of 1 tbs. ammonia in 1 c. cool water (test for colorfastness) • Use dry cleaning fluid, such as Energene or K2R, with plenty of ventilation
MILK OR ICE CREAM	• Blot with clean cloth, then sponge with water • Blot, then sponge with solution of 2 tsp. mild liquid detergent (nonbleach) to 2 c. water; rinse and blot dry with white towels • Use Perky Spotter* or other commercial stain remover • Sponge with mixture of 1 tbs. ammonia in 1 c. cool water (test for colorfastness) • Sponge in few drops of 10 volume (3%) hydrogen peroxide (test for colorfastness)	• Blot with clean cloth, then sponge with water • Blot, then sponge with solution of 2 tsp. mild liquid detergent (nonbleach) to 2 c. water; rinse and blot dry with white towels • Use Perky Spotter* or other commercial stain remover • Sponge with mixture of 1 tbs. ammonia in 1 c. cool water (test for colorfastness) • Sponge in few drops of 10 volume (3%) hydrogen peroxide (test for colorfastness)	• Blot with clean cloth, then sponge with water • Blot, then sponge with solution of 2 tsp. mild liquid detergent (nonbleach) to 2 c. water; rinse and blot dry with white towels • Rub gently with solution of 1 part household chlorine bleach to 9 parts water (test for colorfastness); rinse
PAINT (WATER-BASE)	• Blot, then sponge with solution of 2 tsp. mild liquid detergent (nonbleach) to 2 c. water; rinse and blot dry with white towels (if fresh) • Use Perky Spotter* or other commercial stain remover (if fresh) • Use dry cleaning fluid, such as Energene or K2R, with plenty of ventilation (if dry)	• Blot, then sponge with solution of 2 tsp. mild liquid detergent (nonbleach) to 2 c. water; rinse and blot dry with white towels (if fresh) • Use Perky Spotter* or other commercial stain remover (if fresh) • Use dry cleaning fluid, such as Energene or K2R, with plenty of ventilation (if dry)	• Blot with clean cloth, then sponge with water • Use Perky Spotter* or other commercial stain remover
PAINT (OIL-BASE)	• Use dry cleaning fluid, such as Energene or K2R, with plenty of ventilation	• Use dry cleaning fluid, such as Energene or K2R, with plenty of ventilation	• Blot with clean cloth, then sponge with water • Use dry cleaning fluid, such as Energen, or K2R, with plenty of ventilation
SCUFF MARKS	—	—	• Use nonabrasive polishing cleanser, such as Soft Scrub • Use dry cleaning fluid, such as Energene or K2R, with plenty of ventilation
URINE OR VOMIT	• Blot with clean cloth, then sponge with water • Sponge with solution of 1 part white vinegar to 2 parts water • Blot, then sponge with solution of 2 tsp. mild liquid detergent (nonbleach) to 2 c. water; rinse and blot dry with white towels • Sponge with mixture of 1 tbs. ammonia in 1 c. cool water (test for colorfastness)	• Blot with clean cloth, then sponge with water • Sponge with solution of 1 part white vinegar to 2 parts water • Blot, then sponge with solution of 2 tsp. mild liquid detergent (nonbleach) to 2 c. water; rinse and blot dry with white towels • Sponge with mixture of 1 tbs. ammonia in 1 c. cool water (test for colorfastness)	• Blot with clean cloth, then sponge with water • Blot, then sponge with solution of 2 tsp. mild liquid detergent (nonbleach) to 2 c. water; rinse and blot dry with white towels • Rub gently with solution of 1 part household chlorine bleach to 9 parts water (test for colorfastness); rinse

Cleaning Up after a Fire

If fire has left your home vulnerable to theft or vandalism, take appropriate measures to board up the holes, remove valuables, or hire security. Your insurance company should be involved in the process from the very start. (See "Fire!" on page 244.)

USING A DRY-CLEANING SPONGE

dry-cleaning sponge

mask

smoke damage

A dry-cleaning sponge is the tool of choice for removing loose soot from walls and ceilings.

If the damage is substantial—more than a limited area in one room—you're better off hiring a firm that specializes in postfire cleanup work. You can avoid a lot of additional damage and expense by taking action during the first 24 hours. (See "How to Find a Pro" on page 249.)

However, if the damage is limited, you may be able to do most or all of the cleanup work yourself.

Start by providing plenty of fresh air ventilation so that the smell of smoke will begin to dissipate. Clothing, carpet, and other furnishings may require professional treatment to get rid of the smoke smell, which can linger long after the visible damage from the fire has been cleaned or repaired. (Professionals sometimes use an ozone generator to reduce the odor of smoke after a fire, but the machine can only be used safely in unoccupied areas.)

Use a shop vac to remove dry soot and any chemical residue that's left from the fire extinguisher.

A dry-cleaning sponge, available through cleaning supply and painting supply outlets, is a good tool for removing loose soot particles from latex paint, blown ceilings, and acoustic tiles. The sponge should be used dry, not moistened with water or liquid cleaners. Wipe the ceiling first, then the walls, as shown in

Using a Dry-Cleaning Sponge. Wipe the walls from top to bottom with straight, parallel strokes that overlap a little.

Dry-chemical sponges are not recommended, however, for cleaning oil-based paint, acrylic paint, or vinyl wallpaper or for removing the heavy, greasy soot that's sometimes left after a kitchen fire. For those applications, use Spic and Span or one of the pourable pine-scented cleaners recommended on page 248, applied with a sponge or terry-cloth towel.

If leaking water has carried dirt, rust, or sludge onto carpet or other surfaces, use a little laundry soap or other mild detergent to clean them. Rinse with fresh water and repeat the process if necessary, then dry out the area as quickly as possible.

Carpet and padding that has been deeply soaked will probably have to be discarded, especially if it's been contaminated with sewage. (See "Cleaning Up Sewage Spills" on the opposite page.)

After a serious flood, in which rising water has penetrated wall cavities, the drywall or paneling should be removed well above the water line so that the wet insulation can be removed and the cavities between the studs bays allowed to dry, as shown in *Removing Wet*

Drywall on the opposite page. Professionals use high-powered fans to circulate fresh air up into the stud bays to promote drying.

Likewise, if water has gotten under resilient flooring or tiles, it's usually necessary to remove them so that the wooden subfloor can dry out—otherwise, moisture trapped underneath will warp the wood and invite mildew and rot.

A house that has experienced serious flooding must dry out thoroughly—even if it takes weeks or months— before damaged flooring, drywall, and other coverings are replaced. If you've experienced this kind of flooding, consider seeking professional advice from a firm that specializes in flood damage. (See "How to Find a Pro" on page 249.)

REMOVING WET DRYWALL

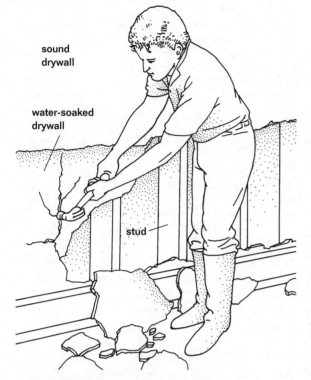

sound drywall

water-soaked drywall

stud

Break away drywall to just above the water flood line. The ragged edge can then be trimmed straight with a utility knife.

CLEANING UP SEWAGE SPILLS

A sewage spill inside the house, whether from a broken pipe or a backed-up fixture or drain, presents a real danger of bacterial infection.

As with all cleanup work, speed is of the essence. If the spill covers more than about 6 square feet or has permeated wall-to-wall carpet or drywall, call a professional right away. (See "How to Find a Pro" on page 249.)

To clean up a smaller spill, protect yourself with rubber boots, gloves, and a respirator. Clear the area of other people, especially anyone who suffers from asthma or other respiratory disease. Open windows and doors to provide plenty of ventilation.

Depending on the surface, use a wet-dry vac, mop and bucket, and/or a snow shovel, as shown in *Shoveling Sewage* on this page, to remove the sewage and water. Dispose of the sewage in a proper municipal sewer (not a storm drain) or septic tank, or bury it, and sprinkle it with lime.

(See "How to Find a Pro" on page 249.)

the cleaning remedies listed in the table on page 250, try the following method:

Last Resort Department

If a stain on vinyl flooring won't go away using the cleaning remedies listed in the table on page 250, try the following method:

1. Saturate a clean, white terry-cloth towel with full-strength bleach.

2. Place the towel over the stained area and leave it in place until the towel has dried (overnight, if necessary).

3. Keep the area well ventilated during the treatment.

4. Remove the towel and check to see if stain has lightened.

5. Repeat the procedure, if necessary.

After a thorough rinse, hard surfaces can be disinfected with Lysol or with a solution of household chlorine bleach and water (1 part bleach to 9 parts water).

Soiled throw rugs can be cleaned and disinfected by laundering them with a detergent and color-safe bleach, such as Clorox II, or

SHOVELING SEWAGE

respirator

rubber gloves

rubber boots

snow shovel or other flat shovel

sewage and solid debris

Sewage is certainly a hazardous material and should be treated as such. Make sure you wear protective clothing and promptly wash yourself, your clothes, and your tools when done.

Mildew

If mildew forms, there are both homemade and commercial products available to remove it. For details, see "Mold and Mildew" on page 213. ●

you can have them professionally cleaned.

Lysol (but *not* bleach) can also be used to disinfect a small area of soiled wall-to-wall carpeting. Use natural and fan-forced ventilation, a dehumidifier, and/or a hair dryer to quickly and thoroughly dry the spot. If necessary, apply a deodorizer, such as Exod or Outright, as well. (See the list of cleaners on page 248.)

Wall-to-wall carpeting and padding that has been saturated over a larger area will probably have to be thrown away, as there is no way to disinfect them. The same goes for pillows, cushions, mattresses, and upholstered furniture that have been deeply wetted.

If sewage-laden water has permeated flooring and walls, the flooring and drywall have to be removed (as described above) so that the cavities underneath can be thoroughly cleaned, dried out, and disinfected. This needs to be done as quickly as possible, preferably by a pro.

After the cleanup work is done, disinfect your tools with a chlorine bleach and water solution (1 part bleach to 9 parts water), then rinse them thoroughly with fresh water. If a wet/dry vac or sump pump was used in

Leaking Oil

If your fuel oil tank (indoors or out) is leaking, call your fuel supplier and a cleaning professional right away. Fuel oil is a serious contaminant that can cause a lot of material damage and pose long-term health risks to your family. ●

the cleanup, run a 2-gallon bucket of the water-and-bleach solution through the machine to disinfect it. Wash your work clothes by themselves, using hot water and an appropriate bleach.

CLEANING UP CHEMICAL AND OIL SPILLS

The potential hazards from toxic fumes, fire, or burns are the foremost concern when a chemical or oil is spilled.

The first priority is to provide plenty of fresh-air ventilation. Second, keep space heaters, smoking materials, and other sources of fire or electrical sparks well away from the spill. Third, wear rubber gloves, rubber boots, safety goggles, and, if necessary, a respirator that's designed for use with the chemical spilled. (See "Work Masks and Respirators" on page 199.)

Once these safety precautions have been taken, swab up the mess with clean rags or paper towels. For larger spills, cover the area with cat litter, sawdust, or vermiculite, let it soak for a few minutes, and shovel the saturated muck into a heavy-gauge plastic trash bag.

The final cleanup may require using a rag or brush dipped in solvent—check the container's label to find out what kind of solvent will work. When the last trace of chemical or oil is removed, scrub the floor with Real Pine or one of the other pourable cleaners listed on page 248. Put soiled rags, paper towels, and the absorbent material in a plastic trash bag. Tie the bag securely, then place it inside a second bag, with a double tie. Store the bag where it cannot be reached by children or pets.

Call your local or state environmental agency to see what kind of disposal process is recommended for the material. You may have to store it until your community schedules a hazardous waste collection day.

Poisoned!

HOUSEHOLD HAZARD

Children are quick and curious, so keep hazardous products out of their reach.

UNDERSTANDING POISON

A poison can enter or affect the human body in four ways: through contact with skin, by being splashed in the eyes, through inhalation, or by ingestion. In all cases—even a minor exposure—it's smart to contact the Poison Control Center as soon as possible. If you need to get into the shower to flush the poison off your skin or out of your eyes, have someone else call the Poison Control Center in the meantime.

If you move swiftly and intelligently, there's a good chance that you can safely resolve the problem at home. In fact, statistics show that 75 percent of all poison emergencies can be handled safely at home when the Poison Control Center is called immediately.

Quick Response

1. If poison is on skin or eyes, flush affected areas with water for 15 to 20 minutes in shower.

2. Call Poison Control Center. Look in front pages of telephone directory under *EMERGENCY* for number.

3. If victim has inhaled hazardous vapors, cut off source and open windows and doors for fresh air, or get victim out of house.

4. If victim is unconscious, call 911, ambulance, or 0 for operator assistance.

Hazard

Do not give the victim ipecac syrup or otherwise try to induce vomiting or administer any other antidotes or medicines without getting clear instructions from the Poison Control Center. (See "What Is a PCC?" on page 257.)

7
SELF-INFLICTED EMERGENCIES

An Ounce of Prevention

The average American house contains a veritable hodgepodge of poisons, including drain cleaners, gasoline, herbicides, paint strippers, pesticides, and wood preservatives, to name just a few. Even substances that are usually considered healthful or beneficial, such as cough syrup, heart medicines, and iron supplements, become poisonous when taken in the wrong dosage or by the wrong person. Happily, the careful storage and appropriate use of home, shop, and garden products reduce your risk of poisoning. Here are some good pointers and precautions to keep in mind.

● *Create a safe environment for your children.* This means keeping potentially dangerous substances out of sight and out of reach, preferably in a locked cabinet or in one with a child-safe latch, as shown in *Child-Safe Latch.* Whenever possible, opt for child-resistant packaging. Don't forget that some apparently benign substances—such as vitamins and some cosmetics—may be toxic in large doses.

● *Use products as they are intended to be used.* Observe the precautions spelled out on the product label, especially regarding ventilation, protective clothing, and proper disposal.

● *Whenever possible, store toxic substances in their original containers.* If you must transfer something toxic into a new container, make sure the new container is safe and that it is accurately labeled.

● *Keep a bottle of ipecac syrup in your medicine cabinet in case you need to induce vomiting.* Ipecac (the generic name) is available at any drugstore without a prescription.

● *If someone has a special sensitivity to bee stings or other insect bites, keep an antidote kit in your medicine cabinet.*

● *Post the phone number of your nearest Poison Control Center near the telephone.* If you call the center, they'll send you telephone stickers and other information.

CHILD-SAFE LATCH

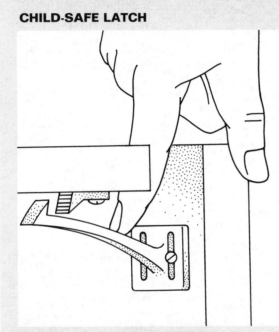

A child-safe latch keeps children away from dangerous poison while causing you minimal inconvenience.

DEALING WITH POISON ON YOUR SKIN OR IN YOUR EYES

Whether the skin, eyes, or both are affected, the object is to dilute the toxic or caustic substance so that it ceases to burn. It's critical to get out of your contaminated clothes and into the shower as quickly as possible. Rinse the affected area for at least 15 minutes.

If the poison has gotten into your eyes, set the shower at a comfortable temperature and hold your face up into the spray. Blink repeatedly, letting the water flush out your eyes.

While you are in the shower, have someone call the Poison Control Center for detailed instructions. A visit to the emergency room or to your doctor may be necessary.

DEALING WITH INHALED POISON

If poison is inhaled, one of two tactics is recommended. The fastest, if the victim can move or be moved, is to get him outside the house, shop, or garage—away from the source of the toxic vapors and into fresh air. If that's not possible, open all the windows and doors in the area to admit fresh air and dilute the toxic fumes.

Try to cap, plug, or remove the source of the poisonous fumes. This might involve putting the lid or cap on a chemical, removing contaminated rags from the area, or shutting down a combustion appliance. (See "Backdrafting Flue" on page 122.)

CAUTION: Take care in trying to help the victim that you limit your own exposure to the toxic fumes.

DEALING WITH INGESTED POISON

Young children, who love to put things in their mouths, are especially prone to swallowing household poisons.

If you believe your child has poisoned himself, your first priority is to find out what exactly he swallowed. Without threatening the child (instruction and discipline can come later), urge him to point out or tell you exactly what he swallowed. It is also important to know how many or how much was swallowed.

Do-It-Yourself Danger

Do-it-yourselfers should be especially alert to the potentially poisonous nature of paint strippers and cement.

The solvent in strippers (methylene chloride) can be absorbed through the skin (even when there's no direct contact), where it metabolizes into carbon monoxide. Thus, without proper clothing and ventilation, you can suffer the symptoms of carbon monoxide poisoning, as described in "Backdrafting Flue" on page 122. (Also see "Work Masks and Respirators" on page 199.)

Cement contains lime, a powerful alkaline, which can result in serious skin burns. So keep your skin and clothing from contact with wet cement. If your pants become damp when working on wet cement, change them quickly and take a shower, flushing the affected skin with plenty of water. Unlike acid burns, which cease to do damage once you rinse the acid off, alkaline will continue to penetrate the skin and cause damage.

What Is a PCC?

Poison Control Centers (PCC) are designed to provide you with immediate help when someone in your household is poisoned. (See the logo of the American Association of Poison Control Centers on this page.)

The centers, staffed by nurses, pharmacists, and physicians, are located all over the United States and are open 24 hours a day, seven days a week to receive emergency calls. There is no fee for the service.

AMERICAN ASSOCIATION OF POISON CONTROL CENTERS
3201 New Mexico Avenue, Suite 310
Washington, DC 20016

When you call the center, the expert will ask you for specific information regarding the type and amount of poison, the age and weight of the victim, and other important details. The PCC experts have immediate access to toxicology resources, including hundreds of thousands of product ingredients, appropriate emergency treatments, and a roster of expert consultants who can be contacted on short notice.

This kind of immediate, specific response to a poison is much better than relying on product labels, which may be inaccurate or incomplete, or on a poison wheel or chart, which can't be specific to the situation.

The Poison Control Center will give you quick advice on what to do and will call you back later to verify that everything is OK. In the unlikely event that the emergency can't be handled at home, the Poison Control Center will call the nearest emergency room for you. This is to save you time and to make sure that the emergency room doctors are aware that you are on your way and have been briefed in advance on the nature of the poison, the condition of the victim, and the best emergency treatment.

Once you find out, take the can, bottle, or package with you to the telephone and call the Poison Control Center for help.

CAUTION: Do not give the child ipecac syrup or otherwise try to induce vomiting. Wait for specific instructions from the Poison Control Center.

Danger Points

While no one's looking, little Amy gets into Grandma's pill box, mistaking those pretty red pills for red-hot candies.

Out in the garden, Aunt Alice accidentally sprays herself in the eye with weed killer.

In the bathroom, the brush slips out of Dad's hand while he's cleaning the toilet bowl, splashing the acid-based cleaner across his bare hand and forearm.

These kinds of incidents are alarmingly common. Sometimes they occur because people don't read the product label and take the necessary precautions. Other times it's just plain carelessness. (See "An Ounce of Prevention" on page 256.)

Since forewarned is forearmed, consider the following list of 20 substances that are sources of poisonings in the home. Keep these substances up high where children can't reach them or in a cabinet with a child-proof latch. Those marked with a **C** are often identified with poisonings in children.

- Alcohol (both beverage and rubbing)
- Ant and roach traps (**C**)
- Antifreeze
- Bites and stings
- Chemical drain openers
- Cleaning products (**C**)
- Cosmetics, personal care products (**C**)
- Cough and cold preparations (**C**)
- Food poisoning
- Herbicides
- Hydrocarbons (furniture polish, gasoline, kerosene, turpentine, etc.)
- Insecticides
- Lime (used as a plant nutrient and an active ingredient in cement)
- Pain relievers (**C**)
- Plants and mushrooms (**C**)
- Prescription drugs (**C**)
- Solvents (for example, paint stripper)
- Toilet bowl cleaners
- Vitamin pills (especially prenatal vitamins and iron supplements) (**C**)
- Windshield cleaning fluid

Tool Strikes Buried Cable or Pipe

DIGGING DANGERS

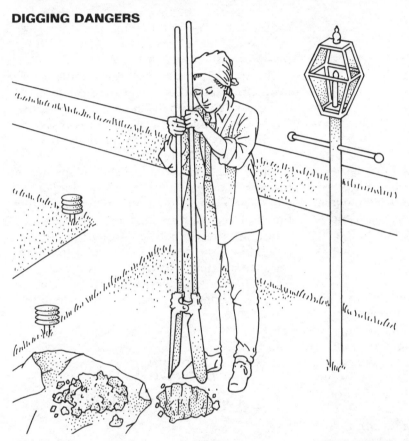

Look around before you start digging to determine what may lie underground.

Quick Response

1. Determine what type of cable or pipe you've hit.

2. Make repairs.

3. Clean up. (See "Spills" on page 247.)

TAKING BAD AIM

Though most people don't realize it, modern houses are surrounded by a maze of subterranean pipes and wires. While some of these belong to public utilities, others, such as septic pipes, landscaping lights, and in-ground sprinkler systems, are the homeowner's responsibility.

If you've had the bad fortune to hit one of these lines or pipes with your post-hole digger or rotary tiller, follow the advice spelled out below. To prevent future accidents, read "Think Before You Dig" on page 261.

Hazards

● If you've hit an electric cable, clear the area until you're sure the circuit is dead. Electricity can travel through soil, especially when it's wet.

● If someone is being shocked, do *not* touch the victim—the current could flow into you. (See "Electrical Safety Tips" on page 102.)

● If you've struck a natural gas or propane line, clear the area and call your gas utility immediately. Extinguish all open flames and cigarettes. Do not operate electrical devices near the leak. If the gas is on fire, do *not* attempt to put it out. Call the fire department. If necessary, spray surrounding combustibles with water to keep them from igniting.

● If you've struck a drain line, protect people and pets from direct contact with leaking sewage.

7

SELF-INFLICTED EMERGENCIES

Utility Emergency Lines

Most gas and electric utilities run a 24-hour emergency line. Post the numbers near your phone with other emergency information. (See "Preparing for an Emergency" on page 10.) ●

LOCATING ELECTRIC CABLE

The type of cable and the depth at which it's buried will usually tell you its character. Incoming utility lines are protected in hard plastic pipe and are buried 2 to 3 feet deep. The pipe may have a strip of red or yellow warning tape running a few inches above it to warn excavators of the underlying danger.

Branch circuit cables that power yard and landscaping lights may be buried up to 2 feet deep (depending on local code requirements) or only a couple inches (if codes were ignored).

While the chances of severing a utility line are slim—because of its depth and armor— you're in a lot more trouble if you do hit one. First of all, there's a lot more amperage in the incoming utility line than in ordinary house and yard circuits. And there's no way to cut off power, so the risk of electrocution is great.

CAUTION: Make sure everyone stays clear of the area while you call the utility's emergency line.

Even if you've just nicked the protective pipe, go ahead and call the utility. Water can seep in through a small crack in the pipe and short circuit the electric service to your entire house.

CAUTION: Do not, under any circumstances, attempt to repair a damaged utility line yourself.

Striking a buried 15- or 20-amp cable that powers a yard light or other outdoor fixture is more likely but less dangerous. First of all, there's less amperage in the line. Second, there's a good chance the circuit is switched off. And third, even if the circuit is live, it's hopefully protected by a ground fault circuit interrupter (GFCI), which eliminates the risk of serious shock. (See "GFCI Spells Electrical Safety" on page 265.)

CAUTION: Regardless of these circumstances, the damaged cable should be treated as though it were live—and deadly—until you can make absolutely sure that it's not.

If you've had some experience doing electrical repairs and feel confident that you can do it safely, you can patch the cable yourself with a UL-approved direct burial splice kit. Make sure that the kit you buy is designed for the cable you're repairing. (Most in-ground residential circuits are wired with UF plastic-sheathed cable.)

The splice is made by slipping a length of heat shrinkable tubing over the broken cable. Once the tube is in place, the stripped ends of the cable (typically three wires) are mechanically rejoined. The tubing is then centered over the joint and heated with a torch or heat gun, which shrink-wraps the tubing around the joint. A second, longer length of tubing is then wrapped around the first and heated, providing a double seal.

Because there are differences from one patch kit to the next, it's important to follow the manufacturer's instructions precisely. *NOTE:* If you don't feel competent or comfortable making the repair, don't hesitate to call an electrician.

LOCATING GAS AND PROPANE PIPING

Natural gas pipes are typically buried 18 inches deep for residential service. Depending on their age, they might be made of plain steel, plastic-coated steel, or plastic. Pipe diameters range from ½ to 2 inches. Some gas utilities run a strip of red or yellow tape just above the pipe to warn excavators.

Propane lines, running from the storage tank to the house, *should* be buried 18 inches deep but often aren't. Made of copper or plastic, they may be as shallow as 2 inches underground.

If you strike a gas or propane pipe with your tool—and smell gas—*clear the area and call the gas utility's emergency line.*

Even if there's no smell of gas or apparent damage to the pipe, it's smart to call the utility. A break may have occurred some distance

Think Before You Dig

To dig a hole in your yard—even a small, shallow hole—without finding out what's underneath, can be both dangerous and expensive. (See *What's Underground?*)

If you hire a subcontractor to do excavation work, don't assume that he has an omniscient view of what's underground. Or even that he'll take the time to find out. You take the responsibility.

Even if no one is hurt, striking a utility cable or pipe can end up costing you hundreds of dollars in repair bills and leave you subject to stiff fines—up to $5,000 in some states!

To avoid problems, start by calling your local Dig Safe Center and tell them you're planning to excavate. Their phone number should be listed in the front of your telephone book or in the Yellow Pages under Utility Locating. Or you can call your gas, electric, or telephone company and ask them for the center's number.

Within a few days, Dig Safe will send a representative to your house, armed with utility maps and perhaps a metal detector, to tell you where underground cables and pipes are hidden.

Using spray paint or small flags, the Dig Safe representative will physically mark each underground utility—red for electric cable, yellow for gas pipe, blue for the water line, green for the sewer, and orange for the telecommunications cable.

But Dig Safe can only go so far. The agency won't have any knowledge of (or responsibility for) underground cables and pipes that you or some former owner installed. These might include electric cables running out from the house to power outdoor receptacles, yard lights, or outbuildings; an in-ground sprinkler system; well water and septic system piping; rainwater and foundation drains; and so forth.

Some homeowners are fortunate in having precise construction records that detail when and where everything was installed, even do-it-yourself work done by prior owners. If you're lacking such records, do the best you can with your memory and common sense. Are you digging between the house and the yard light, where a buried cable might lie? Between the house and the septic system? Close to the well head? Give the matter some serious thought before you fire up that power auger.

It's sometimes possible to determine the exact lay of a cable or pipe by doing a little *gentle* digging. On an outdoor receptacle or light pole, for example, you can follow the cable or conduit to the point where it bends, revealing its angle across the yard. Just to be on the safe side, always do such exploration work with the power off.

To discover the path of a hidden septic pipe, dig down the foundation wall till you uncover the pipe and reveal the angle at which it crosses the yard. Being gravity-fed, it will drop gradually with each foot of run.

WHAT'S UNDERGROUND?

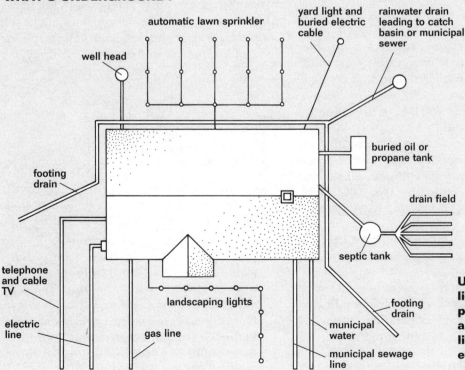

well head

automatic lawn sprinkler

yard light and buried electric cable

rainwater drain leading to catch basin or municipal sewer

buried oil or propane tank

footing drain

drain field

septic tank

telephone and cable TV

landscaping lights

footing drain

electric line

gas line

municipal water

municipal sewage line

Under that grassy surface lies a maze of wires and pipes. Not all the wires and pipes shown here are likely to be present in every house.

from where you struck the pipe—for example, at the point where it's threaded into the meter—making the leak hard to detect.

CAUTION: Do not attempt to repair a damaged gas or propane line yourself. Only gas company personnel and firefighters are trained to turn off the curbside valve that controls the flow of gas.

LOCATING WATER AND SEWAGE PIPES

Municipal water pipes are buried from 3 to 7 feet deep depending on the frostline in your area. The water pipe will generally be made of ¾-inch copper or, in newer construction, plastic. In private well systems, the pipe connecting the well head to the house is usually plastic.

If you break the water line, the resulting leak, at 40 to 80 pounds of water pressure per square inch, can quickly transform your yard into a swamp. Call the municipal water authority to come turn the water off at the main. If you're on a private well system, shut off the pump.

Once the water is off, you can either repair the pipe yourself or hire a plumber. Either way, you'll probably have to excavate the hole further (and pump the water out of it) before you can access the broken pipe well enough to do repair work.

With copper pipe, you'll have to cut out the damaged section and fit a new piece into place. The new pipe can be soldered into place, using slip couplings on either end, or it can be attached with flare fittings, which avoids soldering. Plastic pipe (typically utility-grade polyethylene) is repaired using insert fittings and clamps.

After the repair is complete, have the water turned back on and flush the line out for five minutes.

Sewer pipes, whether connected to the municipal sewer or a septic tank, are buried from 1 to 7 feet deep, depending on the frostline, the grade, and the line's slope (being gravity fed) to the sewer or tank. Sewer pipes are typically 4 inches in diameter and made of PVC plastic (in newer construction) or cast-iron pipe or clay tile (in older construction).

If you crack the pipe, you may not notice a leak, since the flow is intermittent with the use of toilets, showers, dishwashers, and so forth, and is not under pressure. Nonetheless, it's important to have the pipe repaired quickly because the leak will only get worse and eventually cause serious problems.

Repairing PVC pipe is simple, provided you use the right solvent cement (see "Broken Pipes" on page 56) and don't mind tackling a grubby job. But if the sewer line is iron pipe or clay tile, you'd be well advised to call a plumber.

LOCATING TELEPHONE LINES AND CABLE TV

When residential telecommunications lines are laid underground—an increasingly common practice—they're typically buried 24 inches deep. The cables, which are of small diameter and plastic-sheathed, are either buried directly in the ground or housed inside a 4-inch-diameter plastic pipe. Though both telephone and TV cables are low-voltage lines, there's still a possibility of being shocked. Call the phone or cable company and report the damage.

LOCATING OTHER PIPES

As shown in *What's Underground* on page 261, various other pipes may be hidden underground. These could include the following:

● *An in-ground sprinkler pipe:* Pressurized ½- to 1-inch-diameter plastic pipe buried 1 foot deep or less.
● *A rain gutter discharge pipe:* Typically a 4-inch plastic or cast-iron pipe. Nonpressurized. Depth varies from a few inches to several feet, running from the downspout to a municipal storm drain, dry well, or downgrade runoff.

● *A septic system drain field pipe:* Generally a 4-inch plastic pipe with bottomside perforations or vaulted channels with no bottom. Nonpressurized. Depth varies from 1 to 4 feet.

● *A footing drain:* Typically a 4-inch plastic pipe with perforations. Nonpressurized. Runs along the foot of the foundation, channeling groundwater away from the house. (See "Leaky Basement" on page 61.)

● *A sump pump discharge pipe:* 1¼- to 2-inch plastic or metal pipe. Nonpressurized. Depth varies.

Pipe Surprise

If the land around your house was regraded at some point, there may be pipes left there that were once deeply buried and are now much closer to the surface—and therefore more vulnerable—than you expect. Also, there may be forgotten fixtures, such as an old well head or septic system that were abandoned when the house was connected to municipal water and sewer lines. ●

Saw Blade Snags Electric Cable

SNAGGED!

Quick Response

1. If someone is being shocked, do *not* touch him. Unplug tool or turn off power at main service box. (See "Electrical Safety Tips" on page 102.)

2. If the victim has stopped breathing, start CPR (cardiopulmonary resuscitation) immediately and call for help.

3. If there's smoke or fire evident, get *everybody* out and call 911 or fire department. (See "Fire!" on page 244.)

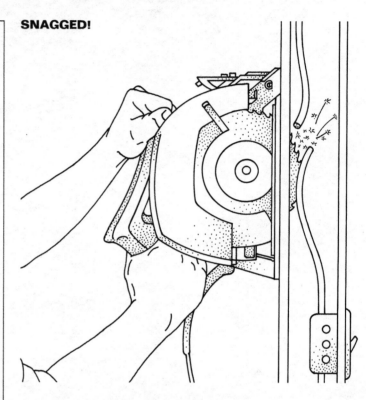

Cutting blindly into walls can lead to some very serious consequences.

Hazards

● Do not attempt to reset the circuit breaker or replace the fuse until you've diagnosed the full extent of the damage and repaired it. (See "Circuit Breaker Trips or Fuse Blows" on page 100.)

● Don't try to repair the damaged cable yourself unless you're sure of your skills and local building codes permit do-it-yourself repairs.

GETTING SNAGGED

Snagging a hidden electric cable is one of the rudest surprises that a do-it-yourselfer can get—especially if the tool isn't properly grounded! At the very least, you'll probably have a blackened saw blade, a noseful of ozone-flavored smoke, and a momentary spike in your blood pressure.

Since the circuit breaker or fuse that protects the circuit you hit will have shut down power to that circuit to prevent a fire, all of the lights and appliances on the circuit won't work. You may be able to temporarily switch some of the more important lights and appliances to another circuit—but be careful not to overload it. (See "Adding Up the Amps" on page 104.)

CAUTION: If smoke persists more than a minute or two after the accident, a fire may be smouldering inside the wall. Get *everybody* out and call the fire department.

REPAIRING THE DAMAGE

If you're tempted to simply splice the broken cable back together and go on about your business, here's a word for the wise: *Don't!*

It's a violation of the National Electric Code to have a concealed junction—that is, to splice wires together in the wall without an exposed junction box or outlet. Making that kind of repair could void your homeowner's insurance in the event of a fire.

One simple (and legal) repair option, if there's enough slack available in the cable, is to install an outlet or exposed junction box to one

Saw Safety

To saw or drill safely into a wall, probe the cavity *before* you start. (See "What's Inside That Wall?" on page 267.) As an added measure of safety, always plug your tool into a receptacle that's protected by a ground fault circuit interrupter. (See "GFCI Spells Electrical Safety" on this page.) ●

side of the break and loop the cable around the hole you were cutting when you snagged it.

If that's not possible or desirable, the entire length of cable must be replaced, wired back to the nearest outlet or junction box.

Some local codes require that this type of repair be done by a licensed electrician. Other code districts will allow you to do the work yourself as long as an electrician inspects the finished work.

GFCI Spells Electrical Safety

The acronym *GFCI* stands for ground fault circuit interrupter. It's a small, inexpensive safety switch that can sense a short circuit and cut off the electricity in the affected circuit before anyone is seriously shocked.

TYPES OF GFCIS

portable cord type

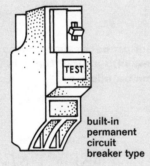

built-in permanent circuit breaker type

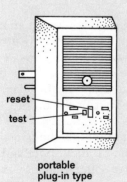

reset
test

portable plug-in type

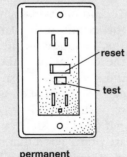

reset

test

permanent receptacle type

GFCIs come in several types to fit any situation.

GFCI receptacles are required by the National Electrical Code for outdoor fixtures (since 1973), bathrooms (since 1975), garages (since 1978), kitchens (select outlets only, since 1987), and crawl spaces and unfinished basements (since 1990).

Portable plug-in and cord-type GFCIs, as shown in *Types of GFCIs,* are easy to use and are especially recommended when working outside with electrically powered tools.

Permanent receptacle-type GFCIs can be installed by an able do-it-yourselfer who's familiar with electrical work and follows the manufacturer's instructions. Otherwise, an electrician is required.

Circuit breaker GFCIs are installed as a permanent fixture in the main service panel, where they protect an entire branch circuit. These should be installed by a licensed electrician only.

GFCI receptacles and adapters should be tested periodically to make sure they're working. Here's how.

1. Press the *TEST* button, which should cause the *RESET* button to pop out.

2. Plug a test lamp into the receptacle to verify that there's no power.

3. Push the *RESET* button back in and verify that the power is back on.

If the *RESET* button does not pop out when you push the *TEST* button, or if the outlet still has power after the *RESET* button pops out, the switch is faulty and must be replaced.

SELF-INFLICTED EMERGENCIES

Drill Punctures Pipe

Quick Response

1. Set any electrical tools or cords safe distance from leaking water.

2. Turn off main water valve. (See "Understanding Your Plumbing System" on page 2.)

3. Clean up. (See "Spills" on page 247.)

4. Patch pipe. (See "Broken Pipes" on page 56.)

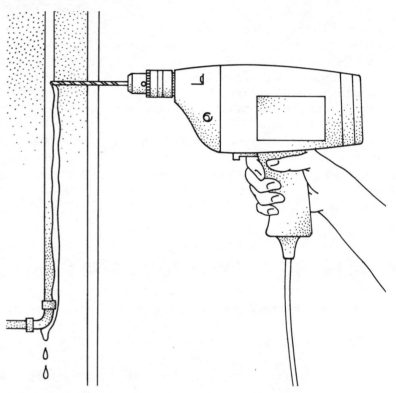

It may not seem probable that you could drill or drive a screw into a pipe, but this is an amazingly common mishap.

Hazards

● If you smell gas, indicating that you've nicked a gas line, do not attempt repairs. Shut off the gas at the meter (or propane tank) and call your gas utility immediately. (See *How to Shut Off the Gas or Propane* on page 119.)

● Water leaking down through the wall cavity and out onto the floor becomes dangerous when there are switches, receptacles, or electric cords close by. For safety's sake, turn off the electricity to the area until the water is cleaned up. If power tools are needed for cleanup or repair, use a long extension cord plugged into another circuit with a GFCI-protected receptacle. (See "GFCI Spells Electrical Safety" on page 265.)

INSPECTING THE DAMAGE

To find out what type of pipe you've hit and the extent of the damage, you'll have to cut a small window in the drywall and look inside the wall cavity. Make the cut shallow so that the saw blade doesn't cause any further damage. (See "What's Inside That Wall?" on the opposite page.)

If you hit a steel or cast-iron pipe, the odds are pretty good that it won't leak. Copper and plastic pipe, however, have softer, thinner walls that are relatively easy to puncture.

Generally speaking, if you've hit a supply line (typically a small-diameter copper or steel pipe) and there's no evidence of a leak, you

What's Inside That Wall?

If you have good blueprints of your house and are sure there haven't been any subsequent in-wall modifications, you can tell exactly where the electric cables, water pipes, and telephone lines are hidden in the walls.

If you don't have reliable blueprints, take the time to probe the wall cavity before you cut or drill deeply into it. One way to do this is to drill a small hole through the drywall only and probe the cavity with a coat hanger, as shown in *Clothes Hanger Probe.* The coat hanger is also a good way to find studs for nailing.

Another approach (if you don't mind the cosmetic damage) is to remove a small section of drywall so that you can see right in.

If you plan to cut a large hole through the wall—to install, for example, a new window or door—be sure to probe the wall in several places before you start. If there's insulation inside the cavity, feel back through it for buried cable or pipe.

NOTE: Don't assume that you won't find water pipes in an exterior wall. Although it's not standard practice to put them there (especially in cold climates), the former owner's younger brother, who fancied himself a plumber, may have done it anyway.

Investigate the space above and below the wall. Sometimes, hidden pipes will reveal themselves where they penetrate an unfinished attic, basement, or crawl space above or below the spot where you plan to cut.

CLOTHES HANGER PROBE

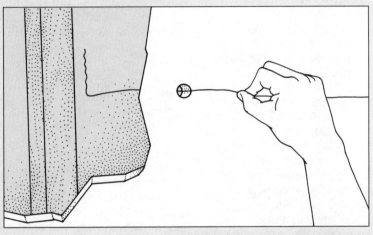

A bent hanger can be used as a probe to detect what is hiding behind a wall without causing a lot of damage.

have probably not punctured the pipe. You can patch the wall and go on about your business.

However, if you've damaged a drain line (typically a large-diameter cast-iron or plastic pipe), the wall cavity should be left open so that you can check the pipe over a period of a few days. Remember, if it has a leak, it will only show intermittently—and perhaps only a trace—when water is flushed through the line.

For very small leaks in plastic drainpipe, try drying the surface thoroughly and patching the hole with a dab of the solvent cement that's recommended for that type plastic.

For other types of repairs, see "Broken Pipes" on page 56.

SELF-INFLICTED EMERGENCIES

Index

Note: Page references in *italic* indicate tables. **Boldface** references indicate illustrations and photographs.

C

Cable, accidental snags or cuts. *See* Saw blade snags electric cable; Tool strikes buried cable or pipe

Carbon monoxide. *See also* Backdrafting flue
  detector, 125
  poisoning, 122
    identifying, 123
    preventing, 125
  sources of, **124**

Carpenter ants. *See* Ants, carpenter

Carpet and Rug Institute, 203

Central air conditioner, 142-45, 147
  buying new, 144
  cleaning, **141**
  troubleshooting, 142-45, 147

Chimney backdraft. *See* Backdrafting flue

Circuit breaker, tripped, 100-108. *See also* Circuit breakers; Electrical system; Electric power, lack of; Fuse, blown; Fuses; Service panel
  causes
    failed appliance motor, 103
    faulty circuit breaker, 103, 108, **108**
    lightning hit, 102, 103
    low voltage, 103
    overloaded circuit, 101-2
    short circuit, 102-3
  hazard, 100
  quick response, 100
  resetting, 106, **106**
  troubleshooting, 101-3

Circuit breakers, 6, **100**. *See also* Circuit breaker, tripped; Electrical system; Fuse, blown; Fuses; Service panel
  calculating load, 104-5
  double-pole, 6, **100**
  faulty, replacing, 103, 108, **108**
  ground fault circuit interrupters (GFCIs) (*see* Ground fault circuit interrupter)
  main, 6
  maintenance, *19*, 101
  problems with, 101-3, 108

resetting, 106, **106**
safety tips, 100, 102, 103
single pole, **100**
what they do, 100-101
wiring for, **108**

Clean-outs, main drain, **3**, 4, 52, 54

Clogs. *See* Fixture, clogged; Main drain, clogged; Rain gutter, clogged; Toilet, clogged

Closet auger, 48-49, **48**

Concrete, cracks in. *See* Masonry walls, cracks in

Cooling, lack of, 141-47. *See also* Central air conditioner; Heat pump; Room air conditioner
  hazard, 102-3, 141
  quick response, 141
  troubleshooting
    central air conditioners, 142-45
    heat pumps, 147
    room air conditioners, 145-46
  ways to stay cool, 145

Cracks. *See* Masonry walls, cracks in

Cuprinol, 151, 174, 175

D

DIY Repair Kit, 174

Downspouts. *See also* Rain gutter, clogged
  clogged, 33
    as cause of leaky basement, 63
    cleaning out, 34, **34**, 36
  damaged, 37
  types, **37**

Dr. Fixit Drain Flusher, 54

Drain auger, 44-45, **45**, 53, **53**

Drain cleaners, 46, 47, 51
  chemical vs. biological, 46

Drainpipes, cleaning, 36

Drill punctures pipe, 266-67, **266**. *See also* Gas leak; Pipes, broken
  hazards, 266
  inspecting damage, 266-67
  preventing, by using clothes hanger probe, **267**
  quick response, 266

Drinking water, contaminated, 185-93

bottled water, 190
hazards, 185
information sources, 193
kinds of contaminants, 188-89
lead, 186, 188, 195
municipal, 185, 186
  assessing, 186
  removing chlorine taste from, 186, *187*
purification systems, in-home, 185, 190-93
  activated carbon filters, **190**, 191
  distillation, 191, **191**
  installing and maintaining, 192-93
  reverse osmosis units, 191-92, **191**
quick response, 185
radioactivity/radon, 189, **189**
signs of, 186, *187*
testing for, 185, 188-89, 190
water softeners, 192, **192**
well water, 185, 187-88
  assessing, 187-88
  contamination from septic system, 187, **188**
  radon, 187, 189, 209, 212

Drywall, removing wet, 253

Dry wells
  cleaning, 36
  installing, 64

Ductwork
  cleaning by professionals, 219, *219*
  maintenance, *19*
  as source of indoor air pollution, 195, 198, 218, *218*

Dursban, 236

Dust masks. *See* Work masks and respirators

E

Electrical emergencies. *See* Blips; Brownouts; Circuit breaker, tripped; Electric power, lack of; Fuse, blown; Fuses; Saw blade snags electric cable; Spikes; Tool strikes buried cable or pipe